Critics' Choice

The Guild
Of
Corinth Theatre Arts
Corinth, Mississippi

Copyright

The proceeds from the sale of this book go to benefit Community Theatre in Corinth and in particular; Children's Theatre, resident director and improvements on the theatre building.

Library of Congress, 88-072306
ISBN 0-9621330-0-0

WIMMER BROTHERS
Memphis   Dallas

Our Compliments To The Chefs

Those who cared enough to share their tried and treasured recipes with us, and those who gave their time and talents writing, drawing, typing, proofing and editing recipes that often said, "just cook til done," thank you, because of you we are *THE CRITICS' CHOICE*.

Too, we would especially like to thank those members of the Theatre Guild who worked long and tirelessly to raise money so that we could go to print. "Break a leg!"

The Cookbook Committee

Mickey Hale
Mallie Norwood
Corinne Pierce
Vicki Sweat
Ann White
Beth Worsham

Foreword

Nobody knows exactly when theatre began or when the magic of a theatrical occasion first created the urge to celebrate the accolades of a premiere performance with an opening night party.

Theatre perhaps began in the shadowy mists of pre-history when some band of hunters returned from an exciting and successful chase and recreated the event for the clan. Perhaps they all dined on roasted mastodon as the hunters mimed the humorous or tragic adventures of the hunt and the first dinner theater was born.

We do know that mystery or religious plays were presented in Egypt 2000 B.C. and no doubt the priest-actors retired to eat roast duck and munch on date and honey cakes after a vivid impersonation of the gods. By the year 450 B.C., the Greeks were presenting awards to such renowned playwrights as Euripides. One can imagine the playwright and his actors dining on gilded peacock and mutton and washing it all down with a good wine. The Romans did much the same with Menander and Plautus. History informs us that Nero relished writing and performing in his own plays and that he did both rather badly. But, we can be certain that every Roman worth his salt attended an opening night baccanale at the imperial palace.

With the coming of the dark ages, European theatre was frowned upon except for clerical or nativity plays, but there can be little doubt that the spectators took along food or bought vendor's fare as they watched some morality play at the local cathedral square.

The Italian Renaissance and the sudden burst of creative genius which came about in Elizabethan England brought theatre back into favor for awhile. Shakespeare and Marlowe were presenting plays for the court, and everyone feasted on venison, pheasant and ale. Later, in France, Molière was writing scathing comedies and enjoying the cuisine which has made his country world renowned.

With the Puritan Rebellion, theatres were closed in England and not reopened until 1660 when Restoration drama arose and gave us the comedy of Congreve or the tragedy of Dryden. In Italy there was the rise of opera as a form of theatrical expression. During the 18th and 19th centuries, theatre was filled with the satire of Goldsmith or the melodrama of Hugo.

In the latter part of the last and the early part of the 20th century, Ibsen, Shaw, and Wilde brought naturalism or realism to the stages of Europe. But that did not mean that the food and drink at dinner and theatre parties had become drab. There is nothing drab about Sarah Bernhart dining on Coq au Vin and champagne. The tradition has followed to the present time.

Whatever the play or the time, good theatre has encouraged and enhanced good dining. They go together hand and glove. Theatre has brought out the affability and camaraderie people feel when they have seen the curtain go down on a rewarding play. Invariably audiences and casts gather in homes or restaurants to celebrate the finer things of life with a rich variety of food and drink.

This collection of recipes has been aimed at providing a rich tapestry of possibilities of food and drink for you. We hope that the richness, flare, excitement and pleasure of a theatrical and personal heritage will be reflected in your luncheons or dinner parties, and that you will have many encores with the recipes in this book.

Larry Cox
Resident Director, CTA
1985 - 1988

Table of Contents

Nutrition Concepts — 7
   Ideas for lowering cholesterol, calories, and sodium
Dramatic Dining — 9
   Special Menus, 11
Overtures, Menus — 49
   Appetizers, 67
   Beverages, 81
Co-stars, Menus — 93
   Salads & Salad Dressings, 99
   Sandwiches, 134
   Soups, 142
Center Stage, Menus — 163
   Meats, 165
   Seafood, 185
   "On the Grill", 204
Break-a-leg, Menus — 221
   Poultry, 222
   Game, 238
Early Reviews, Menus — 245
   Eggs and Cheese, 246
   Pasta, 254
Understudy — 268
   Vegetables, 271
Supporting Roles — 295
   Breads, 297
Finale, Menus — 317
   Cookies, 333
   Desserts, 339
   Cakes, 349
   Pies, 363
Epilogue — 373
   Candies, 375
   Pickles and Relishes, 382
Revivals, Menu — 387
   Heirloom Recipes, 400
Index — 429

The rose denotes recipes that do (or can be made to) meet special dietary needs

NUTRITION CONCEPTS
Risking Reducing Ideas

To reduce cholesterol saturated fats and calories
- Use polyunsaturated margarine instead of butter, lard, bacon or chicken fat
- Choose lean cuts of meat
- Eat smaller portions
- Substitute for animal fats

1 cup Whole Milk = 1 cup of skim or nonfat dry milk plus 2 teaspoons of polyunsaturated oil.

1 Tablespoon Butter = 1 tablespoon polyunsaturated margarine or ¾ tablespoon oil.

1 ounce square Chocolate = 3 tablespoons of cocoa plus 1 tablespoon of polyunsaturated oil or margarine.

Eggs = Use commercially produced cholesterol-free egg substitutes according to package directions. Or use 1 egg white plus 2 teaspoons of polyunsaturated oil.

1 cup Buttermilk = 1 cup lukewarm nonfat milk plus 1 tablespoon of lemon juice. Let the mixture stand for five minutes and beat briskly.

1 Tablespoon Cornstarch = 2 tablespoons flour or 1 tablespoon arrowroot.

1 cup Cream Cheese = 4 tablespoons of margarine blended with 1 cup dry low-fat cottage cheese (plus small amount of skim milk if needed).

1 cup Sour Cream = ½ cup low-fat cottage cheese or cottage cheese plus ½ cup low fat yogurt. Or try this Mock Sour Cream:

2 tablespoons skim milk	1 cup low-fat cottage cheese
1 tablespoon lemon juice	teaspoon salt

Place all ingredients in a blender and mix on medium-high speed until smooth and creamy. This sauce may be added to hot dishes at the last moment. Or serve it cold, with the addition of flavoring or herbs, as a salad dressing or a sauce for a mousse. Yield: About 1¼ cups. Approximate Calories/Servings:
1 Cup = 160   1 Tablespoon = 10

Whipped Cream = Try this recipe for Poly-whipped Toppings:

1 teaspoon gelatin
2 teaspoons cold water
3 tablespoons boiling water
½ cup ice water

½ cup nonfat dry milk
3 tablespoons sugar
3 tablespoons oil

Chill a small mixing bowl. Soften gelatin with 2 teaspoons of cold water, then add the boiling water, stirring, until gelatin is completely dissolved. Cool until tepid. Place ice water and nonfat dry milk in the chilled mixing bowl. Beat at high speed until the mixture forms stiff peaks. Add the sugar, still beating, then the oil and the gelatin. Place in freezer for about 15 minutes, then transfer to refrigerator until ready for use. Stir before using to retain creamy texture. Yield: 2 Cups Approx. Cal./Serv.: 1 Cup = 320
1 Tablespoon = 20

To reduce sodium:
- Watch out for ingredients that are high in sodium:
  - —sodium bicarbonate (baking soda)
  - —baking powder
  - —sodium nitrate
  - —sodium benzoate
  - —monosodium glutamate (MSG)
  - —hydrolyzed vegetable protein
  - —soy sauce
  - —sodium ascorbate
  - —whey solids
  - —sodium

- Use low calorie, low sodium salad dressing.

- Experiment with herbs and spices to liven up the flavor of foods without adding salt.

- Be aware that some commonly used medications contain sodium:
  - —some antacids
  - —some laxatives
  - —some sleeping aids

- Reduce consumption of luncheon meats, ham, bacon, frankfurters and sausage, smoked, pickled and salted foods. Instead, use fresh meats, poultry and fish and specially-processed low sodium luncheon meats.

- Use fresh or frozen fish instead of canned or dried varieties.

- Water in which salty products are cooked can be poured off and replaced with new water.

- Do not automatically add salt to boiling water when cooking pasta, vegetables and cereals.

Reprinted by permission of:
HEALTHCARE NUTRITION SERVICES

Dramatic
Dining

PREFACE

Imagine yourself sitting comfortably in a theatre, waiting impatiently for the show to begin. Well, dramatic cooking can be interpreted the same way. The lights go down, the curtain rises, the show starts. The presentation of new dishes, one more original than the other, delights not only the eyes, but also the taste. No dullness, but excitement, which is the essence of the dramatic cooking itself. Pleasure awaits you in that journey of gourmet food that will stimulate your senses.

The show starts by the arrival of the dishes, covered by a silver dome, bringing your surprise to a greater level. Be ready for a feast for the eyes. At the removal of the silver dome an array of colors will excite your taste buds. The moment has come to eat. While you nibble on your food you will notice the freshness and the quality of the product chosen. The sauce accompanying your meal will tickle your palate. For a few hours you will live what dramatic cooking is all about.

But for now, come with me through the journey of understanding this art, and while you read along you will be impatient to dine with these chefs, or simply try to make the dramatic cooking occur in your own kitchen.

José Gutierrez

Special Menus

A VERY SPECIAL DINNER

Shrimp and Salmon Terrine

Veal Medallions "Pot Pourri"

*Medallions of Chocolate Mousse
with Kumquats and Orange
and Lavender Sherbet*

The aromas, colors and lightness of the flowers are part of this original menu, which will add and revive the romance in you.

JOSÉ GUTIERREZ

Born in France, Jose received the Certificat D'Aptitude Professionelle in the College Enseignement Technique of Monasque, France, consisting of three years vocational training in this academy learning kitchen, dining room, pastry, butchery and wine services and techniques. Prior to becoming the Executive Chef and Manager of the Chez Philippe Restaurant in The Peabody Hotel in Memphis, Chef Gutierrez was Chef de Partie Garde in the Restaurant Paul Bocuse, Collognes Au Mont D'or, France, and was Chef of the Le Restaurant De France of the Hotel Meridien in Houston, Texas.

Dramatic Dining

Shrimp and Salmon Terrine served with Bee Balm Flower Sauce

Shrimp

18 medium shrimp
½ cup dry white wine
½ cup carrots
½ cup onion

1 bunch thyme
2 bay leaves
Water to cover

In a large saucepot, place white wine, carrots which have been peeled and sliced, onions which have been peeled and sliced, thyme and bay leaves. Add enough water to cook shrimp. Boil 1 minute. Remove shrimp and peel.

Mousse

5 salmon
1 egg white
3 ounces whipping cream

¼ teaspoon tomato paste
12 asparagus spears
Salt and pepper to taste

Cut salmon into pieces. Place in food processor with egg whites, salt and pepper. Grind well. Add cream all at once. Mix for about 30 seconds in food processor, but do not over process. Divide mousse into two parts. To one part add the tomato paste. Other half of mousse needs no additional ingredients. Cook mousse in a 12 inch half-moon shaped mold. Use plastic film to line mold, leaving about 7 inch excess film on both sides. Film should be moistened. Procedure: Lay shrimp individually in bottom of mold, covering entire bottom. Use tomato mousse mixture to cover shrimp, following the shape of the mold. Next lay asparagus, which has been cooked AL DENTE in salted water, over mousse, lengthwise. Cover asparagus with second mousse mixture. Cover mold with extra film from sides of terrine. Bake at 400°F oven in water bath for 35 minutes.

Sauce

1½ cups dry white wine
4 shallots

3 bunches Bee Balm flowers
3 cups whipping cream

Place white wine, sliced shallots and flowers in saucepan. Reduce by half. Add cream. Reduce by half. Sauce should thicken. Strain. Season with salt and white pepper to taste.

Special Menus

Presentation

18 small shrimp with heads   1 teaspoon olive oil

Sauté shrimp in olive oil 4 to 5 minutes, until done. Unmold terrine by turning over onto cooking sheet to remove excess water. Remove plastic. Slice terrine. Place portion of sauce on hot plate. Lay 3 slices of terrine on each plate in cloverleaf pattern. Place shrimp alternately between terrine portions. Place a bunch of Bee Balm Flowers in middle of plate. Serves 6.

Veal Medallions "Pot Pourri" Served with Chive Sauce

Sauce

2 shallots, sliced	1 cup whipping cream
½ cup white wine	¼ bunch chives
1 tablespoon dry vermouth	Salt, pepper

Reduce shallots, white wine, vermouth by half. Add cream. Reduce by half. Add chives. Reduce for 5 more minutes. Chives should retain green color. Salt and pepper to taste. Blend in blender until smooth. Pass through strainer. Keep warm until ready to use.

Garnish Portugaise

6 croutons (Baguette size)	2 bunches thyme, bay leaves
1 tomato, large, very red	½ teaspoon parsley, chopped
½ cup onion	½ clove garlic
2 cups oil	Salt, pepper

Boil tomato 12 seconds. Skin, seed, and chop. Slice onion very thin. Sauté in oil until translucent. Add tomato, thyme, bay leaves, salt, pepper, and garlic. Cook until almost dry. Season to taste. Add parsley.

Dramatic Dining

Meat

6 (2 ounce) portions veal medallions

1 teaspoon oil
Salt, pepper

Season veal with salt and pepper. Cook in hot oil until meat is medium rare to medium. Spoon Portugaise portion atop each crouton. Place 3 croutons on each serving plate. Next place veal on croutons. Cover meat with sauce.

Presentation

¼ Frise yellow lettuce
Chervil
10 violas

1 Rose Geranium
4 Chive blossoms
10 violets

Wash flowers and herbs delicately. Place around plate for garnish.

Medallions of Chocolate Mousse with Kumquats and Orange and Lavender Sherbet

Chocolate Terrine

6 egg yolks
2 gelatin leaves
6 ounces butter
¾ ounce Grand Marnier
¾ ounce sour mash whiskey

¾ ounce Amaretto
10 chocolate couvertures
4 egg whites
24 kumquats
1 cup sugar

Dissolve gelatin leaves in cold water. Whip egg yolks atop water bath with 1 tablespoon water until you can see bottom of mixing bowl while whipping. Remove from heat. Add melted butter, drained gelatin. Boil Grand Marnier, whiskey and Amaretto together. Cut chocolate into small pieces. Melt showly. Whip egg whites to stiff peak. Add liquor to mixture. Next add chocolate, then egg whites. In half-moon mold, approximately 8 inches long, line with dampened plastic film to shape of mold. Fill mold half full with chocolate mixture. Place kumquats which have been boiled in cold water, strained, then cooked in water and sugar, in middle of mold across chocolate mixture. Fill with rest of chocolate mixture. Freeze. Slice, 6 small slices per person, then place in cooler until ready for use.

Special Menus

Sherbet

2 cups orange juice
¾ cup sugar

2 bunches Lavender

Boil half of orange juice with sugar and lavender. When cool, mix with remainder of orange juice. Before putting mixture in sherbet machine, place fresh egg on sherbet mixture. If egg sinks, more sugar is needed. If it floats, sugar content is okay. Do not make mixture too sweet. Place in sherbet machine, freeze.

Orange Sauce

1½ cups orange juice
4 teaspoons sugar
2 teaspoons cornstarch

2 teaspoons Grand Marnier or Cointreau

Boil juice with sugar. Add cornstarch which has been dissolved in water. Cook 5 to 6 minutes, whipping slowly. Strain. Cool. When cold, add Grand Marnier or Cointreau.

Presentation: Place 6 thinly sliced pieces of chocolate terrine on plate, three on each side. Place portion of sherbet in center of plate. Place sauce around. Add bunch of lavender atop sherbet. Serve immediately. Serves 6.

Dramatic Dining

SIMPLY ELEGANT

Veloute of Garlic Soup Gratine

Salad of Warm Goat Cheese Terrine

Lamb Tenderloin

Caramelized Apple and Walnut Tart

When peace and simplicity is your cup of tea, come fulfill this desire with the Gourmand Shepherd Menu.

Veloute of Garlic Soup Gratine

1½ cups garlic
1 cup onion
2 white leeks
1½ cups whipping cream

1 ounce butter
2 bay leaves
2 bunches thyme leaves
Salt, pepper to taste

Peel garlic, place in cold water. Boil and drain. Repeat process three times. Slice onions and leeks thinly. Cook slowly in butter. Season with salt and pepper. Cooking process should halt before vegetables change color. Add garlic, cream, thyme and bay leaves to onion/leek mixture. Cook 8-10 minutes. Remove thyme and bay leaves. Place in blender. Pureé, then pass through a strainer.

Garnish

12 baguette slices
½ cup **Swiss cheese**, grated

2 teaspoons chives

Slice baguette. Toast, then rub with garlic on both sides. Pour soup into serving bowl. Top soup with croutons. Sprinkle with Swiss cheese. Place under broiler until golden brown. Sprinkle chives which have been thinly sliced atop soup. Serves 4.

Special Menus

Salad of Warm Goat Cheese Terrine

Mixture

10 ounces goat cheese	½ teaspoon chives
10 ounces cream cheese	½ teaspoon rosemary
½ teaspoon parsley, chopped	1 ounce Greek olives, seedless
½ teaspoon oregano	2 ounces dried tomato
½ teaspoon dill	

Place dried tomato in cold water. Bring to a boil for 1 minute. Skin and chop. Wash herbs and chop thinly. Chop Greek olives. Combine the three above mixtures with the goat cheese and cream cheese. Wet 18 inch strip of plastic film. Put film on surface. Pipe out goat/cream cheese mixture on 2½ inch wide strip, the length of the film, or at least 12 to 13 inches long. Roll, sausage style, in the plastic. Place in simmering water for about 2½ minutes. Immediately place in ice water, and cool for 30 minutes. Remove from ice water, slice with thin hot knife, three slices per person.

Dressing

6 teaspoons olive oil	1 teaspoon mustard
Salt	1 teaspoon Greek olives,
Pepper	chopped
3 teaspoons vinegar	18 Baguette slices

Combine salt, pepper, vinegar, mustard, Greek olives together. Add olive oil slowly.

Salad

1 red leaf lettuce	1 yellow Frise salad

Toss dressing with red leaf and Frise which has been washed and gently torn. Toast baguettes.

Presentation: Three slices of baguette per plate. Place goat cheese mixture atop, proportionately. Place in oven for a few seconds to melt goat cheese mixture. Place salad in middle of plate. Croutons go around salad. Serves 6.

Dramatic Dining

Lamb Tenderloin
served on a bed of Vegetables and Garlic Cake

Meat

Lamb Tenderloin (Rack) Salt
½ teaspoon oil Pepper

Salt and pepper lamb. Sauté in pan on both sides. Place in 500°F oven for 8 to 10 minutes. Meat should be pink inside.

Vegetable Ratatouille

½ onion
½ zucchini
1 tomato (small red)
½ each red and green pepper
1 bunch thyme
1 bay leaf

1 teaspoon olive oil
⅙ cup white wine
1 teaspoon tomato paste
½ teaspoon garlic, chopped
Salt and pepper, to taste

Dice onions, zucchini and peppers into small pieces. Skin and seed tomato. Dice. Sauté onions, then peppers, then zucchini in olive oil. Strain. Cook in pot with white wine, tomato paste, garlic, thyme, bay leaf, salt and pepper for 10 to 15 minutes. Check seasonings and tenderness of vegetables (should be barely crunchy).

Garlic Cake

1 potato
¼ onion
1 teaspoon all purpose flour
¼ teaspoon garlic, chopped

1 egg
2 tablespoons whipping cream
1 teaspoon parsley, chopped
Salt and pepper to taste

Peel and wash potato. Grate. Same process for onion. Mix onion and potato together. Press to remove water. Add flour, chopped garlic, egg, salt and pepper, parsley, and cream. Form to size of sauté pan. Sauté in oil on both sides. One cake per person.

Special Menus

Sauce

Lamb bones from rack
⅓ onion
⅓ carrot
¼ cup white wine
1 teaspoon flour

1 bunch thyme
1 bay leaf
2 teaspoons fresh butter
Salt and pepper, to taste

Sauté lamb bones until golden brown. Peel and slice onions and carrots. Add to pan. Cook 5 to 10 minutes slowly. Add flour. Cook 4 to 5 minutes. Add ½ cup water, white wine, thyme and bay leaf. Cook 15 to 20 minutes. Sauce should be thick and golden in color. Strain. Whip butter into mixture. Season to taste. Presentation: Place 3 inch wide cutter or other circular form on plate. Spoon vegetable portion inside. Press down. Remove circle. Slice lamb thinly. Place on top of vegetables in circular form. Place sauce around vegetables. Potato cake served on side.

Caramelized Apple and Walnut Tart with Apricot Sauce

Tart Shells

8 ounces flour
4 ounces butter
1 egg yolk

2 ounces sugar
3 teaspoons water
Salt, dash

Cut butter into flour. Make well in mixture. Put in egg yolks, salt, sugar and water. Mix to form dough. Refrigerate for 30 minutes. Roll out. Form into two 6 inch tart forms. Edges should be 1 inch in height. Fill shells with beans. Cook 5 to 6 minutes at 450°F. Remove from oven.

Dramatic Dining

Tart Filling

4 egg yolks
3½ ounces sugar
2 cups whipping cream
1 lemon zest
1 orange zest

2 apples, peeled (16 slices per apple)
Walnut pieces, to taste
Powdered sugar

Place peeled apple slices in bottom of tart shells. Add fresh pieces of walnut. Mix egg yolks, sugar, whipping cream and fruit zests. Pour egg yolk mixture over apples and walnuts. Bake at 450°F until almost done. Spread powdered sugar evenly over top of tart. Return to oven. Bake until golden. Remove from oven.

Sauce

20 apricots (fresh or dried)

If using fresh apricots, place in blender after removing seeds, if any. Pureé. Add sugar, if needed, to taste. If mixture is too thick, add a few drops of water. If using dry apricots, soak in water, strain, follow above method.

Caramelized Apples

1 cup apples (cut in ¼ x 3 inch strips)

2 ounces butter
2 ounces sugar

Caramelize apple strips in butter and sugar.

Presentation: Cut tarts into 6 portions each. Spoon apricot sauce on plate. Two slices of tart per person, placed in middle of plate. Serves 6.

Special Menus

AN ITALIAN DINNER

Marinated Italian Salad

Cold Zucchini Soup

Pasta with Scampi Sauce

Amaretto Cheese Cake

CAROL COTTLE

During her youth, Carol's "Nona" (Italian for grandmother) had a boarding house in Utah where Carol helped in preparing and serving three meals a day. Thus, her love of and skills in cooking flowered at an early age. Now, an accomplished cook and hostess, she caters at special occasions for friends in Oxford, MS.

Dramatic Dining

Marinated Italian Salad

1 (14 ounce) can hearts of palm, drained and thickly sliced
1 (14 ounce) can artichoke hearts (plain), drained and quartered
1 pound fresh mushrooms, sliced
2 red onions, thinly sliced
2 green peppers, cut in strips
1 recipe Italian salad dressing mix, made with red wine vinegar
½ cup white vinegar
Romaine lettuce
Cherry tomatoes
Anchovies

Combine all ingredients except greens, tomatoes and anchovies. Marinate overnight in refrigerator. Serve on romaine, garnished with tomatoes and anchovies. Serves 12.

Cold Zucchini Soup

3 to 4 cups chicken stock or broth
6 medium zucchini, cut in chunks
2 onions, coarsely chopped
1 tablespoon fresh basil OR 1 teaspoon dried basil leaves
1 clove garlic
¼ cup snipped parsley
1 cup whipping cream
½ cup milk
Salt and freshly ground pepper
Thin zucchini slices and Parmesan cheese as garnish

Combine broth, zucchini, onion and herbs in large saucepan. Place over medium heat and cook 20 to 30 minutes, stirring occasionally. Transfer to food processor or blender in batches and pureé. Add cream and milk and run through blender again. Season with salt and pepper. Cover and chill. Taste and adjust seasoning before serving. Float a zucchini slice on top and sprinkle with grated Parmesan. Serves 6.

Variation: Substitute ½ teaspoon curry powder (or to taste) for basil, garlic and parsley.

Special Menus

Scampi Sauce

3 tablespoons butter
2 tablespoons minced garlic
1½ pounds fresh shrimp, shelled
¼ cup dry white wine
½ cup tomato sauce
1¼ cups heavy cream
½ teaspoon basil
½ teaspoon oregano
⅛ teaspoon thyme
1⅛ teaspoon Italian hot pepper flakes
2 egg yolks
Salt and white pepper
2 tablespoons finely minced parsley
12 ounces pasta (your choice)

Melt butter in skillet. Add garlic and cook, stirring constantly, for about 1 minute. Add shrimp and cook for 1 minute over medium-high heat, tossing with a wide spatula, until shrimp are bright pink on both sides. Do not overcook shrimp. Add white wine and tomato sauce and cook for 1 minute. Blend in 1 cup of cream, basil, oregano, thyme and hot pepper flakes. Beat egg yolks with remaining ¼ cup cream and add to sauce, stirring over medium heat until sauce thickens. Do not boil. Season to taste with salt and white pepper. Spoon over hot buttered pasta and sprinkle with parsley. Serves 4 to 6.

"At a dinner-party one should eat wisely but not too well, and talk well but not too wisely.", Somerset Maugham, English writer and playwright.

Dramatic Dining

Amaretto Cheesecake

1½ cups graham cracker crumbs
2 tablespoons sugar
1 teaspoon ground cinnamon
1¼ cup plus 2 tablespoons butter or margarine, melted
3 (8 ounce) packages cream cheese, softened
1 cup sugar
4 eggs
⅓ cup Amaretto
1 (8 ounce) carton commercial sour cream
1 tablespoon plus 1 teaspoon sugar
1 tablespoon Amaretto
¼ cup toasted sliced almonds
1 (1.2 ounce) chocolate candy bar, grated

Combine graham cracker crumbs, 2 tablespoons sugar, cinnamon and butter; mix well. Firmly press mixture into bottom and ½ inch up the sides of a 9 inch springform pan. Beat cream cheese with electric mixer until light and fluffy. Gradually add 1 cup sugar mixing well. Add eggs, one at a time, beating well after each addition. Stir in ⅓ cup Amaretto; pour into prepared pan. Bake at 375°F for 45 to 50 minutes or until set. Combine sour cream, 1 tablespoon plus 1 teaspoon sugar, and 1 tablespoon Amaretto; stir well, and spoon over the cheesecake. Bake at 500°F for 5 minutes. Let cool to room temperature; then refrigerate 24 to 48 hours. Cheesecake is best when thoroughly chilled and flavors have time to ripen. Garnish with almonds and grated chocolate. Serves 12.

Special Menus

A CLASSICAL FRENCH MENU

Miniature Mushroom Pies

Crab and Spinach Timbale

Champagne Sorbet

Sautéed Steak with Crushed Peppercorns

Green Beans

Scalloped Potatoes in Garlic and Cream

Gruyere Salad

Grand Marnier Mousse Cake

MARTHA KABBES

Martha has always been interested in food preparation. She worked as Food Economist for United Gas Corporation and was Food Editor for The State Times newspaper in Jackson, MS. Her culinary skills have developed over the years as she has studied with various chefs in that area. Martha lives in Jackson, MS.

Dramatic Dining

Miniature Mushroom Pies

8 ounces cream cheese
8 ounces butter, melted

2½ cups flour

Combine in food processor with on/off motion until mixture forms a ball. Wrap in plastic wrap and chill.

Filling

3 tablespoons butter
1 cup chopped onions
½ pound fresh mushrooms, finely chopped
¼ teaspoon thyme

½ teaspoon salt
Dash of pepper
2 tablespoons all purpose flour
¼ cup sour cream

In a skillet, melt butter, add onions; brown lightly. Add mushrooms; cook about 3 minutes, stirring often. Add thyme, salt and pepper; sprinkle in flour. Stir in sour cream; cook slowly until thickened. Roll out chilled dough in cookie sheet until ¼ inch thick. Cut in 2½ inch circles with cookie cutter. Place ½ teaspoon of mixture on dough circle; fold in half and press together with fork tines. Pierce tops with fork for steam to escape. Freeze. Preheat oven to 350°F. When ready to serve, place frozen pies on cookie sheet; bake 25 to 30 minutes. Yield: About 75.

Crab and Spinach Timbale

¾ cup heavy cream
1 teaspoon lemon juice
½ teaspoon Dijon mustard
1 dash celery salt
1 dash cayenne pepper
5 eggs
Salt and pepper

½ pound lump backfin crab meat, cleaned
2 pounds fresh spinach - remove stems - wash
3 tablespoons butter
3 tablespoons all purpose flour
¾ cup milk
Pinch of freshly ground nutmeg

Special Menus

Whisk together ⅓ of the cream, lemon juice, mustard, celery salt, cayenne pepper, 2 eggs, salt and pepper. Fold in crab meat. Drop spinach into boiling salted water and return to boil. Drain and rinse with cold water. Squeeze dry and chop finely. In a heavy-bottomed saucepan, heat the butter over medium heat. Add flour and whisk 1 minute without browning. Whisk in milk, remaining cream, salt, pepper and nutmeg, stirring constantly until boiling. Remove from heat and mix in spinach followed by remaining 3 eggs. Butter eight 5 ounce timbale molds and half fill with crab mixture. Add spinach mixture and place in shallow pan with 1-inch cold water. Bake in 375°F oven 25 to 30 minutes. Slide a knife around edge of each mold and invert quickly and firmly onto dinner plate. Serve with beurre blanc or lemon mayonnaise sauce. Serves 8.

Champagne Sorbet

2 juicy oranges
½ cup sugar
½ cup water
2½ cups non-vintage champagne

4 tablespoons brandy
¼ teaspoon angostura or orange bitters

Cut peel from the oranges, using a very sharp knife, taking only the rind and none of the pith. Squeeze, strain and reserve the juice. Put the orange rind, sugar and water into a saucepan and heat gently until the sugar has dissolved completely. Raise the heat and boil the syrup 5 minutes; set it aside to cool. When syrup is cold, discard the orange rind and stir the orange juice, champagne, brandy and bitters into the cold syrup. Freeze in an ice cream machine, following manufacturer's instructions, or still-freeze, vigorously whisking the partially frozen ice at least once during the freezing process. Serves 6 to 8.

Dramatic Dining

Steak Au Poivre
(Sautéed Steak with Crushed Peppercorns)

8 individual steaks, 1 inch thick
Cracked peppercorns

1 loaf bread cut into 1 inch thick rounds and toasted on both sides
Oil and butter

Heat together the oil and butter. Lay steaks that have been peppered in pan. Cook to desired doneness. The steaks are medium rare when they feel slightly resistant to touch and you can see a faint pearling of red juice on the surface.

For the Sauce

1 pint heavy cream
2 beef bouillon cubes
1 tablespoon lemon juice

2 tablespoons Madeira
Salt
½ cup brandy

Reduce the cream by half in saucepan. Stir in bouillon cubes, lemon juice and Madeira. When steaks have been cooked, pour in brandy, ignite and stir to deglaze pan. Add this mixture to cream sauce. Serves 8.

To serve: Place steak on toasted bread round and top with sauce.

Haricots Vert
(Green Beans)

1 pound green beans, strings removed
2 to 3 tablespoons butter

Salt and pepper
Fresh mint, minced

Blanch green beans, drain and rinse under cold water. Sauté beans in butter, season with salt and pepper. Toss with fresh mint. Serves 6.

Special Menus

Gratin Dauphinois
(Scalloped Potatoes in Garlic and Cream)

2 pounds potatoes, peeled, sliced ⅛ inch thick
2 cups milk
1½ cups heavy cream
2 cloves garlic, minced

¾ teaspoon salt
½ teaspoon white pepper
1 tablespoon butter
½ cup grated Swiss cheese

Place sliced potatoes in a saucepan with milk, cream, garlic, salt and pepper and bring the liquid to a boil over moderate heat, stirring to prevent sticking. Remove pan from heat. Pour mixture into well buttered gratin dish or a shallow baking dish. Sprinkle the cheese over the mixture and bake on a baking sheet in a preheated 400°F oven for 1 hour. Serves 8.

GRUYERE Salad

Boston lettuce, washed and dried
Romaine lettuce, washed and dried

4 tablespoons diced Gruyere cheese
2 tablespoons finely chopped walnuts

Tear lettuce into pieces. Toss with cheese and walnuts.

Dressing

2 tablespoons wine vinegar
Salt and pepper
1 teaspoon minced shallot
½ teaspoon dried tarragon or 1½ teaspoon fresh
½ teaspoon dried chervil or 1½ teaspoon fresh

1 tablespoon freshly chopped parsley
1 tablespoon chopped chives
2 teaspoons chopped walnuts
6 tablespoons French olive oil

Combine all ingredients in processor or blender and pour over salad. This dressing is better when it is made ahead of time. More tarragon and parsley can be used, if desired. Serves 4.

Dramatic Dining

Grand Marnier Mousse Cake

Cake

1 (12 inch) sponge cake ¼ inch thick, or lady fingers
½ cup water
½ cup sugar
½ cup Grand Marnier

Place sponge cake or lady fingers in bottom of springform pan. Place water and sugar in saucepan. Bring to boil. Cool. Stir in Grand Marnier. Brush surface of cake and set aside.

Topping

½ cup Grand Marnier
2 tablespoons Cognac
2 tablespoons unflavored gelatin
1½ cups sugar
Zest from 2 oranges
3 (8 ounce) packages cream cheese
¾ cup fresh orange juice
2 tablespoons lemon juice
1 tablespoon vanilla
2 cups heavy cream

Combine Grand Marnier, Cognac and gelatin in small saucepan. Stir over low heat until gelatin is dissolved. Process 1½ cups sugar with zest from 2 oranges in food processor until peel is finely chopped, about 1 minute. Add cream cheese. Process until smooth, approximately 30 seconds. Add orange juice, lemon juice and vanilla. Process 30 seconds more. Whip cream. With motor running, pour gelatin mixture through feed tube and process until well mixed, about 5 seconds. Add whipped cream and pulse to combine, 3 pulses. Pour mixture into prepared pan; smooth surface and refrigerate overnight. Garnish with whipped cream, orange segments and mint leaves. Serves 10.

Special Menus

A PATIO LUNCHEON

Fish and Vegetable Salad with Lemon Mustard Dressing

Zuchinni Flan

Sweet Potato Rounds

Mexican Flan

SHEILA PALMER

Sheila, after studying with several chefs in the Jackson, MS, area, became so adept in her skills that she now teaches her own cooking classes in Greenville, MS, and Jackson, MS. Her specialties are French desserts, cake decorating, breads, and luncheons. She also caters in the Jackson area.

Dramatic Dining

Fish and Vegetable Salad

4 filets of redfish
Salt (or seasoned salt) and pepper, to taste

2 cloves garlic, finely chopped
Enough olive oil to brush on both sides of filets

Season filets with salt, pepper, garlic and olive oil. Barbecue in a 400°F oven until flaky. Set aside.

1 (10 ounce) package frozen green peas
4 carrots, scraped
½ cup green onions, finely chopped
½ cup sweet red peppers, chopped (green peppers can be used)

4 hardboiled eggs, chopped
¼ cup capers, drained
3 ripe avocados
Salt and pepper, to taste
2 bunches red leaf lettuce
1 cup uncooked rice

Cook green peas according to directions, drain and set aside. Cook carrots (or steam) until soft but not mushy. Drain and chop. Cook rice according to directions, drain and cool. Marinate the rice in ⅓ the Tangy Lemon-Mustard Dressing (recipe follows) and store in refrigerator in a plastic bag. The rice can be cooked ahead, marinated and refrigerated.

Tangy Lemon Mustard Dressing

¼ cup lemon juice
⅛ cup tarragon herb vinegar
1½ teaspoons Dijon mustard
2 tablespoons honey

2 teaspooons Worcestershire sauce
¼ teaspoon white pepper
½ teaspoon salt
1 cup olive oil

Process juice, vinegar, mustard, honey and Worcestershire and seasonings for 1½ minutes in food processor. Gradually add olive oil while processing. Store in refrigerator. Will keep for about a week. Makes about 1¾ cups.

Special Menus

Flake cooked fish in a large bowl. Add drained, cooked peas and chopped carrots. Add chopped eggs, green or red peppers, green onions and capers. Toss salad with hands, being careful not to shred fish. Add remainder of dressing and toss again. Store in a plastic bag in the refrigerator to marinate. (Salad is best tossed several times prior to serving to allow the dressing to marinate the vegetables and fish. To Assemble: Place red leaf lettuce on a large, oval platter. Drain marinade from rice and arrange rice around the edge of the platter (on the lettuce leaves). Fill the center of the rice ring with the drained, marinated vegetables. Garnish with slices of avocado. Serves 6.

Sweet Potato Rounds

1 cup sugar
½ cup finely packed brown sugar
2 eggs, beaten
½ cup oil
1 (16 ounce) can sweet potatoes, mashed
½ cup juice from sweet potatoes

2 cups all purpose flour
1 teaspoon baking soda
½ teaspoon salt
½ teaspoon nutmeg
½ teaspoon cinnamon
¼ teaspoon cloves, ground
1¼ cup golden seedless raisins
⅔ cup chopped nuts

In mixing bowl combine sugar, eggs and oil. Beat until light and fluffy. Mash sweet potatoes with ½ cup juice from can. Sift dry ingredients with seasonings. Add sweet potatoes alternately with dry ingredients to the egg mixture until well mixed. Stir in raisins and nuts. Pour into 2 greased coffee cans and bake at 350°F for 1 hour 15 minutes. Release from cans and cool on cake rack. Serve in circular slices. Can be filled with seasoned cream cheese or pimiento cheese to form sandwiches. Extremely moist and will keep for several days in an airtight container or zip lock bag. Makes 2 loaves.

Dramatic Dining

Zucchini Flan

1 bunch green onions and tops
3 medium zucchini, shredded with food processor (small julienne blade)
6 eggs
2 cups heavy whipping cream
1 cup evaporated milk
¼ teaspoon nutmeg
¼ teaspoon white pepper

1½ teaspoons salt
Dash red pepper
¾ cup Parmesan cheese, grated
5 ounces Cheddar cheese, grated
5 ounces Swiss cheese, grated
1½ tablespoons butter

Beat the eggs, cream and seasonings in a mixing bowl. Stir in zucchini, onions and cheeses. Butter an oblong pyrex pan and pour in the mixture. Dot with butter. Bake in a preheated 375°F oven for 45 minutes or until puffed and brown. Cook in upper half of oven. Serves 6 to 8.

Mexican Flan

¾ cup sugar
6 eggs plus two egg yolks
2 cans light evaporated milk
1 (14 ounce) can sweetened condensed milk

¼ cup sugar
½ teaspoon cinnamon
1 teaspoon vanilla

Heat oven to 325°F.

Place ¾ cup sugar in cast iron skillet and caramelize over high heat until completely melted. Pour into a standard bread loaf pan and cool completely. Whisk whole eggs and egg yolks until frothy. Add milk, sugar, cinnamon and vanilla. Whisk until completely blended. Pour into cooled bread pan. Place bread pan into a larger pyrex dish filled with 1 inch of hot water. Cook for 1 hour and 20 minutes. Remove loaf pan from pyrex dish and cool on rack. When flan has cooled, refrigerate for several hours before unmolding. To unmold, run knife around edges to free flan completely. Place serving plate on top of bread pan and invert. Allow remainder of caramelized sugar to drain over top. Refrigerate, covered, until serving time. Can be served plain, or garnished with whipped cream and sliced almonds. This dessert can be made several days in advance. Serves 10.

Special Menus

DINNER FOR EIGHT

Salmon Mousse

Spicy Beef Tenderloin

Baked Potatoes

Leaf Lettuce Salad with Special French Dressing

Old - Fashioned Yeast Rolls

Chocolate Mousse

JANIE REISELT

Janie Oliver Reiselt originally from Camden, Arkansas, is one of the great cooks of the young married set. Besides cooking she is into flying, linguistics, and amateur radio. She is a career person in the insurance field. She and her husband are restoring a lovely old home in Corinth.

Dramatic Dining

Salmon Mousse

1 tablespoon unflavored gelatin
2 tablespoons lemon juice
2½ tablespoons chopped onion
2 teaspoons dried green onion
½ cup boiling water
½ cup mayonnaise
⅛ teaspoon white pepper
¼ teaspoon hot sauce
⅛ teaspoon paprika
¾ teaspoon salt
1 teaspoon Worcestershire sauce
1 teaspoon fresh or dried dillweed
1 (15½ ounce) can pink salmon, drained, skin and bones removed
1 cup whipping cream
Parsley (garnish)
Cherry tomatoes (garnish)

Process first 5 ingredients in food processor or blender for 30 seconds. Add remaining ingredients, except whipping cream, and process for 30 seconds. Pour cream slowly into processor tube ⅓ cup at a time (with processor on). Continue processing until well-blended. Pour mixture into well-oiled 4-cup mold. Chill for several hours (or until set). Thoroughly soak a dish towel in hot water and wring out excess water. Place on mold for several seconds (this may have to be repeated several times to loosen mold). Turn out onto platter. Garnish with fresh parsley and cherry tomatoes. Serves 8.

"After a good dinner, one can forgive anybody, even one's own relatives.", Oscar Wilde, Irish playwright.

Special Menus

Spicy Beef Tenderloin

4½ to 5 pounds beef tenderloin (choice or prime beef)
1 cup Burgundy wine
½ cup Jamaican tomato-pepper sauce
½ cup Worcestershire sauce
6 slices bacon
Boiled pearl onions, optional

Place meat in large glass or stainless steel bowl and set aside. Combine wine, Jamaican sauce and Worcestershire sauce until well blended and pour over meat. Cover and refrigerate overnight, turning several times. Wrap roast in bacon and place in a roasting pan (uncovered). Insert a meat thermometer to one-half the depth of meat. Bake 10 minutes at 475°F; lower heat to 325°F and bake to desired doneness as follows: 15 to 18 minutes per pound for very rare meat (140°F on meat thermometer); 22 to 25 minutes per pound for medium roast (160°F); 27 to 30 minutes per pound for well-done roast (170°F). Allow longer cooking time for a large roast, shorter time for a small roast. I prefer the medium doneness, as the meat has the best flavor and the right amount of juiciness. Garnish the roast with boiled pearl onions, if desired. Serves 8.

Leaf Lettuce Salad with Special French Dressing

2 cups vegetable oil
½ cup red wine vinegar
½ cup powdered sugar
2½ teaspoons paprika
1½ teaspoons dry mustard
2½ teaspoons salt
¼ cup lemon juice (preferably freshly-squeezed)
½ cup orange juice
1½ teaspoons Worcestershire sauce
1 clove garlic, forced through garlic press
Green leaf lettuce and red leaf lettuce

Thoroughly mix vinegar and oil in a deep, narrow bowl. Combine dry ingredients and add to oil mixture, beating well. Add fruit juices and garlic - beat thoroughly until well-blended. Keep refrigerated, but allow to reach room temperature before serving. Stir well before using, and spoon over lettuce (combine one-half green leaf and one-half red leaf lettuce) at serving time. Makes about 1 quart dressing.

Dramatic Dining

Old-Fashioned Yeast Rolls

½ cup sugar
1 cup buttermilk
¾ cup shortening
1½ teaspoons salt
1 cup cooked, mashed potatoes

2 packages dry yeast
½ cup warm water (105°F to 115°F)
2 eggs, beaten
6 cups all-purpose flour, sifted
Melted butter or margarine

Combine sugar, buttermilk, shortening, and salt in a medium saucepan, heating until shortening is melted (use low heat). Remove from heat and stir in mashed potatoes. Use potato masher to be sure mixture is well-blended. Cool to lukewarm. Dissolve yeast in warm water (important to be sure water temperature is between 105°F to 115°F for dough to rise properly). Combine sugar mixture, eggs, and half of the flour in a large mixing bowl. Add yeast mixture and beat until smooth. Stir in enough of remaining flour to make a soft dough that is firm enough to be kneaded. Turn dough out on a lightly-floured surface and knead about 8 minutes, adding small amounts of flour to surface as needed to keep dough from sticking. Dough will be smooth and elastic with little "blisters" on surface when properly kneaded. Place in a greased bowl, turning to grease top of dough. If planning to bake rolls now, cover bowl with a dish towel and let rise in a warm place (85°F), free from drafts, until doubled in bulk (about 1 to 1½ hours). Punch dough down and place on a lightly floured surface. Divide dough into thirds, rolling each third into a 10 inch circle (⅛ inch thick). Cut out rolls with a biscuit cutter (or a cup or glass); dip each roll in melted butter and place on baking sheet, folding the roll in half and pinching center edge to seal. Cover and let rise in a warm place as previously described, until doubled in bulk (about 50 minutes). Bake at 425°F for 6 minutes or until golden bown. Makes 3 dozen.

Note: The dough can be stored in refrigerator for up to a week. Cover bowl tightly with aluminum foil - be sure dough is doubled in bulk before making rolls.

Special Menus

Chocolate Mousse

4½ (1 ounce) squares
   semi-sweet chocolate
⅓ cup water
¾ cup sugar

4 egg yolks
2½ tablespoons brandy
3 cups whipping cream
1 egg white

Melt chocolate over hot water in the top of a double boiler. Place water and sugar in a small saucepan; cook over medium heat until sugar is dissolved (stirring frequently). Pour melted chocolate into container of food processor or blender. Process chocolate, slowly adding sugar mixture in a thin stream. Continue processing while adding egg yolks, one at a time; and add brandy, processing mixture until smooth. Set aside and let cool. Combine egg white and whipping cream in a large bowl, beating until stiff peaks form. Fold the chocolate mixture into whipped cream. Spoon into 8 (6 ounce) individual serving dishes and chill at least 2 hours. Serves 8.

Note: This is an especially elegant dessert when served in crystal goblets with thinly-shaved chocolate curls garnishing the top.

"*Everything in France is a pretext for a good dinner.*",
Jean Anouilh, French playwright.

Dramatic Dining

DINNER PARTY FOR EIGHT

Mushrooms Stuffed with Snails

Lemon Sorbet

Veal Chops in Apple-Mustard Sauce

Individual Carrot Souffles

Fresh Asparagus

Orange Salad with Kiwi Dressing

Chocolate Terrine

VICKI SWEAT

While living in Washington, D.C., Vicki attended courses and worked as a chef's assistant at L'Academie de Cuisine. The courses she completed include The French Menu Course, The Professional Theory Course and The Catering Course. Now living in Corinth, MS, she plans to resume catering when her children are older.

Special Menus

Mushrooms Stuffed with Snails

8 tablespoons butter, softened
2 cloves garlic (more for garlic lovers)
2 tablespoons parsley, chopped

Dash of Worcestershire, Cognac, and lemon juice
Salt and pepper
16 canned snails, drained
16 large mushroom caps

Process all ingredients except snails, mushrooms and 2 tablespoons butter in food processor until well blended. Sauté mushroom caps in remaining 2 tablespoons butter for 2 to 3 minutes. Remove mushrooms from sauté pan and place on baking sheet. Place a snail in each mushroom cap and top with butter mixture. Bake at 350°F for 15 minutes. Serve with French bread. Serves 8.

Veal Chops in Apple Mustard Sauce

8 loin veal chops
½ cup butter
2 tablespoons vegetable oil
Salt and pepper, to taste
2 cups apple juice

2 teaspoons thyme
8 teaspoons Dijon mustard
1 Granny Smith apple, thinly sliced

Salt and pepper veal chops. Heat butter and oil in large skillet. Brown veal chops on both sides without burning butter. (Use two frying pans if one is not large enough to hold all the chops. Divide ingredients evenly.) Add apple juice and thyme. Cover and simmer 20 minutes. Add more juice if sauce has been reduced to a syrup. Remove chops and keep warm. Bring liquid to a boil. Add mustard and apples to skillet. Cook 1 minute. Pour sauce over veal chops and serve.

Individual Carrot Soufflés

2 pounds carrots, peeled and sliced
4 tablespoons unsalted butter

Salt and white pepper
4 eggs
1 cup whipping cream

Cook carrots in boiling water until very soft. Drain. Add butter, salt and pepper. Pureé in food processor until smooth. Cool slightly. Add eggs and cream. Blend well. Butter 8 small ramekin dishes and fill with mixture. Bake in a pan of hot water at 350°F for 30 to 35 minutes. Serve hot in mold.

Dramatic Dining

Orange Salad with Kiwi Dressing

8 large naval oranges, peeled and sectioned
6 kiwi fruits

½ cup sugar
½ cup water
Romaine lettuce

To make kiwi sauce, peel and slice kiwi fruit. Boil sugar and water in a saucepan until sugar has dissolved. Put kiwi and sugar syrup in food processor and process until smooth. Cool. Place romaine lettuce leaves on each salad plate. Arrange orange slices on top and dress with kiwi sauce. Serves 8.

Chocolate Terrine

1 cup walnuts, finely chopped
12 ounce package semi-sweet chocolate chips
¾ cup butter
3 tablespoons unsweetened cocoa powder

⅓ cup sugar
5 egg yolks
5 egg whites
Whipped cream (optional)

Butter a 1-quart loaf pan and line with parchment paper. Butter paper also. Sprinkle chopped walnuts over bottom of pan and press into place. Combine chocolate, butter, and cocoa in a saucepan and cook over low heat until chocolate and butter are melted. Remove from heat to cool slightly. In large bowl of electric mixer, add chocolate mixture and sugar. Mix well. Add egg yolks one at a time. Set aside. Beat egg whites with a pinch of salt until stiff. Gently fold whites into chocolate mixture. Turn into loaf pan. Cover with plastic wrap and refrigerate overnight. To serve, carefully invert terrine onto serving platter. Remove parchment paper and replace any loose walnuts. If desired serve thin slices of terrine with a dollop of sweetened whipped cream. Serves 8.

Special Menus

AN INFORMAL BUFFET FOR EIGHT

Smoked Salmon Tartare

Melon Balls in Port Wine

Herbed Pork Roast with Sour Cream Sauce

Sautééd Leeks

Tomatoes Provencale

Mixed Salad Greens Vinaigrette

Apple Tart

Smoked Salmon Tartare

Juice of ½ lemon
4 sour gherkins, finely chopped
1 tablespoon capers, chopped
1 teaspoon shallots, chopped
2 tablespoons olive oil

1 tablespoon Dijon mustard
¼ cup chopped parsley
Salt and pepper, to taste
4 ounces smoked salmon
Toasted French bread rounds

Combine all ingredients except salmon and bread in mixing bowl. Blend until a paste is formed. Chop salmon into small pieces and carefully add to sauce. Top slices of toasted french bread with salmon mixture.

Dramatic Dining

Melon Balls in Port Wine

1 medium size honeydew melon
1 medium size canteloupe
1½ cups port wine

2 tablespoons sugar
Mint leaves (optional)

Use melon ball utensil to carve small ball shapes. Set aside. In a mixing bowl, combine sugar, port and any juice from melons. Add melon balls and let marinate for 30 minutes. Serve in champagne glasses garnished with mint leaves.

Herbed Pork Roast with Sour Cream Sauce

4 to 6 large garlic cloves
2 tablespoons dried marjoram
2 tablespoons dried summer savory
2 teaspoons salt
1 tablespoon freshly ground pepper

4 to 5 pound boneless pork loin roast
Olive oil
1 cup sour cream
Freshly chopped parsley for serving

Mince 4 garlic cloves. Mix with marjoram, savory, salt, and pepper. Unroll the roast. Rub with olive oil and ⅔ of the herb mixture. Reroll the roast like a jellyroll and tie at 1 inch intervals with kitchen twine. Rub the outside of the roast with olive oil and remaining herbs. If you fancy garlic, slice the remaining cloves, pierce the roast all over, and insert the garlic slivers. Roast in a 375°F oven for 1 hour and 45 minutes to 2 hours or until a meat thermometer registers 185°F. Let meat rest for 10 minutes; then slice. To make the sauce, pour grease off pan drippings. Add 1 cup sour cream and whisk until smooth. The sauce will be a mustard color. Check seasoning. To serve, spread a line of sauce across the slices and scatter with chopped parsley.

Special Menus

Sautéed Leeks

8 leeks
2 small onions
4 tablespoons butter

Salt and pepper
2 cloves garlic
1 cup whipping cream

Cut leeks in half lengthwise and wash thoroughly. Trim all but 2 inches of the green part. Chop onions and slice leeks. Cook vegetables in the butter over low heat until soft, 20 to 30 minutes. Season with salt and pepper and garlic. Add cream and cook for 5 more minutes.

Tomatoes Provençale

8 medium size tomatoes
3 large ripe tomatoes, peeled and seeded and cut into chunks
2 tablespoons olive oil

3 teaspoons garlic, chopped
1 teaspoon dried tarragon
3 tablespoons parsley, chopped
3 tablespoons unsalted butter
Salt and pepper, to taste

Heat oil in a skillet and cook tomato chunks for 10 minutes. Remove from heat and add garlic, tarragon, parsley, butter and salt and pepper. Slice off the top of each medium size tomato. Gently remove seeds and water. Fill each tomato with the tomato mixture. Bake at 375°F for 15 to 20 minutes. Serve immediately. Serves 8.

Mixed Salad Greens with Vinaigrette

4 cups torn Boston lettuce
4 cups torn iceberg lettuce

1 bunch watercress, washed and trimmed of stems
1 avocado, cubed (optional)

Combine all ingredients and toss with dressing.

3 teaspoons lemon juice
3 teaspoons lime juice
5 tablespoons salad oil
1½ teaspoons dry mustard

1 teaspoon sugar
Salt and freshly ground black pepper

Dramatic Dining

Apple Tart

10 inch tart pan lined with
   unbaked pastry shell
3 Granny Smith apples, thinly
   sliced
2 eggs

¾ cup sugar
1 teaspoon vanilla
⅓ cup all purpose flour
½ cup butter, melted

Arrange apple slices on top of dough. Combine eggs and sugar. Add vanilla and flour and beat until smooth. Pour over apples. Then pour melted butter over tart. Bake at 350°F for 1 hour or until dough and filling are cooked.

*"There is no love sincerer than the love of food.",
George Bernard Shaw, Irish playwright.*

Overtures

OVERTURES

Just as the composer utilizes the overture to highlight the major motives of the evening, so should the skillful hostess orchestrate her production. Imagine the excitement of opening night. The lights dim as the conductor enters the orchestra pit. A spattering of applause rises to a crescendo, then dies, as the maestro lifts his baton. A hush of anticipation settles over the audience. All the weeks of preparation are over. The stage is set. The play is about to begin.

A successful party is much like a successful play. The hostess can ensure its success by careful planning and preparation. Her stage is her livingroom and/or dining room. The mood is set by her choice of lighting and decorations. But the heart of this play is the food and drink.

If the play is a cocktail hour followed by dinner, the overture should be light and airy. A glass of wine or champagne punch, with nothing heavier than freshly roasted pecans should be served. Mineral water, or non-alcoholic punch should be available.

As a variation to her theme, the hostess could choose to serve the first course in the livingroom. (Many of the recipes in this section are suitable for this purpose.) This eliminates the necessity for any other type of hors d'oeuvres, but be sure the drinks harmonize with the food.

If, however, the event is a cocktail party with no meal to follow, different rules apply. For a two hour cocktail party for 25 people, choose at least eight different hors d'oeuvres. Allow three of each hors d'oeuvres per person.

Be sure to give yourself a few moments before the guests arrive for a last minute check. All the food and drinks are in place. The lights are dimmed. Appropriate background music is playing. The flowers are lovely. All the weeks of preparation are over. The stage is set. The doorbell chimes. The play is about to begin!

Menus

THE FIRST NIGHTER

Mushroom - Liver Paté

Spinach Rolls

Ron's Favorite Shrimp Dip

Chafing Dish Sweet and Sour Meatballs

Georgetown Brie

Shrimp and Crab Salad in Cream Puffs

Marinated Mushrooms

Elegant Vegetable Tray

Mushroom-Liver Paté

¼ pound mushrooms, chopped fine
1 tablespoon butter or margarine
½ pound brunschweiger, at room temperature
½ cup sour cream
2 tablespoons brandy
1 tablespoon chopped green onion
½ teaspoon prepared mustard
Dash of cayenne
Parsley and pimiento for garnish

In skillet sauté mushrooms in butter until dark brown. Mix well with remaining ingredients. Pack in well greased 2 cup mold. Refrigerate 2 hours. To remove, run hot water on bottom of mold and place on bed of lettuce or on plate. Garnish with parsley, and surround with crackers. Makes 2 cups.

DeEtta Wigginton

Overtures

Spinach Rolls

1 (10 ounce) box of frozen puff pastry shells, thawed
1 (8 ounce) package of cream cheese, softened
2 (12 ounce) packages of frozen spinach soufflé, thawed
Garlic salt, to taste
Seasoned salt, to taste

Roll each puff pastry shell into an 8x12 inch rectangle. Spread each with softened cream cheese. Add garlic salt and seasoned salt to spinach soufflé. Mix well. Spread on top of cream cheese, leaving a 1 inch border. Roll up jelly roll fashion. Freeze partially, in order to slice easily. Slice ½ inch thick. Sprinkle with additional garlic salt before baking. Bake on greased cookie sheet for approximately 20 minutes at 375°F. Turn once, after 10 minutes. These may be frozen before they are baked. Approximately 72.

Mary Hedges

Ron's Favorite Shrimp Dip

2 (6½ ounce) cans shrimp
2 cups sour cream
½ cup chili sauce
4 teaspoons lemon juice
2 tablespoons horseradish
4 drops hot pepper sauce

In large mixing bowl, crumble shrimp in small pieces. Add rest of ingredients and mix with spoon until well blended. Chill 2 hours. Serve with ruffled potato chips or thin party crackers.

Ron Hamilton was a former director of the threatre.

Margel Young

Menus

Chafing Dish Sweet and Sour Meat Balls

5 thin slices bread, crusts removed and bread cubed
½ cup milk
1 beaten egg
2 pounds ground beef
Salt, pepper, and garlic salt to taste
Vegetable oil
1 (13 ounce) can pineapple chunks
1 (8 ounce) can tomato sauce, mixed with ¾ cup water
¼ cup white vinegar, mixed with 1 teaspoon salt
¼ cup sugar
½ cup sweet pickles, cut in chunks
1 large green pepper
1 carrot
1 jar spiced crabapples

In a large mixing bowl, combine bread cubes, milk, and beaten egg. Soak for 5 minutes. Add ground beef to the bread mixture. Mix well and form into small meatballs (marble size). Lightly dredge in flour, and refrigerate for 30 minutes. In a heavy, large skillet, put about 1 inch of vegetable oil, and heat to 400°F. (An electric skillet is ideal for this.) Brown the meatballs, and set aside on paper towels. Drain grease (or oil) from the skillet, and add ¾ cup of cold water, tomato sauce, vinegar, sugar, salt, sweet pickle chunks, pineapple chunks (reserving 6). Add meatballs and simmer 10 to 15 minutes, turning often. Keep warm. In 1 tablespoon of hot oil, sauté green pepper, which has been cut in 1 inch squares. Peel the carrot, and slice it diagonally in fairly thin slices, and sauté in the oil. The vegetables should be tender crisp (3 to 5 minutes). Assemble in a chafing dish, topped with the reserved pineapple chunks and garnished with spiced crabapples. Furnish small picks for serving. Makes 140 cocktail size or 40 golf ball size.

Note: The larger size can be used for a main dish over fluffy rice. Freezes well.

Mrs. Carl Norwood

Overtures

Georgetown Brie

1 cup sliced or slivered almonds
1 stick butter
1 wheel of Brie

Parsley
Green grapes
Stone wheat crackers

Toast almonds in 200°F oven until light brown. Melt butter. Run Brie in microwave to heat, ususally one or two minutes. All microwaves vary, so heat a minute or two and test, until warm, not hot and runny. Transfer to serving platter. Sprinkle almonds on top; pour melted butter over top. Garnish with grapes and parsley. 1 wheel of Brie serves 50 people. Recipe may be adjusted for smaller groups.

Beth Worsham
(Mrs. Bob Worsham)

Marinated Mushrooms

Fresh mushrooms
Fresh lemon juice
Garlic salt

Salt
Pepper

Slice mushrooms from top to bottom including stems. Sprinkle generously with fresh lemon juice, garlic salt, cracked pepper and a dash of salt. Marinate in the refrigerate for 15 minutes, drain and serve. *Double this recipe because it really is good.*

Shrimp and Crab Salad in Cream Puffs

12 slices white bread, crusts removed and bread cubed
½ cup minced onions
4 tablespoons melted butter (or margarine)
2 hard boiled eggs, minced
¼ cup parsley, minced

½ cup celery, minced
1 (4½ ounce) can shrimp, minced
1 (6½ ounce) can white crab meat, minced
1½ cups mayonnaise (or salad dressing)

Toss together the bread, onions, butter and eggs. Cover and refrigerate overnight. Next day add the celery, shrimp, crab and mayonnaise. Taste for seasoning. (You may wish to add salt and pepper and a dash of lemon juice.) Fill tiny cream puffs for appetizers. *But so good in a large cream puff for a luncheon.*

Menus

Cream Puffs

½ cup water
4 tablespoons margarine (or butter)

½ cup flour
2 eggs

Preheat oven to 400°F. Bring water and margarine (or butter) to boil in a heavy saucepan. Quickly stir in flour and beat vigorously; turn heat to low and continue beating for about 1 minute (or until mixture forms a ball). Remove from heat and stir in the eggs all at once, beating until smooth. Drop dough by scant tablespoons full about 3 inches apart on cookie sheet. Bake until puffed and golden (about 35 to 40 minutes). Cool puffs. Slit side and pull out any dough left inside. Spoon shrimp and crab salad into puffs, top with puff caps and serve. *This is one recipe you need to double.*

Mrs. Ron Rossi

Elegant Vegetable Tray

1 cup cider vinegar
1 tablespoon sugar
1 tablespoon dill seed
1 tablespoon garlic salt
1½ cups vegetable oil
1 head broccoli, cut into flowerettes
1 head cauliflower, broken in bite size pieces
2 or 3 carrots, cut into thin strips
1 sweet green pepper, cut into thin strips
1 medium zucchini squash, cut in thin rounds
1 medium cucumber (or more), cut in thin rounds
1 (8 ounce) can ripe olives (or more)
8 ounces fresh mushrooms

Put the ingredients for marinade in a large jar with a lid. Shake vigorously and pour over cleaned vegetables. Refrigerate for 24 hours. Drain and arrange on a large silver tray. The vegetables can vary according to your choice.

Mrs. Melinda Moore

Overtures

A WEDDING EVE CELEBRATION

Mushrooms Elegant

Party Spinach Squares

Rumaki with Oriental Sauce

Hot Crabmeat Dip

Shrimp Mold

Cheese Bits

Seasonal Fruits With: Coconut Dressing, Fruit Dip

Savory Cheesecake

Mushrooms Elegant

1 pound medium mushrooms (about 3 dozen)	1½ cups soft bread crumbs
3 tablespoons butter or margarine	½ teaspoon salt
	½ teaspoon ground thyme
	¼ teaspoon turmeric
¼ cup finely chopped green pepper	¼ teaspoon pepper
¼ cup finely chopped onion	1 tablespoon butter or margarine

Heat oven to 350°F. Wash, trim and dry mushrooms thoroughly. Remove stems; finely chop enough stems to measure ⅓ cup. Melt 3 tablespoons butter in skillet. Cook and stir chopped mushroom stems, green pepper and onion in butter until tender, about 5 minutes. Remove from heat; stir in remaining ingredients except mushroom caps and 1 tablespoon butter. Melt 1 tablespoon butter in shallow baking dish. Fill mushroom caps with stuffing mixture; place mushrooms filled side up in baking dish. Bake 15 minutes. Set oven control at broil or 550°F. Broil mushrooms 3 to 4 inches from heat 2 minutes. Serve hot. Makes 3 dozen appetizers.

Mrs. William Alexander (Lois)

Menus

Party Spinach Squares

2 (10 ounce) packages frozen chopped spinach
3 tablespoons butter
1 small onion, chopped
¼ pound mushrooms, chopped
4 eggs
¼ cup bread crumbs
1 (10½ ounce) can cream of mushroom soup
¼ cup grated Parmesan cheese
¼ teaspoon each pepper, dried basil and oregano

Place spinach in a wire strainer, rinse under hot water to thaw, then press out all water; set aside. Melt butter in saucepan; add onion and mushrooms and cook until onion is transparent. In a bowl, beat eggs, then stir in bread crumbs, soup, 2 tablespoons cheese, all seasonings, spinach, and the onion mixture. Blend well. Turn into a well-greased 9 inch square baking pan; sprinkle with remaining cheese. Bake uncovered in a 325°F oven for 35 minutes or until set. Cool slightly; then cover and refrigerate. Cut into 1 inch squares and serve cold, or reheat in a 325°F oven for 10 to 12 minutes. Serves 8 to 10.

Harriett Lipscomb
Abbeville, Mississippi

Hot Crabmeat Dip

1 pound crabmeat
1 pound cream cheese
Green onions, to taste
Garlic, to taste
½ cup butter
Salt
Pepper
Sherry (optional)
Lemon juice

Soften cream cheese. Pick shells out of crabmeat and set crabmeat aside. Sauté onions and garlic in butter. Mix crabmeat, onions, and cheese in a large pot. Heat over low fire and mix well. Add a little milk as needed to thin. Also add salt, pepper, lemon juice, and sherry to taste. Serve in fondue pot, keeping warm. Serve with toasted rounds of French bread. Serves ten.

Liza Golotte
Biloxi, Mississippi

Overtures

Rumaki

Oriental Sauce (Recipe Follows)
6 chicken livers, cut in half
1 (5 ounce) can water chestnuts, drained and cut into 12 slices, or use 12 slices fresh water chestnuts

6 slices bacon, cut in half
¼ cup brown sugar

Place chicken livers and water chestnuts in baking dish with Oriental Sauce. Cover dish and marinate in refrigerator 4 hours. Set oven control at broil and/or 550°F. Remove chicken livers and water chestnuts from marinade. Wrap 1 liver and water chestnut slice in each piece bacon; secure with wooden pick. Roll in brown sugar. Broil 3 inches from heat 10 minutes, turning occasionally, until bacon is crisp.

Oriental Sauce

¼ cup soy sauce
¼ cup salad oil
2 tablespoons catsup

1 tablespoon vinegar
¼ teaspoon pepper
2 cloves garlic, crushed

Mix all ingredients. Makes 1 cup sauce.

Mrs. William Alexander (Lois)

Shrimp Mold

1 (8 ounce) package cream cheese
2 cups sour cream
1 (8 ounce) can of medium size shrimp, chopped

½ cup water
1 package unflavored gelatin
4 teaspoons lemon juice
1 package dry Italian dressing mix

Blend sour cream and shrimp into softened cream cheese. In small saucepan, heat water to boiling, and dissolve gelatin in water. Slowly add lemon juice and dressing mix to gelatin mixture. Fold liquid mixture into sour cream-cream cheese mixture. Pour into a 2 quart mold, and chill 3 hours or longer. Serve with chips or crackers. Serves approximately 25.

Brenda Rogers

Menus

Cheese Bits

1 cup butter, softened
8 ounces sharp Cheddar cheese, softened and shredded
2 cups all purpose flour, sifted

¼ teaspoon red pepper (cayenne)
Pecan halves
1 egg white, slightly beaten

In large bowl, with electric mixer, blend cheese and butter. Sift flour; measure 2 cups, and add pepper. Gradually work flour into the creamed mixture with a wooden spoon. Roll into a log 1 inch in diameter. Cut into ½ inch slices. Top with a pecan half, and brush with egg white. Bake on ungreased baking sheet about 1 inch apart at 425°F for ten minutes. Makes eight dozen.

Note: Do not substitute margarine for butter. Once rolled into a log, this can be wrapped and stored in the refrigerator to slice and cook later. Can be kept in refrigerator for two weeks or frozen to serve later.

Barbara Wayne

Coconut Dressing (Dip for Fruit)

1 small (7 or 8 ounce) can coconut cream (found in drink section of grocery)

1 (8 ounce) package cream cheese
1 cup powdered sugar
Fresh lemon juice, to taste

Mix all together in blender or food processor, until smooth and fluffy. Refrigerate until ready to use. Use as dressing or dip for fresh fruit.

Wanda Banes
Jackson, Mississippi

Overtures

Fruit Dip

1 tablespoon cornstarch
½ cup sugar
2 egg yolks
⅓ cup water

3 tablespoons pineapple juice
2 tablespoons lemon juice
⅛ teaspoon salt

In a small saucepan, mix cornstarch and sugar. Add lightly beaten egg yolks and water. Cook to boiling. Boil 1 minute, stirring constantly. Remove from heat. Add pineapple juice and lemon juice, salt and chill. Serve with fresh fruit (strawberries, chunks of banana, apple, pineapple, watermelon or cantaloupe balls) on toothpicks. Makes about 1 cup.

Jill Robinson Taylor

Savory Cheesecake - first course or appetizer

16 ounce cream cheese at room temperature
1 cup Parmesan cheese
6 large eggs
1 cup sour cream

Finely grate one large onion
Dash hot pepper sauce
Juice of one lemon
Rosemary, oregano or tarragon

Adjust a rack ⅓ up from bottom of oven; preheat to 350°F. In large bowl of electric mixer, beat cheese until soft and smooth; add Parmesan cheese; beat well, scraping bowl as necessary with rubber spatula. The mixture must be smooth. Add eggs, one or two at a time, beating well after each; beat in sour cream and lemon; add herbs. Pour into crust made with ¾ stick of unsalted butter and 1¾ cups round, buttery cracker crumbs. Bake 1⅓ hours. Do not remove from oven; turn off heat; open door 6 to 8 inches and let cake stand until cool. With a small, narrow metal spatula or knife, cut around cake between crust and pan, pressing blade against pan. Carefully remove sides of pan. Refrigerate several hours or a day or two. The cake may be served on the bottom of the pan or flat cake plate. To transfer, use strong and firm, long, narrow metal spatula or knife with about 6-inch blade. Insert between crust and pan; gently ease it around to release. It will be easy if the bottom of the pan has not been buttered and if the cake has been chilled enough. Use a flat-sided cookie sheet or the bottom of springform quiche pan or two wide metal spatulas to transfer. Decorate. Serves 8 to 10.

Martha T. Kabbes
Jackson, Mississippi

A HOLIDAY GALA

Cheese and Ham Puffs

Hot Crab Canapé Pie

Artichoke Dip

Oysters Rossi

Marinated Shrimp

Mushroom Sausage Spread

Wonderful Cheese and Apples

Walnut - Sour Cream Diamonds

Classic Daube Glacé or Mock Daube Glacé

Vegetable Spread

Overtures

Cheese and Ham Puffs

1 (8 ounce) package cream cheese
1 egg yolk, beaten
1 teaspoon onion juice
½ teaspoon baking powder
¼ teaspoon hot pepper sauce
Salt, to taste
2 (2¼ ounce) cans deviled ham
24 small rounds of bread

Cream together the cream cheese, egg yolk, onion juice, hot pepper sauce, baking powder, and salt. Toast the bread rounds on one side. Cover the untoasted side with deviled ham. Then spread the cheese mixture on top of the ham. Bake in moderate oven (375°F) about 10 or 15 minutes, or until slightly brown. Makes 24.

Helen Moore

Dietary Tips

Most labeling gives fat content in grams which makes it a mystery to figure out the fat/cholesterol content of a product. To make it easier, remember each gram of fat is 9 calories. Multiply the number of grams of fat by 9 if this number is 30% or more of the total calorie content then the product is too high in fat for those restricting cholesterol.

Low Fat Herb Dip
½ cup low fat cottage cheese
½ cup low fat Ricotta cheese
2 tablespoons skim milk
2 teaspoons chopped parsley
1 teaspoon fresh lemon juice
½ teaspoon dried dill weed
½ teaspoon Worcestershire
1 tablespoon finely chopped onion
Hot pepper sauce to taste

Process in a blender or a food processor until smooth, if needed add more skim milk. Makes 1 cup.

Menus

Hot Crab Canapé Pie

1 pound lump crabmeat
1 tablespoon horseradish
½ (2¼ ounce) bottle capers, drained
1 teaspoon lemon rind, grated
½ teaspoon monosodium glutamate
Dash hot pepper sauce
2 cups best quality mayonnaise
¾ cup shredded sharp cheese

Mix together crabmeat, horseradish, capers, lemon rind, monosodium glutamate, hot sauce, mayonnaise. Add more seasoning, if you desire (grated onion, Worcestershire sauce, garlic, herbs, or whatever your taste desires). Put into a 10 inch pie plate. Spread out and cover top with cheese. Heat at 350°F about 20 to 25 minutes, or until mixture bubbles. Run under broiler for a few minutes, until cheese is lighty browned. Place pie plate in center of tray, encircled with crackers. Serves 10.

Zetta C. Brunet
(Mrs. R. M. Brunet)

Artichoke Dip

1 (14 ounce) can artichoke hearts, drained and chopped (may use blender)
1 cup mayonnaise
1 cup grated Parmesan cheese

Mix ingredients and place in shallow container, such as pie plate. Bake at 350°F for 20 minutes. Use crisp crackers as dippers. Makes 2½ cups.

Mrs. Charles McDonald (Donna)

Overtures

Oysters Rossi

24 select oysters
1 cup all purpose flour
Salt and pepper, to taste (be careful of the salt)
3 tablespoons melted butter
½ cup fresh lemon juice
1 cup A-1 type sauce
½ cup Worcestershire sauce
2 jiggers dry sherry wine

Sprinkle the oysters with salt and pepper and dredge in flour and brown in a heavy skillet in about 1 inch of vegetable oil. Mix together the ingredients for the sauce. Heat until the sauce bubbles. Put oysters in a chafing dish and pour the sauce over. Serve hot with small toast rounds. Plan on serving three or four to a person. Serves 6 to 8.

Warren Rossi

Marinated Shrimp

2 (16 ounce) bottles Italian salad dressing
2 teaspoons mustard
4 shakes Worcestershire sauce
2 shakes hot pepper sauce
1 teaspoon celery salt
2 teaspoons garlic juice
2 teaspoons lemon juice
3 pounds cooked and peeled shrimp
2 cans crabmeat or one pound lump crabmeat
3 large red onions

Slice onions into ¼ inch slices. Set aside along with shrimp and crabmeat. Combine all other ingredients in a large bowl. Add shrimp, crab, and onions and toss. Cover bowl and chill, tossing now and then. Before serving, drain shrimp, crab, and onions and put on platter. Serve with crackers. Covered and refrigerated, the mixture will be good for several days. Approximately 20 appetizer servings.

Nancy Smith

Menus

Mushroom Sausage Spread

8 ounces fresh mushrooms, chopped fine
2 teaspoons olive oil
½ pound lean sausage, crumbled
3 green onions, chopped fine
2 teaspoons crushed red pepper
4 ounces cream cheese
4 ounces sour cream
2 ounces crumbled blue cheese
¼ cup mayonnaise

Sauté mushrooms in olive oil until dark, and drain on paper towel. Cook sausage and drain. Combine all ingredients and let sit for 4 to 24 hours in refrigerator. Serve at room temperature with Melba rounds, crackers, etc. Makes approximately 3 cups.

Claire Stanley

Wonderful Cheese and Apples

4 ounces Camembert cheese (including rind), cut in small cubes
1 cup shredded Swiss cheese
4 ounces bleu cheese, crumbled
3 (8 ounce) packages cream cheese, softened
2 tablespoons milk
2 tablespoons dairy sour cream
1¼ cups chopped pecans
Chopped fresh parsley
6 to 8 Granny Smith apples, sliced and cored

Let Camembert, Swiss, and bleu cheese stand at room temperature 1 hour. In mixer bowl combine Camembert, Swiss, and bleu cheese with 2 packages of cream cheese; set aside. Line a 9 inch pie plate with foil. Stir milk and sour cream into remaining cream cheese; spread in pie plate on top of the foil. Sprinkle pecans atop cheese layer. Press nuts in. Spoon Camembert, Swiss, and bleu cheese mixture atop nuts and cream cheese layer, spreading to plate edges. Place plastic wrap over cheese; cover tightly. Refrigerate 2 to 3 days before serving. (Flavor is better, if kept up to a week.) To serve, remove plastic wrap. Turn onto a plate; peel off foil. Sprinkle with parsley. Serve with apple slices. Serves 12 to 16.

Wanda Witt

Overtures

Walnut Sour Cream Diamonds

Pastry

1½ cups sifted flour
¾ teaspoon salt
½ teaspoon paprika

½ cup butter
½ cup sour cream

For pastry, resift flour with salt and paprika into bowl. Cut in butter. Add sour cream and mix until well blended. Cover and chill dough ½ hour or longer before using.

Filling

¾ cup chopped toasted walnuts (brown in butter in oven)

¾ cup chopped pimiento stuffed green olives
¾ cup grated Cheddar cheese
2 tablespoons mayonnaise

While dough is chilling assemble filling. Mix together walnuts, olives, cheese and mayonnaise. Divide dough in half. Roll each half into an 8x15 inch rectangle. Cut each rectangle into two 4 inch strips. Spread center of each strip with filling. Fold edges over to enclose it completely, moisten edges to seal. Invert onto baking sheet, seam-side down. Bake in hot oven at 400°F until crisp and golden brown, about 10 minutes. Cool and cut diagonally to make diamonds. Makes about 3 dozen.

Bob Burns
Conyers, Georgia

"Tis an ill cook that cannot lick his own fingers!", William Shakespeare, English dramatist and poet.

Menus

Daube Glacé

- 4 quarts water
- 3 beef bones
- 5 to 6 carrots
- 2 onions, cut in half
- 2 bay leaves
- 2 tablespoons bottled brown Bouquet sauce
- 2 beef rounds or boneless rump roast sliced ¾ inch thick
- 1 tablespoon parsley
- Pinch thyme
- 2 garlic pods
- Celery tops (optional)
- Salt and pepper, to taste
- 1 tablespoon Worcestershire sauce
- Plain gelatin (1 packet for every 1½ cups stock)
- ¼ onion grated
- Juice of 1 garlic pod
- Juice of 1 or 2 lemons
- Salt, pepper, Worcestershire sauce, to taste

Into 4 quarts water, put beef bones, carrots, onions, bay leaves, parsley, thyme, garlic, celery tops, salt and pepper. Simmer for 2 hours, strain and put in refrigerator - next day skim off all fat. Take beef rounds (2 round steaks ¾ inch thick) and cut off fat. Marinate in Worcestershire sauce several hours or overnight. Sear meat thoroughly and season with salt and pepper. Use some stock to scrape bottom of pan to get the dregs and color stock. Add 2 tablespoons brown Bouquet sauce to make a dark stock. Put meat, Worcestershire sauce, bottle brown Bouquet sauce and stock in pot and simmer one hour. Cut meat in bite size pieces and place in molds or loaf pan. Use 1 package of plain gelatin to 1½ cups stock (soften in 1½ tablespoons cold stock or water). Dissolve in stock. Rectify the seasonings: add grated ¼ onion, garlic juice, lemon juice and Worcestershire sauce, salt and pepper to taste. Pour into molds and refrigerate. Loaf pans and molds can be decorated with olives, bell peppers or pimientos and served with mayonnaise. Will keep in the refrigerator 5 to 6 days covered.

Note: Some of the meat and stock can be poured in plastic egg-cartons. Unmold, place on round crackers, and dot with mayonnaise.

Co Grady
Laurel, Mississippi

Overtures

Mock Daube Glacé

2 cans beef consommé
1 cup water or 1 cup sherry
2 envelopes unflavored gelatin
Juice of 2 to 3 lemons
Hot sauce, to taste
Worcestershire sauce, to taste
1 (10 ounce) roll of liver sausage

Heat consommé, soften gelatin in a little of the sherry or water; add gelatin and sherry to consommé. Add the rest of the seasonings. Cover bottom of ring mold with ½ of the mixture and set in refrigerator. When jelled, take out and spread the liver sausage that has been softened with some of the mixture and a little sherry. When this layer has set, pour the rest of the mixture over this. Let set in refrigerator until hard. Unmold and serve with crackers. Serves 15 to 20.

Mickey Hale

Vegetable Sandwich Spread

1 cup celery
1 medium onion
2 peeled tomatoes
1 medium green pepper
1 cup chopped cucumber
1 (¼ ounce) envelope unflavored gelatin
3 tablespoons cold water
1 pint mayonnaise
1 teaspoon salt
¼ teaspoon pepper

Chop all vegetables finely and let stand 2 or 3 hours in bowl; pour off accumulated liquid. Combine gelatin and cold water in top of double boiler to dissolve gelatin. Mix mayonnaise with chopped vegetables. Add gelatin to vegetable mixture. Season with salt and pepper and refrigerate to cool. Spreads 2½ loaves of sandwich bread. Also good as a dip with chips.

Lenoir Stanley

Emergency Appetizer

1 (8 ounce) package cream cheese
1 can lobster or crabmeat
Shrimp cocktail sauce

Put cream cheese on serving plate, top with lobster or crab and top with the cocktail sauce. Serve with water crackers.

Appetizers

Hot Crabmeat Canapé

1 pound crabmeat
2 boiled eggs
1 cup breadcrumbs
2 tablespoons Durkees dressing
2 tablespoons mayonnaise
2 tablespoons Worcestershire sauce
½ teaspoon salt
½ to 1 teaspoon hot sauce
Melted butter or margarine

Pick over the crabmeat, and remove all of the shell-like pieces. Mash the boiled eggs, and mix with the crabmeat. Add ½ cup bread crumbs, Worcestershire sauce, hot sauce, Durkees dressing, and mayonnaise. Put into shells or individual heatproof casseroles. Cover with remaining crumbs. Drizzle with melted butter. Bake 15 to 20 minutes in a 375°F oven. Serves 4 to 6 as a main course, baked in large scallop shells or about 2 dozen, baked in small shells for appetizers.

Note: The small ones should, of course, be baked for a shorter time.

Seafood Dip

1 cup of margarine
1 cup of all purpose flour
2½ cups sweet milk
1 teaspoon paprika
1 teaspoon pepper
¼ teaspoon hot pepper sauce
1 pound crabmeat or 2 (8 ounce) cans crabmeat
1 pound cooked shrimp, cut in pieces
1 (6 ounce) can mushrooms, finely chopped
1 bunch green onions, finely chopped
2 cups parsley, finely chopped

Melt margarine over low heat; remove from heat, and stir in flour, then milk. Return to heat and stir constantly until thick; add seasonings and remaining ingredients. Serve from a chafing dish with toast points. This may also be served in patty shells. Serves 14 to 16.

Mrs. T. Y. Williford, Jr. (Nell)
Greenville, Mississippi

Overtures

Chinese Ribs Norman

4 pounds pork ribs
4 cloves garlic, mashed
2 teaspoons salt
¼ cup honey

¼ cup soy sauce
1 cup undiluted beef consommé
¼ cup tomato paste

Mix all ingredients except the ribs. Place ribs on a cutting board. With a cleaver cut across the ribs at 3 inch intervals. Then cut the ribs between each rib. This will give three small riblets per each rib. (Smaller pieces may be cut if you wish just bite size pieces.) Pour sauce over the ribs which have been put in a shallow baking pan or baking dish. Place in a 450°F preheated oven, covered, for 10 minutes. Stir well and continue baking at 350°F for 1 hour. Serve hot in a chafing dish or at room temperature. Uncover for last 15 minutes.

Note: Yield will depend on how small, or large, the ribs are cut, usually 8 to 10 for cocktails. (Wonderful buffet food!)

Mrs. Leo Norman (Agnes)

Chafing Dish Mexicali Tamale Balls

2 pounds ground beef
4 cloves garlic, minced
1½ cups yellow cornmeal
½ cup flour

1 teaspoon chili powder
2 teaspoons salt
1 teaspoon pepper
¾ cup tomato juice

Sauce

2 (16 ounce) cans tomatoes
1 teaspoon chili powder
1 onion, grated

2 teaspoons salt
2 teaspoons sugar
1 teaspoon pepper

Combine all ingredients, except sauce ingredients. Shape into marble-sized balls. Set aside. Combine the ingredients for the sauce. Blend in the blender for about 2 seconds, put the sauce into a heavy pot and heat. Gently fold in the meatballs; cover, and simmer until the desired thickness. Serve in a chafing dish with colorful picks. Makes 70 to 80 tamale balls.

Appetizers

Burgundy Mushrooms

4 pounds mushrooms
2 cups butter
1 quart Burgundy
1½ tablespoons Worcestershire sauce
1 teaspoon dill seed
1 teaspoon black pepper
1 tablespoon monosodium glutamate
1 teaspoon garlic powder
2 cups boiling water
4 beef bouillon cubes
4 chicken bouillon cubes
2 teaspoons salt

Put everything in large pot. Bring to boil. Reduce to simmer. Cook 5 to 6 hours covered. Remove lid and simmer 3 to 5 hours or until liquid barely covers top of mushrooms. Taste and add up to 2 teaspoons salt if needed. Make ahead. Keeps in refrigerator and freezes well. Serve warm in chafing dish.

June Cassibry
Cleveland, Mississippi

Hot Mushroom Roll Ups

1 pound fresh mushrooms
½ cup butter
1 (10¾ ounce) can cream of mushroom soup undiluted
Dashes of hot pepper sauce, to taste
2 dashes Worcestershire sauce
Sandwich bread
Melted butter

Chop cleaned mushrooms and stems as for Duxelle. Cook in the butter in skillet stirring occasionally until mushrooms are almost dry. Mix with the soup and seasonings. Remove crust from bread. With rolling pin, roll slice one way until very thin. Spread with mixture, roll up and brush with melted butter. At this point may be frozen. When ready to use cut each roll into 4 bites and cook in 375°F oven until toasted. Serve hot. Makes approximately 48.

Mickey Hale

Overtures

Mushroom and Herb Rolls

1 tablespoon minced shallot
1 tablespoon butter
¼ pound mushrooms, finely chopped
1 teaspoon lemon juice
1 teaspoon mixed dried herbs (any combination of dill weed, basil, tarragon, or oregano)
1 (3.5 ounce) package garlic and herb cream cheese
½ (17.25 ounce) package frozen puff pastry
1 egg mixed with 1 tablespoon water (egg wash)

Sauté minced shallot in butter until soft, about 5 minutes. Add mushrooms and lemon juice and cook until mushrooms are soft and juices absorbed. Add herbs, mix well and set aside to cool. Mix cream cheese with cooled mushrooms. Adjust seasonings to taste. Preheat oven to 425°F. Roll out puff pastry to 10x12 inch rectangle. Spread with filling and cut into fifteen 2x4 inch rectangles. Roll up each rectangle and brush with egg wash. Place seam side down on ungreased baking sheet. Bake until golden, about 15 minutes. Serve immediately.

Mrs. Milton L. Sandy, Jr. (Stephanie)

Salmon Dip

1 (1 pound) can red salmon
1 (8 ounce) package cream cheese
1 tablespoon lemon juice
2 teaspoons grated onion
1 teaspoon horseradish
¼ teaspoon salt

Drain and flake salmon; remove bones and skin. Mix all ingredients and serve on crackers. Makes 3 cups.

Miriam R. Propp

Variation: Use two cans minced clams in place of the salmon.

Mrs. John W. Prather

Appetizers

Shrimp Party Spread

2 (8 ounce) packages cream cheese, softened
1 teaspoon shredded onion
2 tablespoons catsup
1 tablespoon Worcestershire sauce
½ teaspoon cayenne pepper
½ teaspoon black pepper
½ teaspoon salt
½ teaspoon hot sauce
2 (4½ ounce) cans shrimp, drained

Combine all ingredients except shrimp in a medium bowl and mix with the electric mixer. Stir in ½ of the shrimp into the cheese mixture, for open sandwiches using can to garnish. For closed sandwiches mix both cans shrimp into cheese. Spread mixture onto bread.

Barbara Wayne

Braunschweiger Mold

½ pound Braunschweiger (liver sausage)
1 (3 ounce) package cream cheese, softened
4 tablespoons mayonnaise
1 or 2 tablespoons half and half cream
1 tablespoon melted butter
1½ teaspoons curry powder (or more to taste)
1 tablespoon dry sherry
¼ teaspoon each salt and pepper
Pinch cayenne pepper
Pinch nutmeg
1 tablespoon Worcestershire sauce

In small bowl of electric mixer, beat sausage, cheese, mayonnaise, and cream. When well blended, beat in remaining ingredients. Turn into lightly oiled mold or put in bowl in which spread is to be served. Chill until ready to serve. Accompany with small round crackers or Melba toast rounds. Makes 2 cups.

Mary Elizabeth Baggenstoss
Tracy City, Tennessee

Overtures

Tuna Mold

1 (10 ounce) tomato soup
1 (8 ounce) package cream cheese
2 envelopes unflavored gelatin
½ cup water
½ cup finely chopped onion
½ cup finely chopped green pepper
½ cup finely chopped celery
2 (3½ ounce) cans tuna (well drained)
1 cup Durkees dressing

Melt cream cheese in the undiluted tomato soup until smooth. Soften gelatin in water and add to soup mixture. Blend, then add rest of ingredients. Put in oiled mold; chill. Serve with plain crackers.

Jewell Dougherty
Memphis, Tennessee

Oyster Cracker Tidbits

1 cup vegetable oil
1 package Ranch Style dressing (dry)
½ teaspoon garlic salt
½ teaspoon dill weed
½ teaspoon lemon pepper
16 ounce box oyster crackers

Empty all ingredients into large bowl and mix. Stir occasionally until oil is absorbed, about 2 hours. Store in cans or in a cannister to keep dry and crisp.

Note: Take my advise and double the recipe.

Mary Davis

Easy Paté

Canned pork paté
2 tablespoons butter
2 tablespoons onion
2 tablespoons cognac

Mix all together well. Put in serving dish and top with bouillon - gelatin.

Appetizers

Spinach Dip Supreme

2 (10 ounce) packages frozen chopped spinach
¼ cup chopped parsley
½ teaspoon black pepper
1 cup sour cream
½ cup minced green onions
1 teaspoon salt
1 cup mayonnaise (no substitute)
1 dash each of Worcestershire sauce and hot pepper sauce

Cook spinach according to directions; drain well and chop very finely. Mix with other ingredients. May be made ahead. Serve hot in a chafing dish as a dip. Makes 3 cups.

Variation: Adding 1 (6 ounce) roll of garlic cheese and 1 (8 ounce) can mushrooms, stems and pieces, will change this to a Mock Oyster Dip!

Mrs. E. J. Knight
Birmingham, Alabama

Delicious Dip

1 (8 ounce) package cream cheese (room temperature)
1 (4 ounce) can chopped black olives
3 teaspoons lemon juice
1 can smoked oysters, chopped
¾ pint mayonnaise (approximate)
5 dashes hot pepper sauce

Mix thoroughly. Serve with cocktail crackers. Makes 3½ cups.

Ed Kossman, Jr.
Cleveland, Mississippi

Overtures

Super Sausage Balls

1 pound sausage, room temperature
2 (5.5 ounce) packages biscuit mix
½ pound sharp Cheddar cheese, grated
½ cup plus 2 tablespoons water
Garlic powder, to taste

Mix all ingredients together. When dough is well blended, roll into balls, about 1 inch in diameter. Bake at 350°F for 15 to 20 minutes on ungreased cookie sheet. Makes about 4 dozen.

Mrs. Travis M. Nelson (Fay)

Artichoke Dip

1½ cups sour cream
1½ cups mayonnaise
1 package Ranch Style dressing (dry)
1 (14 ounce) can artichoke hearts; drained and coarsely chopped

Mix all ingredients together and refrigerate. Serve wtih thin wheat crackers. Makes four cups.

Patsy Walker

Curry Dip for Crudités

1 cup salad dressing
2 teaspoons curry
1 tablespoon catsup
Dash Worcestershire sauce
1 tablespoon onion juice

Mix well and refrigerate until ready to use. Makes one cup.

Tracy Hale Bell
Jackson, Mississippi

Appetizers

Hummus Bi Tahini

2 cups canned chick peas, drained
⅓ cup olive oil
⅓ cup fresh lemon juice
2 to 3 cloves garlic, minced
1 to 2 drops hot sauce
¼ cup tahini (sesame paste)

Put chick peas, olive oil, lemon juice, garlic, and hot sauce in blender or food processor. Mix until smooth. Add tahini. Remix. Adjust consistency by adding more oil and lemon juice. Better if made ahead, overnight or several hours. Serve with warm pita bread.

Frances Seghers
Washington, D.C.

Mexican Caviar

1 (4 ounce) can chopped ripe olives, drained
2 tomatoes, chopped
1 (4 ounce) can chopped green chilies, drained
4 green onions (blades and all), chopped
3 tablespoons salad oil
1½ tablespoons red wine vinegar
Garlic powder, to taste
Salt, to taste
Pepper, to taste
Hot pepper sauce, to taste

In a large bowl, mix olives, tomatoes, green chilies, green onions, salad oil, and red wine vinegar. Add garlic powder, salt, pepper and hot pepper sauce to taste. Refrigerate overnight, stirring once or twice. Serve with corn chips or the equivalent. Makes 3 to 4 cups.

Dale Bishop

Stuffed Ripe Olives

Pull two or three very thin 1 to 2 inch long carrot strips through pitted ripe olives - very colorful.

Overtures

Mississippi Caviar

1 medium onion, sliced thin
½ cup salad oil
½ cup wine vinegar

2 garlic buds, split
2 (15 ounce) cans black-eyed peas, drained well

Mix all ingredients together 2 or 3 days before serving. Drain with pierced spoon before putting in serving bowl. Serve with saltine crackers. Makes about 4 cups.

Patsy Walker

Tex-Mex Dip

2 (10½ ounce) cans bean dip
1 (16 ounce) jar avocado dressing (the refrigerated type)
½ cup mayonnaise
1 cup sour cream
½ package taco seasoning

½ teaspoon lemon juice
1 (4.25 ounce) can chopped ripe black olives
¾ cup chopped green olives
2 large tomatoes, chopped
Shredded Cheddar cheese

In 9 inch square casserole dish, layer bean dip; then avocado dressing. Combine sour cream, mayonnaise, taco seasoning and lemon juice for next layer. Combine olives and sprinkle on top, then chopped tomatoes and top with cheese. Dip with corn chips. Makes 4 cups.

Note: If you can't find the refrigerated avocado dressing, I have substituted guacamole dip using fresh avocadoes. Follow the recipe on dip package.

Evelyn Gernert
Cleveland, Mississippi

Appetizers

Texas Trash

2 large or 3 medium tomatoes
1 large green pepper
1 bunch fresh green onions, including greens
2 avocadoes
1 (8 ounce) jar picante sauce (medium or hot)
2 cups sharp shredded Cheddar cheese
1 large bag corn chips (cheese corn chips go great)

Finely chop the tomatoes, green pepper, onions, and avocadoes. Put in large bowl. Add the jar of picante sauce, stir until well mixed. Spread the mix in a large pie or quiche dish, then cover the top with the shredded cheese. Use the chips to scoop up the mixture. Serves 8 to 10. *Can't stop eating them!*

Colleen M. Brown

"Quickies"

Cubes of sharp Cheddar cheese
Cream cheese topped with caviar, pepper jelly or Jezabel Sauce
1 Carton sour cream mixed with red caviar (Salmon)

Curried Cream Cheese Spread

8 ounces cream cheese, softened
1 teaspoon curry, or to taste
2 tablespoons chutney
¼ cup finely chopped green onion
¼ cup raisins
Slivered almonds
1 fresh pineapple (optional)

Beat the cream cheese with all ingredients except almonds and pineapple. Put in serving dish and top with almonds or put mixture in halved pineapple to serve. Makes 1½ cups.

Linda Shelton
Jackson, Mississippi

Overtures

Frozen Camembert Appetizer

10 ounces ripe Camembert cheese, rind removed
½ cup whipping cream
¼ cup butter, softened
⅛ teaspoon cayenne pepper
1 cup chopped walnuts

In the bowl of a food processor or blender, place cheese, cream, butter, and pepper. Process until smooth. Fold in ½ cup walnuts. Form mixture into a log shape on waxed paper. Coat with remaining nuts. Cover and freeze until firm but not too hard to cut. Or freeze until hard for storage, and defrost to cutting consistency before serving. Serves 8.

Martha Wiles

Cream Cheese Dip

1 (8 ounce) package cream cheese
½ cup plain yogurt or sour cream
2 tablespoons milk
1 (2½ ounce) jar dried beef, cut up
2 tablespoons chopped green pepper
2 tablespoons chopped onion
½ cup chopped pecans

Blend cream cheese, yogurt, and milk until smooth. Fold in beef, green pepper, and onion. Put in ovenproof bowl, put pecans on top, and bake at 350°F for 15 minutes. Serve hot with dip chips. Makes 2 to 3 cups.

Mrs. R. T. Gernert
Cleveland, Mississippi

Cheese Ball With a Difference

2 (8 ounce) packages cream cheese, room temperature
1 cup butter (no substitute)
1 tablespoon garlic powder
½ cup (or more) finely chopped toasted pecans or almonds

Mix the cream cheese, softened butter and garlic together. Roll in chopped nuts and refrigerate until firm. Serve with small crackers.

Mrs. Ron Rossi

Appetizers

Shrimp Cheese Ball

1 (8 ounce) package cream cheese
1½ teaspoons prepared mustard
3 teaspoons grated onion
2 teaspoons lemon juice
1 pound small boiled shrimp, chopped
Dash salt and paprika
Chopped pecans

Let cheese soften. Combine all ingredients, except pecans. Chill overnight. Form into ball or balls and roll in pecans. Serve with crackers.

Lisa Golotte
Biloxi, Mississippi

Susan's Cheese Ball

1 (8 ounce) package cream cheese
1 teaspoon basil
1 teaspoon caraway seed
1 teaspoon dill weed
Lemon pepper

Allow cream cheese to soften. Add basil, caraway seed, and dill weed. Form into ball and coat with lemon pepper. Makes a small cheese ball.

Mary Speer
Indianola, Mississippi

Cheese Ball

2 (8 ounce) packages cream cheese
1 (6½ ounce) can crushed pineapple (drained)
¼ cup chopped onions
¼ cup chopped bell pepper
1 tablespoon diced pimiento
1 tablespoon seasoning salt
1 cup chopped nuts
Paprika

Mix cream cheese, pineapple, onions, bell pepper, pimiento, seasoning salt and ½ cup chopped nuts and form into a ball. Sprinkle with additional nuts and desired amount of paprika. Refrigerate for 1 hour to allow cheese ball to get firm. Serve with crackers.

Pam Page

Overtures

Bleu Cheese Ball

1 (8 ounce) package cream cheese, softened
8 ounces bleu cheese, crumbled
¼ cup butter, softened
1 (14½ ounce) can pitted ripe olives, well drained and sliced
1 teaspoon Worcestershire sauce
Dash of hot pepper sauce
½ cup chopped walnuts
Chopped parsley or chopped walnuts or combination of both to cover ball

Blend cheeses and butter. Add olives, Worcestershire sauce, hot pepper sauce, and walnuts. Chill slightly for ease in shaping. Shape into one large ball or two smaller ones. Cover with parsley or finely chopped walnuts, or combination of both. Serve with assorted crackers. Good with tart apple slices.

Tracy Bell
Jackson, Mississippi

Bar Cheese

1 pound pasteurized process cheese spread
½ cup margarine
3 ounces cream cheese
⅔ cup horseradish
¼ cup bacon drippings
8 ounces sweet French salad dressing
Hot pepper sauce, to taste

Melt all ingredients in double boiler or in a two part casserole in a microwave oven. Beat until smooth. Pour into crocks or containers (covered). Can be frozen. Will keep in refrigerator two weeks. Makes 1 quart.

Dorothy Griffith
(Mrs. George Griffith)

Beverages

Christmas Mull

1 gallon cranberry juice
2 (6 ounce) cans frozen lemonade, thawed
2 (6 ounce) cans frozen orange juice, thawed
1 cup sugar
1 teaspoon whole cloves
½ teaspoon allspice
Peel from ½ orange cut into strips
Peel from ½ lemon cut into strips
2 tablespoons butter

Mix juices and sugar in large kettle; put spices and peels into a cheese cloth bag. Drop bag into juices and bring to a boil; reduce heat, but keep mixture hot. Add butter. Stir well and serve. Makes just over a gallon.

Connie G. Rast

Hot Buttered Rum

2 cups butter
1 pound powdered sugar
1 pound light brown sugar
2 teaspoons cinnamon
2 teaspoons nutmeg
1 quart ice cream, vanilla
Rum
Whipped cream
Cinnamon sticks

Combine butter, powdered sugar, brown sugar, cinnamon, and nutmeg. When well blended mix in ice cream. Freeze. To serve, thaw butter mixture slightly. In large mug combine 3 tablespoons of butter mixture, 1 jigger of rum. Fill mug with boiling water. Top with whipped cream. Add cinnamon stick as a stirrer.

Mrs. Phillip Sell

"I only drink to make other people seem more interesting.",
George Jean Nathan, theater critic.

Overtures

Hot Spiced Tea

1 cup sugar
5 tea bags
10 cups water
4 cinnamon sticks
24 whole cloves
Juice of 3 lemons

1 (46 ounce) can pineapple juice
1 (6 ounce) can frozen orange juice
1 (6 ounce) can frozen lemonade

Boil water and spices for 10 minutes. Strain out spices. Steep 5 tea bags in water mixture for 5 minutes. Add sugar, pineapple juice, lemon juice, orange juice and lemonade. Serve hot. Makes 20 cups.

Pam Wyont

Instant Mocha

5 cups non-fat dry milk powder
2 cups pre-sweetened cocoa powder

1 ¾ cups powdered non-dairy coffee creamer
¾ cup instant coffee crystals

Combine all ingredients. Store in tightly covered container. To serve, mix ⅓ cup mix with ¾ cup hot water. Makes 30 cups.

Rita Strachan

Bourbon Slush

1 (12 ounce) can frozen orange juice
1 (12 ounce) can frozen lemonade

1 (2 liter) bottle lemon-lime soda
2 cups sugar
2 cups bourbon

Mix ingredients and freeze; set out 1 hour before using. Makes 14 measuring cups.

Mrs. Ron Rossi

Beverages

Champagne Punch

2 quarts sauterne wine
1 (46 ounce) can pineapple juice

Juice of 6 lemons
1 cup sugar
1 quart champagne

Mix sauterne, pineapple juice, lemons and sugar and refrigerate overnight. Add champagne at last minute. About 24 servings.

Anne M. Gernert
Atlanta, Georgia

After Theatre Punch

1 dozen small juicy oranges, thinly sliced
½ dozen large ripe lemons, thinly sliced
1 (20 ounce) can crushed pineapple
2 (11 ounce) cans mandarin orange slices, crushed in the juice from the can

1 pint Napoleon (4 star) brandy
1 fifth good rye whiskey
1 fifth Irish whiskey
1 pint Grenadine
1 (16 ounce) jar maraschino cherries with juice
1 pint strong green tea
Chilled good dry champagne

At least two days, (preferably a week) before expected use, put all the above (except champagne) into a stone, glass or plastic container (do not use metal). Let this stand at room temperature, covered tightly. Stir well 2 or 3 times a day. About 1 day before time to use, strain mixture through cheese cloth and put the liquid in a closed plastic container into the freezer (it will not freeze). When ready to serve put cold mixture in punch bowl and charge it with the well chilled champagne. Use one cup of mixture per 1 fifth champagne. Use more if you like it stronger. Use very little ice in the bowl.

Served at reception for opening of GIGI, CTA 1986 season

Overtures

Mocha Punch

Punch

½ cup strong brewed coffee
½ cup granulated sugar
½ cup vanilla ice cream
1½ quarts cold whole milk

Topping

½ cup heavy cream
2 tablespoons instant cocoa
1 tablespoon granulated sugar
⅛ teaspoon cinnamon
Shaved chocolate

In the large bowl of electric mixer put all punch ingredients and blend together with electric mixer. Refrigerate until ready to serve. Prepare the topping just before serving. Whip cream until thickened. Gradually add cocoa, sugar, and cinnamon. Continue whipping until cream holds its shape. Top each serving with this and some shaved chocolate. Serves 10.

Note: Punch recipe may be doubled, quadrupled, etc., and stored in refrigerator until needed. Make topping only as needed. A good and pretty way to serve to a crowd is to freeze some of the punch mixture in 1 quart ring molds. Unmold ring in punch bowl; pour chilled punch over mold. Float topping in the center of the ring. Garnish with shaved chocolate.

Tracy Hale Bell
Jackson, Mississippi

Cranberry Rum Slush

12 ounce can frozen cranberry juice
1½ cups rum
Juice of 1 lemon
8 cups crushed ice

Combine all ingredients in a blender. Enjoy!

Lynda Bullard

Beverages

Henry's Celebration Punch

½ pound powdered sugar
1 fifth sauterne
3 ounces brandy
3 ounces maraschino
3 ounces orange flavored liqueur

½ cup lemon juice
3 bottles champagne, or 1 bottle soda water and 2 champagne

Mix all ingredients together except champagne, stir well and chill. When ready to serve put into punch bowl add block of ice and pour in champagne. Makes 1 gallon.

Henry Hobbs
Brookhaven, Mississippi

Southern Mint Juleps

The Syrup
2 double handfulls fresh mint
3 cups sugar

6 lemons
3 cups water

Wash mint. Mix sugar and water in a saucepan and bring to a boil. Remove from heat and add mint. Crush mint with a wooden spoon. Juice the lemons and set the juice aside. Add the lemon rinds to the hot syrup and allow the mixture to cool for 30 to 45 minutes to room temperature. Add the lemon juice. Strain, bottle and refrigerate. (This freezes well.) Serves 16.

Mixing the Julep

2 jiggers prepared syrup
2 jiggers bourbon

1 fresh sprig mint
Crushed ice

Pack crushed (or shaved) ice to the top of each glass or silver julep cup. Pour over the ice 2 jiggers of the syrup and 2 jiggers of bourbon. Lightly rub the rim of the glass or cup with the sprig of mint before garnishing the drink with it. The glass or cup will "frost" beautifully. *This is a sipping drink!*

Mrs. Hull Davis
(Her grandmother's recipe)

Overtures

World Famous Bloody Mary Mix

1 (46 ounce) can tomato juice
⅔ cup lemon and lime juice
   (fresh squeezed)
¼ cup tomato catsup
¼ cup Worcestershire sauce

2 teaspoons salt (heaping)
1 teaspoon celery salt
¾ teaspoon black pepper
½ teaspoon dill weed
½ teaspoon sweet basil

Half fill blender with tomato juice, put remainder in glass half gallon container. Add other ingredients and blend thoroughly. Pour into glass container with remaining tomato juice. Refrigerate overnight (can be kept refrigerated for two weeks). Serve in 12 ounce glass with ice and 40% vodka and 60% mix. Shake mix well before preparing drink. Serves 8 to 10.

George Griffith

Amaretto Liqueur

3 cups sugar
2 cups water
Lemon peel from 1 lemon
6 tablespoons almond extract

1 tablespoon chocolate extract
3 cups vodka
½ cup bourbon

In two quart saucepan combine sugar, water, and lemon peel. Bring to boil and simmer for 20 minutes. Remove from heat and add almond and chocolate extracts. Remove lemon peel and add vodka and bourbon. Pour into pint bottles to store. Enjoy in coffee, on ice cream, or in a cocktail glass with half and half cream. Makes 1 quart.

Lynn Wroten

"The trouble with the world is that everybody in it is three drinks behind.", Humphrey Bogart, stage & screen actor.

Beverages

Kahlua

3 cups water
3 cups sugar
12 tablespoons instant coffee

One fifth of vodka
4 teaspoons pure vanilla

Combine water, sugar, and instant coffee in two quart saucepan. Simmer for one hour. Remove from heat, and cool completely. Add bottle of vodka and vanilla. Pour into pint bottles to store. Makes for cheerful Christmas spirits. Makes 1¼ quarts.

Lynn Wroten

Peach Brandy

Wide mouth gallon glass jar with top
12 peaches (washed, unpeeled)

2½ pounds sugar
1 fifth gin

Put peaches in jar. Pour in sugar and gin. Put top on jar. Every day or two twist jar around to help dissolve sugar. After about a week when all the sugar has dissolved, add more gin to cover peaches (peaches will shrink). Store in a secure place (I use the bottom of my linen closet). Taste after two months; you may add more sugar or gin to taste. When ready to bottle, remove peaches (they are great on ice cream or pound cake). Strain liquid through several layers of cheese cloth so it will be beautifully clear. Bottle and enjoy. Makes ¾ gallon.

Note: I make this when peaches are at their best (June or July) and bottle it the last of November for Christmas gifts.

Mickey Hale

Overtures

Quick Lemonade

1½ cups sugar
¾ cup bottled real lemon juice

2 lemons—juice and peeling
3 quarts water

Mix and stir. Pour over ice. Serves 20

Mrs. R. C. Liddon

Lemon Tea

6 quarts water
4 quart size tea bags
1 cup sugar
2 (12 ounce) cans frozen lemonade concentrate, thawed and undiluted

Fresh mint leaves (optional)
Lemon slices (optional)

Bring water to a boil and add tea bags. Remove from heat, cover and let stand for 20 minutes. Remove tea bags, add sugar and lemonade concentrate to tea. Stir until thoroughly mixed. Serve over ice. Garnish with mint leaves and slices of lemon if desired.

Lenoir Stanley

Diet Pina Colada

1 cup non-fat dry milk
1 cup unsweetened orange juice
1 cup unsweetened pineapple juice

1½ teaspoons vanilla
1½ teaspoons coconut extract
1 cup crushed ice

Mix all ingredients in blender until frothy and cold. Makes 2 servings. This is low in calories.

DeEtta Wigginton

Beverages

Surprise Punch

1 cup sugar
2 cups water
1 (46 ounce) can unsweetened pineapple juice
1 (12 ounce) can frozen orange juice, diluted according to directions

2 (6 ounce) cans frozen lemonade, diluted according to directions
1 (24 ounce) can apricot nectar
1 (1 ounce) bottle almond extract
2 (32 ounce) bottles ginger ale, optional

Make a simple syrup from the sugar and water, cool. In large container mix all ingredients together and chill. When ready to serve, ginger ale may be added. Serves 15 to 20.

Note: I often freeze this into a slush and add ginger ale. Most refreshing and cooling in the summer. May decorate with fresh mint.

Mrs. Thelma Hedgepeth
Brookhaven, Mississippi

Pink Punch

3 (6 ounce) cans frozen pink lemonade
2 (6 ounce) cans frozen orange juice
1 (46 ounce) can orange and pineapple juice
2 (46 ounce) cans fruit punch

3 quarts water
2 (2 ounce) packages cherry drink mix
3 cups sugar
2 (32 ounce) bottles ginger ale
1 (64 ounce) bottle lemon-lime carbonated drink

Boil water and sugar until dissolved; cool. Add all ingredients except last two. Refrigerate. Just before serving add chilled ginger ale and lemon-lime drink. Serves 50.

Grace Teague
Ramer, Tennessee

Overtures

Orange Smoothie Punch

5 cups cold water
1 cup non-fat dry milk

1 (12 ounce) can frozen orange juice (unsweetened)

Mix water with milk powder and frozen juice. Stir well or blend in blender. Chill and serve or pour over ice cubes. Serves 8.

Ms. Joyce Pruett
Sherrard, Illinois

Punch for a Tea

3 cups orange juice
1 cup bottled lemon juice
1 cup pineapple juice
1 cup grape juice

1½ cups tea infusion
1 cup sugar
1 cup hot water
1 quart of ginger ale

Mix fruit juices and tea. Boil sugar and water 5 minutes. Cool. Combine with juices. Chill thoroughly. Just before serving add ginger ale. Serve over block of ice. Serves 20.

Mrs. R. C. Liddon

Spiced Cider Punch

2 gallons apple cider
8 (3 inch) sticks cinnamon
2 teaspoons whole cloves
2 quarts pineapple juice
6 quarts ginger ale

8 quarts orange juice
2 quarts lemon juice
2 (28 ounce) cans crushed pineapple

Simmer 2 cups of cider with spices in pan for about 15 minutes. Cool and remove spices. Chill all juices until cold. Combine all ingredients. Pour into punch bowl, add ice, and garnish with orange, lemon and cherry slices. Makes one hundred, 4 ounce servings.

Grace Teague
Ramer, Tennessee

Co-Stars

CO-STARS

Versatility is the hallmark of these co-stars. Often called upon to play supporting roles, they are equally effective as the stars of the show.

A favorite winter meal may consist of individual tureens of steaming clam chowder, a crisp green salad lightly coated with a vinaigrette dressing and sandwiches.

In Spring, luncheon in the garden may feature a cold soup, sandwiches, and a fresh fruit compote. Equally appealing is a "Tailgate" menu, where thermoses of hot soup are accompanied by robust ham or turkey sandwiches and a platter of crisp crudités.

Soups and salads each play another important role as separate courses in elegant dining or as an addition to a family meal. Just as bit-players in a show are constantly being cast in different roles, so these co-stars are frequently found in new and surprising places.

Menus

BRIDGE LUNCHEON FOR 12

Fresh Fruit with Redeal Fruit Dip

Marinated Asparagus with Mushrooms and Toasted Walnuts

Good Time Chicken Salad

Grand Slam Congealed Salad

Strawberry Frozen Yogurt Topped with Fresh Strawberry

Mr. Dick Atkins

Redeal Fruit Dip

½ cup sugar
2 tablespoons all purpose flour
1 cup pineapple juice

1 egg, beaten
1 tablespoon butter
1 cup whipping cream, whipped

Combine first 5 ingredients in a heavy saucepan; cook over medium heat, stirring constantly until smooth and thickened. Let cool completely; fold in whipped cream. Serve with fresh fruit. Makes about 2 cups.

Fresh Fruit Center Piece

Note: Base of arrangement of styroform covered with green foil paper. The base needs to be stacked to give a tier effect. Use whole fresh pineapple on bottom, then cut another pineapple lengthwise and attach to side with florist picks. Use large clusters of grapes (different colors) to cover base. Use canteloupe halves as containers for fruit and dip.

Co-Stars

Marinated Asparagus with Mushrooms And Toasted Walnuts

3 (15 ounce) cans asparagus or fresh cooked, drained asparagus
1 (16 ounce) package fresh mushrooms
1 (4 ounce) bag shelled English walnuts
1 (14 ounce) bottle Italian dressing

Wash and slice mushrooms. Toast walnuts until lightly brown. Place asparagus, mushrooms and walnuts in container and cover with Italian dressing. Let stand in refrigerator overnight. Drain well before serving.

Note: To designate servings of asparagus, small strips of pimiento can be laid over about 4 pieces.

Good Time Chicken Salad

6 large chicken breasts
1 cup slivered blanched almonds
2 cups green seedless grapes, halved
1 cup mayonnaise or until moist
Salt and lemon pepper to taste

Cook chicken and debone. Cut up and add other ingredients. Serve in pastry shells.

Grand Slam Congealed Salad

1 (6 ounce) box lemon gelatin
1 envelope plain gelatin
2 cups carrots, grated
1 cup nuts, chopped
1 (20 ounce) can crushed pineapple, drained

and chill to heavy syrup, according to directions. Add re-
gredients. Pour into individual molds; muffin papers in
n be used. When served, top with cottage cheese and gar-
e of olive.

Menus

SOUP'S ON

Leek Soup

French Onion Soup

Mallie's Chicken Soup

Assorted Breads and Crackers

Frozen Fruit Salad

Italian Cream Cake - p.358

This is a nice and different way to entertain. Have soups in tureens and guests may help themselves. (Most take a little of one then go try another, etc.) A good change from brunch or salad luncheon.

French Onion Soup

2 tablespoons butter
4 large onions, thickly sliced
6 cups beef stock
1 cup cream sherry
Black pepper

6 slices French bread, lightly toasted
3 tablespoons fresh Gruyere or Parmesan cheese, grated

In large saucepan, melt butter over medium heat and cook onions until they are golden. Add stock, sherry and dash of pepper. Simmer for 45 minutes. Place bread slices in bottom of ovenproof bowls and ladle in soup. Sprinkle cheese over bread and broil until cheese is melted. Serves 6.

Margel Young

Co-Stars

Leek Soup
Soupe Au Poireau

Serve this soup one of two ways, just as it comes from the microwave oven, or put through a blender to make a cream soup. It is good and refreshing, whether served piping hot or chilled.

¼ pound bacon, diced
1 cup chopped onion
1 cup finely chopped carrots
1 cup finely chopped celery
2 bunches leeks
4 medium-size potatoes, diced
1 tablespoon dried parsley flakes
1 teaspoon salt
Pepper to taste
¼ cup dry white wine, optional
1 cup water
1 teaspoon chicken bouillon concentrate
1 pint half and half

Cook the bacon in a casserole, uncovered, until it is brown and crisp (this will take about 4 to 5 minutes). Discard all but 2 tablespoons of the bacon drippings. Cut the leeks in half lengthwise. Wash them very carefully. Cut the leeks in ½ inch slices, crosswise, using all the white part and as much of the green part that is not too tough and coarse. Put the bacon, bacon drippings, onion, carrot, celery, leeks, potatoes, parsley, salt, pepper, wine, water and chicken bouillon in a large casserole and cook, covered, in the microwave oven, stirring from time to time, until the vegetables are tender. (This should take about 15 to 20 minutes.) Add the cream and 1½ cups chicken broth. Heat to a simmer. Put through a blender and serve as a cream soup. Tip: If you like your soup a bit thicker, mix 2 tablespoons flour with a little water and blend into the soup before the final heating. Traditionally, this is not a thick soup. Serves 6 to 8.

Barbara Redmont
Jackson, Mississippi

Menus

Mallie's Chicken Soup With "Better Than Zest"

5 chicken quarters
1 stick margarine
2 tablespoons vegetable oil
1 teaspoon salt
4 ribs celery, including leaves, chopped
2 large onions, diced
2 pints canned or frozen chicken broth
1 carrot, diced
8 cups water

3 cloves garlic, pressed
1 tablespoon flour
½ cup water
½ cup chopped parsley
"Better Than Zest" to taste (p. 383)
Salt, pepper and hot sauce to taste
Sprigs of parsley for garnish

In a heavy soup pot, sauté the chicken pieces in the margarine and vegetable oil until lightly brown on all sides. Add the chicken broth and the 8 cups of water, the onions, celery and carrot and 1 teaspoon salt. Bring to a boil, cover, and turn heat to low; and simmer until chicken is done (about 1 hour). Uncover and remove chicken to cool. Add the chopped parsley and pressed garlic and simmer uncovered for about 30 minutes to reduce the stock. Skin the chicken and dice. Return to the soup pot and keep warm. Now is the time to add "Better Than Zest" to taste. Add one frozen cube (which is about 1 tablespoon), stirring gently until thawed and blended into the soup. Taste for the special lemony flavor this is your "goal". The soup may be thickened slightly with your mixture of 1 tablespoon flour and ½ cup water which has been shaken vigorously in a small, capped jar. Re-heat the soup, being very careful not to let it burn, until it thickens. Taste again and add more "Better Than Zest" if necessary. Rice may be mixed into the soup or serve a mound on top of each serving of the soup. Sprinkle with parsley, of course. Serves 16.

Ms. Mallie Norwood

Co-Stars

Frozen Fruit Salad

1 (16 ounce) can fruit cocktail
1 (8 ounce) can crushed pineapple
1 cup mini marshmallows
½ cup sugar
½ cup maraschino cherries, chopped
2 bananas, sliced
2 tablespoons lemon juice
1 (8 ounce) carton sour cream

Combine fruit cocktail, crushed pineapple, marshmallows, sugar, maraschino cherries, bananas, and lemon juice. Add sour cream. Freeze in muffin tins or small molds. If using muffin tins, line with paper baking cups, and fill not quite full. This way, you can put a piece of cardboard on top of each pan and stack several on a freezer shelf. After completely frozen, it is easy to remove the paper from each serving. Also, you can store unused portions in a freezer bag for several weeks. Serves 24.

Mrs. Robert (Betty) A. Jennings
Memphis, Tennessee

"To make a good salad is to be a brilliant diplomatist...the problem is entirely the same in both cases. To know how much oil one must mix with one's vinegar.", Oscar Wilde, Irish playwright and poet.

Salads

Frozen Banana Salad

2 cups sour cream
1 (15½ ounce) can crushed pineapple, drained
Juice of 1 lemon or 2 tablespoons lemon juice

3 bananas, mashed
¾ cup sugar
½ cup pecans, chopped

Combine all ingredients, mix well and freeze until firm. Serves 6 to 8.

Mrs. Leo Norman

Black Cherry Salad

1 (16½ ounce) can pitted Bing cherries
1 (8 ounce) can crushed pineapple

1 (3 ounce) package cherry flavored gelatin
1 (3 ounce) package cream cheese (room temperature)
¾ cup chopped pecans

Drain the cans of Bing cherries and crushed pineapple, and add enough water to the juices to make 2 cups. Heat the liquid and cherry gelatin. Pour a small amount over the cream cheese; then add remainder of liquid and blend well. Chill the mixture until firm. Beat with mixer until fluffy. Fold in the Bing cherries, crushed pineapple, ¾ cup pecans (chopped). Pour into mold and chill several hours. Serves 6 to 8.

Mrs. Bob Lee (Carol)

Blueberry Salad

1 (3 ounce) package lemon gelatin
1 (3 ounce) package grape gelatin
1 cup boiling water

½ cup cold water
1 tablespoon lemon juice
1 (15 ounce) can blueberry pie filling

Dissolve gelatin in boiling water. Stir as you mix. Add cold water and lemon juice. Continue to stir well. Add blueberry pie filling. Pour into mold; and refrigerate until well chilled. Serves 6.

Mrs. Dolan Bugg (Rita)

Co-Stars

Grapefruit Salad

1 (3 ounce) package lemon gelatin
½ cup boiling water
1 envelope plain gelatin
3 tablespoons cold water
½ cup grapefruit juice

1 cup ginger ale or lemon-lime drink
¼ cup sugar
2 cups drained grapefruit sections

Dissolve lemon gelatin in ½ cup boiling water. Add 1 envelope plain gelatin, which has been dissolved in 3 tablespoons cold water. Add ½ cup grapefruit juice, 1 cup ginger ale, and ¼ cup sugar. Mix well. When it begins to set, add 2 cups drained grapefruit sections cut in bite size pieces. Pour into molds. Serves 8.

Note: This can be used for a low calorie salad by substituting nutra-sweet gelatin and nutra-sweet and diet soda for the gelatin, sugar, and soda.

Mrs. Orma R. Smith (Margaret)

Fruit Salad

3 bananas
2 (8 ounce) can Mandarin oranges

2 cups fresh seedless grapes (or 1 can seedless grapes)
1 cup strawberries, fresh or frozen (no sugar added)

Mix all ingredients together.

Sauce:

½ cup sour cream
1 tablespoon honey

1 tablespoon orange juice

Mix sauce and pour over the fruit. Gently toss.

Note: The sauce may be doubled. Serves 10.

Carol Baker
Michie, Tennessee

Salads

Cranberry Salad

1 (16 ounce) can whole
   cranberry sauce, melted
1 (3 ounce) box cherry gelatin
½ cup hot water
1 ground orange and juice

1 apple, diced
1 (8¼ ounce) can crushed
   pineapple
1 cup pecans, chopped
¼ cup chopped celery

Dissolve gelatin in hot water. Juice of orange and pineapple will take the place of extra liquid. Combine cranberry sauce, orange, apple, pineapple, pecans, and celery, and add to gelatin mixture. Put in refrigerator to congeal. Serves 12.

Mrs. Pete Pannell

Five Fruit Salad

3 bananas, sliced
1 (15 ounce) can chunk
   pineapple, drained, liquid
   reserved
1 (10 ounce) box frozen
   strawberries, undrained

1 (8 ounce) can Mandarin
   orange slices, drained
1 (15 ounce) can peach pie
   filling

Dip sliced bananas in reserved pineapple liquid; then discard liquid. Mix bananas with pineapple, strawberries, orange slices, and peach pie filling. Serves 10.

Mrs. Minnie Ulmer

Orange Pineapple Salad

1 (3 ounce) package orange
   gelatin
¾ cup boiling water
1 cup orange juice

1 (8 ounce) can crushed
   pineapple, drained
3 oranges, sectioned
½ cup pecans, chopped

Dissolve gelatin in boiling water; add orange juice. Chill until thickened. Add fruit and nuts. Pour into molds and chill. Serves 6 to 8.

Margaret Perkins

Co-Stars

Frozen Fruitcake Salad

1 cup dairy sour cream
½ of 4½ ounce carton frozen
   whipped dessert topping,
   thawed
½ cup sugar
2 tablespoons lemon juice
1 teaspoon vanilla

1 (13 ounce) can crushed
   pineapple, drained
2 medium bananas, diced
½ cup red candied cherries,
   sliced
½ cup green candied cherries,
   sliced
½ cup chopped walnuts

In mixing bowl, blend together sour cream, dessert topping, sugar, lemon juice and vanilla. Fold in fruit and nuts. Turn into 4½ cup ring mold. Freeze several hours or overnight. Unmold onto lettuce-lined plate. Garnish with additional candied cherries, if desired. Let stand 10 minutes before serving. Serves 8.

Rachel Goddard

Pear Salad

1 cup chopped celery
½ cup golden seedless raisins
1 teaspoon lemon juice
1 teaspoon lemon pepper
1 tablespoon honey
½ cup mayonnaise

4 slices cooked crumbled
   bacon
2 large pears, cored and
   chopped
3 tablespoons lemon juice
½ cup crumbled bleu cheese
Lettuce leaves

Combine chopped celery and raisins with lemon juice, lemon pepper, honey and mayonnaise. Chill for 15 minutes. Fry bacon and drain. Pour lemon juice over chopped pears. Combine chilled celery mixture with pears; add crumbled bacon. Chill for approximately 2 hours. Arrange large lettuce leaves on plates. Spoon salad onto lettuce leaves; sprinkle crumbled bleu cheese on each serving. Serves 4.

Brenda Rogers

Salads

Cottage Cheese and Pineapple Salad

1 (3 ounce) package lemon gelatin
1 (3 ounce) package lime gelatin
2 cups boiling water
1 (16 ounce) can crushed pineapple, drained
1 (12 ounce) carton small curd cottage cheese
1 (5 ounce) can undiluted evaporated milk
1 cup commercial salad dressing
1 cup pecans, chopped (optional)

Dissolve gelatin in boiling water and let cool but not set. Add pineapple, cottage cheese, evaporated milk, salad dressing, and pecans. Mix well and mold in a 2 quart dish. Serves 15.

Mrs. Frank Hinton

Cheekwood Port Wine Salad

2 (3 ounce) packages raspberry gelatin
2 cups boiling water
1 cup port wine
2½ cups (20 ounce can) undrained, crushed pineapple
1 (16 ounce) can jellied cranberry sauce
½ cup chopped nuts

Dissolve gelatin in boiling water. Cool slightly. Add remaining ingredients and mix thoroughly to dissolve the cranberry sauce. Place in 12 salad molds and chill until firm. Serves 12.

Note: Excellent with turkey or chicken or on a luncheon salad plate.

Ms. Aline E. Lampley
Assistant Manager
The Pineapple Room at
Cheekwood
Nashville, Tennessee

Co-Stars

Pretzel Salad

2 cups crushed pretzels
½ cup sugar
¾ cup margarine, softened
1 (8 ounce) package cream cheese, softened
1 cup sugar

1 (10 ounce) carton whipped topping
1 (6 ounce) package strawberry gelatin
2 (10 ounce) package frozen strawberries
2 cups boiling water

Mix pretzels, sugar, and margarine together. Spread in a 9x13 inch casserole dish. Bake at 350°F for 10 minutes. Mix cream cheese, sugar, and topping together. Spread over cooled pretzel layer. Dissolve gelatin in 2 cups boiling water. Add frozen strawberries, stirring until dissolved. Put in refrigerator until partially firm. Spread on top of cream cheese layer. Refrigerate until firm. Serves 12.

Elaine Key

Strawberry Nut Salad

2 (3 ounce) packages strawberry gelatin
1 cup boiling water
2 (10 ounce) packages frozen, sliced strawberries

1 (1 pound) can crushed pineapple, drained
3 medium bananas, mashed
1 cup chopped nuts
1 pint sour cream

Dissolve gelatin in boiling water. Fold in strawberries until thawed. Mix bananas, pineapple, and nuts; add to gelatin mixture. Pour half of mixture into 12x8 inch dish. Chill until firm. Leave other part of gelatin mixture sitting out. Spread the mixture in the dish with sour cream. Gently pour remaining mixture over sour cream. Refrigerate until congealed. Delicious with ham, turkey, or chicken. Serves 12 to 14.

Mrs. A. M. Farris

Salads

Artichoke Madrilene

1 package unflavored gelatin
½ cup cold water
1 (13 ounce) can red Madrilene
¼ cup fresh lemon juice
¼ teaspoon salt
2 tablespoons sugar
Dash pepper
1 large grated carrot
½ cup chopped celery
1 (8½ ounce) can artichoke hearts

Soak gelatin in cold water. Heat Madrilene then dissolve gelatin in it. Add lemon juice, and seasonings. Arrange vegetables in lightly oiled ring mold. Pour gelatin mixture over and chill to set.

Congealed Beet Salad

1 (3 ounce) package lemon gelatin
1 cup boiling water
¾ cup beet juice
2 tablespoons white vinegar
1 tablespoon minced onion
¼ teaspoon salt
1½ tablespoons cream style prepared horseradish
¾ cup diced celery
1 cup finely diced beets

Dissolve the gelatin in the hot water. Add the beet juice, vinegar, onion, salt, and horseradish, and chill until it begins to stiffen. Add the celery and beets; pour into an oiled mold and chill until firm. Serve on lettuce leaves with a spoonful of sour cream on top. Serves 6.

Doris D. Dixon

Broccoli and Cauliflower Salad

1 head broccoli
1 head cauliflower
1 cup celery, chopped
½ cup onion, chopped
6 pieces bacon, fried and crumbled
1 cup mayonnaise
¾ cup grated Parmesan cheese

Wash broccoli and cauliflower, and separate flowerets. Add chopped celery, onion, and crumbled bacon. Mix in mayonnaise and Parmesan cheese. Chill at least 24 hours before serving. Serves 12.

Lynn Wroten

Co-Stars

Artichokes A La Redmont

5 quarts water
3 tablespoons salt

6 artichokes

In a large pot, bring the water to a boil and add 3 tablespoons of salt. Add the artichokes, and boil 35 minutes or until done.

Vinaigrette Sauce:

1/3 cup vinegar
1 cup olive oil
1/2 teaspoon mustard powder

1/2 teaspoon salt
1/4 teaspoon white pepper

Combine the vinegar, olive oil, powdered mustard, salt, and white pepper in a bowl and whisk together. Or put ingredients in a bottle and shake well.

1 1/2 dozen flat anchovy filets (a small tin contains 1 dozen filets)
1 cup minced celery, strings removed

1/4 cup minced parsley
3/4 cup minced green onions
1 teaspoon salt
1/2 teaspoon white pepper

In a bowl combine the minced anchovies, celery, parsley, green onions, leaf scrapings, 1 teaspoon salt and 1/2 teaspoon of pepper. Divide the mixture into six equal portions. Use your hands to form the portions into balls, and squeeze out any excess liquid from the vegetables.

2 ripe tomatoes
3 cups chopped lettuce (1 large head of Boston or Bibb lettuce)

1 hard boiled egg, minced
3 teaspoons red caviar or roe (black)

To assemble the salad, begin by slicing each of the two tomatoes into three slices vertically, and then cut the slices in half. Put 1/2 cup of the chopped lettuce on each of six salad plates. Place an artichoke heart in the center and a ball of the mixed vegetables on each heart. Arrange two tomato slices on the plate on each side of the heart so that the inside of the slice is against the heart. The end slices should be placed skin side down. Sprinkle egg on top, then the caviar. Serves 6.

Salads

Fresh Broccoli Salad I

1 large bunch broccoli, broken into flowerets
⅔ cup chopped green olives
1 small onion, grated
4 hard cooked eggs, chopped
½ pound fresh mushrooms, chopped
1 whole egg

2 tablespoons Parmesan cheese
1 clove garlic, crushed
½ teaspoon Dijon mustard
Salt to taste
Freshly ground pepper
½ cup vegetable oil
⅓ cup lemon juice

Toss broccoli, olives, onions, eggs and mushrooms. Place egg, cheese, garlic, mustard, salt and pepper in blender, mix lightly. Add oil and lemon juice and mix. Pour dressing over salad one hour before serving. Serves 6 to 8.

Barbara Redmont
Jackson, Mississippi

Fresh Broccoli Salad II

Salad

2 bunches fresh broccoli
1 cup green olives, sliced
8 green onions, chopped

5 hard boiled eggs
1 pound bacon, fried, drained, crumbled

Dressing:

1 cup mayonnaise
¾ cup Parmesan cheese

1 (16 ounce) bottle Italian dressing
Salt and pepper

Wash broccoli and separate into flowerets. Break into small buds. Toss broccoli, olives, green onions, eggs, and bacon. Combine mayonnaise, cheese, dressing and seasonings to taste. Pour over the broccoli mixture. Refrigerate. Serves 12 to 15.

Co-Stars

Broccoli Salad

2 (10 ounce) boxes frozen chopped broccoli, cooked and drained
1 (8 ounce) package cream cheese
1 (10¾ ounce) can beef consommé
1 (4 ounce) jar chopped pimiento, drained

2 tablespoons Worcestershire sauce
3 tablespoons lemon juice
½ teaspoon black pepper
½ teaspoon salt
1 cup mayonnaise
1 teaspoon liquid hot pepper sauce
4 hardboiled eggs, chopped fine
2 envelopes plain gelatin, dissolved in ¼ cup water

On medium heat, gradually warm soup and cream cheese. Whip with a wire whisk until smooth and blended. Add dissolved gelatin, and let cool. In a large bowl, combine broccoli, pimiento, Worcestershire sauce, lemon juice, salt, and pepper, mayonnaise, pepper sauce, and hard-boiled eggs. Stir until blended; add soup mixture and stir. Grease a 1½ quart mold. Chill in mold until firm. To unmold, place a wet, hot dish rag over bottom of mold, or run a little warm water over bottom of mold. Serves 12.

Note: Options: 1. Add 2 cans tiny shrimp; 2. Add 1½ cups finely diced ham; 3. Omit cream cheese. Very rich. Needs "heavy" plain roast beef.

Lynn Elliott

Cauliflower Salad Bowl

4 cups thinly sliced raw cauliflower
1 cup chopped pitted ripe olives

⅔ cup chopped green pepper
½ cup chopped pimiento
½ cup chopped onion

In medium bowl, combine cauliflower, olives, green pepper, pimiento, and onion. Make dressing (recipe follows) and pour over cauliflower mixture. Refrigerate, covered, until well chilled. Toss just before serving. Serves 8.

Salads

Dressing

½ cup salad oil
3 tablespoons lemon juice
3 tablespoons wine vinegar

2 teaspoons salt
½ teaspoon sugar
¼ teaspoon pepper

Beat oil, lemon juice, vinegar, salt, sugar, and pepper in a small bowl until well blended.

Lynda Bullard

Charlengne Salad with Hot Brie Dressing

Garlic croutons as many as you wish
1 head curly endive

1 head iceburg
1 head Romaine

Place croutons in a large salad bowl. Cover with mixed greens and toss. Add dressing and toss again. Serve immediately.

1 cup olive oil
1 teaspoon minced green onion
2 teaspoons minced garlic
½ cup wine vinegar

2 tablespoons lemon juice
4 teaspoons Dijon mustard
10 ounces Brie cheese, rind removed and cut in pieces

Warm olive oil in large skillet on low heat for 10 minutes. Add green onion and garlic and cook until translucent, stirring occasionally. Blend in vinegar, lemon juice and mustard. Add Brie and stir until smooth. Season with pepper. Toss hot dressing with salad. Serve immediately. Serves 14 to 16.

Barbara Redmont
Jackson, Mississippi

Co-Stars

Chinese Salad

1 (3 ounce) package sugar-free orange gelatin
¾ cup boiling water
½ cup cold water
Ice cubes
1½ tablespoons soy sauce
1 tablespoon lemon juice
½ cup sliced celery
½ cup drained bean sprouts
¼ cup sliced water chestnuts
1 tablespoon sliced green onion

Completely dissolve gelatin in boiling water. Combine cold water and ice cubes to make 1 cup. Add to gelatin. Add soy sauce and lemon juice. Stir until ice is melted and gelatin is slightly thickened. Remove any unmelted ice. Add remaining ingredients and spoon into casserole or individual molds. Serves 4 to 6.

Cucumber Mousse

¾ cup boiling water
1 (3 ounce) package lime gelatin
1 cup peeled, grated cucumber
1 cup mayonnaise
2 tablespoons grated onion
1 cup sour cream
¼ teaspoon salt

Dissolve gelatin in boiling water. Chill until it thickens. Blend cucumber, mayonnaise, onion, sour cream, and salt; stir into gelatin. Mold and refrigerate. Can be served as salad or on crackers as an appetizer.

Miriam R. Propp

Kidney Bean Salad

½ teaspoon salt
2 (16 ounce) cans kidney beans, drained
1½ cups thinly sliced celery
⅔ cup onions, chopped
½ cup dill pickle, chopped
⅓ cup green pepper, chopped
½ cup French dressing

Salt the beans. Let stand while preparing remaining vegetables. Then combine all ingredients and toss well. Marinate 2 to 3 hours before serving. Serves 8 to 12.

Deborah D. Glorioso
Jackson, Mississippi

Salads

Nana's Corn Salad

1 (17 ounce) can white crisp shoe peg corn (do not substitute)
1 large firm tomato, peeled
1 tablespoon fresh lemon juice
1 heaping tablespoon mayonnaise
¼ teaspoon salt
¼ teaspoon coarse pepper
1 medium onion (diced fine)
1 medium bell pepper (diced fine)

Drain corn. Dice firm part of tomato and lay on paper towel; pat dry. Mix all ingredients. Chill for several hours in refrigerator. This is great because you do not have to cook. Serves 6 to 8. *(May be doubled.)*

Ms. Whitney Hodges
Columbus, Mississippi

Easie's Cucumber Salad

½ teaspoon salt
½ teaspoon sugar
¼ teaspoon red pepper
¼ cup red wine vinegar
1 teaspoon celery seed
1 cup sour cream
1 small Vidalia onion, chopped in big chunks
2 medium sized cucumbers

Mix salt, sugar and red pepper in wine vinegar, and stir until dissolved. Add sour cream and celery seed. Peel cucumbers; slice, and put in sour cream mixture. Mix with chunks of onion. Refrigerate for at least 2 to 3 hours before serving. Serves 3 to 4.

Note: Recipe can be doubled.

Mrs. O. B. Wooley, Jr. (Easie)
Jackson, Mississippi

Co-Stars

Layered Salad

1 head lettuce torn in bite size pieces
1 package frozen peas, thawed
¼ cup celery, chopped
¼ cup green pepper, chopped
¼ cup onion, chopped
1 (7½ ounce) can sliced water chestnuts, drained
1 pint mayonnaise
2 tablespoons sugar
Parmesan cheese
8 slices crisp bacon
4 hard boiled eggs
Tomatoes

Layer first six ingredients in order listed in large salad bowl. Completely seal the top with the mayonnaise. Sprinkle with 2 tablespoons sugar. Cover with Parmesan cheese. Refrigerate overnight. Top with 8 slices crumbled crisp bacon, hard boiled eggs and chunks of tomatoes. Serves 8.

Mrs. A. M. Farris

Macedonian Salad

2 medium eggplants
2 cups diced tomato
2 cups diced cucumber
1 cup diced green pepper
1 cup diced red pepper
½ cup sliced red onion
½ cup chopped fresh parsley
½ cup olive oil
½ cup wine vinegar
¼ cup dry red wine
2 tablespoons lemon juice
2 cloves garlic, minced
½ teaspoon oregano
½ teaspoon thyme
½ teaspoon basil
½ teaspoon salt
¼ teaspoon pepper

Peel eggplant, cut into ¾ inch slices. Salt lightly. Broil until light brown on both sides (4 to 5 minutes per side). Cool. Cut into bite size pieces. Combine eggplant, tomato, cucumber, red and green peppers, green onion and parsley in large bowl. Combine remaining ingredients in large jar with screw top. Shake thoroughly. Pour over vegetables. Toss gently and refrigerate for several hours. Serve on salad greens.

Salads

Mandarin Orange Salad with Tarragon Dressing

3 green onions, chopped
¼ cup chopped pecans
⅓ cup chopped fresh parsley
Boston lettuce leaves

2 cups Mandarin oranges, drained
1 cup purple or red grapes, halved with seeds removed

Dressing

3 tablespoons vinegar
¼ teaspoon salt
¼ teaspoon pepper

1 tablespoon tarragon
½ cup salad oil

Mix onion, pecans, parsley, oranges and grapes. Mix dressing ingredients together. Pour ¼ cup of dressing over salad and refrigerate for 1 hour. Arrange lettuce leaves on salad plates and mound orange mixture. Add the remaining dressing.

Mushroom Salad

1½ pounds fresh mushrooms
¾ cup olive oil
1 tablespoon lemon juice
¼ cup wine vinegar
1 teaspoon seasoned salt
Fresh ground pepper

2 tablespoons minced parsley
2 tablespoons minced pimientos
4 green onions, minced
Watercress, for garnish
Lettuce

Wash, drain, dry and slice mushrooms. Mix remaining ingredients. Pour over sliced mushrooms. Marinate 4 hours before serving on beds of lettuce leaves with watercress garnish.

"Seeing is deceiving. It's eating that's believing.",
James Thurber, American playwright.

Co-Stars

Potato Salad

8 medium potatoes
8 large hard boiled eggs
1 onion, chopped
3 to 4 sweet pickles, chopped
1 teaspoon mustard

½ cup mayonnaise
1 cup sour cream
Freshly ground pepper, to taste
Salt to taste

Boil potatoes in the skins until soft when pierced with a fork. Peel and dice potatoes and mix with chopped onions while potatoes are still hot. Chop boiled eggs and add to potatoes. Add pickles, salt and pepper. Mix well. Add mustard, mayonnaise and sour cream. Mix thoroughly and chill. Serves 10.

Note: Mayonnaise and sour cream may be adjusted as to one's taste.

Martha Wiles
Memphis, Tennessee

Vera's Cabbage Salad

1 medium head cabbage
4 red onions, medium sized

4 bell peppers

Shred cabbage into thin strips. Cut onions and pepper into rings.

Dressing

1 cup salad oil
1½ cups vinegar

¾ cup sugar
½ teaspoon red pepper

Mix and use as a marinade for cabbage mixture. Serves 8 to 10.

Vera Wagner
Memphis, Tennessee

Salads

Cruise Street School Slaw

12 heads white cabbage (or more)
1 gallon dill pickles

2 gallons salad dressing
4 large bottles catsup
2 quarts prepared mustard

Grind cabbage and pickles coarsely and mix together. Add salad dressing, catsup and mustard and mix thoroughly. Keep cool.

The Cruise Street School used to have a Hot Dog Supper every year. This was their slaw recipe. We prepared it in the cafeteria using the big pans and meat grinders or vegetable graters. But today's food processors ought to simplify the work and cut down on the time. The children loved this slaw. Will feed 300 for hot dogs.

Mrs. Richard B. Warriner (Ellen)

Freezer Slaw

1 medium head cabbage
1 teaspoon salt
1 carrot
1 sweet pepper
1 cup vinegar

1½ cups sugar
¼ cup water
1 teaspoon mustard seed
1 teaspoon celery seed

Grate cabbage and mix with salt. Let stand for one hour and squeeze out excess water. Grate carrot and sweet pepper. Add to cabbage mixture. Mix vinegar, sugar, water, mustard seed and celery seed together and bring to a boil. Let cool to lukewarm and pour over cabbage mixture. Put in containers and freeze. Thaw and serve. Yield: 3 pints.

Note: Originally published in Savannah's Proud As A Peacock *cookbook. Reprinted here by special permission of Savannah Junior Auxiliary.*

Mrs. Russell Neill (Linda)
Savannah, Tennessee

Co-Stars

24 Hour Slaw

½ purple cabbage
½ green cabbage
1 purple onion
1 bell pepper
1 tablespoon celery seed

1 tablespoon dry mustard
1 tablespoon salt
1 cup sugar
¾ cup vegetable oil
1 cup white vinegar

Slice cabbage, onion and bell pepper. Combine celery seed, mustard, salt, sugar, vegetable oil, and vinegar, and bring to a boil. Mix with sliced vegetables immediately. Store in refrigerator. Serves 8.

Note: This is good with barbecue!

Nancy N. McLemore

Spinach Salad with Hot Bacon Dressing

½ pound bacon
4 teaspoons brown sugar
½ cup sliced green onions or scallions
½ teaspoon salt
3 tablespoons vinegar
¼ teaspoon dry mustard
Dash paprika

1½ pounds spinach, washed and trimmed
Sliced fresh mushrooms
Sliced celery
Hard boiled eggs
Garnish: tomato wedges and chopped parsley

Dice bacon and fry over medium high heat. Reduce heat, and add brown sugar, green onions or scallions, salt, vinegar, mustard, and paprika. Pour hot dressing over spinach, mixed with mushrooms, celery, and sliced hardboiled eggs. Garnish with tomato wedges and chopped parsley.

Joan Hennessy

Salads

Frozen Tomato Salad

1 (16 ounce) carton cottage cheese
1 (8 ounce) package cream cheese
1 (16 ounce) can crushed pineapple, not drained
1 (46 ounce) can tomato juice
2 cups unsweetened pineapple juice
1 medium onion, grated
1 quart mayonnaise
2 tablespoons Worcestershire
Hot pepper sauce, to taste

Place cottage cheese and cream cheese in blender or food processor; blend until smooth; mix with the rest of the ingredients. Pour into container and freeze. If freezing in refrigerator, stir several times while freezing. Makes a little less than a gallon. May be frozen in paper muffin cups (placed in muffin tins) and stored in plastic bags in the freezer for several months.

University Club
Memphis, Tennessee

Tomato Soup Aspic

2 envelopes unflavored gelatin
½ cup cold water
1 can tomato soup
3 (3 ounce) packages cream cheese
1 cup chopped celery
½ cup chopped green pepper
½ cup chopped stuffed olives
1 heaping tablespoon grated onion
2 tablespoons lemon juice
1 cup mayonnaise
1 tablespoon Worcestershire sauce
1 teaspoon hot sauce
Salt to taste

Soften gelatin in cold water. Heat soup in a double boiler; add cream cheese. Whip with rotary beater, and add gelatin. Stir until dissolved. Cool; add celery, pepper, olives, onion, lemon juice, mayonnaise, Worcestershire sauce, hot sauce, and salt. Pour in oiled mold or pan, and chill until firm. Serves 6 to 8.

Note: To freeze, omit the celery and green pepper. Thaw in refrigerator overnight.

Doris D. Dixon

Co-Stars

Tomato Aspic With Artichoke Hearts

3 cups tomato vegetable juice
2½ packages plain gelatin
Red pepper, to taste
Liquid hot sauce, to taste

1 stalk celery, minced
½ onion, minced
1 (16 ounce) can artichoke hearts, drained

Let half the tomato vegetable juice come to a boil. Stir gelatin in ½ cup water then add to hot juice. Mix chopped celery and onions in cold juice with red pepper and hot sauce. Pour into hot juice. Put 1 artichoke heart in each individual mold, then fill mold with vegetable juice mixture. Place in refrigerator, let congeal. If made in ring mold, double recipe and cut the artichoke hearts in half. Serve with homemade mayonnaise. Serves 6 to 8.

Mrs. Ted Bushey (Mary)

Tomato Ice

3 large tomatoes (peeled, seeded, and chopped)
¼ chopped onion
¼ cup chopped celery
1 tablespoon sugar
1 tablespoon fresh lemon juice

½ teaspoon Worcestershire sauce
¼ teaspoon salt
2 sprigs mint
¼ teaspoon dried mustard
2 drops hot pepper sauce

Combine and pureé all ingredients. Put in shallow container and freeze. When frozen cut in big pieces and place in food processor again. Pour back in dish and freeze again.

Salads

Fresh Vegetable Marinade

4 stalks fresh broccoli
8 large fresh mushrooms, sliced
1 medium green pepper, chopped
3 stalks celery, chopped
1 small head cauliflower, broken into flowerets

1 cup sugar
2 teaspoons dry mustard
1 teaspoon salt
½ cup vinegar
1½ cups vegetable oil
1 small onion, grated
2 tablespoons poppy seeds

Remove flowerets from broccoli; cut into bite size pieces. Reserve stalks for other use. Combine broccoli flowerets, mushrooms, peppers, celery, and cauliflower. Toss lightly. Combine sugar, mustard, salt, vinegar, oil, onion, and poppy seed; mix well; and pour over vegetables. Chill at least 3 hours. Serves 10 to 12.

Rita Strachan

Sweet and Sour Salad

1 (17 ounce) can green sweet peas, drained
1 (16 ounce) can green beans, drained
1 small jar pimientos (optional)
1 medium onion, sliced and separated into rings

¾ cup vinegar
¼ cup vegetable oil
¾ cup sugar
½ teaspoon salt
½ teaspoon celery seed
¼ teaspoon pepper

In large bowl, combine peas, beans, pimientos, and onion. Combine vinegar, oil, sugar, salt, celery seed, and pepper; pour over mixture. Cover and chill several hours or overnight. Serves 10.

Lenetia Childers

Variation: Add to the above: 1 can shoe peg corn, 1 can water chestnuts, 1 can bamboo shoots, ½ cup celery, chopped. Serves 14.

Mrs. Bob O'Brien

Co-Stars

Vegetable Mold

1 pint mayonnaise
1 teaspoon salt
Dash of garlic powder
Dash of pepper
2 packages unflavored gelatin
1 bell pepper
1 cup celery

1 cucumber
1 large carrot
2 medium tomatoes
1 grated onion
3 tablespoons dry parsley
Dillweed

Soften 2 packages gelatin in ¼ cup cold water. Add ¼ cup boiling water to dissolve. Combine in mixing bowl the mayonnaise, salt, pepper, and garlic powder. Add the gelatin to the mayonnaise mixture gradually. Add dillweed and parsley. Add chopped bell pepper, celery, cucumber, carrot, tomatoes, and grated onion. Pour all into a 6 cup mold that has been greased with mayonnaise. Refrigerate. Serves 8 to 10.

Goldie Himelstein
Moorhead, Mississippi

Wild Rice Salad

2 cups cooked wild rice and long grain white (may use minute)
2 hard boiled eggs, chopped

½ cup black olives, sliced
1 cup celery, chopped
1 small jar pimiento, chopped

Dressing

1 cup mayonnaise
1 teaspoon horseradish mustard

1 teaspoon lemon juice
1 teaspoon grated onion
1 teaspoon curry powder

Mix with rice and serve with cold rare roast beef.

Mrs. Phil Nelson

Salads

Chicken Tomatoes

6 large tomatoes
½ cup plus 2 tablespoons mayonnaise
¾ teaspoon curry powder
½ teaspoon salt
¾ teaspoon lemon juice
⅛ teaspoon pepper

1 cup cooked rice
1 cup cooked, diced chicken
½ cup diced celery
2 tablespoons chopped green onion
¾ cup cooked green peas
1 tablespoon chopped pimiento

Scoop out pulp of tomatoes; invert, and drain. Combine mayonnaise, curry powder, salt, pepper and lemon juice. Add rice, chicken, celery, onion, peas, and pimiento; mix well. Fill tomatoes with mixture and chill. Serve on bed of lettuce. Serves 6.

Mrs. Charles McDonald (Donna)

Chicken Salad Mousse

2 (10¾ ounce) cans chicken rice soup (undiluted)
2 envelopes gelatin, unflavored
6 ounces cream cheese, softened and cut into small pieces
6 tablespoons mayonnaise
4 large or 6 small (about 2 pounds) chicken breasts, steamed and diced

1 (16 ounce) can early English peas, drained
1 cup celery, finely diced
½ cup salad olives, chopped
1 (2 ounce) jar pimientos, chopped
10 green onions, diced (include tops)
1 large bell pepper, finely diced
1 teaspoon salt

Mix soup and gelatin; heat, but do not boil. Add cream cheese; let melt; cool. Add mayonnaise. Add chicken, peas, celery, olives, pimiento, onions, pepper, and salt. Pour into a 3 quart oblong casserole dish (9x13 inch), sprayed with cooking oil. Refrigerate overnight. Cut into squares. Garnish with mayonnaise and paprika. Serve on lettuce. Serves 15.

Mrs. Frank Hinton

Co-Stars

Curry Vegetable Salad

1⅓ cups precooked rice
1½ cups boiling water
½ teaspoon salt
¼ cup French dressing (recipe page 130)
¾ cup mayonnaise
1 tablespoon minced onion
¾ teaspoon curry powder
½ teaspoon salt
⅛ teaspoon pepper
½ teaspoon dry mustard
½ cup diced celery
½ cup thinly sliced radishes
½ cup thinly sliced cauliflower
½ cup sliced carrots
1 cup frozen peas

MAKE THIS A DAY AHEAD!! In saucepan, combine water, rice, and salt; cook rice according to package directions. Lightly toss in French dressing. Cool; refrigerate. In bowl, blend mayonnaise with onions, curry powder, salt, pepper and mustard. Add to rice mixture. Refrigerate. Combine vegetables with rice mixture the day of serving, at least one hour before serving. Serves 6 to 8.

Claire Stanley

Chicken Salad

5 cups cooked chicken breasts, boned and diced
2 cups pineapple chunks, drained
¾ cup toasted almonds or cashews
2 cups seedless grapes
2 cups celery, diced
1 cup mayonnaise
1 cup sour cream
1 teaspoon curry powder
1 teaspoon salt
Lettuce

Combine chicken, pineapple, nuts, grapes and celery in a large salad bowl. Mix together the mayonnaise, sour cream and seasonings. Stir into the salad mixture and chill an hour. Serve over lettuce. Serves 4 to 6.

Mrs. Bill Alexander

Salads

Corned Beef Salad

1 envelope unflavored gelatin
1 tablespoon cold water
1 (3 ounce) package lemon gelatin
1 can beef consommé
1 can warm water
3 hard boiled eggs, chopped
1 cup diced celery
1 (7 ounce) can corned beef, chopped
1 small onion, grated
½ green pepper, diced
2 or 3 tablespoons chopped pimiento
¾ cup mayonnaise

Soak unflavored gelatin in one tablespoon cold water. Heat one can water and pour over lemon gelatin, stirring until well dissolved. Combine lemon gelatin and gelatin mixtures, adding consommé which has been warmed. Add eggs, celery, corned beef, onion, pepper, pimiento, and mayonnaise, stirring well. Pour in oblong pan to set. Serves 10 to 12.

Helen Cranwell

Pork Apple Salad

2 cups cooked and diced pork (leftover roast is good)
1 cup diced celery
1½ cups diced apples
1½ cups grated carrots
1 (14½ ounce) can English green peas, drained
Mayonnaise to taste
Lettuce leaves

Combine all ingredients. Use enough mayonnaise to make a moist salad. Refrigerate overnight. Serve on lettuce leaves on individual salad plates. Serves 6 to 8.

Ms. Joyce Pruett
Sherrard, Illinois

Co-Stars

Layered Ham 'N Potato Salad

Ham Layer

1½ cups diced, cooked ham
¼ cup chili sauce
1 tablespoon finely chopped onion
2 teaspoons prepared mustard
1 teaspoon bottled horseradish
½ cup water to soften 1 envelope plain gelatin
½ cup mayonnaise

Combine ham, chili sauce, onion, mustard and horseradish. Soften the gelatin in the ½ cup water. Stir ¼ into the mayonnaise and add to the ham mixture. Turn into a 10X6X½ inch baking dish. Chill until almost set. (Keep remaining gelatin at room temperature.)

Potato Layer

2 cups diced, cooked, white potatoes
2 cups diced celery
2 tablespoons diced green, sweet pepper
1 tablespoon finely diced onion
1 teaspoon salt
⅛ teaspoon pepper
1 cup mayonnaise
Remainder of the gelatin

Mix potatoes, celery, green pepper, onion and mayonnaise. Taste and add salt and pepper. Stir in the reserved gelatin and spread the potato salad on top of the ham mixture. Chill at least 8 hours. Cut into squares for serving. Serves 8.

Taco Salad

1 pound ground beef
½ teaspoon chili powder
1 cup Cheddar cheese, shredded
1 large head lettuce, shredded
2 medium tomatoes, chopped
2 cups taco chips, broken
½ cup black olives, sliced
1 cup ranch dressing, milk or buttermilk type
1 sliced avocado
Taco chips, unbroken

Brown ground beef with chili powder. Drain. Combine with next 6 ingredients. Garnish with avocado and serve with taco chips. Good hot or cold.

Salads

West Indies Salad

1 pound fresh lump crabmeat
1 medium onion, finely chopped
2 stalks celery, finely chopped
½ bell pepper, finely chopped
4 ounces vegetable oil

3 ounces cider vinegar
4 ounces ice water
Salt
Pepper

Combine onion, celery and bell pepper. Spread ½ of this mixture over bottom of large mixing bowl. Separate crabmeat lumps and place on top of vegetable mixture in bowl, then spread balance of mixture on top of crabmeat. Now salt and pepper to taste. Pour over all; first, the vegetable oil, next the vinegar and lastly, the ice water. Cover and place in refrigerator to marinate from 2 to 4 hours. When ready to serve toss lightly, but do not stir. Do not substitute any of ingredients as results would not be the same. Serves 4.

Lenoir Stanley

Oriental Salad

1 (10 ounce) package frozen peas
1½ cups of pre-cooked rice (instant)
2½ pounds shrimp
1½ cups thinly sliced celery
¼ cup chopped onion
½ cup salad oil
3 tablespoons red wine vinegar

1 tablespoon soy sauce
¾ teaspoon curry powder
1 teaspoon salt
½ teaspoon monosodium glutamate
½ teaspoon celery seed
½ teaspoon sugar
¼ cup slivered almonds

Cook rice according to directions and set aside. Green peas should be cooked by package directions and set aside. Cook and peel shrimp. In large bowl, mix rice, peas, shrimp, celery, onions, and almonds. Combine oil, vinegar, soy sauce, curry powder, salt, monosodium glutamate, celery seed, and sugar. Mix well, and pour over rice mixture. Better if made day ahead. Serves 8 to 10.

Mrs. O. B. Wooley, Jr.
(Easie Mercier)
Jackson, Mississippi

Co-Stars

Shrimp Topped Salad

2 (6 ounce) packages lemon gelatin, dissolved in ¾ cup hot water
2 (8 ounce) packages cream cheese
1 cup half and half or whole milk
2 cups thinly sliced celery
1 cup thinly sliced, stuffed olives
2 cups whipping cream (whipped)
18 lettuce cups

Dissolve gelatin in boiling water. Blend cream cheese and milk or cream and add to dissolved gelatin; cool until it starts to set. Add celery and olives. Fold in whipping cream. Pour into 13x9x2 inch oblong dish; refrigerate for 12 hours.

Shrimp Topping

2 tablespoons lemon juice
2 cups salad dressing and mayonnaise (mixed)
2 teaspoons green onion, finely chopped
½ cup finely chopped green pepper
4 (4½ ounce) cans shrimp, drained

Mix lemon juice, salad dressing-mayonnaise mixture, green onions, green pepper and shrimp. Serve as topping for salad. Serves 18.

Jewel Dougherty
Memphis, Tennessee

Nancie's Salad

1 head cauliflower, in flowerets
1 bunch broccoli, flowerets
1 bunch green onions, sliced
½ bunch radishes, sliced
6 ounces Monterey Jack cheese, shredded
1 pound shrimp, cooked, deveined
1 (8 ounce) bottle creamy Italian dressing

Mix vegetables, cheese and shrimp together. Toss with dressing. Chill before serving. Serves 6 to 8.

Nancie McGehee
Watertown, New York

Salads

Turkey-Wild Rice Salad

1 package long grain and wild rice mix (cooked with seasoning)
2 cups cooked extra long grain rice
3 cups chopped turkey
4 tablespoons oil
1 cup salad dressing
8 hard-cooked eggs, chopped
2 cups chopped celery
1 cup chopped green pepper
1 cup chopped onion
4 tablespoons red wine vinegar
Salt and pepper, to taste

Combine rices, turkey, oil, salad dressing, hard cooked eggs, celery, green pepper, onion, and vinegar. Toss gently. Refrigerate overnight; salt and pepper before serving. Serves 16.

Mrs. Carl Welch

Exotic Luncheon

2 quarts cut up cooked turkey or chicken
2 pounds seedless green grapes
1 cup diced dates
1 (20 ounce) can water chestnuts
2 cups sliced celery
1 (4 ounce) can Mandarin orange sections
1 (4 ounce) can pineapple tidbits
2/3 cup toasted slivered almonds
3 cups mayonnaise
1 tablespoon curry powder
2 tablespoon soy sauce

Mix and combine turkey or chicken, grapes, dates, water chestnuts, celery, oranges, pineapple. Mix mayonnaise, curry powder, and soy sauce to make dressing; pour over salad ingredients and toss. Chill several hours. Spoon into nest of Bibb or Boston lettuce. Sprinkle with almonds. Serves 12.

Martha T. Kabbes

Co-Stars

Apricot Cream Dressing

1 (8 ounce) carton sour cream
¼ cup chopped pecans or walnuts
¼ cup flaked coconut
2 tablespoons apricot preserves

Combine sour cream, nuts, coconut, and preserves, and serve over honeydew balls or other fruit. Yield 1½ cups.

Mildred A. Smith

Bleu Cheese Special Dressing (2 cups)

4 ounces blue cheese crumbled, ¾ cup
1 cup mayonnaise
½ cup dairy sour cream
½ to 1 clove garlic minced
2 teaspoons finely cut green onions and tops
1 tablespoon wine vinegar
1 tablespoon lemon juice
1 teaspoon sugar

Blend well.

Mrs. A. C. Wiggins
Cleveland, MS

Salad Dressing A La Steak House

1 (3 ounce) package cream cheese
3 tablespoons light cream
1 tablespoon mayonnaise
½ teaspoon lemon juice
½ teaspoon grated onion
Dash of cayenne or hot pepper sauce
1½ teaspoons Worcestershire sauce
6 tablespoons commercial sour cream
6 tablespoon crumbled bleu cheese
3 teaspoons catsup
½ teaspoon salt

Mix cream cheese, cream, mayonnaise, lemon juice, grated onion, cayenne or pepper sauce, Worcestershire sauce, sour cream, bleu cheese, catsup, and salt in blender or food processor. Yield 1½ cups.

Katherine Brown Worde
Durham, N.C.

Salad Dressings

Celery Seed Dressing

½ cup sugar
1 teaspoon dry mustard
¼ teaspoon salt
1 teaspoon celery seed

⅓ cup honey
1 tablespoon lemon juice
4 tablespoons white vinegar
1 cup salad oil

Mix sugar, mustard, salt, and celery seed. Add honey, lemon juice, and vinegar. Mix with electric mixer on medium speed. Pour oil into mixture slowly, beating constantly, until ingredients are mixed and dressing thickens. Chill and serve over fruit. Yield 1 pint.

Mrs. Hull Davis (Bitsy)

Come Back Sauce

2 cloves garlic, chopped fine
1 cup mayonnaise
¼ cup chili sauce
¼ cup catsup
1 teaspoon prepared mustard
½ cup vegetable oil
1 tablespoon Worcestershire sauce

Dash black pepper
Dash of liquid pepper sauce
Dash of paprika
Juice of 1 medium onion
Juice of 1 lemon
2 tablespoons water

Mix well in large mixing bowl the garlic, mayonnaise, chili sauce, catsup, mustard, vegetable oil, Worcestershire sauce, pepper, liquid pepper sauce, paprika, onion juice, lemon juice, and water. Blender can be used. Store in refrigerator. Yield about one quart.

Note: Recipe is from Dennery's Restaurant in Jackson, Mississippi.

Becky Laughlin

Co-Stars

Fruit Marinade

1 (6 ounce) can frozen lemonade, thawed and undiluted
¼ cup orange marmalade
2 tablespoons orange flavored liqueur, Cointreau, or white rum

Mix together lemonade, marmalade, and liqueur, and serve over any fresh fruits.

Note: Marinade and fresh peaches may be used over ice cream.

Jewel Dougherty

Zesty French Dressing

1 (15 ounce) can tomato sauce
1½ cups vegetable oil
½ cup vinegar
1 cup sugar
1 tablespoon prepared mustard
1 teaspoon pepper
1 teaspoon salt
1 tablespoon paprika
1 tablespoon celery seed
3 cloves garlic, minced

Combine tomato sauce, oil, vinegar, sugar, mustard, pepper, salt, paprika, celery seed, and garlic in blender. Yield: Approximately 3½ cups.

Claire Stanley

Louis Dressing

1 cup mayonnaise
¼ cup chili sauce
¼ cup dry sherry
2 tablespoons chopped parsley
1 teaspoon grated onion
½ teaspoon Worcestershire sauce
Salt, to taste

Mix mayonnaise, chili sauce, sherry, parsley, onion, Worcestershire sauce and salt in a small bowl. Chill at least 2 hours. Good on crabmeat and other seafood. Yield: 1½ cups.

Mrs. John D. Mercier

Salad Dressings

Honey Dressing

1 cup mayonnaise
4 tablespoons prepared
  mustard
4 tablespoons vinegar
4 tablespoons honey
3 sprigs parsley, chopped
¼ medium sized onion, diced
  fine
1 dash salt
½ teaspoon sugar
½ teaspoon monosodium
  glutamate
1 cup vegetable oil

Combine mayonnaise, mustard, vinegar, honey, parsley, onion, salt, sugar, monosodium glutamate in blender and mix. Add oil slowly and mix well. Refrigerate. Yield: 2½ cups.

Rachel Goddard

Homemade Mayonnaise

1 quart vegetable oil
1 egg
1 teaspoon salt
½ teaspoon dry mustard
4 tablespoons lemon juice

Put egg, salt, and mustard into blender; add 1 tablespoon lemon juice. Blend well, and begin to add, very slowly, the oil, letting it pour in a small steady stream into the blender. Keep mayonnaise pushed away from sides of blender. Use lemon juice intermittently to thin the mayonnaise, or add after all oil has been added. The key to perfect mayonnaise is not to add the oil too rapidly. Wonderful on a summer tomato sandwich! Yield: 1 quart.

Note: First aid for separated mayonnaise: Remove all ingredients from blender and put 2 tablespoons water into blender. Slowly pour mixture back into blender while it runs.

Rosemary Fisher

Co-Stars

Mollie's Remoulade Sauce

2 boiled eggs, chopped
3 ribs celery, chopped
1 tablespoon Worcestershire
2 tablespoons sauterne wine
3 tablespoons prepared
  mustard
5 tablespoons creole mustard

1 teaspoon salt
1 teaspoon sugar
¼ teaspoon red pepper
2 cups mayonnaise
2 green onions, chopped
1 garlic clove, chopped

Place all ingredients in blender and blend until smooth and creamy. Make one day in advance, but may be stored one week. Makes 2½ cups. *To serve:* Arrange boiled shrimp on a bed of lettuce of pour sauce over all.

Ann White

Roquefort Cheese Dressing

1 cup salad oil
¼ cup tarragon or wine vinegar
1 teaspoon salt
½ teaspoon paprika
1 teaspoon sugar

½ teaspoon dry mustard
Few dashes white pepper
¼ pound Roquefort or bleu
  cheese

Combine oil, vinegar, salt, paprika, sugar, mustard, and pepper, and beat to a smooth emulsion. Crumble cheese coarsely into mixture. Stir until just blended. Lumps of cheese should be present to make this dressing more interesting. Makes about 1½ cups.

Russian Dressing

1 cup mayonnaise
2 hard boiled eggs, grated
1 teaspoon dill relish
Generous dash of garlic salt
Dash of celery salt

Salt and pepper, to taste
Dash of Worcestershire sauce
1 teaspoon drained capers,
  optional

Mix all ingredients. Refrigerate in a covered container. Recipe can be doubled. Use on green salads and on Dining Car Special Sandwich. Makes 1½ cups.

Salad Dressings

Thousand Island Dressing

2 eggs, hard boiled
1 cup sweet pickle, chopped fine
Celery and onion as desired, chopped fine

2 tablespoons mayonnaise
2 tablespoons vinegar, cider vinegar preferred
2 tablespoons catsup
Salt, pepper, and sugar to taste

Chop hard boiled eggs fine. Mix gently with pickle, celery, onion, mayonnaise, vinegar, catsup, salt, pepper, and sugar. Serve on lettuce wedges or any green salad. Serves 8.

Classic Rustic Inn Salad Dressing

1 tablespoon salt
1 teaspoon celery salt (more if desired, to taste)
½ teaspoon red pepper
1 (12 ounce) bottle catsup
1 pint white vinegar (2 cups)
1 quart mayonnaise

1 (12 ounce) bottle steak sauce
½ cup Worcestershire sauce
1 cup sugar
2 cups vegetable oil

Mix all ingredients together in a large mixing bowl. Store in refrigerator. Stores well. Makes approximately one gallon (recipe may be cut in half).

Sidney Williams

Sweet Salad Dressing

2 egg yolks
2 tablespoons flour
¼ cup orange juice
¼ cup lemon juice

¼ cup pineapple juice
¼ cup sugar
1 cup cream, whipped

Mix egg yolks, flour, orange juice, lemon juice, pineapple juice, and sugar together in top of double boiler. Cook over hot water, stirring constantly, until thick. Cool. When ready to serve, mix with 1 cup of whipped cream. Serve generously over fresh fruits, mixed for salad. Use about 2 tablespoons for each serving. Will keep about 10 days. Serves 16.

Mrs. R. C. Liddon

Co-Stars

Cheese Angels

1 (5 ounce) jar Old English cheese - room temperature
½ pound American cheese grated
1 (3 ounce) cream cheese - room temperature

½ cup butter or margarine, softened
1 egg

Season with

⅛ teaspoon onion salt
⅛ teaspoon garlic salt

⅛ teaspoon salt
⅛ teaspoon cayenne pepper
1 loaf white sandwich bread

Mix all ingredients in electric mixer until smooth. You may wish to adjust the seasoning a bit to your taste. Trim crusts from bread and cut bread into fourths. Spread mixture over one piece of bread, put a second piece of bread on top and cover the whole sandwich as if icing a cake. Arrange sandwiches on a cookie sheet and cook at 325°F until puffed and slightly browned—about 10 minutes. Makes approximately 30 sandwiches.

Nette Williford

Green Bean Sandwiches

Cans of vertical pack green beans (may have to use whole green beans)

Italian dressing
Sandwich bread

Durkee's dressing
Mayonnaise

First Day: Drain green beans and marinate in Italian dressing overnight. Second Day: Cut crust from bread and spread each slice with dressing (½ Durkee's and ½ mayonnaise). Drain beans and place 3 or 4 beans on each slice of bread. Roll slices of bread lengthwise and secure with toothpicks. Place in tightly covered plastic container and refrigerate overnight. Third Day: Remove toothpicks and cut rolls in 3 or 4 pieces. Good to serve at teas.

Mrs. Clifford Worsham

Sandwiches

Chicken Salad for Sandwiches

8 chicken breasts, cooked and chopped (about 4 cups)
4 eggs, hard boiled
3 teaspoons salt
2 cups chopped sweet pickle
2 cups chopped celery
Mayonnaise and Durkees

Moisten with the mayonnaise and Durkees. Set aside.

Dressing

2 eggs
1/3 cup vinegar
2 teaspoons sugar
1/4 teaspoon dry mustard
1 teaspoon Dijon style mustard
1 tablespoon butter (or margarine)
Pinch cayenne pepper

Beat the eggs slightly. Place in the top of a double boiler over simmering water. Mix the vinegar, sugar, the mustards and the pepper, and gently stir into the eggs. Continue stirring and add the butter. When the dressing thickens, remove from heat and cool to room temperature. Add 1/2 cup cooked dressing to the chicken mixture and refrigerate overnight before spreading sandwiches. This is marvelously moist. Makes 16 to 20 sandwiches.

Ms. Anne M. Gernert
Atlanta, Georgia

Nutty Cheese Sandwich

1/4 pound Roquefort cheese
1 cup chopped salted almonds
Butter (as much as needed)
Dark rye bread as needed

Mash Roquefort cheese with chopped almonds and spread over toasted bread which has been buttered on one side. Then pop into the oven at 350°F for about 6 to 7 minutes. Serve quickly. Makes 4 sandwiches. A tossed salad added makes a tasty lunch.

Kathleen A. Masters

Co-Stars

Cucumber Sandwiches

2 cucumbers, peeled and sliced
¾ cup cider vinegar
1 cup water
1 teaspoon salt (coarse Kosher preferred)
1 (8 ounce) package cream cheese softened
Salt, pepper and garlic salt, to taste
1 heaping tablespoon mayonnaise
½ teaspoon Worcestershire
1 loaf day old white bread
½ stick softened butter (or margarine)
Mayonnaise to mix with the cream cheese

Peel cucumbers and slice (not too thinly). Soak cucumbers in 1 cup water, ¾ cup vinegar and 1 teaspoon salt for 30 minutes ONLY. Put 6 ice cubes on top of the mixture. Drain cucumbers and pat dry. Cut bread rounds. (A small liqueur glass is just the right size!) Spread each round lightly with butter. Mix the cream cheese with enough mayonnaise to a spreadable consistency. Season lightly with salt, pepper, garlic salt and Worcestershire. Spread on the buttered side of each slice of bread. Place 1 cucumber slice on each of one half the bread slices. Lightly salt, pepper and garlic salt the cucumber. Press another prepared bread round on top and press gently together. Continue until all sandwiches are completed. Place on a cookie sheet that has been covered with a slightly damp towel. Cover with another slightly damp towel. Cover with plastic wrap. Chill for at least 3 hours before serving. These will keep for 2 days!

Variation: If the cucumbers have large seeds, cut lengthwise, scrape out the seeds and grate coarsely. Proceed as above through the soaking stage. Then mix with the cream cheese mixture, adding finely diced canned water chestnuts for crunch. A dash of Louisiana red hot sauce adds a new dimension. Makes "a lot".

Mrs. Everett Meeks

Sandwiches

Delmonico Sandwich

8 slices whole wheat bread, toasted (unbuttered)
16 slices baked ham (or 8 slices ham and 8 slices breast of turkey)

3 (14½ ounce) cans asparagus pieces, drained
1 recipe Remoulade sauce

Place toasted bread on plate; top with 2 ham slices, a generous spoonful of asparagus and cover with Remoulade sauce. Garnish with parsley.

Remoulade sauce

1 cup mayonnaise
1 boiled egg, mashed
1 tablespoon horseradish
1 teaspoon grated onion and juice

Worcestershire sauce, to taste
3 tablespoons chopped parsley

Mash egg and add to mayonnaise in a quart jar; add other ingredients and shake well. Refrigerate overnight before using. Makes 12 sandwiches.

Rosemary Fisher

Ham Sandwich Loaf

1 loaf of French bread unsliced
½ to ¾ pound shaved ham
4 slices of American cheese

4 slices of Swiss cheese
Leaf lettuce
Mayonnaise

Slice French bread loaf in half horizontally. Spread top and bottom halves with mayonnaise. Layer shaved meat on bottom half of loaf. Alternate American and Swiss cheese slices at an angle over meat. Top with lettuce. Place top on loaf. Make angled cuts through loaf to make 7 or 8 individual sandwiches but leave sandwich in a loaf shape. *Shaved turkey or beef may be substituted for the ham. Sliced tomatoes, mustard and Durkee's may be added.*

Bitsy Davis

Co-Stars

Dining Car Special Sandwich
(a knife and fork sandwich)

1 slice bread, toasted
1 slice baked or boiled ham
1 slice iceburg lettuce cut about 1 inch thick
1 slice white meat of turkey (or chicken)
1 piece lean bacon, cooked and crumbled
Garnish of olives, sweet pickle
1 slice Swiss cheese
½ cup Russian dressing (p 132)

Toast the bread. Do not trim. Place ham, turkey and cheese on the toast. Slice across the head of lettuce to make the "lettuce slice" and place on top. Cover with ½ cup Russian dressing (serve more on the side). Top with crumbled bacon and garnish with pickles and olives. (This was a chef's special on one of the older passenger trains and was a luncheon favorite.) Makes one sandwich.

Jonnie Norwood
NMRC
Oxford, MS

Deluxe Ham Sandwiches

½ cup melted butter
1½ tablespoons prepared mustard
1 cup chopped onion
2 tablespoons poppy seeds (optional)
1 dozen buns or potato rolls
12 slices ham
12 slices Swiss cheese

Mix together butter, mustard, onions and poppy seeds. Butter both sides of rolls with mixture. Place 1 slice of ham and 1 slice of Swiss cheese on each roll. Wrap individually in foil. Bake at 250°F for ½ hour. May make these ahead and freeze until needed. Bake 1 hour if frozen. A great make-ahead meal for company and special occasions or brunches or buffets. Serves 12.

Linda Gunther
Glen, Mississippi

Sandwiches

Pimiento Cheese Spread

2 pounds medium sharp cheese, grated
3¼ cups mayonnaise (do not use homemade)
1 teaspoon garlic salt
1½ teaspoons seasoned salt
1 teaspoon onion juice
¾ teaspoon Louisiana hot sauce
2 teaspoons Worcestershire sauce
2 (7 ounce) jars chopped pimientos, drained
Black pepper, to taste

Put all ingredients in large bowl of electric mixer and blend on medium speed until thoroughly blended. Yield: 4 pounds.

Irma Downs Bell
Memphis, Tennessee

Tal's Pimiento Cheese Goodies

10 ounces sharp cheese, grated
8 ounces cream cheese
2 tablespoons grated onion
1 tablespoon finely chopped bell pepper
6 ounces pimiento mashed
1 teaspoon Worcestershire sauce
½ teaspoon liquid hot sauce
½ cup mayonnaise or to taste
1 tomato, peeled
1 sweet onion

Combine all ingredients except tomato and onion with electric mixer. This is an open faced sandwich. Toast bread on one side. Turn oven off. Turn bread over and let stay in oven. Thinly slice peeled tomato and sweet onion. Spread pimiento cheese on untoasted side of the bread and put a slice of tomato and a slice of onion on each sandwich. Run under broiler on low rack for 6 minutes.

Mrs. T. Y. Williford, Jr.
Greenville, Mississippi

Co-Stars

Polish Sausage Subs

1 pound Polish (Kielbasa) sausage sliced
1 green bell pepper, cut into strips
1 medium onion, thinly sliced
1 clove garlic, minced
¼ cup olive oil
2 teaspoons Italian seasonings
6 submarine rolls

Heat oil in large skillet. Add sausage and sauté 5 minutes. Add vegetables and seasonings. Cook until onions and peppers are soft. Add more olive oil if mixture becomes dry. Spoon mixture onto submarine rolls. Serves 6.

Harriett Lipscomb
Abbeville, Mississippi

Royal Sandwich Loaf
4 Layers

1 loaf unsliced sandwich type bread, sliced lengthwise into slices ½ to ¾ inch thick, crusts trimmed; soft butter to spread.

Ham Filling

1 cup ground boiled or baked ham
3 tablespoons chopped pimientos
2 to 3 tablespoons mayonnaise
1 teaspoon prepared mustard

Mix well and set aside.

Egg Salad Filling

3 hard boiled eggs, mashed with a fork
2 to 3 tablespoons mayonnaise
1 teaspoon prepared mustard
½ teaspoon Worcestershire type sauce
Salt, pepper and celery salt, to taste

Mix well and set aside.

Pimiento Cheese Filling

(p. 139)

Sandwiches

Cucumber Filling

(p.) 136

Use the cucumber sandwich variation that uses grated cucumber.

Icing

4 packages cream cheese at room temperature, mixed with about ⅓ cup cream. Season with salt, pepper and garlic salt and ½ teaspoon of cider vinegar. Food coloring may be used sparingly. This amount may be a little too much but it will give enough to "swirl".

Put one slice of the bread on a waxed paper (or foil) covered cookie sheet. Spread lightly with softened butter. Put ham filling on the bottom slice, covering generously. Top with slice of bread #2, buttering the bottom that is against the ham layer. Spread butter on the top of the second layer and cover it generously with the egg salad filling. Put buttered side down and press gently. Again butter the top of this piece of bread and cover generously with pimiento cheese spread. Repeat for the cucumber layer. Trim all edges neatly with a rounded knife blade, or the back of a tablespoon, proceed to "ice" the loaf. Leave some swirls. Place uncovered in the refrigerator overnight. Then loosely cover until serving time. Cut into thick slices vertically and place cut sides down on individual serving plates. Garnish with olives, etc., before slicing. Excellent for luncheon dish or for buffet.

Tuna Fish Salad For Sandwiches

1 (9¼ ounce) can solid white tuna, packed in water
2 hard cooked eggs, chopped
½ cup celery, diced
½ cup sweet pickle, diced
Juice of 1 lemon
Mayonnaise, to taste
Paprika, salt, white pepper, to taste

Drain tuna and dice fine; add eggs, celery, and pickles. Pour lemon juice over all; mix with enough mayonnaise to hold together and make nice spreading consistency. Serves 6 to 8.

Co-Stars

Cheese-Asparagus Soup

1½ tablespoons butter
1½ tablespoons all purpose flour
½ cup whipping cream
½ cup chicken broth

1½ cups cut cooked asparagus
1 teaspoon salt
Dash of white pepper
1¼ cups shredded Cheddar cheese

Melt butter; blend in flour, and cook until bubbly. Gradually add milk, stirring until well blended. Cook over low heat, stirring constantly, until smooth and thickened. Add asparagus and seasonings. Mix well. Add cheese; stir until cheese is melted. Serves 4.

Barbara Redmont
Jackson, Mississippi

Creole Bean Soup

2 cups of dried beans and peas (a mixture), washed and drained
3 quarts chicken stock
1 teaspoon salt
½ pound smoked ham, cubed
1 (20 ounce) can tomatoes, undrained, mashed

3 large onions, chopped
8 stalks celery, chopped
3 cloves of garlic, minced
1 pound thin sliced Polish sausage (Kielbasa)
2 cups raw chicken, cubed
1½ cups fresh parsley, chopped
1 cup red wine

Simmer beans, stock, salt and ham cubes 2½ to 3 hours. Add tomatoes, onions, celery and garlic. Simmer uncovered until thick and creamy, about 1½ to 2 hours. Add sausage and chicken; continue cooking 30 to 45 minutes. Add parsley and the red wine. This improves with age and is best made the day before. Serves 12.

Mrs. Bob Ayers
Sewanee, Tennessee

Sandwiches

Broccoli Bisque

2 (10 ounce) packages frozen chopped broccoli, thawed
½ cup chopped onion
1 stick butter or margarine
2 cups chicken stock

¾ teaspoon basil
1 teaspoon salt
¼ teaspoon pepper
1 tablespoon lemon juice
1 cup light cream

In a saucepan, sauté onion in butter for 5 minutes. Add broccoli, stock, basil, salt and pepper. Cover and simmer for 15 minutes. Pureé in blender until it is smooth. Add the lemon juice and cream. This may be served hot or cold. Serves 6.

Helen Moore

Brussels Sprouts Cream Soup

1 pound Brussels sprouts, pared and cleaned
1 quart water
1 large onion chopped (or 1 bunch fresh green onions)
1 dash cayenne pepper
Black pepper
Salt

1 teaspoon garlic powder (or 2 cloves finely chopped fresh garlic)
4 tablespoons butter or margarine
1 cup sour cream (or 1 cup plain yogurt)

Cut Brussels sprouts in fourths, place in water, bring to a boil, then add chopped onions, dash of cayenne pepper and garlic powder. Let simmer about 45 minutes or until tender. Use a potato masher and mash until all is a coarse pulp. Add salt and black pepper to taste. Then mix butter in soup. Just at serving time, add a dollop of sour cream over individual steaming soup dish. Good with croutons or garlic rounds. Serves 4 to 6.

Co-Stars

Barley Soup

¼ cup whole barley
6 cups water
1 cup carrots
½ cup celery
¼ cup onions, chopped
2 cups tomatoes, chopped

1 cup peas, fresh or frozen
½ to 1 cup boiled and diced
   chicken
Butter, optional
Salt, optional
Pepper, optional

Cook barley and 6 cups water for 1 hour. Add other ingredients and cook until tender. Season with butter, salt and pepper, as desired.

Note: This recipe is good for someone on a restricted diet.

Rachel Goddard

Carrot Soup

8 to 10 carrots, cut in chunks
2 pods garlic
½ onion, finely chopped
2 cups chicken stock or 2
   (10½ ounce) cans of chicken
   consomme
Salt and pepper, to taste

Dash of cayenne pepper
1 teaspoon celery seed
1 quart milk
½ pint sour cream
Pimiento strips and seasoned
   croutons

Cook carrots, onion and garlic in the chicken stock or consomme until tender. Remove from heat. Pureé in blender. Return to pot and add seasonings, milk and sour cream. Heat slowly until the sour cream is dissolved and mixture is very hot. Serve garnished with pimiento strips and seasoned croutons. Serves 8.

Betty Ann Perkins
Brookhaven, Mississippi

Soups

Carrot-Cauliflower Cream Soup

6 cups water
4 large carrots, diced
1½ cups cauliflower, uncooked
1 teaspoon parsley
3 fresh green onions (including tops), chopped
2 tablespoons butter or margarine
Salt and pepper, to taste
1 teaspoon garlic powder
¼ cup sour cream

Bring water to a boil; add carrots, cauliflower, parsley, onion, salt, pepper and garlic powder. Cook for 15 to 20 minutes, partially covered. Cream butter and sour cream together and add to soup just before serving. Garlic bread goes nicely with this dish. Serves 4 to 6.

Kathleen A. Masters

Cheese Soup

¾ cup chopped carrots
¾ cup chopped celery
¾ cup chopped onion
¼ cup chopped green onions
1 stick butter or margarine
½ cup flour
2 tablespoons cornstarch
⅛ teaspoon baking soda
40 ounces canned chicken stock
1 quart milk
1 pound box process cheese spread

Sauté carrots, celery, and onions in butter until soft. Mash with potato masher. Add flour, cornstarch, soda and blend well. Slowly add chicken stock, milk and cheese. Blend; heat thoroughly, but do not boil. Better if made day before serving. Serves 10.

Mrs. O. B. Wooley, Jr. (Easie)
Jackson, Mississippi

Co-Stars

European Cheese Soup

1 small onion
2 stalks celery
1 green pepper
2 carrots
4½ tablespoons butter
4 tablespoons flour

4 cups chicken stock
3 cups Cheddar cheese, grated
2 cups milk
2 tablespoons sherry
Salt, pepper
Chopped parsley

Chop onion, celery, green pepper and carrots in very fine pieces. Melt butter over low heat in large pot, and cook vegetables about 10 minutes. Stir in flour with wire whisk as smoothly as possible, and add stock. Cook, stirring constantly, until soup boils and thickens slightly. Add cheese, continue cooking and stirring until melted; then add milk and sherry gradually, and season soup to taste with salt and pepper. Cook pot of soup over medium-low heat for 15 to 20 minutes until heated thoroughly. Serve with a sprinkling of chopped parsley if desired. Serves 6.

Margel Young

Ham Chowder

2 tablespoons butter
½ clove garlic
1 cup onion, chopped
1 cup celery, chopped
2 cups diced ham
2 cups diced potatoes
2 cups water
1 bay leaf

¾ teaspoon salt
½ teaspoon dried leaf thyme
½ teaspoon red Louisiana hot sauce
2 cups milk
1 (16 ounce) can tomatoes, drained and chopped

Sauté garlic, onion, celery and ham in butter. Add potatoes, water and seasonings. Simmer covered until potatoes are tender. Add milk and tomatoes and heat, but do not boil. Yield: 6 to 8 cups.

Mrs. T. Y. Williford, Jr.
Greenville, Mississippi

Soups

Duck Gumbo

4 ducks or 8 breasts
1 onion
1 apple
¾ cup butter
1 cup flour
2 cups onions, chopped
1 bunch green onions, tops included, chopped
2 cups celery, chopped
½ cup green bell pepper, chopped
6 ounces tomato paste
2 (16 ounce) cans tomatoes, cut up
1 teaspoon thyme
1 teaspoon oregano
2 bay leaves
2 teaspoons parsley, chopped
¼ cup sugar
1 teaspoon pepper
1 teaspoon red pepper
1 teaspoon filé powder
1 pound smoked sausage, sliced
Salt to taste

Boil duck with onion and apple until well done. Remove meat and skin from bones. Reserve duck stock. Discard skin and cut duck into bite size pieces and set aside. Melt butter in large boiler; add flour to make a roux. Cook over medium heat until dark brown. Add 2 quarts of strained duck stock and stir well. Add all vegetables and seasonings and cook 1 hour. Add duck meat and cook another hour or until duck is tender. Slice and add summer sausage the last 30 minutes. Add filé the last 5 minutes. Can thin with more duck stock or water if needed. Freezes well. Serves 10 to 12.

Mrs. Bob Worsham (Beth)

Reducing Soup

3 carrots, chopped
1 head cabbage, shredded
1 bunch celery, chopped
2 large onions, chopped
1 (28 ounce) can tomatoes, chopped, liquid included
Bouillon crystals or cubes

Cover with water. With every cup of water use 1 teaspoon bouillon crystals or 1 bouillon cube. DO NOT ADD SALT. Sprinkle with black pepper. Bring to a boil and simmer 45 minutes covered. Serve hot or cold.

Mrs. Herman Baggenstoss
Tracy City, Tennessee

Co-Stars

Mary Ann's Hodgepodge Soup

2 pounds ground beef
1½ cups onions, chopped
1½ cups celery, chopped
2 (31 ounce) cans ranch style beans
1 (ranch style) can water
3 (10¾ ounce) cans minestrone soup
1 (10 ounce) can tomatoes and green chili peppers, chopped
1 (16 ounce) can stewed tomatoes
2 tablespoons chili powder
Worcestershire sauce, to taste
Louisiana red hot sauce, to taste
Garlic powder, to taste
1 (8¾ ounce) can whole kernel corn

Sauté meat, onions and celery. Drain and add other ingredients. Cook slowly for at least 30 minutes. *Delicious!* Serves 6 to 8.

Mrs. Phil Nelson
Jackson, Mississippi

Jalapeño Chili

1 pound dried pinto beans
2 teaspoons salt
2 slices salt pork
6 pounds ground beef
6 tablespoons vegetable oil
6 onions, chopped
4 cans (16 ounce) stewed tomatoes, mashed
6 cloves garlic, mashed
3 teaspoons oregano
2 teaspoons cumin
½ cup chili powder
2 teaspoons sugar
2 to 6 dashes red Louisiana hot sauce
6 jalapeño peppers, chopped
2 teaspoons cinnamon

Simmer beans in water with salt and salt pork until cooked (3 to 4 hours). In a large boiler heat oil. Crumble beef and brown. Add all ingredients and simmer 1 hour. Stir in beans and cooking water. Cook 30 to 40 more minutes. Freezes well. Yield: 8 to 10 quarts.

Mrs. Bob Worsham (Beth)

Soups

Potato Soup

6 potatoes, peeled and cut into bite-size pieces
2 onions, chopped
1 carrot, sliced or diced
3 stalks celery, diced
4 chicken bouillon cubes
1 tablespoon parsley flakes (or 2 tablespoons fresh chopped)
5 cups water
1 tablespoon salt (or more if desired)
Pepper, to taste
⅓ cup butter
Dash garlic salt
1 (13 ounce) can evaporated milk

Mix and cook all ingredients, except milk, slowly until vegetables are tender. Can mash them if desired. Stir in milk last hour of cooking. Serves 8 to 10.

Sandra Fulghum

Creamy Potato Soup

4 cups peeled and cubed baking potatoes
1 cup of ¾ inch sliced celery
1 cup coarsely chopped onion
2 cups water
2 teaspoons salt
1 cup milk
1 cup whipping cream
3 tablespoons butter
⅛ teaspoon pepper

Combine potatoes, celery, onion, water and salt in a large Dutch oven. Simmer covered about 20 minutes or until potatoes are tender. Mash mixture with potato masher until desired consistency. Stir in remaining ingredients. Return to heat. Cook, stirring until soup is heated. Yield: 7 cups.

Claire Stanley

Co-Stars

Vichyssoise

4 large Spanish onions, chopped
1 tablespoon butter
2½ cups diced potatoes
2 cups chicken stock
¼ teaspoon paprika
Salt and pepper, to taste
2 cups milk
1 cup heavy cream
Chopped chives

Sauté onions in heavy skillet with butter until soft but not brown. Add the potatoes, chicken stock and seasonings. Simmer covered for 45 minutes. Put mixture into electric blender and mix until smooth. Chill, then add milk and cream. Serve topped with chives. Serves 6 to 8.

Helen Moore

Low Cholesterol Potato Soup

2 medium potatoes, cut up
1 large onion, sliced
2 tablespoons polyunsaturated margarine
2 tablespoons flour
3 cups skimmed milk
1 cup potato water
1 tablespoon chopped parsley
1 tablespoon chopped chives

Boil potatoes and onions together in salted water until tender. Drain, reserving liquid. Rub vegetables through coarse strainer. Make white sauce with margarine, flour, and liquids. Combine with vegetable pulp. Season with chopped parsley, chives, salt and pepper. Mix thoroughly and heat. Yields 5 cups.

Margaret Perkins

Soups

Gazpacho

1 (46 ounce) can tomato juice
2 cucumbers, peeled and diced
2 bell peppers, diced
2 tomatoes, chopped
3 tablespoons lemon juice
2 cloves garlic, pressed
2 tablespoons parsley, chopped
¼ teaspoon black pepper

Mix all ingredients and chill for 3 hours. Serve ice cold. Serves 8.

William McMullin

Quick Gazpacho

2 stalks celery
1 cucumber
1 (10¾ ounce) can tomato soup
1 (6 ounce) can Bloody Mary mix
4 ounces sour cream
Fresh dill

Chop celery and cucumber in food processor. Add tomato soup, Bloody Mary mix, sour cream, a bit of fresh dill and mix. Chill before serving. Serves 2.

Frank Chapin
Washington, D.C.

Cold Spinach Soup

2 (10 ounce) packages frozen chopped spinach
½ cup chopped green onion
3 tablespoons butter
3 (14½ ounce) cans chicken broth
Dash nutmeg
1 (8 ounce) package cream cheese, cut in cubes

Sauté onions in butter until soft. Add spinach. Cover and cook on low until spinach is thawed - about ten minutes. Add broth and nutmeg. Simmer 5 minutes. Cool. Pour soup into blender 4 cups at a time with some of cream cheese until all is blended. Chill at least 4 hours in glass container.

Ann White

Co-Stars

Chilled Spinach and Cucumber Soup

2 tablespoons butter
1 bunch scallions, sliced
4 cups diced peeled cucumbers
3 cups chicken broth
½ cup sliced, peeled potatoes
Pinch of salt
Lemon juice, to taste
Pepper, to taste
1 cup light cream

In saucepan sauté sliced scallions in butter until soft. Add cucumbers, chicken broth, chopped spinach, potatoes, salt, lemon juice and pepper. Simmer until potatoes are tender. Pureé in food processor. Add 1 cup of cream and chill. Serves 8.

Barbara Redmont
Jackson, Mississippi

Taco Soup

1½ pounds ground chuck
1 (15 ounce) can pinto beans
1 (10¾ ounce) can cream of celery soup
1 (10¾ ounce) can cream of potato soup
1 small onion, chopped
1 (1¼ ounce) package taco seasoning
2 (16 ounce) cans tomato wedges
1 (8 ounce) can tomato sauce

Brown ground chuck and onion in large pot; drain well. Add remaining ingredients and simmer 1 hour. (Or put in crockpot and cook on low for 2 to 3 hours.) Garnish with crushed corn chips and grated Cheddar cheese.

Cindi Irwin
Blue Mountain, Mississippi

Soups

Fresh Tomato Soup

1 large onion, chopped
2 cloves garlic, minced
2 stalks celery, chopped
¼ cup butter
3 to 4 pounds tomatoes, peeled and coarsely chopped*
4 cups water
4 teaspoons instant chicken bouillon
1 (8 ounce) can tomato sauce
½ teaspoon black pepper
2 tablespoons basil
2 tablespoons cornstarch

Using a large pan (I use a Dutch oven) melt butter. Add onion, garlic, celery and sauté until tender. Add tomatoes, water in which chicken bouillon has been dissolved, tomato sauce and black pepper. Simmer for 15 minutes. Add basil. Thicken mixture with cornstarch mixed with enough cold water to dissolve, adding slowly. Cook 5 to 10 minutes longer. If too tart for individual taste, add one or two pinches of soda. *One quart canned tomatoes may be substituted for the fresh ones. Yields 3 quarts.

Mrs. Ben W. Matthews (Melanie)
Jackson, Tennessee

Tomato Dill Soup

2 tablespoons butter
¼ cup chopped onion
2 (14½ ounce) cans tomato soup
1 (14½ ounce) can chicken broth
1 cup whipping cream
1 tablespoon dried dill
Salt and pepper, to taste

Melt butter in saucepan. Add chopped onion and sauté until soft. Add soups and dill. Bring to a boil; reduce heat and simmer for 15 minutes. Add cream, salt and pepper. Stir to blend. Serve hot or cold. Serves 4.

Harriett Lipscomb
Abbeville, Mississippi

Co-Stars

Teedee's Vegetable Beef Soup

1½ pounds stewmeat or other lean beef, cut in ½ inch cubes
2 tablespoons vegetable oil
2 quarts water
2 (16 ounce) cans of tomato wedges cut up or an equal amount of fresh tomatoes
1 large onion, chopped
2 large fresh carrots, diced or sliced crosswise
2 (16 ounce) packages of frozen soup vegetables
½ cup uncooked rice
Salt and pepper, to taste
½ cup tiny peas, optional

Brown stewmeat in oil. Place beef, water, tomatoes, onion and fresh carrots in a large Dutch oven. Bring to boil; reduce heat to simmer. Add desired amount of salt and pepper, and cook for 40 minutes. Add frozen soup vegetables and rice, and cook another 25 or 30 minutes. Adjust seasonings. You may add any left over vegetables you may have, as this just enhances the soup flavor. One half cup of tiny English peas added 5 minutes before serving adds color. This freezes well and probably is more tasty made the day before serving. Serves 8 to 10.

Teedee Williford
Cleveland, Mississippi

Cold Zucchini Soup

1½ pounds zucchini, peeled and sliced
⅔ cup chopped yellow onion
¼ cup chopped green pepper
2½ cups chicken stock
1 cup heavy cream
½ teaspoon dill weed
Salt, to taste
Hot pepper sauce, to taste

In a 3 quart saucepan, place zucchini, onion, green pepper and stock. Cover and simmer 30 minutes. Cool. Pureé in blender. Add cream and dill. Blend well. Season with salt and hot pepper sauce. Serve cold. Serves 6 to 8.

Helen Moore

Soups

Wonton Soup

18 wonton wrappers

Filling Ingredients

1 pound finely ground pork
1 egg beaten

1 tablespoon soy sauce
½ teaspoon pepper

Combine filling and place a spoonful on each wonton wrapper. Fold wrapper around filling, using a little water to seal edges.

Soup Ingredients

8 cups chicken broth (canned will do)
1 cup shredded Bok Choy (Chinese cabbage) or fresh spinach

2 tablespoons chopped green onions
1 (6 ounce) can mushroom slices

Combine soup ingredients in a large saucepan. Bring to a boil. Add wontons. Cook about 5 minutes or until all wontons float to the surface. Wontons may be frozen on a tray, then sealed in a bag and kept in the freezer. Increase cooking time about 5 minutes to cook frozen wontons. Serves 6.

Crab Stew

Carolyn Hamilton

4 tablespoons butter or margarine
3 tablespoons finely diced onion (or to taste)
3 (heaping) tablespoons plain flour

1 quart milk
1 pound fresh crabmeat, picked clean of bits of fiber
Dry sherry, optional

Sauté onion in butter until limp. Add flour slowly, stirring constantly. Add milk slowly, stirring constantly. After it begins to thicken, add crabmeat. Salt to taste; heat and serve. If desired, a tablespoon of dry sherry may be added to each bowl as it is served.

Charles McCall
Lyons, Georgia

Co-Stars

Good Winter Soup

2 small ham hocks
1 large onion, chopped
2 green peppers, chopped
1 clove garlic, chopped
1½ cabbages, thin sliced

1 (16 ounce) can tomatoes and liquid
2 tablespoons barley
¾ teaspoon marjoram
¼ teaspoon cayenne pepper
Salt and pepper, to taste

Cook pork in 2 quarts water for 1 hour. Remove hocks and set aside to cool. Skim all fat but 1 tablespoon. If you have time, it is best to cool stock and take off hardened fat. Heat 1 tablespoon fat in casserole. Cook onion and peppers until light brown. Add garlic, stir a minute. Add cabbage, raise heat and cook, stirring for a few minutes until slightly wilted. With scissors cut up tomatoes in can. Add to soup, then add stock, barley, marjoram, pepper and bring to simmer. Remove skin and fat from hocks. Cut into pieces and add to soup. Simmer about 1 hour. Season to taste and serve. Keeps well. Let cool; refrigerate and reheat. Serves 4.

Mrs. R. T. Sawyer (Helen)
Starkville, Mississippi

Clam Chowder

2 cans (6½ ounce) minced clams
1 cup finely chopped onions
2 cups diced potatoes
1 cup diced celery
¾ cup flour

¾ cup butter
1 quart half and half
1½ teaspoons salt
½ teaspoon sugar
Pepper, to taste

Drain juice from clams into vegetables. Add enough water to cover. Simmer until vegetables are done. While simmering the above, make a white sauce from butter, flour and cream. Cook until thick. Add vegetables and liquid. Add clams, sugar, salt and pepper. Heat only until hot. (Clams get tough when cooked too long, so watch when reheating also.) Makes 16 cups.

Marie Holley Anderson

Soups

Crescent City Oyster Soup

⅓ cup olive oil
4 slices French bread
2 sprigs parsley, chopped
¾ cup red wine
1 tablespoon ketchup

1½ dozen oysters with liquid
1 clove garlic
1 cup oyster juice
¼ teaspoon pepper
½ teaspoon oregano

Heat 2 tablespoons oil in large, deep skillet. Add bread and brown on both sides. Remove bread, add rest of oil and garlic. Cook 3 minutes, then remove garlic. Add remaining ingredients to oil and simmer 10 minutes. Put slice of bread in each bowl and pour in soup. Serves 4.

Margel Young

Oyster Stew

1 pint oysters (small stewing oysters, if available)
2 teaspoons paprika
2 teaspoons Worcestershire sauce
½ teaspoon celery salt

¼ cup butter
1 cup cream
2 cups milk
Salt, pepper and hot pepper sauce, to taste

Boil and stir oysters with liquid in the jar with the paprika, Worcestershire sauce, celery salt and butter until the oysters are well curled around the edge (3 or 4 minutes). Add milk and cream and warm, but do not bring to boil. Add salt, pepper and hot pepper sauce to taste. Serves 4.

Lee Sweat

Co-Stars

Seafood Gumbo

1½ cups chopped onion
4 tablespoons bacon fat
2 tablespoons flour
6 cups canned tomatoes
3 cups water
2 pounds frozen cut okra
1 cup diced green pepper
2 cloves garlic, crushed
3 cans good quality crabmeat
1 pound fresh or frozen shrimp, peeled and deveined
1 pound oysters and juice, use fresh or canned (oysters optional)
Salt and pepper to taste, hot pepper sauce if desired
1 tablespoon Worcestershire sauce
1 small pinch thyme
1 bay leaf
1 tablespoon gumbo filé powder

Sauté onion in bacon fat until soft, then stir in flour. Add tomatoes and water. Simmer for 30 minutes. Add okra, peppers and garlic and cook 1 hour. Add crabmeat and shrimp; salt and pepper to taste. Cook 30 minutes. Add other ingredients (except filé powder) and cook for another 30 minutes. Dissolve the filé powder in cold water (about ½ cup) and add to the gumbo. Cook about 10 minutes longer. Serve in soup bowls over rice. Serves 12 to 14.

Rosemary T. Williams

Snapper Soup

2 cups onion, chopped
½ cup carrots, chopped
3 ribs celery
1 (2½ ounce) can mushrooms, stems and pieces
3 tablespoons vegetable oil
2 quarts water
3 (10 inch) catfish, dressed (or any bland white fish)
Salt and pepper, to taste

Sauté onions, carrots, celery and mushrooms in the oil. Cook until vegetables are limp but not brown. Add 2 quarts of water, salt, pepper and fish. Bring to a boil and simmer for 30 minutes. Cool. Strain. Discard vegetables and fish. Use liquid for fish stock.

Soups

Roux:

2 tablespoons bacon drippings   3 tablespoons all purpose flour

Cook over low heat, in heavy skillet, until walnut brown, being careful not to burn the flour. Set aside.

2 tablespoons butter	Pinch of dried thyme
2 tablespoons carrots, chopped	1½ ounces tomato paste
2 tablespoons celery, chopped	2 quarts fish stock
½ cup onions, chopped	4 ounces roux
1 clove garlic, crushed	Salt and pepper, to taste
½ bay leaf	3 drops caramel coloring

Sauté carrots, celery, and onions in butter. Add seasonings and salt and pepper. Stir in tomato paste. Add fish stock and bring to a boil. Stir in roux and simmer for 20 minutes. Add coloring carefully. Check for seasoning and strain. Set aside and keep barely warm, while finishing the soup.

2 tablespoons butter	1 pound red snapper, chopped fine
1 cup onions, chopped	
½ cup celery, chopped	2 ounces sherry (dry)

Sauté onions, celery until limp. Add fish and toss gently. Add sherry and continue simmering for 2 or 3 minutes. Add to soup. Stir briefly. Taste for seasonings and heat, but do not boil. Serve immediately. Serves 4 to 6.

Billie Wadlington

Hot Cheese Crackers

Put small pieces of cheese on your favorite crackers, sprinkle with powdered Worcestershire sauce. Heat in microwave til cheese is melted.

Co-Stars

Fish Chowder

1 pound salt pork, cut into ¼ inch dice
1½ cups onions, sliced
4 stalks celery and leaves, diced
3 cups peeled white baking potatoes, cut in ½ inch dice
1½ pounds haddock
2 cups heavy cream
Salt and pepper, to taste
2 tablespoons butter

In a large kettle, fry out (or render) pork slowly until fat melts and pieces are crisp and brown. Remove crisp fat pieces and drain on a paper towel. Save 2 tablespoons of the fat (discarding the remainder). Sauté onions and celery in the pork fat until soft. Add a layer of raw potatoes and enough water to come to the top of the potatoes but not to cover them. Place haddock on top of the potatoes. Cook, covered, (stirring a couple of times) until the potatoes are done. The fish will be done when the potatoes are done! This takes about 15 minutes. Flake the haddock into bite-sized pieces with a fork. Add cream, salt and pepper to taste and the butter. Serve with the pork (scraps) and garnish with snipped parsley, if desired. Serves 6 to 8.

There are as many recipes for fish chowder as there are cooks in New England. In Connecticut they add tomatoes, which is unthinkable in Maine! Fish chowder is better made the day before so it can season through. Since the chowder will curdle if allowed to boil, reheat in the top of a double boiler over simmering water. Chowder is delicious on a cold winter night served with cornbread, pickles and a salad.

Ms. Alice Mary Pierce
Portland, Maine

To Reduce Calories

Chill soups, stews, sauces and broths. Remove hardened fat (saves 100 calories per tablespoon of fat removed. (H.N.S.)

Center Stage

CENTER STAGE

The most dramatic moments in theatre usually take place in the center of the stage. Here, all eyes focus on the star of the show.

The star in good dining is usually a meat or seafood entree. Nothing in the theatre could surpass the visual drama of a crown roast of pork surrounded by bright red spiced crabapples or the tantalizing appeal of lobster thermidor, each portion served in its own individual cassoulet.

In summer, when most southerners move outdoors, the grill becomes the center of attention. A wide variety of entrees, from shish-kebabs to char-broiled salmon steaks, are the star attraction.

Whether your dining is formal or informal, elegant or casual, remember that "Stars" can be difficult and usually require more time and attention than the rest of the cast.

SUMMER SIZZLER

Grilled Ham Steak with Sauce - p.209

Baked Beans Casserole - p.272

Vera's Cabbage Salad - p.114

Corn Light Bread - p.298

Strawberry Pie - p.369

MIDSUMMER NIGHT'S DREAM

Grilled Shrimp Kabobs - p.211

Elegant Beef Bits - p.214

Grilled Parmesan Corn - p.218

Fresh Vegetable Marinade - p.119

Debbie's Bread - p.300

Mocha Ice Cream Dessert - p.341

Center Stage

EASTER DAY LUNCH

Roasted Leg of Lamb - p.184

Asparagus Casserole - p.271

Nutty Wild Rice - p.285

Mandarin Orange Salad with Tarragon Dressing - p.113

French Bread - p.300

Caramel Barvarian Cream - p.343

BY THE SEA

Bass and Cashews - p.187

Broccoli Puff - p.274

Lemon/Parsley Potatoes - p.281

Tomato Ice - p.118

Lemon Meringue Pie - p.367

Meat

Beef Brisket in Beer

3 to 4 pound brisket
1 onion, sliced
Salt and pepper
½ cup chili sauce

2 tablespoons brown sugar
1 clove garlic, crushed
1 (12 ounce) can beer

Salt and pepper beef and place in 9 inch square casserole dish. Place sliced onion over top of beef. Mix together in a separate bowl the chili sauce, brown sugar, garlic and beer. Pour over beef and cover dish tightly with foil. Bake at 300°F for 3 hours. Uncover and bake 30 more minutes. Refrigerate for several hours or overnight. Skim off congealed fat from surface. Remove meat and trim off fat. Slice and return to sauce in the casserole dish. Reheat or freeze for later. Serves 6.

Phyllis Spearman
Brookhaven, Mississippi

Sure Fire Rib Roast

1 rib roast: Allow 2 to 2½ servings per pound.

(I've always used about a 10 pound roast.)

Preheat the oven to 350°F. Place completely thawed out beef, fat side up, in a shallow roasting pan. Put the roast in the oven at 1 o'clock in the afternoon and bake for exactly 1 hour. Turn off oven and DO NOT OPEN OVEN DOOR ALL AFTERNOON. 45 minutes before serving time, turn the oven on again to 350°F. After taking the roast from the oven, allow it to rest for 10 minutes before carving. Carve in slices across the grain, using the tip of the knife to loosen the slices as you carve. This method is for rib roast only. No matter what the weight of the roast, it will come out medium rare.

Joan Hennessy

Center Stage

Alley Galley's Beef Burgundy
From A Very Special Place To Dine

1 large onion, thinly sliced
1 tablespoon melted butter
1 pound boneless, lean beef cut into strips
1 tablespoon all purpose flour
Salt and pepper, to taste
Dash of dried marjoram leaves (optional)
Dash of thyme (leaf thyme crumbled is best)
½ cup beef bouillon
1 cup dry red wine
1 (4 ounce) can mushrooms, drained
Hot cooked noodles

Sauté onion in butter until tender but not browned. Remove from skillet and set aside. Add beef to skillet and sauté until brown. Stir in the flour, salt, pepper, marjoram, thyme, bouillon and wine. Cover and cook over low heat for 3 hours. Stir in mushrooms and sautéed onion. Serve over noodles cooked according to package directions. Serves 3 to 4.

Variation: A dollop of sour cream on top is divine.

Gene and Bobby A. Greene
The Waldron Room at Alley Galleys
A unique place to dine.

Busy Day Pot Roast

3 or 4 pound boneless chuck roast
Flour
2 tablespoons cooking oil
½ cup dry red wine
½ cup soy sauce
½ cup water
1 tablespoon parsley
¾ cup finely chopped celery
¾ cup finely chopped onion

Pat flour into roast and brown slowly in Dutch oven. Mix remaining ingredients and pour over roast. Bring to a boil and then cover and simmer for 3 hours. Serve with rice and spoon some sauce over the rice. Good with cabbage slaw dressed in mayonnaise and lemon juice dressing. Serves 6.

Ann Whitfield

Meat

Lazy Creamy Swiss Steak

2 pounds round steak
1 large onion, thinly sliced

1 (10¾ ounce) can mushroom soup, undiluted
Salt and pepper, to taste

Cut steak into serving pieces. Season and place in crockpot (slow cooker). Put onions on top of the steak and cover with the mushroom soup. Cover and cook for 8 to 10 hours! Serves 6 to 8.

Variation: Can be put in a covered roasting pan, covered and bake in the oven at 325°F.

Tip: Garnish with a dollop of sour cream on each serving.

Ms. Joyce Pruett
Sherrard, Illinois

Oven Swiss Steak

½ to ¾ pound boneless round steak
3 tablespoons all purpose flour
½ teaspoon salt
Shortening for frying
1 (8 ounce) can of cooked tomatoes

¼ cup chopped celery
¼ cup chopped carrots
1 tablespoon chopped onion
¼ teaspoon Worcestershire sauce
2 tablespoons shredded sharp American cheese

Cut meat into 2 portions. Mix flour and salt and pound into the meat. Set aside remaining flour. Brown meat in small amount of hot shortening. Place meat in small shallow baking dish. Blend remaining flour with drippings in skillet. Add remaining ingredients, except the cheese and cook, stirring constantly, until mixture boils. Pour over the meat. Cover and bake at 350°F for 2 hours or until the meat and vegetables are tender. Sprinkle cheese over the meat. Return to oven to allow cheese to melt. Serves 4.

Nancy Norman McLemore

Center Stage

Beef Eggplant Curry

1 pound beef, cubed
1 large eggplant, cubed
Olive oil for sautéing
2 large potatoes, cubed
1 large onion, chopped
½ can tomato paste

1 cup water
½ teaspoon curry powder
½ teaspoon garlic powder
½ teaspoon lemon pepper
½ teaspoon salt

Sauté beef cubes and onion until brown. Sauté eggplant in small amount of olive oil and add to beef. I boil my diced potatoes almost done and add those. Add tomato paste, water and seasonings. Pour in casserole. Cover and bake 1 hour at 350°F.

Mildred Sawyer

Swedish Beef Stew

2¼ pounds shoulder of beef on the bone
3 tablespoons all purpose flour
3 tablespoons butter or margarine
2 teaspoons salt

10 allspice corns
2 bay leaves
1⅓ cups of water
2 carrots
2 yellow or red onions

Take approximately 2¼ pound of shoulder beef on the bone and cut the meat into 1x1 inch cubes. Turn them in 3 tablespoons of flour. Brown the meat in butter in a frying pan and transfer to a large saucepan. Sprinkle meat with salt and other seasonings. Add water to the frying pan; scrape the bottom well and pour resulting stock over the meat. Add 2 peeled and sliced carrots, 2 peeled and sliced onions and allow to simmer for 1½ hours until the meat is tender. If necessary, add more water. Serve the beef stew with boiled potatoes. Serves 6 to 8.

Eric Brunskog
Stockholm, Sweden

Meat

Beef Stew

2 pounds lean beef chuck, cut into 1 inch cubes
2 tablespoons flour
2 tablespoons vegetable oil
1 medium onion, peeled and crushed
1 clove garlic, peeled and crushed
¾ cup sliced celery
1 tablespoon vegetable oil
2 cups water
1 bay leaf
1½ teaspoons salt
¼ teaspoon pepper
3 tablespoons catsup
4 medium-sized carrots, peeled and sliced
6 medium-sized potatoes, peeled and quartered

Coat beef cubes with the 2 tablespoons flour and set aside. Heat the 2 tablespoons vegetable oil in a Dutch oven over moderately high heat (about 275°F). Add onion, garlic and celery and cook until lightly browned. Remove vegetables with a slotted spoon and set aside. Add the 1 tablespoon vegetable oil to the Dutch oven and brown meat on all sides over moderately high heat (about 300°F), stirring frequently. Return browned vegetables to the Dutch oven and add the 2 cups water, bay leaf, salt, pepper and catsup and bring to a boil. Reduce heat to moderately low (about 225°F); cover and cook 1½ hours. Add carrots and potatoes and cook, covered, 45 minutes more, until meat and vegetables are fork-tender. Serves 6 to 8.

Mrs. Bob (Carol) Lee

"The best thing about liver is how virtuous it makes you feel after you've eaten some.", Bruce Jay Friedman, American playwright & screen writer.

Center Stage

Swiss Bliss

2 pounds round steak or chuck, cubed
1 envelope onion soup mix
1 (2½ ounce) can mushrooms, drained
1 green pepper, sliced
1 (16 ounce) can tomatoes, drained and chopped (reserve juice)
1 teaspoon steak sauce
1 tablespoon cornstarch
¼ teaspoon salt, pepper, to taste
Cooked rice

Grease a 2 quart casserole. Arrange steak cubes on bottom of casserole. Sprinkle with soup mix, mushrooms, green pepper, tomatoes, salt and pepper. Mix tomato juice (from can of tomatoes), steak sauce and cornstarch and pour over meat and vegetables in casserole. Cover and bake for 3 hours at 325°F. May need to add a little water in last hour of baking time. Serve over rice. Serves 6 to 8. Leftovers freeze well.

Mrs. Robert Jennings (Betty)
Memphis, Tennessee

Beef Stroganoff

2 pounds beef tenderloin, cut into ½ inch cubes
3 cups fresh mushrooms, sliced thin
1 large onion, chopped
3 tablespoons butter
¼ cup butter
5 tablespoons flour
1 cup beef bouillon
1 pint sour cream
1 tablespoon Worcestershire sauce
2 tablespoon steak sauce
1 tablespoon hot pepper sauce

Sauté meat, mushrooms and onion in 3 tablespoons butter until meat is brown but pink and vegetables tender. Melt butter, add flour (1 tablespoon at a time), stirring constantly. When it begins to bubble, add bouillon slowly stirring constantly. When sauce begins to thicken add sour cream and seasonings, then meat mixture. Refrigerate. Best made the day before. If using meat other than tenderloin, cook until tender before adding to sauce. Serve over browned noodles. Serves 6 to 8.

Corinne Pierce

Meat

Browned Noodles

4 to 5 ounces noodles
2 teaspoons salt

3 tablespoons butter (must use butter)
2 tablespoons minced parsley

Drop noodles into 2 quarts of salted water. Cook uncovered until tender. Drain and rinse with hot water. Drain well. Melt butter, cook until lightly browned. Pour over noodles and sprinkle with parsley.

Linda Gunther
Glen, Mississippi

Garnished Beef Stroganoff

2 large onions, chopped
3 tablespoons vegetable shortening
2 pounds lean round steak (slivered)
1½ cups tomato juice
2 bay leaves, broken
2 teaspoons soy sauce
2 tablespoons Worcestershire sauce

1 teaspoon hot pepper sauce
1 teaspoon each of salt, pepper and paprika
2 cloves garlic, minced
5 tablespoons all purpose flour
2 (2½ ounce) cans mushrooms (SAVE JUICES)
1 pint sour cream
1 can fried onions for garnish
1 cup rice, cooked

Sauté onions in shortening. Pour into deep pot. Sauté slivered beef and pour into pot. Add tomato juice, seasonings and sauces. Let boil and cook slowly for 30 minutes. Taste meat for tenderness. DON'T OVERCOOK! Set aside until ready to serve. When ready to serve, heat tomato-meat mixture and thicken with flour mixed with the juice from the canned mushrooms. Add mushrooms and sour cream. Serve on rice and top with crisp, canned, fried onions. Serves 6.

Mrs. Orma R. Smith

Center Stage

El Dorado Casserole

1 pound ground beef
1 medium onion, chopped
1 package taco seasoning mix
½ teaspoon garlic powder
2 (8 ounce) cans of tomato sauce
1 cup water
1 cup pitted ripe olives, sliced
1 (8 ounce) carton sour cream
1 cup small curd cottage cheese
1 (4 ounce) can green chili peppers, chopped and drained
1 (7 ounce) package tortilla chips, crushed
1 (8 ounce) bar Monterey Jack cheese with jalapeño peppers, shredded

Cook ground beef and onion until browned, stirring often. Drain off grease. Add taco seasoning mix, garlic powder, tomato sauce, and 1 cup water to meat mixture. Let this simmer a little while. In a large 3 quart casserole dish, put half the tortilla chips and half the meat mixture. Combine sour cream, cottage cheese and green chilies. Put half of this mixture over the meat mixture. Sprinkle with half the olives and about half the cheese. Repeat layers. Bake at 350°F for 30 minutes. Pass warm tortilla chips to eat along with the casserole. Serves 6.

Dale Bishop

Hamburger Pie

⅓ cup onions, chopped
½ pound ground beef
1½ tablespoons vegetable oil
½ cup mayonnaise
½ cup milk
1 tablespoon cornstarch
1½ cup Cheddar cheese (shredded)
Salt
Pepper

Brown ground beef and onions in vegetable oil and drain. Blend mayonnaise, milk and cornstarch. Stir in meat, cheese, salt and pepper. Pour in unbaked pie shell (9 inch deep dish). Bake at 350°F for 35 to 40 minutes. Serves 6 to 8.

Mrs. Charles Ellington (Sara)

Meat

Peppy Mexican Crescent Pie

1 (8 ounce) can crescent dinner rolls
1 pound ground chuck
2 garlic cloves, minced
1 tablespoon chili seasoning
1 tomato, sliced thinly
2¾ cups shredded Cheddar cheese

¼ cup jalapeño peppers, chopped
1 cup sour cream
⅔ cup mayonnaise
¼ cup black olives, chopped
¼ cup chopped onion

Press crescent rolls into a 10 inch pie plate, creating a crust. Sauté ground chuck, garlic and chili seasoning in skillet. Drain. Spread evenly in pie plate. Thinly slice tomato evenly over the meat mixture. Mix 1¾ cups of shredded cheese with jalapeño peppers. Spread over tomato. Make a mixture with the sour cream, mayonnaise, black olives, and onion. Spread on top and cover with remaining cheese. Bake at 325°F for 20 minutes or till crust is brown. Serve with a tossed salad for a complete meal. Serves 6.

Rita Strachan

Italian Mini Meat Loaves

¾ cups oats
1 (8 ounce) can tomato sauce
1 (2½ ounce) can sliced ripe olives, drained
2 tablespoons finely chopped onion

½ teaspoon Italian seasoning
1 pound lean ground beef
½ teaspoon garlic powder
½ cup (2 ounces) shredded mozzarella cheese

Heat oven to 375°F. In a bowl combine oats, ¼ cup tomato sauce, ¼ cup sliced olives, 2 teaspoons onions, and Italian seasoning. Add ground beef mixing thoroughly. Shape to form four 4x2 inch loaves. Place in 8 inch square glass baking dish or 9 inch glass pie plate. Bake 25 to 30 minutes or until meat is done. Drain. Combine remaining tomato sauce, olives, the remaining onions and garlic powder. Cook over low heat 3 to 5 minutes or until hot. Spoon sauce over meat loaves; sprinkle top with cheese and return to oven for 2 minutes or until cheese is melted. Serves 4.

Kathleen A. Masters

Center Stage

Meat 'N Pepper Cornbread Skillet

1 tablespoon margarine or less
½ cup chopped onion
1 pound lean ground beef or ground turkey
1 (8 ounce) can tomato sauce (low salt type preferred)
2 teaspoons chili powder, or to taste
1 teaspoon salt (omit for low salt diets)
¼ teaspoon pepper
6 or 7 green pepper rings
1 small (8½ ounce) package cornbread mix

Lightly brown onion and meat in shortening in the frying pan. A 9 inch pan works best. Add tomato sauce and seasonings. Simmer while preparing cornbread batter, according to instructions on the box. Press pepper rings through meat in the skillet so they will form a design when served. Pour cornbread batter over the meat. Place skillet in hot oven (425°F) for 20 to 25 minutes, until cornbread is done. Remove from oven. Put a large plate, face down, over the skillet and invert onto the plate. Serves 4.

Note: Sometimes I open a larger can of tomato sauce and pour the extra over the top when serving. Good for low sodium diets.

Nancy Arganbright
La Crosse, Wisconsin

Hamburger And Bean Casserole

½ cup chopped celery
½ cup chopped onion
½ cup chopped bell pepper
Margarine for sautéing
1 pound browned ground beef
1 (15½ ounce) can of pork and beans
1 tablespoon Worcestershire sauce
¼ cup brown sugar
¼ cup catsup

Brown the celery, onion and bell pepper in margarine. Brown the ground beef. Mix together the pork and beans, Worcestershire sauce, brown sugar and catsup. Mix everything together. Put in a large casserole dish. Bake 1 hour at 350°F. Serves 6.

Optional: Top with strips of bacon.

Meat

Ham Loaf

1½ pounds ground smoked ham
1 pound ground roast pork
½ package, prepared herb stuffing mix
½ bell pepper, chopped fine
½ onion, chopped fine
2 whole eggs, well beaten
1 cup milk
½ teaspoon or more black pepper
1½ cups brown sugar
1 tablespoon dry mustard
¼ cup cider vinegar
¼ cup water

Mix the first 8 ingredients together and shape into loaf. Mix the last 4 ingredients together. On bottom of greased loaf pan place ½ of the sauce, then ham loaf. Baste top with the other half the last hour of cooking. Cook 2 hours at 325°F. Makes 1 loaf. Serves 8 to 10.

Sis McPeters
Memphis, Tennessee

Ham Loaf With Sweet and Sour Sauce

2 pounds ground ham
2 pounds ground beef
1½ cups milk
3 eggs
2 cups graham cracker crumbs
Salt and pepper, to taste

Beat eggs slightly and mix with the ham, ground beef, milk and graham cracker crumbs. Shape into a loaf. Place into greased metal loaf pan. Preheat oven to 350°F while making the sauce.

Sauce

½ cup cider vinegar
2 cups tomato juice
1 teaspoon dry mustard
1½ cups brown sugar

Mix well and pour over the ham loaf. Bake at 350°F for 1 to 1½ hours. Check closely and cover loosely with aluminum foil if the loaf dries out. Serves 6 to 8.

Mrs. Joyce Pruett
Sherrard, Illinois

Center Stage

Ham and Broccoli Roll-Ups

1 bunch broccoli, cooked and drained
5 thin slices ham
½ cup mayonnaise
3 tablespoons flour
1½ cups milk
⅓ cup Parmesan or Cheddar cheese
Fine dry bread crumbs

Roll ham around the broccoli sprears. Place in a shallow casserole dish folded side down. In small saucepan, stir together mayonnaise, flour and gradually stir in the milk. Cook over low heat stirring constantly until thickened. Pour sauce over rolls. Sprinkle with crumbs. Broil 2 minutes or until bubbly. Serves 5.

Dorothy Griffith

New Orleans Style Red Beans With Ham And Sausage

1 pound dried red kidney beans
2 quarts water
3 tablespoons bacon drippings (no substitute)
1 large onion, chopped
1 green pepper, chopped
1 carrot, chopped
3 stalks celery, chopped
¼ cup all purpose flour
1½ pounds ham, chopped
1 pound smoked sausage (Kielbasa)
1 tablespoon sugar
1 tablespoon vinegar
2 bay leaves
1 tablespoon parsley
⅛ teaspoon red pepper; salt and pepper to taste, garlic salt
1 cup water

Soak kidney beans overnnight in the 2 quart water. Cook in the same water until tender. Set aside. Heat bacon drippings in a large Dutch oven. Sauté the onion, green pepper, carrot, and celery until wilted but not brown. Add the flour and lightly brown. Add the 1 cup water, ham, sausage, sugar, vinegar, bay leaves, parsley, red pepper, and garlic salt. Drain the red beans, reserving the cooking water. Add the beans to the other ingredients. Simmer for 30 minutes, correct for seasonings, adding more of the cooking water if necessary. Let simmer about 30 more minutes. Serve over hot, cooked rice. Serves 8.

Caroline Hamilton

Meat

Holiday Ham And Sauce

1 whole ham
Cloves

1 quart champagne

Score ham and insert cloves over the ham. Pour champagne over ham. Bake 15 minutes per pound in a 300°F oven, basting frequently.

3 tablespoons brandy
1 cup brown sugar, packed

½ cup mustard

Note: I prefer Dijon type mustard.

Make a paste by combining brandy, brown sugar, and mustard. Spread evenly over baked ham. Bake at 450°F for 20 minutes, basting as needed with champagne sauce until brown and glazed.

Sauce

1 cup brown sugar, packed
1 cup vinegar
4 beaten eggs

3 tablespoons dry mustard
1 tablespoon flour
1 (12 ounce) jar currant jelly

Heat and stir sugar and vinegar in top of double boiler until sugar dissolves. Add sugar and vinegar gradually to eggs and then return to top of double boiler. Combine mustard and flour. Add a small amount of the vinegar/sugar mixture to flour and blend until smooth. Stir this into remaining liquid in top of double boiler. Add the currant jelly to the liquid. Cook in double boiler over boiling water until thickened, stirring constantly. Serve sauce with ham.

Note: The jelly can be omitted and still produce excellent results. Too, Champale or beer may be substituted for champagne.

Dr. Mona Carlyle

Center Stage

Moussaka

3 medium sized eggplants
1 cup butter
3 large onion, finely chopped
3 pounds ground lamb
3 tablespoons tomato paste
1¾ cup red wine
1¾ cup chopped parsley
¼ teaspoon cinnamon
Salt and freshly ground pepper, to taste
6 tablespoons flour
1 quart milk
4 eggs, beaten until frothy
Nutmeg, several shakes
2 cups ricotta or cottage cheese
1½ cups fine bread crumbs
1½ cups freshly grated Parmesan cheese

Preheat oven to 375°F. Peel eggplants and cut into ½ inch slices. Brown slices quickly in 4 tablespoons of butter. Set aside. Heat 4 more tablespoons butter in same skillet and cook onions until brown. Add ground meat and cook 10 minutes. Combine tomato paste with wine, parsley, cinnamon, salt and pepper. Stir this mixture into meat and simmer, stirring frequently, until liquid has been absorbed. Remove from fire. Make a white sauce by melting 8 tablespoons butter and blending in the flour. Add milk gradually to butter/flour mixture, stirring constantly. When mixture is thickened and smooth, remove from heat. Cool slightly and stir in beaten eggs, nutmeg and ricotta (or cottage) cheese. Grease an 11x16 inch pan and sprinkle bottom lightly with bread crumbs. Alternate layers of eggplant and meat sauce in pan, sprinkling each layer with Parmesan cheese and bread crumbs. Pour ricotta cheese sauce over top. Dot with butter. Bake 1 hour, or until top is golden. Cool a bit and cut into squares to serve.

The Day Before: Roast ½ leg of lamb, 350°F till done.

The Day Of: Take off meat and grind it. This makes much more than what the recipe calls for but it's much better.

Mrs. Jotham Pierce
Falmouth Foreside, Maine

Meat

Sweet And Sour Pork

1½ pounds pork tenderloin, cubed
2 beaten eggs
2 cups water
1 cup all purpose flour
Oil for frying pork
3 green peppers, cut in 1 inch pieces
2 cups pineapple chunks, drained
¾ cup brown sugar
3 tablespoons molasses
3 tomatoes or 1 (16 ounce) can
2 tablespoons cornstarch
1 teaspoon salt
Freshly ground pepper
1 cup vinegar
Cooked rice

Combine the eggs, flour, salt and ¼ cup of the water. Add pork and stir until coated. Fry pork until golden, drain. Combine green peppers, pineapple, brown sugar, vinegar, molasses, pepper, and 1½ cups water. Bring to a boil. Add tomatoes and simmer for 5 minutes. Combine cornstarch with ¼ cup water, stir into mixture. Cook until thick. Add pork and simmer for 15 minutes. Serve on a bed of rice. Serves 6.

Miriam R. Propp

Fried Rice With Pork And Shrimp

3 cups cooked long grain rice
6 slices of bacon, chopped
4 eggs
⅛ teaspoon pepper
3 tablespoons oil
1 tablespoon grated fresh ginger
8 ounces cooked pork, cut in strips
8 ounces cooked shrimp, chopped
8 green onions, chopped
4 tablespoons soy sauce

Cook bacon in wok over medium heat, stirring frequently. Drain bacon, remove all but 1 tablespoon of drippings. Beat eggs with pepper, pour egg mix into wok and tilt until egg covers bottom of wok. Cook until set and remove eggs. Slice into thin strips. Add remaining oil and ginger. Stir fry 1 minute. Add rice, bacon, green onion, pork, shrimp, and soy sauce. Stir until hot through. Add eggs and any additional seasoning you desire. Serves 6 to 8.

Linda Cox

Center Stage

Skillet Pork Chops And Rice

6 pork chops
1 tablespoon cooking oil
1 green bell pepper, sliced in rings
1 onion, cut in rounds
1 (16 ounce) can stewed tomatoes
1 cup raw rice
1 quart water (lightly salted)
½ cup flour
Salt and pepper, to taste

Salt and pepper the pork chops and dredge in flour. Heat the oil in a heavy iron skillet and brown the chops on both sides. Drain any excess oil. Set aside. Bring 1 quart of lightly salted water to a boil and stir in the rice. Boil for 7 to 8 minutes only. Drain. Place drained rice on top of the chops. Put 1 slice of onion on each chop and cover with a ring of green pepper. Pour the stewed tomatoes over the rice. Lightly salt and pepper the tomatoes. Cover and steam in a 375°F oven for about 45 minutes. Serves 6.

Ms. Jerrie Doran

Pork Tenderloin Picante

1 whole pork tenderloin
1 egg, beaten
½ cup bread crumbs
2 tablespoons vegetable oil
1 (8 ounce) jar mild picante sauce
½ cup grated Parmesan cheese

Use toothpicks to secure deboned loin halves together. Dip tenderloin in egg, then in bread crumbs until well coated. Brown on all sides in oil in hot skillet. Place meat in shallow baking dish. Pour picante sauce over meat. Top with Parmesan cheese. Cover with foil. Bake 30 minutes in 350°F oven. Uncover. Bake 10 minutes more or until meat thermometer reaches 170°F. Serves 4.

Helen Mercier (Mrs. John D.)

Meat

Barbecued Spareribs With Orange Sauce

4 pounds spareribs
1½ tablespoons lemon pepper
1 (6 ounce) can frozen orange juice
¾ cup catsup
¾ cup hot barbecue sauce
½ cup margarine
2 tablespoons brown sugar
1 tablespoon soy sauce
3 teaspoons prepared mustard
5 finely chopped green onions

Sprinkle ribs with lemon pepper; cut in serving size pieces. Place ribs in roasting pan. Mix remaining ingredients and pour over ribs. Cover and bake at 350°F for 35 to 45 minutes. Serves 4.

Note: I boil ribs in a large saucepan for 20 minutes before baking. This makes them tender and cuts down on baking time.

Brenda Rogers

Curried Sausage And Rice Casserole

1 cup chopped onion
1 cup chopped celery
1 cup chopped green pepper
Margarine for sautéing
1 pound hot sausage
1 cup uncooked rice
1 (4 ounce) can mushroom pieces, drained
1 tablespoon margarine
1½ teaspoons curry powder
2 (10½ ounce) cans beef bouillon
Salt, to taste

In large skilltet sauté onions, peppers and celery in a little margarine. Pour 2 cans bouillon over this. Cook mushrooms in margarine and add to the mixture. Add curry powder. Cook sausage in a skillet, scrambling it until it is broken up and slightly brown. Add this to the mixture and then add the raw rice. Mix well. Put in a 2 quart casserole with tight fitting cover and cook about 1 hour at 325°F, stirring about half way through. Test rice at this time. It may be done. If so take out. Rewarms well in the microwave. Serves 6.

Mary W. Bushey

Center Stage

Sausage Soufflé

6 large eggs
½ pound bulk sausage
Sausage drippings plus enough melted butter to measure ⅓ cup
1 small onion
1 rib celery (finely chopped), optional

⅓ cup all purpose flour
1½ cups milk
¾ teaspoon cream of tartar
Softened butter or margarine for buttering soufflé dish.
Fine bread crumbs for dusting soufflé dish.

Separate eggs, one at a time, while still cold. Cook sausage in large skillet until browned. Measure drippings from pan. Add melted butter if necessary to measure ⅓ cup. Heat drippings and butter over medium heat. Add onion and celery and cook until vegetables are soft. Add flour and stir until smooth. Add all of milk and cook until mixture thickens. Preheat oven to 350°F. Beat egg whites and cream of tartar with mixer until foamy; then beat on high until stiff. Thoroughly blend egg yolks and sausage into sauce. Fold in egg whites. Turn soufflé mixture into a 1½ to 2 quart soufflé dish that has been generously buttered and dusted with bread crumbs. Bake on middle rack for 45 to 50 minutes until mixture is high and browned. Serve immediately. Serves 6.

Mrs. David Roberts (Kim)

Cheesy Sausage Casserole

1 pound pork sausage
½ cup chopped onion
½ cup chopped celery
1 (11 ounce) can cream of celery soup

1 (11 ounce) can Chedder cheese soup
3 tablespoons Parmesan cheese (grated)
1 (5 ounce) package egg noodles

Prepare noodles as package directs. Brown the sausage, onion and celery in a skillet on top of the stove. Pour off grease. Mix noodles, sausage mixture and soups in 13x9 inch pan or casserole dish. Sprinkle Parmesan cheese over the top. Bake in a 350°F oven for 20 minutes or until bubbly. Serves 6 to 8.

Rita Bugg (Mrs. Delan)

Meat

Chinese Casserole

1 pound mild sausage
½ pound hot sausage
5 green onions and tops, chopped
1 large green pepper, chopped
1 medium bunch celery, chopped
1 (3.5 ounce) box, 2 envelopes, chicken noodle soup
4½ cups water
1 cup raw brown rice
1 (6 ounce) can sliced water chestnuts, drained
1 (2½ ounce) package sliced almonds

Fry sausage until browned. Drain on paper towels. Sauté all vegetables in sausage grease. Drain. Cook soup in water according to directions of the box. After soup is cooked, add rice and vegetables, browned sausages, water chestnuts and almonds. Cook in a 9x13 inch greased dish. Bake, uncovered, 1½ hours at 350°F. Serves 10.

Mrs. Mike Byrnes III

Veal Bouchet

12 pieces veal scalloppine, pounded thin
Salt and pepper, to taste
½ cup all purpose flour
Clarified butter or vegetable oil for sautéing
½ cup white wine
1½ cups thinly sliced mushrooms
1 tablespoon chopped shallots
2 cups whipping cream

Season the veal with the salt and pepper and dust lightly with flour. Cover the bottom of a sauté pan with a thin film of butter or oil. When it is very hot, add veal pieces without crowding the pan. Brown lightly on both sides and remove. Repeat as necessary to cook all the veal. Keep warm. Drain grease from the pan. Add shallots and wine and simmmer over high heat for about 1 minute. Add mushrooms and cream, salt and pepper. Lower heat and allow sauce to reduce and become creamy, stirring it now and then. Place veal on serving plates or platter and pour sauce over them. Serves 6.

Martha Wiles
Memphis, Tennessee

Center Stage

Roasted Leg Of Lamb

6 to 7 pound leg of lamb
1 teaspoon salt
½ teaspoon pepper
1 lemon
1 medium sized onion
6 or 8 mint leaves
1½ cups water

Rub lamb with salt and pepper. Slice onion and lemon in thin slices. Place the slices on top of the lamb (the fat side should be up). Put mint leaves on top of the lamb. Wrap in aluminum foil and place in roasting pan on top of the rack. Bake at 250°F for 45 minutes to the pound. For the last hour remove the foil, lemon, onion and mint. Add about 1½ cups water to the drippings in the pan. Baste frequently and continue cooking until a golden brown. Serves 8.

Helen Moore

Roast Leg Of Venison

5 to 7 pound leg of venison
½ cup vinegar plus 3 tablespoons fresh lemon juice
4 cloves of garlic, peeled
6 cups water
1½ cups brown sugar
2 tablespoons ground nutmeg
1 tablespoon leaf thyme
1 tablespoon dry mustard
2 teaspoons salt
1 teaspoon black pepper
Dash of cayenne pepper
3 bay leaves
1 onion cut into rings
1 cup water
2 tablespoons cornstarch

Make slits in the roast and stuff with garlic cloves. Mix the vinegar and lemon juice and rub over the meat. Preheat the oven to 325°F. Place roast uncovered in a turkey roaster and bake for 45 minutes. Mix everything but 1 cup water and 2 tablespoons cornstarch together and bring to a boil. Mix the water and cornstarch and add to the boiling liquid. Cook until thickened, about 3 minutes. Pour the gravy over the venison, cover and bake for 2½ to 3 hours, basting frequently. Add a little more water if necessary. Serve the gravy separately. 1 to 2 tablespoons sour cream and ⅓ cup of chopped fresh parsley adds to this gravy. Serves 8 to 10.

Mrs. R. T. Sawyer (Helen)
Starkville, Mississippi

Seafood

Crab With Sherry

2 cups crabmeat
2 hard boiled eggs, chopped
1 cup mayonnaise
1 teaspoon onion, cut fine
1 teaspoon parsley, chopped

2 teaspoons lemon juice
½ teaspoon Worcestershire sauce
3 tablespoons sherry
1 cup buttered bread crumbs

Mix all ingredients, saving out ½ cup bread crumbs for top. Place in shells or ramekins and cover with remainder of crumbs. Bake at 400°F for 15 minutes. Serves 6. May be prepared in the morning and stored in refrigerator. Take out in time to allow for room temperature before baking.

Pauline McCall

Eastern Shore Crabcakes

½ stick of margarine
½ bunch of parsley, chopped
1 medium onion, chopped
½ cup all purpose flour
1 cup milk

2 eggs
1 pound crabmeat
Cracker crumbs
3 eggs, beaten well
Vegetable oil, for frying

Sauté onion and parsley in margarine, add flour and stir until blended. Beat the milk and 2 eggs and add to hot mixture stirring constantly until thick and coming away from sides of pan. Add crabmeat and mix well. Season with salt and pepper to taste. Form into flat cakes and dip into eggs and then roll in cracker crumbs. Fry in deep fat until golden brown, turn and fry the other side. Serves 4 to 6.

Note: A very old recipe handed to me by a little grandmother from Crisfield, Maryland.

Mary W. Bushey

Center Stage

Crabmeat Casserole

3 tablespoons butter
4 tablespoons flour
1 cup milk
¼ teaspoon salt
Dash white pepper
¼ cup green onions, chopped

8 ounces Monterey Jack cheese, shredded
1 pound crabmeat
2 tablespoons white wine (optional)
Bread crumbs, for topping

Melt butter, add flour, mix well and add milk, salt and pepper. Cook until sauce thickens. Add cheese, onions, and wine. Stir in crabmeat. Salt and pepper if needed. Put in buttered casserole dish and bake at 350°F until bread crumbs are brown. Serves 4.

Lisa Golotte
Biloxi, Mississippi

Stuffed Crabs

1 pound crabmeat
⅔ cup chopped yellow onions
⅔ cup chopped celery
¾ cup chopped bell pepper
½ pod garlic, chopped fine
¼ cup chopped green onion
¼ cup chopped parsley

½ loaf French bread (stale or toasted)
Salt and pepper, to taste
Water to moisten - may also use 1 beaten egg
Vegetable oil for sautéing

Sauté vegetables in cooking oil or margarine, adding green onions and parsley last. Add bread crumbs and crabmeat. Stuff in cleaned crab shells and bake at 350°F about 25 minutes or until golden brown. Makes approximately 11 large crabs. May be frozen for later use.

Lisa Golotte
Biloxi, Mississippi

Seafood

Bass And Cashews

½ cup margarine
6 bass fillets
Salt
Lemon pepper
10 tablespoons slivered cashew nuts, chopped
½ cup sliced mushrooms
8 tablespoons vermouth

Melt margarine in a skillet. Sprinkle fillet with salt and lemon pepper. Cook fillets in margarine 4 minutes on each side. Remove and place on hot plate. Brown the cashews and mushrooms in the margarine that the bass was cooked in. Spread over fillets. Then pour vermouth into skillet and stir with wooden spoon, scraping the pan and blending the vermouth with the margarine, cashew and mushroom residue. Simmer for 5 minutes. Put a tablespoon of this mixture over each fillet and serve immediately. Serves 3 to 4.

Lenoir Stanley

Baked Fish With Vegetables

4 fish fillets (orange roughy, grouper or any firm white fish)
2 ribs celery
1 green pepper
1 bunch green onions
¼ cup margarine
1 tablespoon parsley flakes
Juice of a lemon
¼ cup white wine

Line a pan with aluminum foil. Place fish on foil. Cut celery in 1 inch cubes. Cut green pepper in strips and onions in 1 inch pieces. Put all on top of fish. Combine other ingredients and pour over fish. Wrap foil and seal edges. Bake at 425°F for 20 minutes or until fish flakes easily with a fork. Sauce is good on rice. Serves 4.

Note: This recipe calls for no salt. You may season with salt and pepper if you desire.

Ann Whitfield

Center Stage

Baked Stuffed Fish

½ cup margarine
1 cup minced onion
2 cups diced celery
2 cups cooked rice
1 ½ teaspoons salt
½ teaspoon pepper

½ teaspoon sage
½ teaspoon thyme
1 cup chopped stuffed olives
Fish (6 to 8 pound Red Snapper)

Melt margarine in skillet. Add onions and celery. Sauté until tender (about 3 minutes). Add rice and rest of ingredients. Stuff dressed fish with mixture. Heat oven to 500°F. Bake fish 10 minutes, then reduce heat to 400°F. Bake until easily flaked with fork. Garnish with thin slices of lemon and stuffed olives. Delicious with garlic French bread. Serves 8 to 10.

Lacey Robertson

Stuffed Red Snapper

½ cup margarine
½ pound fresh mushrooms
2 tablespoons minced onion
3 tablespoons dry white wine
1 teaspoon lemon juice
2 tablespoons minced parsley

Fresh pepper
2 cups bread crumbs
1 cup boiled shrimp, chopped
4 fillets of red snapper
½ cup margarine

Sauté mushrooms and onion in ½ cup margarine. Add wine, lemon juice, parsley, pepper, and bread crumbs to make a moist dressing. Dip fish in melted butter, top with shrimp and dressing. Bake 30 to 35 minutes at 350°F. Serves 4.

Rosemary Landreth
Selmer, Tennessee

Seafood

Stuffed Flounder

¼ pound butter or margarine
1 pound fresh or canned crabmeat
½ pound fresh or canned shrimp (if fresh, should be raw, peeled and deveined)
1 cup finely chopped onion
½ cup snipped parsley
½ cup chopped green onion tops
1 teaspoon lemon juice
¼ teaspoon grated lemon rind
1 clove garlic, minced
1 (6 ounce) can button mushrooms
2 cups fine bread crumbs
⅛ teaspoon thyme
2 eggs
Salt, red pepper, black pepper, to taste
8 whole flounders
Non-stick vegetable spray

Melt butter, add crabmeat and shrimp. Cook over low heat until well heated if canned seafood is used. Cook until shrimp are pink if fresh seafood is used. Add vegetables. Cook until onions are transparent and wilted. Add lemon juice and rind. Add mushrooms. Cook about 5 more minutes. Remove from heat. Add bread crumbs, beaten eggs and seasonings. Mix thoroughly, but gently. Wash flounders which have had pockets slit in each. Rub inside and out with salt and pepper. Fill cavities generously with stuffing. Arrange on large flat pan which has been covered with heavy duty foil and sprayed heavily with vegetable spray. Bake uncovered in 375°F oven. Baste well and often with:

¼ pound butter or margarine
1 teaspoon lemon juice
½ cup dry white wine

Do not attempt to turn flounder over. Lower temperature to 300°F after 20 minutes. Cook 15 to 20 minutes longer. Serves 8.

Rosemary T. Williams

Center Stage

Salmon Steaks With Sauce Picante

4 salmon steaks (¾ inch thick, each)

Place salmon in a 12x7 inch, oven-proof glass baking dish, placing thicker edges toward the outside and smaller sections toward center of dish. Cover with glass lid or waxed paper secured tightly across top. If salmon is frozen, remember to thaw before cooking. Cook in microwave oven 10 to 12 minutes on high temperature setting. Salmon is done if it flakes when lifted gently with a fork near center. Let stand, keeping covered, for 5 minutes before serving.

¼ cup butter or margarine
½ teaspoon dry mustard
1½ teaspoons dried parsley flakes

⅛ teaspoon white pepper
¼ teaspoon garlic powder
1½ teaspoons lemon juice (preferably freshly squeezed)

Place butter in 1-cup glass measure. Microwave on medium-high for about 1½ minutes, or until melted. Add remaining ingredients and mix well. Pour sauce over salmon before serving. Serves 4.

Mrs. Fred Reiselt (Janie)

Trout With Almonds

4 medium sized trout, 1 to 1½ pounds each
¾ cup of all purpose flour
⅔ cup butter or margarine
½ cup heavy cream

⅔ cup toasted, slivered almonds
Salt and pepper, to taste
1 lemon, sliced thin

Clean, wash and scale trout. Dry thoroughly and roll lightly in flour. Melt the butter in a frying pan. When it is hot, but not brown, put in trout. Cook over low heat 5 to 7 minutes; turn carefuly and cook on other side for the same length of time. When golden brown, salt and pepper them and lay them carefully on a heated serving platter. Add cream to the butter remaining in pan; mix rapidly; add almonds and stir carefully so that the almonds will not be broken and heat again just to the boiling point. Do not boil sauce. Spoon sauce over trout; add thin rounds of lemon and serve immediately. Serves 4.

Rosemary T. Williams

Seafood

Oven Fried Catfish

4 catfish fillets
2 tablespoons low fat yogurt
2 teaspoons vegetable oil
2 tablespoons fresh lemon juice
¼ teaspoon paprika

½ teaspoon salt
⅛ teaspoon pepper
4 tablespoons dry whole wheat bread crumbs

Drain fish. Combine yogurt, oil, lemon juice and seasonings in shallow dish. Sprinkle bread crumbs on wax paper. Dip fish in yogurt mixture, then press in crumbs, lightly coating both sides. Place fish on lightly greased cookie sheet or shallow pan. Bake at 450°F for 7 to 10 minutes or until it flakes when tested. Garnish with lemon. Serves 4.

Note: This recipe is good for dieters.

Mrs. R. T. Sawyer (Helen)
Starkville, Mississippi

Beer Batter Fried Fish

1½ to 2 pounds fish fillets (any kind of good fish), cut into ¾ inch strips or bite size pieces

Peanut oil

Batter: 1 cup biscuit mix, 1 egg, (12 ounces) beer, salt and pepper

Mix batter ingredients thoroughly with a fork and let stand for a few minutes. Pat fish fillet strips dry with paper towels. Dip fish in batter and fry in deep, hot peanut oil until golden brown. Strained peanut oil can be reused. Serves 6.

Sara Hudson

Center Stage

Oyster Chop Suey

6 cups water plus 1 cup for steaming
1 teaspoon salt
1 cup raw rice
½ cup margarine or butter
1 cup sliced celery
1 cup sliced onions
1 (16 ounce) can Chinese bean sprouts
1 (8 ounce) can water chestnuts, drained
1 (8 ounce) can bamboo shoots, drained
1 (8 ounce) can oysters, not drained
2 tablespoons all purpose flour
2 tablespoons soy sauce
Salt and pepper, to taste

In an open saucepan bring 6 cups water to a boil. Add the salt. Stir in the rice and boil for 20 minutes. Pour rice into a strainer and wash under hot water. Replace pan on stove adding 1 cup water. When it boils, place strainer containing rice over the boiling water. Lower heat and steam the rice. Melt margarine (or butter) in a skillet and sauté onion and celery until limp but not brown. Drain bean sprouts but save the juice. Add soy sauce, stir sprouts into the skillet and add oysters in their juice. Add water chestnuts, sliced thinly, and bamboo shoots. Mix flour and bean sprout juice and stir into the mixture, stirring gently until it thickens. Serve over the fluffy rice. Serves 6.

Rev. Roy McAllily
Batesville, Mississippi

Scalloped Eggplant And Oyster Casserole

1 medium size eggplant
2 tablespoons butter
1 small onion, chopped
¼ cup chopped celery
¼ cup chopped parsley
3 tablespoons butter
1¼ cups cracker crumbs
4 tablespoons Italian seasonings
1 pint oysters, liquor reserved
Salt, to taste
Grated Parmesan cheese
1 cup liquid made from adding milk to oyster liquor to make 1 cup

Seafood

Peel and dice eggplant, cook until done in boiling salted water. Drain. Sauté onion, celery in butter (2 tablespoons) until transparent. Add parsley. Melt 3 tablespoons butter and toss with cracker crumbs and add Italian seasonings. Drain oysters, reserve liquor. Layer ½ eggplant, sautéed vegetables and cracker crumbs, then all of oysters in one layer. Salt (optional). Repeat layers ending with cracker crumbs. Pour 1 cup liquid over. Then top with Parmesan cheese. Bake at 350°F, until done, about 40 minutes. Serves 4 to 6.

This is a tradition at Christmas dinner at our house. Doubled, this serves from 12 to 16 nicely. If doubled, use larger casserole, do not increase layers.

Mickey Hale

Scalloped Oysters

1 pint oysters
1 cup cracker crumbs
½ cup bread crumbs
½ cup melted butter
4 tablespoons oyster liquid

2 tablespoons cream
Salt
Pepper
Nutmeg

Drain oysters, reserving liquid. Mix crumbs and butter together. In shallow, buttered baking dish, put a thin layer of crumb mixture, then a layer of oysters. Sprinkle with salt, pepper, and a few gratings of nutmeg. Drizzle 2 tablespoons of oyster liquid and 1 tablespoon of cream all over. Repeat. Top with remaining crumbs. Bake in 450°F oven for 30 minutes. Serves 4 to 6. Excellent for Thanksgiving turkey.

Note: Have only two layers of oysters. If you have three layers, the middle layer will not cook properly.

Alice Mary Pierce
Portland, Maine

Center Stage

Oysters Rockefeller, Classic

8 strips bacon, cooked crisp
2 cups chopped spinach
½ cup minced parsley
½ cup chopped celery and leaves
2 green onions and tops
½ cup butter

4 tablespoons tomato paste
⅓ cup lemon juice
4 drops Anisette
Salt, pepper, paprika, to taste
2 tablespoons white wine
4 dozen oysters on half shell
Rock salt

Put bacon, spinach, parsley, celery, and onions through meat grinder. Melt butter in saucepan, add spinach mixture and the remaining ingredients except oysters and rock salt. Cook about 5 minutes to blend seasonings. Heat a layer of rock salt in pie pans until very hot. Place oysters on half shell on salt. Put a spoonful of sauce on each oyster. Cook in oven at 475°F for about 7 minutes or until oysters curl and sauce is lightly browned. Serves 8 as appetizer, 4 as a main course.

Oysters Rockefeller

5 dozen oysters on half shell
Large bunch spring onions
Large bunch parsley
¼ pound butter or margarine
5 jars baby food spinach
1 tablespoon celery salt
¾ tablespoon anchovy paste
2 tablespoons Worcestershire sauce

2 tablespoons hot pepper sauce
1 tablespoon ground horseradish
2 teaspoons basil
1 teaspoon marjoram
2 tablespoons absinthe
1 tablespoon Peychaud bitters

Chop onions and parsley, cook slowly in butter in covered pan until soft, about 20 minutes. Run through food blender, put back in pot and add next 8 ingredients. Bring to a boil then remove from fire and add absinthe and Peychaud bitters. Stir well, let cool, after which put in refrigerator until ready for use. Wash and drain oysters. Put them in oyster shells, set shells on a pan of hot ice cream salt, and run them under broiler for 5 minutes. Cover them with sauce, and run under broiler until sauce melts and brown. Serves 10.

Mrs. O. B. Wooley, Jr. (Easie)
Jackson, Mississippi

Seafood

Salmon Casserole

1 (10¾ ounce) can cream of celery soup
½ cup salad dressing or mayonnaise
½ cup milk
¼ cup shredded Parmesan cheese
1 pound can salmon, drained and flaked
1 (10 ounce) package frozen peas, cooked
4 ounces (2 cups) noodles, cooked
1 tablespoon chopped onion

Combine soup with salad dressing, milk and cheese. Blend well. Stir in salmon, peas, noodles, and onion. Pour into a 1½ quart casserole. Bake in 350°F oven for 25 minutes. Serves 6.

Mrs. Herman Baggenstoss
Tracey City, Tennessee

Salmon Loaf

Loaf

1 (15 ounce) can salmon (pick out bones and save liquid for sauce)
1 cup cracker crumbs
2 eggs (well beaten)
1 teaspoon lemon juice
½ cup milk
1 teaspoon salt

Mix ingredients in order given; mold into shape desired. Bake at 350°F until brown (about 30 minutes).

Sauce

Liquid from can of salmon
3 tablespoons butter, melted
2 tablespoons all purpose flour
1 cup sweet milk
Salt and pepper, to taste

Mix thoroughly in order given; cook over moderate heat until thickened. Pour over salmon loaf before serving. Serves 6.

Amy Foster
Jackson, Tennessee

Center Stage

Salmon Loaf With Cucumber Sauce

2 (15 ounce) cans salmon
¾ to 1 cup Italian bread crumbs
2 tablespoons grated onion
1 tablespoon minced parsley
½ teaspoon salt
½ teaspoon celery salt
⅛ teaspoon pepper
3 tablespoons melted butter
1 egg, beaten
2 hard boiled eggs, sliced
12 stuffed olives

Combine salmon, bread crumbs, onion, parsley, salt, celery salt, pepper, 2 tablespoons butter and beaten egg. Mix well. Pour half of the mixture into a 9x5x3 inch loaf pan. Top with sliced boiled eggs and stuffed olives. Cover with the rest of the salmon mixture. Brush the top with the remaining 1 tablespoon butter. Bake at 350°F for 30 minutes. Serve hot or cold, with cucumber sauce. Serves 6.

Cucumber Sauce

2 tablespoons butter
2 tablespoons flour
½ teaspoon salt
⅛ teaspoon pepper
1 cup milk
½ cup grated cucumber

Melt butter in small saucepan. Remove from heat. Add flour, salt and pepper. Put back on heat. Add milk slowly. Stir constantly until thickened. Remove from heat, add cucumber. Stir. Serve with salmon loaf.

Melinda Hinton Moore

Baked Crabmeat And Shrimp

1 medium green bell pepper, chopped
1 medium onion, chopped
1 cup celery, chopped
1 (6½ ounce) can crabmeat, flaked
1 (6½ ounce) can shrimp
⅛ teaspoon black pepper
1 teaspoon Worcestershire
1 cup mayonnaise
1 cup buttered bread crumbs

Combine all ingredients in a medium mixing bowl, except the bread crumbs. Place in a 1½ quart casserole dish (greased). Sprinkle with buttered bread crumbs and bake at 350°F for 30 minutes. Serves 6.

Mrs. J. R. Laughlin (Becky)

Seafood

Shrimp And Artichoke Casserole

½ cup lemon juice
3 tablespoons butter
½ pound fresh mushrooms
2 pounds of shrimp, medium to large, peeled and cleaned
1 (14 ounce) can artichoke hearts
4½ tablespoons butter
4½ tablespoons all purpose flour
¾ cup milk
¾ cup whipping cream
½ cup dry sherry
1 tablespoon Worcestershire sauce
Salt and pepper, to taste
½ cup Parmesan cheese
Paprika (if desired)

Sauté shrimp and mushrooms in 3 tablespoons butter and lemon juice. In 2 quart casserole, layer artichoke hearts, putting shrimp and mushroom mixture on top. In saucepan, use flour, butter, milk, and whipping cream to make a sauce. Add sherry and Worcestershire to this mixture. Pour over artichoke and shrimp; sprinkle with Parmesan cheese and paprika. Bake in a 350°F oven for 30 minutes. Serve over rice. Can prepare day before and refrigerate. Serves 6.

Penny Long

Shrimp And Cheese Strata

6 slices white bread
1 pound boiled, peeled shrimp
½ pound pasteurized process cheese spread
¼ cup butter or margarine, melted
½ teaspoon dry mustard
3 whole eggs, beaten
2 cups milk
Salt, to taste

Pull bread into bite size pieces. Cut cheese into bite size pieces. Arrange shrimp, bread, cheese in several layers in greased 2 quart casserole. Pour margarine or butter over this mixture. Beat eggs. Add mustard and salt to eggs. Then add milk. Mix together and pour over casserole ingredients. Let stand minimum of 3 hours or overnight in refrigerator, covered. Bake 1 hour at 350°F in covered casserole. Serves 6.

Mrs. John W. Prather

Center Stage

Eggplant And Shrimp Casserole

1 pound shrimp, boiled or frozen
2 pounds eggplant, peeled and cubed
2 tablespoons olive oil
1 tablespoon green onion, chopped
1 teaspoon minced garlic
½ teaspoon crushed red pepper flakes
½ teaspoon salt
2 teaspoons sugar
½ teaspoon black pepper
2 tablespoons soy sauce
1 cup chicken stock
1 tablespoon cornstarch dissolved in 2 tablespoons chicken stock

If using frozen shrimp, prepare according to package instructions. Set aside. Heat oil to 350°F. Deep fry eggplant cubes until soft. Drain on paper towels. Set aside. Heat the 2 tablespoons oil in a 10 inch skillet. Add onion, and garlic. Sauté until just tender. Add all other ingredients, except eggplant and shrimp. Bring to a boil then add eggplant and shrimp and cook 1 minute. Serve over hot rice. Serves 8.

Mrs. Travis M. Nelson

Crispy Coconut Shrimp

1 pound medium-sized, fresh shrimp
¼ cup all purpose flour
½ teaspoon salt
½ teaspoon dry mustard
1 egg
2 tablespoons heavy cream
¾ cup flaked coconut
⅓ cup packaged bread crumbs
Vegetable oil (approximately 3 cups)
Chinese mustard sauce (recipe follows)

Shell and devein shrimp, but leave tails intact. Combine flour, salt and dry mustard in a small bowl; beat egg and cream in another small bowl. Combine coconut and bread crumbs on a sheet of wax paper. Dip shrimp first in flour mixture, then in egg-cream mixture, and finally in coconut crumbs coating well. At this point shrimp can be refrigerated in a single layer until ready to cook. Pour oil into a medium saucepan to 2 inch depth. Heat to 350°F on deep fat thermometer. Fry shrimp a few at a time in hot oil for about 2 minutes, turning once. Remove with a slotted spoon to paper towels to drain. Keep warm in 200°F oven until all shrimp are cooked. Serve with sauce. Makes about 24 shrimp.

Seafood

Chinese Mustard Sauce

⅓ cup dry mustard
1 tablespoon honey

2 teaspoons vinegar
¼ cup cold water

Mix until well blended. Refrigerate. Makes about ⅓ cup.

Joan Hennessy

Shrimp Mitchell

½ cup lemon juice
1 cup butter
½ teaspoon white pepper
2 tablespoons soy sauce

1 teaspoon coarse black pepper
1 tablespoon garlic powder
10 extra large fresh shrimp, shells on

Combine lemon juice, butter, peppers, soy sauce and garlic powder in a large iron skillet. When it comes to a slow boil, add shrimp, shells on, into mixture. Cook 15 minutes. Remove shrimp and turn mixture on medium-high to thicken (about 15 to 20 minutes). Add shrimp back to mixture and serve with rice. Serves 2.

Note: Mom's Favorite (Billye Tullos, Mobile, Alabama)

Yvonne Gallaher

Shrimp Creole

5 pounds cleaned raw shrimp
2 sticks butter
3 green peppers
4 onions, chopped fine
4 cups celery, chopped fine
2 cloves garlic, chopped fine
½ cup parsley, chopped fine

½ teaspoon black pepper
1 teaspoon salt
1 teaspoon curry powder
1 teaspoon thyme
½ teaspoon red pepper
3 (51 ounce) cans tomatoes

Sauté peppers, onions, garlic, celery, and parsley in butter. Add tomatoes and seasoning. Cook slowly for 30 minutes. Add shrimp and cook 20 minutes longer. Serve with rice. Serves 10.

Martha Ball
New Orleans, Louisiana

Center Stage

Shrimp De Jonghe

2 to 3 pounds deveined, shelled shrimp
1 cup toasted bread crumbs
¼ cup chopped green onions
½ cup snipped parsley
½ teaspoon garlic salt
½ teaspoon tarragon (dried)
¼ teaspoon nutmeg
Salt and pepper, to taste
4 tablespoons butter for topping, melted
1 cup melted butter (no substitute)
¼ cup dry sherry (not sweet)

Combine crumbs, onion, parsley and seasonings in a medium skillet (preferable heavy aluminum or black iron). Add butter, stir until butter is melted and the crumbs begin to color slightly. This is best done on medium to low heat. Add shrimp and toss until they become pink. Add sherry. Remove from the stove, toss again. Place in baking dishes or shells and drizzle the 4 tablespoons of melted butter over. Bake in a preheated 400°F oven for 10 to 15 minutes. Serves 6 to 8.

Warren Rossi

Mike's Peel 'Em And Eat 'Em

1 to 1½ gallons water
1 (12 ounce) can of beer
1 bag shrimp boil
2 tablespoons liquid crab boil
1 tablespoon salt
Dash of hot sauce
Juice and rind of 4 lemons
4 to 6 pounds raw shrimp in the shell

In large pot put everything but shrimp and bring to rapid boil. Put in shrimp, boil rapidly until pink and opaque. About 6 minutes for small, 10 to 12 minutes for medium to large is about right. Do not overcook. Remove from heat, drain and chill, enjoy. Serves 6 to 8.

Mike Hale's Seafood
Hattiesburg, Mississippi

Seafood

Wild Rice And Shrimp Casserole

- 1 (10¾ ounce) can cream of mushroom soup
- 2 tablespoons chopped green pepper
- 2 tablespoons chopped onion
- 2 tablespoons melted butter
- 1 tablespoon lemon juice
- 2 cups cooked wild rice (4 ounce box)
- ½ teaspoon Worcestershire sauce
- ½ teaspoon dry mustard
- ¼ teaspoon pepper
- ½ cup cubed Cheddar cheese
- ½ pound uncooked shrimp

Mix all ingredients together thoroughly. Pour into greased 1½ quart casserole. Bake in 375°F oven 35 to 45 minutes. *If frozen uncooked shrimp is used, thaw it in several layers of paper towels to remove excess moisture.)* Serves 4.

Mrs. Carroll Hudson

Shrimp Stroganoff

- 4 tablespoons margarine
- 2 pounds shrimp, cleaned but not cooked
- ¼ cup green onions
- 1½ teaspoons salt
- ¼ teaspoon pepper
- ½ pound mushrooms, sliced
- 4 ounces vermicilli spaghetti
- Chicken stock
- 1 cup sour cream
- ¼ cup dry sherry or more, to taste

Sauté onions and mushrooms in margarine until tender and most of liquid has been absorbed. Add shrimp and sauté until done (about 3 minutes). Add salt and pepper. Cook spaghetti in chicken stock. (Bouillon cubes can be used to make the stock - 2 per cup of water). When ready to serve, add sour cream, toss with spaghetti and season with the sherry. This can be made and frozen. Heat in oven at 350°F for 15 minutes. Serves 6.

Helen Moore

Center Stage

Shrimp In Beer

5 pounds large shrimp
2 cans beer
1 pint cider vinegar
1/8 to 1/4 cup red pepper
1/8 to 1/4 cup black pepper
1/4 cup salt
2 tablespoons celery seed (tied in a cloth)

Bring all ingredients except shrimp to a boil. Drop shrimp in and simmer 5 minutes. Serve hot with melted butter and minced parsley. Serves 5 or 6.

Mrs. Nap Cassibry (June)
Cleveland, Mississippi

Holiday Seafood Newberg

1 package (6 ounce) frozen king crabmeat
1 pound scallops
1 pound raw shrimp
1/4 cup butter
1/3 cup all purpose flour
1 cup light cream
1 can (10 3/4 ounce) condensed chicken broth
1/3 cup sherry
1 can (6 ounce) sliced mushrooms (drained)
Salt and pepper

Thaw and drain crabmeat. Drop scallops and shrimp into boiling water (salted). Cook until scallops are white, and shrimp, pink. Drain, shell and devein shrimp. In a large saucepan, melt butter and stir in flour. Gradually stir in cream, chicken broth and sherry. Cook while stirring until sauce bubbles and thickens. Fold in mushrooms and shellfish. Reheat until bubbly. Season to taste with salt and pepper. Spoon that mixture over patty shells or rice. Serve immediately. Serves 6.

Giny Hurlbert
Clearwater, Florida

Seafood

Baked Seafood

3 (6 ounce) cans crabmeat or 1 pound fresh or imitation crabmeat
3 (6 ounce) cans shrimp or 1 pound fresh shrimp
8 ounces fresh mushrooms, sliced
½ green pepper, chopped fine
½ cup green onion, chopped fine
½ cup pimiento, chopped
1 cup celery, chopped fine
2 tablespoons butter
1 cup mayonnaise
½ teaspoon salt
⅛ teaspoon cayenne pepper
1 cup half and half
1 tablespoon Worcestershire sauce
3 cups cooked rice

Sauté mushrooms, green pepper, green onion and celery lightly in 2 tablespoons butter. Combine mayonnaise, salt, cayenne pepper, half and half and Worcestershire sauce. Combine all ingredients together. Put in a greased casserole dish. Cover with topping, recipe follows. Sprinkle with a little cayenne pepper. Bake at 300°F for 45 minutes. Serves 8.

Topping

8 buttery round crackers, crumbled
8 saltine crackers, crumbled
4 heels of loaf bread, crumbled
1 stick of butter, melted

Mix all together.

Melinda Hinton Moore

Center Stage

Tips For Outdoor Cooking

1. Good quality hardwood charcoal briquets are the best and easiest fuel to use.
2. Make you fire fit your grill and the meat or other food you are preparing. A small grill (portable) would call for probably no more than a dozen and a half briquets, whereas a large grill would call for more, depending on the size of the meat being cooked. The larger the meat, the more briquets needed. If cooking a large piece of meat that will take several hours, a small fire on the side, perhaps in a coal skuttle is good to keep going so you can shovel in new briquets as needed.
3. Use tongs to turn meat rather than a fork, as piercing the meat causes the juices to escape.
4. Hickory, apple wood and pecan chips (first soaked in water) add a lovely different flavor to meats when placed on the fire four or five at a time.
5. A water pistol or squirt bottle is good to have next to the fire should it flare up.
6. A hinged grill or broiling basket is excellent for cooking fish. Grills with a rotisserie often come with a broiling basket or can be secured through the store handling the cooker.
7. Put your guests to work helping to cook. They love it!!

Louie's Special Barbecue Sauce

½ cup melted margarine
Juice of one lemon
3 tablespoons vinegar
3 tablespoons Worcestershire sauce
1 teaspoon pepper
1 teaspoon salt

Melt margarine and add all other ingredients. Stir well and brush on meat. Stir before each application as mixture will separate. I melt the margarine in the microwave in a measuring cup and just put the other ingredients in. This sauce is wonderful on chicken, pork chops, and shrimp. It may also be used on beef kabobs. Makes 1 cup.

This is the original recipe of Louie DeMoville of Okolona, MS, and Sandestin, FL, an outstanding backyard chef.

Rosemary Fisher

On the Grill

Rich's Barbecue Sauce

½ cup butter or margarine
1 cup water
2 tablespoons vinegar
¾ teaspoon dry mustard
2 teaspoons sugar
1 medium sized onion, minced
3 cloves garlic, minced

1 teaspoon salt
⅛ teaspoon red pepper
1 tablespoon Worcestershire sauce
½ teaspoon black pepper
½ medium sized bell pepper, minced

Combine all ingredients and simmer for ½ hour. This sauce is excellent for chicken, pork, or fish. Makes 2 cups.

C. J. "Rich" Richardson, Jr.
Cleveland, Mississippi

Tip For Smoking Fowl

When smoking turkey or chicken, rub with honey before putting in smoker and it will come out a beautiful golden color.

Stan's Charcoaled Chicken

2 chickens, halved or quartered or 8 to 10 chicken breasts
1 cup cooking oil
½ cup lemon juice
1 tablespoon salt

1 teaspoon paprika
2 teaspoons crushed basil
2 teaspoons onion powder
½ teaspoon crushed thyme
½ teaspoon garlic powder

Combine all ingredients and mix thoroughly in bowl. Place chicken in broiler pan and pour mixture over chicken. Let marinate for several hours on both sides. Best if allowed to marinate in refrigerator overnight and grilled outside. Brush chicken with marinade while cooking. Serves 8 to 10. You may wish to grind pepper over chicken.

Stan R. Jones
Memphis, Tennessee

Center Stage

Barbecue Sauce - Chicken

1 (6 ounce) jar horseradish mustard
¾ pound margarine
1 cup white vinegar
1 tablespoon salt
1 cup Worcestershire sauce
2 teaspoons chili powder
1 cup water

Melt margarine. Add all other ingredients and stir. Bring to a boil. Remove from heat and let cool. Marinate chicken before grilling and brush chicken frequently while grilling. Serves 10 halves. Reserve extra sauce for the table.

Lynn Elliott

Tips On Barbecuing Chicken

Buy small frying chickens and quarter them. Cut away and discard visible excess fat from chicken. Sprinkle both sides of chicken pieces with seasonings, salt, fresh ground pepper. Brush with barbecue sauce. Cook over a medium-hot charcoal fire covered for about 1 hour. Place skin side up first. Turn every 10 minutes (or more often initially) basting the top before each turn and taking care to move around any pieces that seem to be on a hot spot. Use tongs rather than a fork to turn. A few chips of water soaked apple wood placed on the fire add immeasurably to the flavor.

"Strive mightily, but eat and drink as friends...",
William Shakespeare, English dramatist and poet.

On the Grill

Duck Shish-Kabob

Breast of 4 ducks
1½ cups Italian salad dressing
Lemon pepper
½ teaspoon garlic salt
2 tablespoons beer
Medium onion, cut in quarters

Bell pepper, cut in 1½ inch squares
Tomatoes quartered or use cherry tomatoes
Mushrooms

Cut duck in 1 inch squares. Place in flat dish and sprinkle with lemon pepper and garlic salt. Combine beer and salad dressing and pour over duck. Beer removes the wild taste. Marinate 6 to 8 hours. Boil onion pieces, bell pepper until just tender. Marinate onion, bell pepper, tomatoes and mushrooms with duck for 1 hour. Alternate duck and vegetables on skewers. Cook on medium grill 10 to 15 minutes turning to brown each side. Serve over rice. Serves 6.

John Beall Clark
Jackson, Mississippi

Dove Breasts

12 to 15 dove breasts
2 medium onions quartered
Bell pepper cut in 1½ inch squares

Bacon

Marinade

1½ cups Italian salad dressing
2 tablespoons beer

1 teaspoon lemon pepper
½ teaspoon garlic salt

Quarter onion and bell pepper and boil until barely tender. Put a piece of bell pepper and onion in arch of breast. Wrap bacon around breast and secure with toothpick. Marinate 6 to 8 hours. Cook on medium, grill 15 to 20 minutes turning as needed to brown. Serve over brown rice. Serves 4 to 5.

John Beall Clark
Jackson, Mississippi

Center Stage

The Swine Lake Ballet Barbecue Sauce

12 ounces wine vinegar
4 tablespoons salt
3 tablespoons dried minced garlic
1 tablespoon dried horseradish
¼ cup cooking oil
¼ cup soy sauce
1 tablespoon black pepper
6 bay leaves
1 teaspoon ginger
½ cup dried onion flakes
1 cup white wine
1 (10 ounce) can diced tomatoes and green chilies
1 cup water
1 cup commercial barbecue sauce, hot
2 cups commercial barbecue sauce with onions
4 dashes Worcestershire sauce
¼ cup dark corn syrup
1 (10 ounce) can tomato sauce
1 (12 ounce) can vegetable - tomato juice
½ cup lemon juice

1. Don a leotard, tights, tutu, and toe shoes. 2. Combine all ingredients in a large pot and bring to boil. Turn heat down and simmer for 1 hour, stirring occasionally. IMPORTANT: While sauce is simmering, listen to "Swan Lake".

The Swine Lake Ballet

The Swine Lake Ballet is a group of Corinth Professional men who have participated the past several years in the finals of the International Barbecue Contest, Memphis in May, Memphis, TN. They have lots of fun as well as turning out great barbecue.

Eddie Knight's Barbecue Sauce For Ribs

12 pounds lean pork ribs, uncut
1 pint apple cider vinegar
½ pound butter or margarine
4 lemons, sliced
1 teaspoon red pepper
1 teaspoon black pepper
1 tablespoon dry mustard
2 tablespoons Worcestershire type sauce
½ teaspoon salt, or to taste
½ teaspoon Louisiana type red hot sauce
½ teaspoon garlic powder

On the Grill

Cut excess fat off ribs and salt and pepper to taste. Let charcoal fire burn down to ashes. Mix vinegar and butter and sliced lemons and bring to a boil. Simmer 15 minutes. Mix peppers, dry mustard, hot sauce into the Worcestershire sauce and stir into vinegar and butter sauce. Keep warm. When coals are burned to a silver ash, apply sauce generously on the whole ribs and cook very slowly — basting frequently for about 2 hours. Ribs will be brown, slightly crusty but not dry when done. Cut between every other rib when serving. A party special!

E. J. Knight
Pickwick Dam, Tennessee

Ham Steak

1 two inch thick centercut pre-cooked ham steak
1 (16 ounce) jar crabapples, juice reserved

1 teaspoon dry mustard, or to taste
½ cup brown sugar

Sauce

Mix juice from crabapples, dry mustard and brown sugar. Place ham steak over a medium hot charcoal fire about 8 inches from fire. Cook 10 minutes on each side basting 3 or 4 times with the seasoned crabapple juice. Slice meat at an angle to desired thickness and serve with reserved sauce.

Note: Leftovers excellent for sandwiches.

Mrs. Ben Pierce

Sauce For Ham Steak

4 tablespoons lemon juice
2 teaspoons salt

2 tablespoons Dijon mustard
1 cup honey

Combine all ingredients. Refrigerate or freeze until needed. Cut 2 inch thick slices of precooked ham. Cook 15 minutes on both sides and baste with above sauce.

Variation: For low sodium diet, reduce salt.

Mrs. Bob Worsham (Beth)

Center Stage

Pork Chops

Desired number of loin pork chops cut 1¼ inches thick.

Season liberally with:

Salt
Fresh cracked pepper

Garlic powder or garlic salt
Lemon pepper seasoning

Place grill about 6 to 8 inches from a hot charcoal fire. Put 3 or 4 water soaked chips of applewood on the fire as they will add favorably to the taste of the meat. Place meat over the fire, close the top and cook about 6 minutes to the side. This is excellent, served with applesauce, green peas and a green salad.

Note: If your charcoal cooker does not have a top, make a loose tent of aluminum foil.

Mr. C. J. Richardson
Cleveland, Mississippi

Pork Ribs

8 pounds of ribs, cut in 3 rib pieces

Salt
Fresh cracked pepper

Sauce

Your choice of Louie's Special Barbecue Sauce, Eddie Knight's Barbeque, Rich's Barbecue Sauce, Stan's Charcoaled Chicken Sauce, or Swine Lake Barbecue Sauce.

Parboil ribs in salted water to cover for 20 minutes. Drain and sprinkle with fresh cracked pepper and lemon pepper. Cook over a slow charcoal fire about 12 inches from the heat, basting frequently and turning often. Best if top is down but not absolutely necessary. Cook about 1 hour. Allow ¾ pound per person.

Charlie McCall
Lyons, Georgia

Grilled Shrimp Kabobs

½ cup orange juice
¼ cup white vinegar
¼ cup vegetable oil
¼ cup soy sauce
½ teaspoon salt
¾ pound of raw shrimp
Lemon wedges

Combine orange juice, vinegar, oil, soy sauce and salt. Shell and devein raw shrimp and add to marinade; chill 1 hour. Remove shrimp from marinade and thread with lemon wedges on skewers. Broil shrimp and lemon skewers over medium coals 3 to 4 minutes, turning often. Marinade may be heated and served with kabobs. Serves 2.

Mrs. Hull Davis (Bitsy)

Beef Shish-Kabob

1 cup wine vinegar
1 cup vegetable oil
1 cup soy sauce
2 teaspoons onion salt
4 teaspoons Italian seasoning
¼ teaspoon garlic powder
3 pounds boneless sirloin steak, cut in cubes
1 pound fresh mushrooms
2 large onions, quartered
2 bell peppers, quartered
Cherry tomatoes, as desired

Combine wine vinegar, oil, soy sauce, onion salt, Italian seasoning and garlic powder in large bowl. Mix well. Add steak, mushrooms, onions and peppers. Let marinate at least 6 hours. Put on skewers and add tomatoes. Cook on grill, turning often. Serve over rice if desired.

Note: This recipe is easily doubled and the steak freezes well. Also the mushrooms are good as an appetizer before cooking if marinated separately. Cooking time 8 minutes or less over a medium hot fire.

Variation: Steam vegetables for 8 minutes before skewering.

Mary Hedges

Center Stage

Shish-Kabob Tips

Lamb and pork kabobs can be made in much the same way as beef kabobs, using the marinade above or another of the oil-butter-lemon based sauces listed in this chapter.

Lamb: A leg of lamb cut in 1½ inch to 1¾ inch slices and then cubed is your best bet. Marinate in your chosen sauce at room temperature for 3 hours along with your chosen vegetables (either raw or steamed a bit). Cook over a hot ash-covered fire quickly, turning as the meat browns, about 4 minutes per side. The lamb should be pink inside. Serve over saffron rice.

Pork: Cut lean pork (from chops or tenderloin) into 1½ inch cubes. Marinate in a oil-butter-lemon based sauce for an hour along with the vegetables to be used. Skewer and cook over a hot fire about 6 or 7 minutes. You may want to skewer the meat on separate skewers from the vegetables, as pork needs to cook longer than the vegetables. Put the meat on 3 minutes before the vegetables. Turn all frequently and serve over rice.

Caution: Do not overcook just because this is pork.

Beef Tenderloin

1 (5 pound) beef tenderloin
Bacon
Mushrooms (canned)
Salt
Lemon-pepper marinade

Cut bacon strips and lay across tenderloin about every inch and a half. Stick 3 large mushrooms on the side of each bacon strip with toothpicks. Start fire 30 minutes before you want to cook. Cook 20 minutes per side on grill. Cook on flat side first and then turn over completely. If mushrooms are secured tightly, they will not fall off when you turn roast. Does best with grill top closed. Serves 10.

Ed Kossman, Jr.
Cleveland, Mississippi

On the Grill

Buffet Beef Tenderloin

Marinade

1 cup red dry wine
2 cans beef broth
1 small bottle soy sauce

1 bottle garlic juice
1 bottle onion juice
1 tablespoon sugar (A MUST)

Mix all ingredients in a large container and marinate the beef tenderloin overnight if possible. Grill on hot grill approximately 10 minutes on each side. Serve with bottled horseradish sauce.

Barbara Witt

Bearnaise Sauce

¼ cup tarragon vinegar
¼ cup dry white wine
2 tablespoons chopped fresh tarragon, or 1 teaspoon dried tarragon leaves

1 tablespoon finely chopped green onion
3 egg yolks
½ cup butter

Have all ingredients at room temperature. In a small saucepan combine vinegar, wine, green onions and tarragon. Simmer until reduced to ¼ cup. Strain mixture into top of double boiler. With wire whisk, beat in egg yolks. Cook over hot, not boiling, water beating constantly. Beat in butter 1 tablespoon at a time, beating well after each addition. Serve with fillets of beef.

Ann White (Mrs. Elbert)

Outdoor Cooking Tip

Serve your next grilled steak with this delicious butter:

Mustard Butter

1 stick unsalted butter, softened
1½ tablespoons coarse grain mustard

1 teaspoon fresh lemon juice
Salt and pepper, to taste

Process all ingredientds in food processor until smooth. Chill, then shape into a log. Wrap in plastic wrap and freeze until needed.

Center Stage

Elegant Beef Bits For Cocktails

1 centercut sirloin steak cut 1 inch thick
6 tablespoons butter or margarine, melted
¼ cup vegetable oil
Juice of 1 lemon
1 tablespoon Worcestershire sauce
1 tablespoon tarragon vinegar
½ teaspoon garlic powder
Salt and pepper (fresh cracked)

Cut sirloin into 1 inch squares, let come to room temperature, then salt and pepper a bit. Mix all other ingredients, heat almost to a boil and pour over steak bits. Let marinate for an hour, stirring 3 times. You may refrigerate at this point until ready to use. To cook, have a hot charcoal fire, throw steak bits on grate and rake back and forth over fire for 3 or 4 minutes with a large metal spatula. Put on a heated platter and use toothpicks to spear and dip in a mushroom sauce.

Sauce

1 (4 ounce) can mushroom sauce
2 tablespoons butter
1 tablespoon chives
Worcestershire sauce, to taste

Mix together and heat.

Note: In order to prepare this, one must have grating on their cooker close enough together so that 1 inch thick cubes of meat will not fall through. A 1x2 foot piece of hardware cloth laid across your regular grating will do the trick and the recipe is worth the trouble.

Mrs. Ben Pierce

On the Grill

Barbecued Brisket

3 pound beef brisket
Garlic salt, to taste
¼ cup liquid smoke
1 teaspoon tenderizer

Sprinkle brisket with garlic salt and marinate overnight in liquid smoke. Wrap in foil, after adding tenderizer, and bake for 1½ hours at 325°F.

Sauce

¾ cup brown sugar
⅓ cup vinegar
3 tablespoons lemon juice
½ cup catsup
2 teaspoons Worcestershire sauce
½ cup chopped onion
¼ teaspoon pepper
Salt, to taste

Heat ingredients for sauce in pan. Brush on meat and cook on grill until flavor penetrates meat and meat is tender. Cooking time, approximately 1 hour on a low fire. Serves 8 to 10.

Variation: After marinating overnight and adding tenderizer, cook in smoker overnight, basting with sauce well before and after cooking.

Mrs. Charles Ellington (Sara)

Smoked Roast

Sirloin tip roast (5 pounds or more)
3 lemons, more for larger roast
Salt
Red pepper
Black pepper
Rosemary
Hot pepper sauce
2 teaspoons dry mustard
2 cloves garlic, mashed
Worcestershire sauce
Vegetable oil or olive oil

Squeeze lemon juice over roast. Rub liberally with all ingredients. Marinate 8 to 12 hours, turning every 2 hours. Put meat thermometer in and cook on covered grill until desired doneness, approximately 3 to 4 hours. Serves 10.

Bob Worsham

Center Stage

Ed's Roast

8 or 9 pound loin tip*
10 to 12 ounces purchased barbecue sauce
6 to 8 ounces wine vinegar
1 teaspoon hot pepper sauce

3 or 4 tablespoons lemon juice (bottled)
Salt and pepper, to taste
3 tablespoons soy sauce

*Or Pike's Peak Rump Roast (Beef)

Mix all ingredients in mixing bowl. Place roast in bowl of sauce. Spoon sauce over roast, cover, and marinate for 24 hours, if possible, turning once. Charcoal grill must have a cover. Start fire 30 minutes before cooking. Cook 15 to 20 minutes per pound, turning 3 or 4 times without basting. A spit is not necessary. Any size or kind of roast may be used. Serves 18 to 20.

Ed Kossman, Jr.
Cleveland, Mississippi

Fish
Whole, Fillets, Or Steaks

Lightly salt fish with sea salt and let stand for 30 minutes. Secure whole fish, fillets or steaks in a greased hinged grill or broiling basket. When the charcoal is ash covered, place the fish over the fire and baste on both sides with Stan's or Louie's Barbecue Sauce (see first of this chapter). With 1 inch fillets or steaks, cook fish about 4 minutes to a side, basting at each turn. Whole fish weighing up to 2 pounds, cook 8 to 10 minutes to a side. Fish is done when it flakes easily. This can be cooked on aluminum foil placed over the grill if you don't have a hinged grill or broiling basket. Turn once using this method.

Variations: Add 4 water soaked apple wood chips or bits of green willow sticks to the fire. You may wish to marinate the fillets or steaks in the sauce to which you have added your favorite herb or herbs — parsley, basil, coriander or rosemary.

On the Grill

Vegetable Accompaniments

Tomatoes

Cut whole tomatoes in half crosswise; salt and pepper, set on grill with meat (cut side down first) for 2 minutes; turn, baste with your barbecue sauce, sprinkle with Parmesan cheese, fresh diced parsley and cook for another 4 minutes depending how hot your fire is.

Potato Kabobs

Boil little red potatoes until firm-tender; rub with vegetable oil and roll in fresh ground pepper and coarsely ground salt; put on skewers and grill until browned a bit. A light basting with your barbecue sauce will zap up the flavor. When finished, sprinkle lightly with finely diced parsley to enhance appearance.

Squash - Yellow or Zucchini

Cut in half lengthwise and then in 4 inch lengths. Parboil for 3 minutes; salt and pepper with fresh ground pepper. Baste with whatever barbecue sauce you are using and cook on grill during last 6 minutes of your meats' cooking time.

Corn On Cob

Shuck corn and remove silks. Place on a piece of foil with a generous pat of butter and wrap in a semi-loose seal. Place on coals for 8 minutes turning twice.

Variation: Sprinkle liberally with cajun-style seasoning, seal in foil and cook 20 or 30 minutes on the grill, turning occasionally.

Onions

Split a medium onion from top almost to bottom so that it is in quarters. Butter generously, wrap securely in foil and punch a few holes in the top part so that the steam can escape. Cook on covered grill for about 1 hour or you can start them in your oven and finish up outside.

Potatoes

Boil baking potatoes until just short of being done. They could be microwaved. Cut in half crossways, place a ½ inch slice of onion the same circumference as the potato between the 2 halves. Set on a piece of foil, salt with sea salt, pepper, butter generously and wrap securely. Finish cooking on grill with the meat. About 15 or 20 minutes on a covered grill.

Center Stage

Grilled Parmesan Corn

8 ears fresh corn
¾ cup margarine
½ cup grated Parmesan cheese

1 tablespoon chopped parsley
½ teaspoon salt

Remove silks and husks from corn. Combine margarine, cheese, parsley and salt. Spread mixture on corn. Place each ear in aluminum foil; wrap tightly. Grill over medium heat for 30 minutes, making sure to turn corn several times. Yield: 8 servings.

Brenda Rogers

Lagniappe

Charcoal-grilled fruit: Cut the fresh fruit of your choice (tart apples, pears or peaches) in half, top to bottom, and squeeze lemon juice over exposed surfaces. Brush with melted butter, sprinkle with cinnamon, and brown sugar. Dust the apples lightly with salt. Grill quickly just until hot and splash a bit of brandy or sweet liqueur over all.

"It isn't so much what's on the table that matters, as what's on the chairs", W.S. Sullivan (Gilbert & Sullivan), English lyricist.

Break-a-leg

"BREAK A LEG"

One of the most curious traditions in the theatre is that it is bad luck to wish good luck. Out of this superstition grew the expression "Break a leg".

In marked contrast, getting the longest piece when breaking the wishbones is considered good luck. Perhaps for double insurance, the next time you crack a wishbone with someone, you might also say "Break a leg"!

AFTER THE HUNT BRUNCH

Christmas Brunch Quail - p.239

Garlic Cheese Grits - p.280

Spinach and Artichoke Casserole with Blender Hollandaise - p.286

Cheekwood Port Wine Salad - p.103

Assorted Breads:
Buttermilk Orange Muffins - p.307
Blueberry Bran Muffins - p.306
Pumpkin Bread - p.305

PICNIC

Lemon Chicken - p.228

Ham Sandwich Loaf - p.137

Fresh Broccoli Salad - p.107

Potato Salad - p.114

Assorted Cheeses and Fruits

Easy Brownies - p.336

Break-A-Leg

Barkley's Chicken Casserole

5 or 6 pound hen, stewed and diced
1 cup uncooked rice
1 large onion, chopped
1 cup diced celery
2 (4 ounce) cans mushrooms
1 green pepper and/or 1 pimiento, diced
1 cup sliced almonds
1 tablespoon A-l sauce
Salt and pepper, to taste
Chicken broth as needed (about 3 cups)

Mix all ingredients and steam for 20 minutes. Correct seasoning, if necessary. Top with buttered bread crumbs, brown in oven on 350°F. (The first part may be done the day before adding your bread crumbs and browning just before serving. Serves 6.

Mrs. T. Y. Williford, Jr.
Greenville, Mississippi

Chicken Breast Supreme

6 whole chicken breasts, deboned
2 cartons sour cream
1/4 cup lemon juice
4 teaspoons Worcestershire sauce
4 teaspoons celery salt
2 teaspoons paprika
4 cloves garlic, chopped or garlic powder
4 teaspoons salt
1/2 teaspoon pepper
1 1/2 cups fine bread crumbs
1/2 cup vegetable shortening
1/2 cup butter

Mix sour cream and all the seasonings together and place chicken in the mixture. Marinate overnight. Take chicken out and roll in crumbs. Fold chicken into squares with sides tucked in. Melt shortening and butter in casserole dish. Put chicken breasts in dish and spoon the shortening mixture over them. Bake uncovered for 45 to 60 minutes at 350°F. Serves 8.

Nancy Norman McLemore

Poultry

Brunswick Stew

2 chickens or squirrels
1 onion, sliced thin
3 slices bacon
1 gallon water
1 quart peeled tomatoes
2 ears corn, grated

3 Irish potatoes, peeled and cubed
½ pint shelled butter beans
½ pod red pepper
1 tablespoon grated bread
1 tablespoon butter

Cook chicken (or squirrel), onion, bacon and water together until meat is tender. Remove bones, skin and return meat to broth. Add tomatoes, corn, potatoes, butter beans and pepper. Cook until all vegetables are tender. Add bread and butter. Season to taste with salt and pepper. Serves 8.

Nancy Smith

Curried Chicken Divan (with a special twist)

2 (10 ounce) packages broccoli or 2 (10 ounce) packages French-style green beans
6 to 8 small, cooked, boned chicken breasts, sliced
2 (10½ ounce) cans cream of chicken soup

1 cup mayonnaise
1 teaspoon lemon juice
½ teaspoon curry powder
½ cup grated Cheddar cheese
¼ cup chopped pecans
1 (6 ounce) can sliced water chestnuts

Cook broccoli or beans and drain. Arrange in a greased 11x7 inch casserole. Place chicken over vegetables. Combine soup, mayonnaise, lemon juice, curry, nuts and water chestnuts. Pour over chicken. Top with cheese and bake in 350°F oven 30 to 45 minutes. Serves 6 to 8.

Mrs. Herman Baggenstoss
Tracy City, Tennessee

Break-A-Leg

Chicken Cerise

6 to 8 chicken breasts, deboned
All purpose flour
Salt
Pepper
Paprika
Ginger, few grains
4 tablespoons butter
2 tablespoons grated onion or green onion, including tops
1 cup boiling water
4 tablespoons cornstarch
1 (10 ounce) can pitted Bing cherries and juice
2 cups chicken soup stock
2 chicken bouillon cubes
1 cup chicken broth
½ cup cooking sherry
Wild rice, cooked according to directions

Preheat oven to 300°F. Cut whole deboned chicken breasts in half. Dredge in flour and rub with salt and pepper. Rub liberally with paprika and ginger. Melt butter and brown chicken breasts. Transfer to baking dish and pour butter over chicken. Sprinkle with onion and pour boiling water over top. Bake covered in preheated oven 1 hour. Uncover and brown. While chicken is browning, sprinkle cornstarch in a skillet or pan. Add juice from cherries slowly to cornstarch, stirring constantly, until smoothly mixed. Add soup stock, bouillon cube and chicken broth. Stir and cook until thickened. Stir in cherries and cooking sherry; season with salt and pepper to taste. Place breast on bed of wild rice; spoon sauce over chicken and garnish with parsley. Serves 6 to 8.

Variation for Low Cholesterol: Roll breasts in wheat flour and brown in safflower oil. Cook in oil and butter buds with water. Serve on brown rice.

Fay Berman
Lexington, Mississippi

Poultry

Country Captain

10 to 12 pieces chicken (breasts, thighs and drumsticks)
1 cup tomatoes
1 large onion, chopped
1 large green pepper, chopped
½ cup butter
Garlic salt, to taste
1 tablespoon parsley flakes
2 tablespoons vinegar
2 tablespoons prepared mustard
1 teaspoon Worcestershire sauce
1 teaspoon curry powder
1 teaspoon thyme
1 teaspoon black pepper
½ cup golden raisins
1 (2 ounce) can mushroom pieces
Slivered almonds

Roll chicken pieces in flour and paprika and brown in butter. Place in roaster. Sauté onion, green pepper and dash of garlic salt in melted butter until tender. Add tomatoes and all seasonings. Cook slowly until well blended. Add mushrooms. Pour sauce over chicken and bake in slow oven (350°F) for 1 hour. Add raisins and cook 15 minutes more. Sprinkle generously with slivered almonds. Serve over rice. Serves 6 to 8.

This is a great company dish, preparing earlier improves the flavor.

Mrs. Travis M. (Fae) Nelson

Mrs. Donald's Chicken

10 boned chicken breasts
1 (2½ ounce) jar of dried beef
2 (10½ ounce) cans of mushroom soup
1 cup sour cream
½ cup sherry

Wrap chicken breast around 3 or 4 slices of beef. Mix soup, sour cream and sherry. Pour ½ of mixture into greased 9x13 inch baking dish. Lay chicken on top of soup mixture. Pour remaining mixture over the chicken and bake 3 hours at 300°F covered. Uncover and cook 15 more minutes. Serves 8 to 10.

Ann White

Break-A-Leg

Chicken And Dumplings

1 medium fryer, cut up
2 to 3 quarts water
1 teaspoon salt
½ onion, chopped (optional)
½ teaspoon celery salt (optional)

Cut fryer into parts and cook in the salted seasoned water in a large pan until tender. Set aside.

Dumplings

2½ cups all purpose flour
½ cup boiling water
¼ teaspoon baking powder
1 teaspoon salt
½ cup shortening or margarine

Pour the ½ cup boiling water over the shortening. Mix salt and baking powder with the flour. Add the shortening and water and stir well with a fork to make a soft dough. Roll on a floured board until thin (pie crust thickness) and cut into 1 inch squares or 1x3 inch strips. Drop into the chicken broth (removing the chicken pieces from the broth first) and simmer for about 25 minutes. Serves 6.

Julie Chambers

Hot Chicken Salad

2 cups diced cooked chicken
3 chopped hard boiled eggs
2 tablespoons grated onion
¼ cup finely chopped green pepper
1½ cups cooked rice (regular rice, not instant)
¾ cup mayonnaise mixed with ¼ cup cold water
½ cup slivered almonds
1 (10½ ounce) can cream of chicken soup, undiluted
Salt and pepper, to taste
2 cups crushed potato chips

Mix all ingredients together except potato chips. Pour into 8x10 inch casserole dish. Top with crushed potato chips and sprinkle with paprika. Bake for 30 minutes at 350°F. Serves 8 to 10.

Note: You can use entire chicken by adding chicken broth until mixture is creamy. This will increase your casserole to a 9x13 inch dish.

Sandra Fulghum

Poultry

Chicken Gertrude

1 (5 pound) stewing hen
1 tablespoon salt
A few celery leaves

Water to cover chicken (about 1 quart)

Place hen in a large kettle with water, salt and the celery leaves. Simmer, covered for several hours or until tender. Allow to cool in the broth. Skim fat from the broth. Remove chicken from bones and cut into bite size pieces.

Sauce

3 tablespoons butter or margarine
3 tablespoons all purpose flour
1½ cups chicken broth
1 cup light cream
1 teaspoon salt and a dash of pepper
½ teaspoon monosodium glutamate
1 pound fresh mushrooms, sliced

4 tablespoons butter or margarine
2 cups grated sharp yellow cheese
1 cup rice, cooked according to package directions
1 cup slivered almonds
1 tablespoon minced onion
½ cup chopped almonds

In a heavy saucepan, melt the butter. Stir in the mushrooms. Sauté briefly, then add the flour and, while stirring constantly, add the chicken broth and the cream. As the sauce thickens add the cheese, and pepper and salt and the monosodium glutamate. In a large bowl combine the chicken, the cream sauce, the cooked rice and the slivered almonds and the onion. Pour into a 2 quart casserole. Sprinkle with the chopped almonds. Bake in a moderate oven (350°F) until bubbly and lightly browned. Excellent buffet dish. Serves 4 to 6.

Ms. Mary Davis

Break-A-Leg

Lemon Chicken

2 chickens, cut into quarters
2 cups fresh lemon juice
2 cups all purpose flour
2 teaspoons salt
2 teaspoons paprika
1 teaspoon pepper
½ cup corn oil
2 tablespoons grated lemon rind
¼ cup brown sugar
¼ cup chicken broth
1 teaspoon lemon extract
2 lemons, sliced paper thin

Combine chicken pieces and lemon juice in a bowl. Cover and marinate in refrigerator overnight, turning occasionally. Drain chicken and pat dry. Combine flour, salt, paprika, and pepper in a plastic bag. Add chicken pieces by twos and shake well, coating completely. Preheat oven to 350°F. Heat corn oil in large skillet until hot and fry chicken pieces, a few at a time, until well browned and crisp. Arrange browned chicken in a single layer in a large shallow baking pan. Sprinkle with lemon rind and brown sugar. Mix chicken broth and lemon extract together and pour around chicken pieces. Set a lemon slice on each piece of chicken and bake 35 to 40 minutes.

Serve hot or cold - very good for picnics.

Carolyn Hamilton

Chicken Loaf

1½ cups milk
1½ cups chicken broth
4 eggs, beaten
2 cups soft bread crumbs
4 cups cooked chicken, diced
1 cup cooked rice
¾ cup diced celery
2 tablespoons chopped pimiento
1 teaspoon salt

Combine the milk and broth in a bowl and blend in eggs. Add bread crumbs. Let this mixture set for several minutes. Then add diced chicken, rice, celery, pimiento and salt. Spread evenly in a buttered 9x13x2 inch casserole. Cover and put in the refrigerator overnight. Bake 1 hour at 350°F. Cut in squares and serve with sauce. Loaf will freeze well either before cooking or after. Thaw in refrigerator before cooking or reheating. The sauce must be done at the time of serving.

Poultry

Sauce

4 tablespoons margarine
6 tablespoons all purpose flour
2 cups chicken broth
1 tablespoon chopped parsley
1 teaspoon salt
½ teaspoon paprika
1 tablespoon lemon juice
1 (3 ounce) can mushrooms, drained
1 cup light cream or evaporated milk

Melt margarine in saucepan; stir in flour; add broth slowly, stirring constantly until thick. Add remaining ingredients and heat thoroughly. Serves 12.

Doris D. Dixon

Chicken L'Orange

4 deboned chicken breasts
Salt, white pepper, and curry powder, to taste
½ cup butter, melted
1½ cups orange juice
1 small can pineapple chunks or tidbits
⅓ cup walnuts, chopped
⅓ cup raisins
¼ teaspoon cinnamon
½ cup warm water
3 tablespoons all purpose flour
Soy sauce, to taste
2 cups raw white rice, cooked according to directions*
4 green onions (bottoms and green tops), chopped
4 tablespoons margarine or butter, melted
Celery salt

Skin chicken breasts and rub liberally with salt, pepper and curry powder. Dip breasts in melted butter and place in a baking dish. Bake in preheated 400°F oven for 10 minutes, turning frequently. Bring to a boil the orange juice, pineapple, nuts, raisins and cinnamon. Pour over the chicken pieces and bake another 30 minutes at 350°F. Remove chicken from pan and set aside. In a saucepan add the flour to the water, stirring constantly. Add the soy sauce and pour into the original baking dish and stir and scrape drippings. Mix cooked rice, green onions and enough butter to moisten. Season with celery salt. Place 1 cup rice on each of four serving plates. Arrange 1 chicken breast on top and pour a generous amount of sauce over the rice and chicken. Serves 4.

*2 cups of raw rice will yield 8 cups of cooked rice, so there will be ample rice for hearty eaters.

Ms. Beth Worsham

Break-A-Leg

Chicken Jambalaya

½ cup extra long grain rice
1 small fryer
1 tablespoon margarine
1 onion, chopped
1 (10¾ ounce) can cream of mushroom soup
2½ cups chicken broth
¼ teaspoon salt
Dash garlic salt
2 teaspoons chopped pimiento for color (optional)
⅓ cup slivered almonds, toasted

Soak rice for 2 to 3 minutes and rinse. Boil fryer until tender. Remove meat from bones and cut in bite size pieces. Sauté onion in margarine. Combine soup, broth, salt, rice, chicken, and pimiento and put in (10 inch square) buttered casserole. Top with almonds. Bake at 350°F 1½ hours or until set. Cover for 1 hour. Remove cover for remainder of cooking time. Serves 2 to 3.

Margaret Perkins

Chicken Noodle Casserole

1 (4 pound) hen
1 quart water (or more to cover hen)
Salt
1 cup chopped green peppers
1 cup chopped green onions
1 cup chopped celery
8 tablespoons margarine
½ pound processed cheese food
1 (7 ounce) jar stuffed olives (drained and diced)
1 (6 ounce) can sliced mushrooms
1 (10 ounce) can cream of mushroom soup
1 (14½ ounce) package artichoke-spinach noodles
Cheese crackers, crushed and drizzled with margarine

Boil hen in salted water. Reserve broth. Cut chicken into bite-sized pieces. Sauté onions, peppers and celery in margarine. Add cheese and stir until melted. Add olives, mushrooms and soup. Boil noodles in reserved broth until tender. Mix with chicken mixture and pour into greased casserole. (If mixture is too stiff, add broth.) Bake at 300°F for 45 minutes. Top casserole with crushed crackers for last 15 minutes cooking. Serves 8 to 10.

Mrs. Carl Welch

Chicken Mimosa

8 chicken breasts
4 tablespoons melted butter

⅓ cup toasted slivered almonds

In a 12x16 inch pan place chicken breasts in one layer and drizzle with melted butter. Bake in a 350°F oven for 40 minutes.

Sauce

1 cup orange juice
1 cup champagne
½ cup orange marmalade
½ cup yellow raisins
2 tablespoons butter

2 large apples, peeled and thinly sliced
1 teaspoon cinnamon
¼ teaspoon nutmeg

In a saucepan stir together all sauce ingredients and simmer mixture for about 20 to 25 minutes or until apples are softened (not mushy). Pour apple and raisin wine sauce evenly over the top and continue to bake for 30 minutes or until chicken is tender. Before serving, sprinkle with almonds. Serves 8.

Giny Hurlbunt
Clearwater, Florida

Southern Fried Chicken With A Difference

1 quart buttermilk
1 teaspoon baking soda
1 large frying chicken, cut up
1 to 1½ cups all purpose flour

Salt and pepper
Enough cooking oil to cover half of chicken

Mix buttermilk and soda in deep, large mixing bowl. Wash and partially dry chicken. Soak chicken in buttermilk mixture 30 minutes. Pour chicken and buttermilk into colander to drain. Roll chicken in flour seasoned with salt and pepper. Fry in hot oil in covered skillet about 15 minutes on each side.

Dr. Robert E. Crowe

Oriental Chicken

½ cup butter
½ cup all purpose flour
1 tablespoon salt
1 cup cream
3 cups milk
2 cups chicken stock
2 cups diced chicken - large dice
½ cup sautéed mushrooms
½ cup blanched slivered almonds
1 cup sliced water chestnuts
¼ cup pimiento, cut in strips
¼ cup sherry

Melt butter in top of double boiler. Add flour and salt and cook until bubbly. Add cream, milk and chicken stock, stirring until smooth. Cook over hot water for 30 minutes. Just before serving, add the rest of the ingredients and heat thoroughly. Serve over cheese soufflé; in pastry shell, over rice, or what have you; but over souffle is the most delightful thing you will ever taste. You may reserve the mushrooms, sauté whole and top each service with one. Fresh asparagus served across a grilled tomato completes a beautiful plate. Serves 8 to 10.

Mrs. Roberta Wiggins
Cleveland, Mississippi

Pecan Chicken

½ cup butter or margarine
1 cup buttermilk
1 slightly beaten egg
1 cup flour
1 cup chopped pecans
¼ cup sesame seeds
1 tablespoon salt
1 tablespoon paprika
½ teaspoon black pepper
8 half chicken breasts
24 whole pecans

Melt ½ cup butter or margarine in a 9x13 inch baking dish. Combine 1 cup buttermilk and egg in a deep plate. In another deep plate mix flour, chopped pecans, sesame seeds, salt, paprika and pepper. Dip chicken breasts in buttermilk and then in flour-pecan mixture. Put breasts in baking dish and turn until coated with melted butter. Arrange chicken with skin side up and place 3 pecan halves on each piece. Bake at 350°F for 1½ hours until golden brown and tender and nuts are toasted. Baste during baking. Serves 8.

Mrs. Hull (Bitsy) Davis

Poultry

Ruth Malone's Chicken Pie

1 (5 pound) hen, 8 cups cut-up meat
Pastry for top and bottom of casserole
8 medium sized potatoes, boiled, peeled and diced
8 hard-cooked eggs, diced
2 ounces pimiento, drained and diced
1 green pepper, diced
2 tablespoons all purpose flour
2 cups rich chicken stock
1 teaspoon salt
½ teaspoon pepper
1 cup milk

Wash hen, pat dry and rub salt in cavity and on outside. Place in large heavy pot with cover. (Cook giblets separately for gravy.) Add water to within 3 inches of top. Cover and bring water to boil over high heat. Lower heat and simmer chicken until tender, approximately 2 hours, or longer. When the leg can be moved back and forth easily, the chicken is done. Let hen cool in broth, with lid of pot removed. While hen is cooking, prepare pastry. Line casserole, saving a circle of pastry to cover top of pie. Skim fat from broth and reserve. Save broth for sauce. Strip meat from bones, discarding gristle and skin. Cut meat into pieces about 2 inches long. In pastry-lined casserole, layer potatoes, eggs, pimiento, green pepper and chicken. Repeat until all is used to fill casserole, with chicken as the last layer. Make a paste of flour and small amount of chicken broth in a saucepan. While stirring over medium heat, gradually add remaining broth, seasonings and finally the milk. Continue stirring until sauce thickens. Pour gravy into filled casserole until it reaches within inches of top. Place pastry over the chicken-vegetable filling. Prick pastry in several places to let out steam. Spread 1 tablespoon chicken fat over crust. Bake at 400°F until pastry is brown and filling is heated through. Serves 10 to 12.

Ruth Malone
Camden, Arkansas

Break-A-Leg

Chicken Livers And Brown Rice

1 pound chicken livers, halved
1 teaspoon salt
½ teaspoon pepper
1 cup all purpose flour
½ cup margarine
1 medium onion, chopped
3 ribs celery with leaves, chopped
½ cup fresh parsley, chopped
1 (4 ounce) can sliced mushrooms, undrained
1 (10 ounce) can cream of chicken soup
1 soup can milk
⅛ teaspoon thyme
⅛ teaspoon marjoram
½ cup brown rice
2 cups chicken broth

Cook brown rice in chicken broth according to package directions. While this cooks melt margarine in large skillet. Sprinkle livers with salt and pepper and coat with flour. Sauté livers in the margarine over medium heat until lightly browned. Remove from pan. Add onion, celery and parsley to pan and cook 10 to 15 minutes, stirring until tender. Stir in chicken soup, milk, thyme and marjoram and mix well. Add the chicken livers and cooked brown rice and heat well. Serve over toast triangles or place in greased 2 quart casserole and heat in 350°F oven until bubbly (about 30 minutes). Serves 4 to 6. *This dish freezes well.*

Doris D. Dixon

Rolled Chicken Breasts

4 whole deboned chicken breasts, pounded flat
Salt
Pepper
4 thin slices ham
4 thick slices Cheddar cheese or 12 tablespoons grated Cheddar
1 cup all purpose flour
2 eggs
Milk, enough to make medium batter
Toothpicks

Poultry

Preheat oven to 300°F. Rub chicken breasts liberally with salt and pepper. Lay one slice of ham and cheese (or substitute 3 tablespoons grated cheese) on each breast. Fold ends of breast, then sides to center; secure with toothpicks. Make batter of flour, eggs and milk. Dip each breast in batter and place in baking dish.

White Wine Sauce

2 tablespoons butter
2 tablespoons all purpose flour
2 cups milk
¼ teaspoon salt

White pepper
Button mushrooms
¼ cup cooking sherry or dry white wine

To make wine sauce, melt butter and stir in flour. Slowly add milk, stirring constantly. Salt and pepper to taste. Use sauce plain or add mushrooms and sherry. Pour over breasts and bake 1 hour. Serve on bed of white rice. Spoon sauce over breasts and rice. Garnish with parsley. Serves 4.

Variation: If you are in a hurry, use this alternate sauce; 1 can mushroom soup mixed with ½ can water and ½ can sherry.

Blanche Whitehead Beall
Lexington, Mississippi

Chicken And Wild Rice Casserole

1 (6 ounce) package long grain and wild rice mix
2½ cups chicken broth
2 cups cubed cooked chicken
1 (10 ounce) package frozen French style green beans
1 (8 ounce) can sliced water chestnuts, drained

1 (10 ounce) can cream of celery soup
¼ cup onion, chopped or grated
½ cup mayonnaise
½ cup (or more, if desired) slivered toasted almonds
1 (2 ounce) jar pimiento

Cook wild rice mix in chicken broth. Combine with remaining ingredients. Pour into a 9x13 inch baking dish and bake, uncovered at 350°F until hot (about 25 to 30 minutes). Serves 10 to 12.

Mrs. Robert (Betty A.) Jennings
Memphis, Tennessee

Break-A-Leg

Vol Au Vent

1 hen, 4 to 5 pounds
6 sprigs parsley or 2 teaspoons dried flakes
2 large carrots
2 stalks celery
½ bell pepper
2 small onions
1 (8 ounce) can mushrooms
1 (2 ounce) can pimiento
1 (16 ounce) can green peas
4 tablespoons all purpose flour
1 cup sherry
Pie crust
Paprika

Cook hen, skin, remove meat from bones and cut in bite size pieces. Chop carrots, celery, onions, pepper and parsley and cook until tender in 1 cup chicken broth. Now add chicken, mushrooms, chopped pimiento and peas and bring to a boil. While this is cooking, beat flour and wine together until smooth and gradually add to the boiling mixture. Stir until thickened. Divide into 10 individual casseroles or 1 large casserole. Cover with pie crust, prick with a fork and brush with butter. Bake in 450°F oven for 20 to 30 minutes or until brown. Sprinkle with paprika. Serves 8 to 10.

Mrs. Herman Baggenstoss
Tracy City, Tennessee

Cornish Hens

Melted butter or margarine
4 Cornish hens
Salt and pepper
2½ cups cooked rice
6 green onions using top and bottom, chopped
½ cup water chestnuts, chopped
1½ cups fresh spinach - chopped medium coarse
1 tablespoon pine nuts or 2 tablespoons salted roasted pistachio nuts, chopped
¾ cup chicken bouillon
3 Cornish hen livers, chopped (optional)

Wash Cornish hens, dry. Salt and pepper inside and out. Mix chicken bouillon, rice and remaining ingredients. Stuff hens with rice stuffing and wire legs together with cooking "twist 'ems". Place in shallow roasting pan, brush hens with melted butter and place in preheated 325°F oven for 1 hour, basting with butter 1 or 2 times more. Prepare a small additional side dish of the rice stuffing if you plan to halve the birds. These brown beautifully and make a stunning dish, broccoli and carrots or other vegetables placed around them. Serves 4.

Mrs. Ben Pierce

Poultry

Turkey Breast Mole'

1 (4 or 5 pound) turkey breast
1 teaspoon salt
2 tablespoons cooking oil
2 medium tomatoes, peeled and chopped
½ cup chopped onion
1 (4 ounce) can chopped green chilies
½ cup blanched almonds
⅓ cup raisins
1 (6 inch) corn tortilla, cut up
2 tablespoons sesame seeds

1 clove garlic, minced
½ teaspoon crushed red pepper
¼ teaspoon salt
¼ teaspoon ground cloves
¼ teaspoon ground cinnamon
¼ teaspoon ground coriander seed
⅛ teaspoon pepper
½ of a square unsweetened chocolate, melted
Toasted sesame seeds (for garnish)

In large Dutch oven combine turkey breast, the salt and enough water to cover the turkey. Bring to boiling; simmer 1¼ to 1½ hours or until meat is tender. Drain, reserving 1½ cups broth. Cool turkey breast slightly. Pat dry with paper toweling. In Dutch oven brown turkey breast in hot oil. Drain off fat.

To Prepare Mole' Sauce

In blender combine: tomatoes, onion, chili peppers, almonds, raisins, broth, tortilla, sesame seeds, garlic, all the spices, salt and pepper. Cover and blend nearly smooth. Stir in melted chocolate. Pour sauce over turkey breast in Dutch oven; cover and simmer for 20 minutes. Serves 8 to 10.

To Serve: Slice turkey, arrange on platter, spooning over turkey. Sprinkle with toasted sesame seeds.

Lynn Wroten

Break-A-Leg

Cold Glazed Duckling

1 (4½ to 5 pounds) duckling
3 tablespoons honey

3 tablespoons dry sherry
⅛ teaspoon ground cinnamon

Split duckling length ways, removing neck and backbone. Place duckling, skin side down, under a moderate broiler flame for 20 minutes. Turn and prick skin in 6 or 8 places with a fork to let fat run. Broil, skin side up until light brown, about 20 to 30 minutes. Place skin side up on wire rack in an uncovered roasting pan and bake about 1 hour at 325°F, basting every 10 minutes with a mixture of honey, sherry and cinnamon, until drumstick separates easily. Cool, refrigerate and serve cold. Great on picnics. Serves 4.

Carolyn Hamilton

Doves Elegant

Dove breasts (any number desired)
Salt
Pepper

½ cup butter
1 (4 ounce) jar mushrooms
Lemon juice
Worcestershire sauce

Rub breasts liberally with salt and pepper. Melt butter and brown doves on all sides. Put doves in baking dish and squeeze lemon juice over the top. Sprinkle with Worcestershire sauce and cover with mushrooms. Cover and bake at 350°F for about 30 minutes. Serve with either white or wild rice.

Mrs. Leonard Patterson
Sumner, Mississippi

"And men sit down to that nourishment which is called supper...", William Shakespeare, English dramatist and poet.

Game

Mississippi Delta Duck

Vinegar
Salt and pepper
1 wild duck or 4 breasts
1 small onion
1 apple
4 stalks celery
2 cups orange juice
2 teaspoons soy sauce
1 teaspoon powdered or crushed thyme
4 strips bacon

Soak duck overnight in water with plenty of salt and vinegar. Drain duck and pat dry. Salt and pepper inside and out liberally. Stuff whole duck with onion, apple and celery and sprinkle with thyme. If using breast, cut up or quarter onion, apple and celery around breasts. Place bacon on duck, may secure with a toothpick. Sprinkle with soy sauce and pour orange juice over duck. Bake 3 hours at 325°F. Thicken juices for gravy. Remove bacon. Slice duck or put breast on a platter of wild rice and garnish each with a twisted orange slice and parsley. Serve gravy on the side. Serves 4.

Beth B. Worsham

Christmas Brunch Quail

12 quail
1 pound hot sausage
12 slices bacon
1/3 cup white wine
Salt and pepper, to taste
1 cooking bag (large)

Prepare plastic cooking bag according to directions on box. Wash and dry quail. Place 1 heaping tablespoon of hot sausage in the cavity of each bird. Salt and pepper birds to taste and wrap one slice of bacon around each bird. Place cooking bag in a roasting pan, then fill the bag with the quail. Add wine to the bag and close bag securely. Bake in 350°F oven for 1 hour. During the last 10 minutes of baking, split open the bag and continue cooking to brown quail. Watch carefully and don't let the quail dry out. Serves 6.

Jan Riley
Tupelo, Mississippi

Break-A-Leg

Roasted Quail

6 quail
Salt
Pepper
1 stick butter or margarine
1 onion, chopped
1 can sliced mushrooms

½ cup water
1 teaspoon Worcestershire sauce
Dash garlic salt
2 slices lemon

Salt and pepper quail. Brown on top of stove in melted butter and place in roaster. Sauté onion and mushrooms in butter. Add water, Worcestershire, garlic salt and lemon to onion and mushrooms. Pour over quail. Cover and cook at 350°F for 1 to 1½ hours. Baste birds often. Water may be added if necessary while cooking in order to have desired amount of gravy.

Mrs. Hull Davis

Variation: Omit water and use 1 cup white wine or cooking sherry also add 2 tablespoons lemon juice.

Mrs. Lacie Robertson

Trail's End Quail

½ cup chopped green onions
2 slices bacon, diced
1 can sliced mushrooms, drained
1 cup margarine
24 quail
3 tablespoons flour

1 cup white wine
2 cups stock (made from chicken bouillon cubes)
¼ teaspoon tarragon
¼ teaspoon basil
¼ teaspoon chervil

Sauté onions, bacon and mushrooms in margarine till lightly browned; remove ingredients; brown quail in remaining fat (add more margarine if necessary). When brown, remove birds. Make a sauce by adding flour, wine, chicken bouillon, onions, bacon, mushrooms and herbs. Place quail in long baking pan. Pour sauce over birds. Cover with aluminum foil. Bake at 350°F for 2 to 2½ hours or until birds are tender. Serve over wild or brown rice. Serves 10 to 12.

Mrs. Rudolph Janzen, Jr. (Donna S.)

Game

Quail In Casserole

4 quail
Salt and pepper
⅓ cup salad oil
1 medium onion, minced
1 carrot, finely chopped
1 tablespoon minced green pepper
¾ cup sliced fresh mushrooms
2 tablespoons all purpose flour
4 chicken bouillon cubes
2 cups boiling water
⅓ cup white wine

Rub the whole birds lightly and salt and pepper, then brown in oil (or part oil and part butter). Remove to heated casserole. In the same oil sauté carrot, onion, green pepper and mushrooms slowly about 5 minutes. Blend in flour, then gradually stir into heated stock, made by dissolving bouillon cubes in boiling water. Season to taste with salt and pepper. Pour this sauce and wine over quail. Cover and bake in 350°F oven about 1 hour or until birds are tender. At this point you must decide whether to throw the birds away and drink this lovely sauce or to serve both over a bed of fluffy rice. Serves 4

Variation: Eight to 12 doves or 4 chicken quarters can be substituted for quail.

Corinne Pierce

Quail And Wild Rice

12 quail
Salt and pepper
Bacon
2¼ cups margarine
1 box (6 ounce) seasoned long grain wild rice

Salt and pepper quail. Wrap bacon around each bird. Place in baking dish. Pour 3 tablespoons melted margarine on each bird. Cover with foil and bake in 350°F oven for 1 hour. Remove foil and brown. Cook rice by directions on package. Serve with quail on top.

Mrs. John D. Mercier (Helen)

Break-A-Leg

Pheasant Breast Marinade

¼ cup sherry
½ cup sauterne
¼ cup soy sauce
¼ cup olive oil
1 large clove garlic, sliced
1 teaspoon ginger

¼ teaspoon oregano
1 teaspoon tarragon
2 tablespoons cold water
3 pheasant breasts boned (6 halves)

Combine first 9 ingredients. Arrange pheasant breasts in flat glass baking dish and pour mixture over. Marinate in refrigerator for 24 hours, turning breasts several times. To cook, remove from marinade and let drain on paper towels. Sprinkle with seasoned salt and white pepper. Sauté in olive oil until done (about 5 minutes on each side). Serve over wild rice.

Note: This marinade is also good with chicken breasts.

Mrs. Dolores Johnson

"To drink is a Christian diversion, unknown to the Turk or the Persian: Let Mahometan fools live by heathenish rules, and be damned over teacups and coffee, but let British lads sing, crown a health to the king, and a fig for your sultan and sophy!", William Congreve, English dramatist.

Early Reviews

EARLY REVIEWS

From Shoney's to the Peabody, brunch has become a weekend way of life. Brunch has also become an important way to entertain. You may want to combine breakfast and lunch as an easy way to entertain weekend guests. Brunch is also an excellent way to entertain during the holidays, providing a more relaxed, informal atmosphere for both hostess and guests.

Whatever the occasion, your menu can be as simple or as elaborate as you choose. All of the favorite breakfast meat, egg, and bread entrees can be used. In the spring, a whole menu can be based on fresh home-grown fruits and vegetables, from tender asparagus spears swimming in butter to fresh strawberries - plain, sugar coated, in pies, cobblers, or preserves.

Be innovative! Be daring! The "Reviews" are worth it.

Menus

SPRING GARDEN LUNCHEONS

Cold Spinach Soup - p.151

Country Cheese Pie - p.253

Fresh Fruit with Celery Seed Dressing - p.129

Individual Homemade Bread Loaves - p.299

Walnut Lace Cups with Ice Cream - p.338

SPRING LUNCHEONS

Cheese Souffle - p.248

Oriental Chicken - p.232

Grilled Tomatoes topped with Asparagus

Ella Mae's Rolls - p.312

Lemon Cream Sherbet - p.342

Early Reviews

A "COOL KITCHEN" SUMMER SUPPER OR LUNCHEON

Cold Chicken Pasta - p.255

Chinese Salad - p.110

Bread Sticks

Sherry-Mint Melon Balls - p.345

Crisp Cookies from the Bakery

Brunch Casserole

3 dozen eggs
¼ cup milk
2 cans (10¾ ounce) cream of mushroom soup
½ cup dry sherry
1 (10¾ ounce) can mushrooms (buttons and stems)

½ pound sharp Cheddar cheese, grated
¼ pound butter
Paprika
Pimiento, optional
Cubes of ham, optional
Cubed green pepper, optional

In a medium size mixing bowl, beat eggs and milk. Heat mushroom soup, sherry and mushrooms in a medium saucepan. In a large skillet, scramble eggs until just set. Put a layer of eggs in a 9x13 inch greased baking dish, a layer of sauce and a layer of cheese. Repeat layers. Dust top with paprika. Place in a cold oven and turn heat on 250°F for 1 hour. Can be prepared ahead (even the night before) and stored in refrigerator. Serves 6 to 8.

Jill Robinson Palmer

Cheese & Eggs

Brunch Casserole

1 cup butter
¼ cup flour
1 cup milk
1 cup cream (whipping cream is fine)
¼ teaspoon thyme
¼ teaspoon marjoram
¼ teaspoon basil

¾ pound Cheddar cheese, shredded
1½ dozen hard boiled eggs, sliced thin or chopped
1 pound bacon, sautéed, drained and crumbled
¼ cup chopped parsley
Buttered bread crumbs

Melt butter in medium saucepan. Stir in flour. Gradually stir in milk and cream and cook, stirring until cream sauce is smooth and thickened. Add spices and cheese and cook, stirring until cheese is melted. Place layer of cooked eggs in casserole; sprinkle bacon over eggs; sprinkle parsley over bacon. Add layer of cheese sauce. Repeat two more layers. Sprinkle top with buttered breadcrumbs. Bake uncovered at 350°F for 30 minutes. Can be made a day ahead. Serves 8 to 10.

Mrs. Charles McDonald (Donna)

Cheese And Potato Omelet

4 tablespoons butter or margarine
3 cups thinly sliced potatoes
1 (1.4 ounce) package onion soup mix

8 eggs
¾ cup milk
½ cup shredded Cheddar cheese

In a medium skillet melt butter and cook potatoes until tender. Beat together soup mix, eggs, and milk. Pour into skillet with potatoes and cook covered over low heat for 25 minutes. Top with cheese and serve. Serves 4.

Judy Martin

Early Reviews

Ham Omelet Supreme

1 pound cheese, shredded (Cheddar or your choice)
2 cups diced, cooked ham
½ cup butter or margarine
1 dozen eggs
½ cup all purpose flour
Salt and pepper, to taste
1 pint small curd cottage cheese
1 teaspoon baking powder
5 or 6 drops red hot sauce

Butter a 9x12 inch baking dish with the ½ cup butter. Barely blend the eggs and add to them ½ cup flour, salt and pepper, the baking powder, hot sauce and the cottage cheese. Add the ham and cheese and mix thoroughly. Spoon into the buttery baking dish and bake at 400°F (in a pre-heated) oven for 15 minutes. Reduce heat to 375°F and bake 10 to 15 minutes longer (or until just set). This can be baked at a lower temperature for a longer time and can also be mixed, covered and refrigerated overnight. Remove from refrigerator 1 hour prior to baking. Delicious for brunch. Serves 12 to 15.

Ms. Joyce Pruett
Sherrard, Illinois

Cheese Soufflé

3 tablespoons butter
¼ cup all purpose flour
1 ⅞ cups milk
1 teaspoon salt
Dash cayenne pepper
1 teaspoon prepared mustard
2 drops Worcestershire
1 cup shredded American cheese, packed
6 eggs

Make cream sauce by melting butter and blend in flour. Cook till bubbly. Add milk, salt, cayenne pepper, mustard and Worcestershire and bring to a boil. Stir constantly. Boil 1 minute - TIME IT. Remove from heat and cool slightly. Add cheese. Beat egg yolks until thick and add to cheese mixture stirring constantly. Beat egg white until stiff. Fold into cheese mixture carefully. Pour into well-buttered baking dish, ¾ full. Bake 300°F in a hot water bath for 2 hours or until silver knife comes out clean. Serves 6. *This soufflé keeps a day in refrigerator after baking.*

Mrs. Roberta Wiggins
Cleveland, Mississippi

Cheese & Eggs

Creole Eggs

½ cup chopped celery
1 tablespoon butter or margarine
1 tablespoon margarine for sautéing
1 tablespoon flour
1 cup milk
½ dozen hard boiled eggs, shelled
½ cup chopped green bell pepper
½ cup chopped onion
1 (15 ounce) can tomatoes, sieved
1 (4 ounce) can mushrooms (pieces and stems are all right)

Sauté celery, peppers and onion until done in 1 tablespoon margarine. Add tomatoes and simmer while making a white sauce of the 1 tablespoon butter (or margarine), 1 tablespoon flour and 1 cup of milk. Add drained mushrooms. Mix with the vegetables. Cut the eggs in thick slices (or cut in half) and place in a 2 quart casserole. Cover with the sautéed vegetables. Sprinkle with bread crumbs. Dot with butter and bake until hot.

Mrs. Lou V. Vaught

Fabulous Cheese Casserole

18 slices day old bread buttered
3 tablespoons minced white onion
3 tablespoons minced scallions
2 pounds Cheddar cheese, shredded
8 eggs slightly beaten
5 cups milk
2 teaspoons dry mustard
2 teaspoons Worcestershire
Salt and pepper, to taste

Cut 6 slices of bread in 3 strips each and fit tightly on bottom of lightly greased 4 quart casserole. Sprinkle with salt and pepper and ⅓ of each kind of onion. Add ⅓ of the grated cheese evenly over the top and press down. Repeat twice more. Mix eggs, milk, mustard and Worcestershire and pour over the casserole. Refrigerate 8 hours or overnight. Remove from refrigerator and let reach room temperature. Bake uncovered at 325°F for about 1 hour. Serves 8 to 10.

Mrs. Leonard Pierce (Helen)
Bangor, Maine

Early Reviews

Baked Fondue

16 slices bread
10 ounces American processed cheese, cubed
5 eggs
2 cups milk
1 teaspoon salt
½ cup margarine

Cut crust off the bread and cut into ½ inch cubes. Reserve 1½ cups of bread cubes. Also cube cheese in smaller cubes. Toss remaining bread and cheese cubes together in large bowl. Combine eggs, milk and salt and beat until smooth, then pour over bread and cheese. Stir gently until well mixed. Turn into a shallow, greased baking dish (approximately 13x9x2 inch). Sprinkle the 1½ cups of reserved bread cubes over the top. Melt the ½ cup of margarine and dribble over the entire mixture, especially the dry bread cubes. Cover with plastic wrap and refrigerate overnight or 8 hours. Return to room temperature, remove wrap and bake for 1 hour at 350°F. Serves 12.

Variation: Add 1 to 2 cups of either cubed ham, halved green olives, mushrooms or crumbled bacon.

Janice Wilcox Grady

Fancy Eggs Scrambles

1 cup diced Canadian bacon
¼ cup chopped green onions
7 tablespoons margarine
12 beaten eggs
1 (3 ounce) jar mushrooms, drained and chopped
Cheese Sauce
2½ cups soft bread crumbs (3 slices)
⅛ teaspoon paprika

In skillet cook bacon and onions in 3 tablespoons margarine. Add eggs and scramble till just set. Fold eggs and mushrooms into cheese sauce. Turn into 12x7x2 inch casserole dish. Combine 4 tablespoons melted margarine, bread, paprika and put on top of eggs. Chill until 30 minutes before baking; bake uncovered at 325°F for 30 minutes.

Cheese & Eggs

Cheese Sauce

2 teaspoons margarine
2 tablespoons all purpose flour
½ teaspoon salt
⅛ teaspoon pepper

2 cups milk
1 cup Cheddar cheese, shredded

Melt margarine in a heavy saucepan. Stir in flour, salt and pepper. Slowly add milk, and cook, stirring constantly, until bubbly and thickened. Stir in the cheese and continue stirring until the cheese is melted. Serves 8.

Sandra Fulghum

Scrambled Egg Casserole

4 slices raw bacon, diced
1 (6 ounce) roll jalapeño cheese
2 (6 ounce) cans sliced mushrooms, drained
¼ cup margarine
½ cup flour

4 cups milk
20 eggs
Red pepper
1 teaspoon salt, or to taste
1 cup evaporated milk
¼ cup margarine

Sauté bacon in skillet until done. Do not drain. Add drained mushrooms and ¼ cup margarine. Stir, add flour slowly, mix well, add 4 cups milk slowly, stirring well. Add cheese and melt. Add pepper. When thick, set aside. Break 20 eggs in large bowl, beat with salt and evaporated milk. Melt ¼ cup margarine in large skillet. Scramble eggs until set (not runny or dry). Butter 9x13 inch casserole dish. Layer with ½ of sauce. Pour in all eggs and cover with remaining sauce. Cover and refrigerate overnight. Serves about 15.

Note: If possible, let stand at room temperature about an hour before placing in 350°F oven and bake until set in center.

Mrs. E. J. Knight
Birmingham, Alabama

Early Reviews

Ham Strata

12 slices bread, trimmed
Sliced sharp Cheddar cheese to cover bread
2 cups diced ham
2 (10 ounce) packages frozen broccoli florets or the equivalent of fresh

7 or 8 eggs
3 cups milk
½ teaspoon salt
¼ teaspoon dry mustard
Onion flakes sprinkled over top

Butter 3 quart rectangular casserole generously. Layer bottom with bread slices, add sliced cheese, ham and cooked broccoli. Whip eggs in blender, add milk, salt and mustard to eggs. Pour slowly over bread and let soak in. Sprinkle lightly with onion flakes—do not forget the onion flakes as they are important. IMPORTANT: Refrigerate 6 to 8 hours or overnight. Bake uncovered 1 hour 20 minutes at 325°F. Bake long enough to be able to cut into squares to serve. Serves 6 to 8.

Note: This will freeze well if covered properly.

Corinna and Ginny Bushey

Cheesy Onion Pie

6 ounces cracker crumbs (soda crackers will do)
5 tablespoons melted butter
2 large Spanish onions
1½ cups hot milk

3 eggs
½ pound shredded sharp cheese
Salt and pepper, to taste
Dash garlic powder

Mix cracker crumbs with melted butter and firmly press down into a buttered pie dish. Sauté onions in butter until golden in color. Spread them over cracker crust. Heat milk to boiling point and quickly remove from heat and very slowly add to the beaten eggs stirring with a wooden spoon. Add the cheese, black pepper, salt and garlic powder. Pour over onions and bake at 320°F for 45 minutes. Serves 4 to 6.

Note: A dish of your favorite mustard on the side adds a zesty touch.

Kathleen Masters

Cheese & Eggs

Country Cheese Pie

1 (9 inch) uncooked pie shell
1 pound farmer cheese, grated
6 tablespoons plain yogurt
½ teaspoon ground coriander
¼ teaspoon ground nutmeg
1 tablespoon minced chives or scallions
1 teaspoon sugar
3 eggs well beaten
¼ cup Parmesan cheese
Salt and pepper, to taste

Preheat oven to 375°F. Prick bottom of pie shell and bake for 10 minutes. Mix together in a bowl; farmer cheese, yogurt, coriander, nutmeg, chives, sugar, salt, and pepper. (Taste cheese for salt before adding any salt; some brands are rather salty.) Stir with a wooden spoon until smooth. Add eggs and stir thoroughly again. Pour batter into the pie shell and smooth the top with a spatula. Sprinkle the Parmesan cheese on top. Bake for 45 minutes or until top is nicely browned and puffy. Serve immediately. Serves 4 to 6.

Note: Batter can be prepared ahead and refrigerated; remove from refrigerator 30 minutes before baking, or increase baking time by 5 to 8 minutes.

Karen Lambert

Bacon And Ham Quiche

2 (9 inch pie shells) prebaked
4 slices bacon cooked and broken
1 bunch green onions minced and cooked in 1 tablespoon butter
1 (4 ounce) can sliced mushrooms, drained
4 thin slices ham-shredded
½ pound Swiss cheese grated
4 whole eggs
1½ cups evaporated milk
1 clove garlic pressed
½ teaspoon salt
½ teaspoon dry mustard
1 dash nutmeg
1 dash black pepper

Layer bacon, ham and onions in pie shell. Beat eggs with milk and add seasonings. Pour over meat. Bake 35 minutes in 350°F oven. Will freeze.

Janalee Holley Wilkins

Early Reviews

Chicken With Pasta And Curry Sauce

12 ounces fettuccine, broken into 2 inch pieces
12 ounces spinach noodles
6 to 8 tablespoons olive oil

2 or 3 tablespoons white wine vinegar
Salt and pepper

Boil pasta until tender but still firm to the bite. Drain. Toss with oil and vinegar. Season with salt and pepper. Cover and refrigerate until serving time.

8 chicken breasts
2 tablespoons vinegar
6 to 8 tablespoons vegetable oil

Salt and pepper
1 teaspoon Dijon mustard
1 clove garlic, diced

Simmer chicken until cooked, about 40 minutes. Cool and cut into bite-sized pieces. Mix remaining ingredients together and toss with chicken. Cover and refrigerate.

1 large can black olives, finely chopped (label states "6 ounces drained")
1 pint container cherry tomatoes, halved

2 cups broccoli florets, blanched
1 (10 ounce) package frozen peas, defrosted

About 30 minutes before serving, arrange lettuce leaves around outer edge of platter. Gently toss pasta with chicken, olives, and vegetables. Arrange in center of platter. Serve with curry sauce.

Note: Olives are in a can that states "6 ounces, drained".

Curry Sauce

½ cup mayonnaise
¾ cup sour cream
¼ cup plain yogurt
Juice of one lemon

Juice of one orange
½ medium onion, finely chopped
Curry powder, to taste

Combine all ingredients. Chill for 24 hours. Serves 12 to 16.

Vicki Sweat

Pasta

Cold Chicken Pasta

12 ounces vermicelli
1½ cups Italian dressing
15 mushrooms, sliced
½ cup frozen Chinese pea pods, thawed
2 large tomatoes, chopped
3 cups chicken chunks
1 tablespoon dried basil
¼ cup parsley, fresh

Cook and drain pasta. While warm, toss with ½ cup of dressing. In another bowl mix mushrooms, peas, tomatoes, parsley with 1 cup of salad dressing. Chill pasta and vegetables. When ready to serve, toss chicken, pasta, vegetables and basil together. Serves 8.

Anne M. Gernert
Atlanta, Georgia

Chicken With A Twist

6 ounces corkscrew macaroni
3 cups cooked chicken, boned and cubed
½ cup Italian dressing
½ cup mayonnaise
3 tablespoons lemon juice
1 tablespoon mustard (prepared)
1 medium onion, chopped
¾ cup sliced black olives
1 cup diced celery
¼ teaspoon black pepper
Salt, to taste
1 cucumber, chopped
Lettuce leaves

Cook macaroni, following the directions on the package. Mix cooled cubed chicken, dressing, and cooled macaroni. Blend in mayonnaise, lemon juice and mustard; add onion, olives, celery and cucumber. Add salt and pepper. Mix well and chill 2 hours or more. Serve on lettuce leaf. Serves 8.

Mrs. Price Schuauk (Jane Fraley)
Ft. Lauderdale, Florida

"Only dull people are brilliant at breakfast.",
Oscar Wilde, Irish playwright.

Early Reviews

Shrimp Pasta Salad For A Crowd

Salad

- 2 chopped onions
- 2 cups chopped dill pickles
- 2 cups chopped celery
- 2 cups black olives
- 2 pounds cooked and peeled shrimp, chopped
- 2 dozen hard boiled eggs, chopped
- 2 pounds cooked spaghetti (shells and spirals)

Mix all ingredients together in large bowl.

Dressing

- ½ cup olive oil
- 1 quart mayonnaise
- 2 tablespoons hot sauce
- 2 tablespoons Worcestershire sauce
- 2 tablespoons lemon juice
- 2 or 3 teaspoons salt
- 1 tablespoon creole mustard

Beat together olive oil and mayonnaise, add remaining ingredients stirring well after each addition. Pour dressing over salad and mix well. Chill at least overnight. Serves 35 to 40.

Mrs. R. T. Sawyer (Helen)
Starkville, Mississippi

Chicken And Snow Pea Pasta Salad

- 1 cup raw spiral pasta, cooked
- 2 cups cooked chicken breast, cubed
- 2 cups snow peas, blanched
- ½ cup minced green onion
- 1 can sliced water chestnuts

Combine the above ingredients and lightly toss. Add the following:

- ¼ cup mayonnaise
- ¼ cup salad dressing
- 2 tablespoons white wine vinegar
- ⅛ teaspoon ginger
- 3 tablespoons low salt soy sauce
- ¼ teaspoon pepper

Mix and refrigerate overnight. Sprinkle with toasted almonds. Serves 8.

Vermicelli Salad

1 pound vermicelli
1 (14 ounce) bottle Italian dressing
½ cup black olives, sliced
½ cup green olives, sliced
1 (4 ounce) can mushrooms, drained and sliced
1 (17 ounce) can early green peas, drained
1 (4 ounce) can water chestnuts; drained and sliced
1 (3 pound) chicken, cooked in seasoned water; drained, cooled and chopped
½ cup slivered almonds or pine nuts
Dried basil, to taste
Salt and pepper, to taste

Cook vermicelli until al dente. Combine ½ bottle of Italian dressing with remaining ingredients. Toss. Add remaining Italian dressing to taste. Serves 8.

Claire Stanley

Pasta Casserole

1 (18 ounce) package macaroni twists
1 tablespoon salt
4 (or more) quarts water
6 tablespoons butter
1 large onion, chopped
2 cups broccoli florets
5 tablespoons butter
5 tablespoons flour
5 cups milk
10 ounces sharp Cheddar cheese
Salt, to taste

Cook macaroni in salted water al dente. Drain. Toss in 6 tablespoons salted butter. Sauté onion in 2 tablespoons butter until soft. Mix onion and broccoli with macaroni and pour into 3 quart casserole. Make cheese sauce: Melt 5 tablespoons butter, slowly add 5 tablespoons plain flour until bubbly, stirring constantly. Add milk slowly, stirring constantly until medium thick. Add cheese and stir until melted. Pour over macaroni twirls, sprinkle with additional grated cheese and cook at 350°F until hot and bubbly. (About 40 minutes.) Do not cover. Serves 12.

Variation: Add 2 or 3 cups cooked diced chicken to macaroni before adding cheese sauce.

Mrs. Bob Kittredge
Cumberland Foreside, Maine

Early Reviews

Spinach Lasagna

1 box lasagna
1 tablespoon oil
2 boxes chopped spinach
1 carton ricotta or cottage cheese
2 eggs, beaten
Mozzarella cheese
Parmesan cheese
2 jars good quality spaghetti sauce with mushrooms

Cook lasagna according to directions on package adding oil to prevent pasta from sticking. Drain and squeeze dry spinach. Mix ricotta cheese with eggs. Drain lasagna. Spoon 1 layer spaghetti sauce in bottom of one large oblong (9x13x2 inch) casserole. Top with lasagna noodles then with egg and cheese mixture then spinach. Continue layering until desired layers are reached. End with sauce. Sprinkle generously with cheeses. Bake at 350°F for 1 hour. Serves 8.

Ann Whitfield

Stuffed Shells Florentine

1 tablespoon salt
4 quarts water
1 (12 ounce) package jumbo stuffing shells
1 (32 ounce) jar, or can, spaghetti sauce
1½ pounds ricotta or cottage cheese
⅓ cup grated Parmesan cheese
1 pound Mozzarella cheese, shredded
2 eggs, slightly beaten
¼ cup chopped parsley
½ teaspoon salt
1 (10 ounce) package frozen spinach cooked, and well drained

Add shells to boiling water for 15 minutes; partly drain, leaving shells standing in warm water. Mix ricotta, Parmesan and ½ of Mozzarella cheeses, eggs, parsley, salt and spinach. Remove 1 shell at a time. Stuff each shell with mixture. Pour ½ of spaghetti sauce into bottom of large casserole. Arrange stuffed shells in casserole. Pour remaining sauce over shells. Sprinkle remaining mozzarella on top. Cover and bake at 375°F for 30 minutes. Serves 8.

Marie Holley Anderson

Pasta Mustardo

2 pounds ground beef
1 large green pepper, chopped
1 large yellow onion, chopped
1 (16½ ounce) can niblet, or whole style, corn
1 (1½ ounce) can dry mustard*
¼ teaspoon basil

1 garlic clove
½ teaspoon oregano
1 (32 ounce) can tomato juice
1 pound package elbow macaroni
1 tablespoon brown sugar
1 tablespoon tomato paste
1 to 2 tablespoons olive oil

Sauté onions in olive oil in frying pan or skillet until translucent. Add ground beef and cook until browned. Add corn, drained, and green pepper. Salt and pepper to taste; simmer 3 minutes. Drain and transfer mixture to large soup or stew pot. Add tomato juice, paste and sugar. Add crushed garlic clove. Add all other dry spices and macaroni. Simmer on very low heat for at least 1 hour. Serve with toasted garlic/buttered French or Italian bread and salad. Serves 12.

*The amount of dried mustard in this dish might seem a mistake or excessive, but the dish is more subtle than might be expected. Other shapes or variety of small pasta noodles may be substituted if preferred.

Linda and Larry Cox
Picture Show Pasta House
Corinth, Mississippi

Red Wine Tomato Sauce

2 large onions, chopped
2 cloves garlic, minced
½ cup olive oil
15 large tomatoes
2 cups red wine
12 ounces tomato paste

1½ teaspoons salt
¼ teaspoon pepper
2 heaping teaspoons oregano
1 tablespoon basil
1 teaspoon rosemary
4 carrots, grated

Sauté onions until golden. Peel tomatoes, cut into ⅛'s. Add the rest of the ingredients to pot and simmer 2 to 3 hours. Serves 8.

Early Reviews

Carbonara

¼ pound lean smoked bacon, thick sliced
¼ cup cooked ham strips, warmed
2 eggs, beaten
⅓ cup freshly grated Parmesan cheese
¼ teaspoon freshly milled black pepper
1 tablespoon olive oil
1 tablespoon chopped parsley
½ pound vermicelli

Cut bacon into strips and sauté slowly in skillet until crisp. Drain bacon on paper toweling, set aside. Combine eggs, cheese and olive oil, set aside. This mxiture must be awaiting the freshly drained hot pasta. Cook vermicelli al dente in 2 to 3 quarts of salted water. Quickly drain pasta, return to pot. Quickly pour egg/cheese mixture over pasta. Toss with fork until egg/cheese mixture sets, 1 or 2 minutes. Add bacon and ham, toss. Top with parsley. Serve immediately with an extra bowl of grated cheese. Serves 4.

David M. Sandy

Pesto

2 cups fresh basil, chopped
2 tablespoons parsley, chopped
3 tablespoons olive oil
2 cloves garlic, cut up
3 tablespoons broken walnuts
2 tablespoons Parmesan, grated

Put all ingredients in food processor and blend well. This freezes beautifully.

Note: Freeze in muffin cups. ½ of the recipe is enough for 8 ounces Linguine, cooked AL DENTE. With added Parmesan cheese, a salad and French bread a most tempting meal.

Dr. Russell Burns
Brookhaven, Mississippi

Pasta

Delicious Lasagna

1 pound lean ground beef
¾ pound sausage
2 tablespoons fresh parsley flakes
1 teaspoon basil
2½ cups tomatoes, chopped
1 (6 ounce) can tomato paste
Salt, to taste
1 garlic pod, minced

1 egg, beaten
2 (12 ounce) cartons dry cottage cheese
½ cup Parmesan cheese
1 tablespoon parsley flakes
10 ounce package lasagna noodles
Mozzarella cheese cut in thin slices

Brown ground beef and sausage together. Drain off grease. Add parsley, basil, tomatoes, tomato paste, salt, garlic and simmer 1 hour. To beaten egg add cottage cheese, Parmesan cheese and 1 tablespoon parsley flakes. Cook lasagna noodles until tender and rinse in cold water. In a deep rectangular greased baking dish (9x13x2 inch) put:

1 layer noodles
½ cottage cheese mixture
1 layer meat mixture

1 layer sliced mozzarella cheese
(Repeat layers)

Bake at 350°F for about an hour. May be frozen and cooked at a later date. Do not put Mozzarella on until ready to bake. Serves 10.

Mrs. John Shea (Linda Lee Meade)
Former Miss America
Memphis, Tennessee

"No man is lonely while eating spaghetti.", Robert Morley, English actor.

Early Reviews

Italian Spaghetti

2 large onions, chopped
2 cloves garlic, minced
1 green pepper, minced
½ cup vegetable oil or shortening
2 pounds lean beef, ground
1 teaspoon salt
½ teaspoon black pepper
⅛ teaspoon red pepper
1 teaspoon chili powder
1 teaspoon Louisiana red hot sauce
1 (11½ ounce) can, cream of mushroom soup
1 (11½ ounce) can, cream of tomato soup
1 (6 ounce) can, tomato paste
1½ pounds long spaghetti
1 cup grated Parmesan cheese

Sauté onions, garlic and green pepper in the vegetable oil until the onions are golden. Add meat, brown slightly, cover and simmer 15 minutes. Combine mushroom soup, tomato soup, tomato paste and seasonings. Add to meat mixture. Cover and cook slowly for 2½ to 3 hours. *(I often put in a heavy pot with cover and cook in oven at 300°F.)* When you are ready to serve, cook spaghetti in boiling, salted water until tender. Drain and rinse with hot water. Drain again and arrange on hot plates. Pour sauce over each serving and sprinkle with Parmesan cheese. Pass additional sauce and cheese. Serves 8 to 10. *This sauce freezes well.*

Mrs. R. C. Liddon

White Wine Tomato Sauce (No Oil)

10 pounds Italian plum tomatoes
1 pound onions, chopped
½ pound bell pepper, chopped
4 carrots, grated
2 cups celery, roughly chopped with leaves
1 bunch parsley, finely cut
1 to 2 cups fresh basil, thyme, sage, oregano and marjoram
3 tablespoons sugar
Salt and pepper, to taste
2 cups white wine

Simmer all ingredients for 3 to 4 hours, stirring occasionally. Pureé in food processor. Cook for another 2 hours to thicken. Serve over green noodles for color. Makes 2 quarts.

Spaghetti Ring

1 cup spaghetti elbows
1 cup soft breadcrumbs
1½ cups scalded milk
¼ cup margarine or butter
2 pimentos, minced
1 tablespoon chopped onion
1 tablespoon chopped parsley
1½ cups Cheddar cheese, shredded
1 teaspoon salt
3 eggs, beaten
Dash of pepper

Cook spaghetti according to directions on package and drain. Pour scalded milk over crumbs. Add other ingredients. Mix with spaghetti and turn into a greased 5 cup ring mold. Set mold in pan of hot water and bake in oven at 350°F for 45 minutes.

Note: This is an easy recipe but is a bit tricky to turn out of the mold. Be sure to grease mold well and cook the full time.

Serve with a mushroom-tomato sauce; or fill ring with creamed peas, creamed shrimp or other creamed vegetables. You can use a canned sauce, if you like, but the following is a "grand one".

Tomato Sauce For Spaghetti Ring

3 tablespoons olive oil (or salad oil)
1 small clove garlic, diced
1 cup onion, chopped
½ cup green pepper, chopped
½ small carrot, chopped
1 (32 ounces) can tomato chopped (not drained)
1 bay leaf
¼ cup of green celery leaves, chopped
½ teaspoon salt
Pepper, to taste
1 teaspoon sugar

Sauté onion in oil. Add other ingredients and cook slowly for 40 minutes. Rub through sieve before serving.

Mrs. Richard Warriner

Reviews

Chicken Spaghetti

1 (16 ounce) package spaghetti
1 (4 pound) hen
3 ribs celery
1 bay leaf
½ cup butter or margarine
1 onion, chopped
1 clove garlic, minced
½ green pepper, chopped
2 tablespoons fresh parsley, chopped
1 (16 ounce) can tomatoes, chopped
1 quart chicken broth
1 tablespoon Worcestershire sauce
1 teaspoon salt
Cayenne pepper, to taste
1 can ripe, pitted olives, sliced (can states 6 ounces, drained)
8 ounces fresh mushrooms, sliced
1 pound grated Cheddar cheese

Stew hen in water to cover with celery and bay leaf, and salt to taste. Cool, debone and cut in bite size pieces. Reserve broth. Cook spaghetti according to package directions. Drain. Sauté onion, pepper, garlic and parsley in butter. Add tomatoes, Worcestershire sauce, salt, cayenne pepper and chicken broth. Cook 30 minutes. Add mushrooms and olives. In a quart baking dish arrange in layers. Begin with a layer of spaghetti, then a layer of chicken, a layer of tomato sauce and a layer of cheese, continue layers until all ingredients are used. Top with cracker crumbs. Bake 45 minutes at 350°F. Serves 10 to 12.

Wanda Witt

Chicken Tetrazzini

6 tablespoons margarine
½ cup chopped onion
5 tablespoons flour
2 cups chicken broth
1 (13 ounce) can evaporated milk
1 cup grated medium sharp Cheddar cheese
2 (4 ounce) cans sliced mushrooms, drained
¼ cup chopped parsley
1 (4 ounce) jar diced pimientos, drained
2 teaspoons salt
⅛ teaspoon pepper
2 tablespoons lemon juice
Grated rind of 1 lemon
8 ounces vermicelli
3 cups cooked chicken, cubed
¼ cup grated Parmesan cheese

Pasta

Melt margarine in large skillet. Sauté onions until soft. Blend in flour and stir until smooth. Add broth and milk slowly, stirring until smooth and thickened. Add salt, pepper, lemon juice, lemon rind, parsley, mushrooms, pimientos and cheese. Stir until cheese melts. Keep over low heat, uncovered, 10 to 15 minutes. Cook, vermicelli in boiling water 6 to 8 minutes. Drain, then mix with sauce and chicken. Spoon into a greased 2 quart casserole and sprinkle with the Parmesan cheese. Bake at 375°F for 30 to 40 minutes. Serves 6. *Freezes well.* To freeze omit the Parmesan cheese and add after dish has thawed in refrigerator for baking.

Doris Dixon

Meat Sauce For A Crowd

1 pound bacon, fried and crumbled
3 pounds ground beef
3 large onions, finely chopped
2 sweet peppers, finely chopped
3 cups celery, finely chopped
3 cloves garlic, finely chopped
1 (32 ounce) jar spaghetti sauce
1 (16 ounce) can chopped tomatoes
1 (16 ounce) can tomato sauce
1 (6 ounce) can tomato paste
3 (4 ounce) cans mushrooms or stems and pieces
2 cups water
1 tablespoon salt
1 teaspoon black pepper
4 red pepper seeds

Fry bacon in heavy pot until crisp. Fry onions, peppers, celery and garlic in bacon grease until limp. Add ground beef and cook until raw look disappears. Drain excess fat before adding spaghetti sauce, tomatoes, sauce and paste. Pour the water into empty cans and jar so you can get all the sauce and paste possible. Add salt and black pepper. Simmer for 1 hour. Add the bacon, mushrooms and red pepper seeds. If no dried red pepper seeds available, add 1 teaspoon of ground red pepper. Simmer about 40 minutes longer. You may have to add a little water from time to time. This sauce may be made in advance and reheated or frozen for this above dish or to use with spaghetti. If used for spaghetti, have grated cheese to sprinkle on top. Serves 20 to 25.

Marie Holley Anderson

Early Reviews

Spaghetti With Veal And Peppers

2 pounds boneless veal, cut into thin strips
¼ cup flour
¼ cup olive oil
2 green peppers, chopped
1 (4 ounce) cans mushrooms, drained

2 (28 ounce) cans, tomatoes, undrained but chopped
2 (8 ounce) cans tomato sauce
1 teaspoon basil
1 teaspoon oregano
Hot cooked spaghetti

Dredge veal in flour, sauté in oil in Dutch oven. Add green peppers and cook, stirring occasionally. Add next 6 ingredients. Cover and simmer 1 hour. Serve over spaghetti and sprinkle with Parmesan cheese. Serves 8.

Ann Whitfield

Seafood Lasagna

8 lasagna noodles
1 cup chopped onion
2 tablespoons butter
1 (8 ounce) package cream cheese
1½ cups cottage cheese
1 beaten egg
2 teaspoons dried basil

2 (10¾ ounce) cans cream of mushroom soup
⅓ cup milk
⅓ cup dry, white wine
1 pound shelled shrimp
1 (7½ ounce) can crabmeat
¼ cup Parmesan cheese
½ cup grated Cheddar cheese

Cook noodles and drain; arrange 4 noodles in bottom of greased 13x9x2 inch baking dish; cook onion in butter; blend in cream cheese; and stir in cottage cheese, egg, basil, ½ teaspoon salt, and ⅛ teaspoon pepper. Spread half atop noodles. Combine soup, milk and wine, stir in shrimp and crabmeat. Spread half over cheese layer. Repeat layers. Sprinkle with Parmesan cheese and bake, uncovered, in 350°F oven for 45 minutes. Top with Cheddar cheese, and bake 3 to 5 minutes more. Let stand for 15 minutes before serving. Serves 12.

Rosemary Fisher

Pasta

Confetti Fettucini

¼ cup olive oil
2 chicken breasts, cut in julienne strips
1 red onion, julienned
1 sweet red pepper, julienned
1 sweet green pepper, julienned
2 cloves garlic, minced
Salt, to taste
2 large ripe, peeled tomatoes, seeded and diced
12 ounces cooked, drained fettucini

Sauté chicken in 2 tablespoons of oil for 2 minutes, stirring constantly. Set aside. Sauté onions, peppers, and garlic in 2 tablespoons olive oil for 10 minutes. Add chicken and cook for 2 minutes. Add tomatoes. Cook until warm. Toss with well drained pasta to blend well. Serve with freshly grated Parmesan cheese. Serves 4.

Barbara Redmont
Jackson, Mississippi

Nick's Shrimp Givesti

2¼ pounds large shrimp, shelled and deveined
1½ sticks salted butter
1½ cups chopped onions
½ pound mushrooms, sliced
½ cup chopped scallions
1½ cups chicken stock
½ cup water
¼ pound shell pasta (small)
½ teaspoon pepper
2 cups canned tomatoes and juice
Parmesan cheese
1½ sticks salted butter

In a large saucepan sauté shrimp, 1½ sticks salted butter until pink. Stir in onions, mushrooms, and scallions. Sauté mixture for 7 minutes or until vegetables are soft. Transfer shrimp and vegetables with slotted spoon to a dish and keep warm. Add to the saucepan the chicken stock and water and bring to a boil. Stir in pasta shells and cook, stirring occasionally for 15 minutes, or until pasta is al dente. Return shrimp to pan and heat. Add salt and pepper to taste. Sprinkle with Parmesan cheese and pour 1½ sticks butter melted and heated until golden brown, over mixture. Serves 4 to 6.

Claire Stanley

Early Reviews

Shrimp Fettuccini

3 pounds boiled shrimp
3 sticks margarine
3 onions, chopped
3 cloves garlic, chopped
4 teaspoons parsley, chopped
¼ cup flour
1 pint half and half cream
⅔ pound Jalapeño cheese
1 pound fettucini egg noodles
⅓ cup evaporated milk

Sauté onions, peppers and celery in margarine. Add parsley, garlic and cook 10 minutes. Add flour, cream, cheese and simmer 15 to 20 minutes. Boil and drain noodles. Add noodles and shrimp to mixture. Pour into buttered individual casseroles. Bake 20 minutes at 350°F or until hot and bubbly. Serves 8.

Mrs. Nap Cassibry (June)
Cleveland, Mississippi

Opening Night "Show-Off"

1 (8 ounce) package vermicelli or thin spaghetti
½ cup butter or margarine
½ cup all purpose flour
1 cup chicken broth
1 cup heavy cream
1 cup shredded Swiss cheese
4 tablespoons sherry
1 (6 ounce) can mushrooms, sliced
3 pounds shrimp, cooked, peeled, deveined
White pepper, to taste
Grated Parmesan cheese
Slivered almonds

Cook spaghetti, drain. Make cream sauce out of butter, flour, broth and cream over low heat stirring constantly until sauce thickens. Blend in cheese, sherry and white pepper. Heat and stir until cheese melts; add mushrooms. Remove from heat. Add shrimp. Add spaghetti to sauce. Turn into large shallow casserole. Sprinkle with Parmesan cheese and slivered almonds. Heat under broiler (5 to 7 inches) until lightly brown. Serve immediately. Serves 10 to 12.

Mickey Hale

Under Study

UNDERSTUDY

Every director lives in fear of something happening to the star of the show. In order to avoid complete disaster he will have an understudy ready to replace the star at a moment's notice. While the understudy will never duplicate the performance of the leading role, this sometimes provides the opportunity she needs to be discovered as a star in her own right.

The wise cook will be equally as well prepared as the wise director. Having a pantry adequately stocked for emergencies is a necessity in a well organized kitchen. For, whether the roast burns, or the soufflé falls, when the doorbell rings and the guests arrive, "the show must go on"!

Vegetables

Artichoke Casserole

1 bunch green onions
2 (6 ounce) jars marinated
   artichoke hearts
1 clove garlic

4 eggs, beaten
8 ounces Cheddar cheese,
   shredded
32 ounces crackers, rolled

Finely mince onions using tops. Cut artichokes in thirds. Reserve oil, sauté onions and garlic in oil. Combine all ingredients. Bake in 9x9 inch dish at 350°F, 15 to 20 minutes or until set.

Asparagus Casserole

6 tablespoons flour
6 tablespoons melted butter or
   margarine
3 cups milk
Salt and pepper, to taste
1 tablespoon Worcestershire
   sauce (optional)
2 (14½ ounce) cans asparagus

1 (15 ounce) large can small
   peas
1 (4 ounce) jar Old English
   cheese spread
½ (or more) cup cracker
   crumbs
Slivered almonds

Make cream sauce with flour, butter, milk, salt and pepper to taste. (I add 1 tablespoon Worcestershire sauce.) Cook in 9x13x2 inch casserole. Cover vegetables with sauce, top with spoonfuls of cheese, sprinkle with cracker crumbs. Then cover top with slivered almonds. Cook at 350°F for 15 to 20 minutes. Serves 12 to 14.

Mrs. A. C. Wiggins
Cleveland, Mississippi

Understudy

Baked Bean Casserole

1 pound ground chuck
1 large onion, chopped
3 or 4 (31 ounce) cans pork and beans
½ cup tomato catsup
2 to 4 tablespoons prepared mustard
½ cup brown sugar
2 or 4 tablespoons Worcestershire sauce

Brown beef and skim off fat. Chop onion and add to the beef as it browns. Put all ingredients in bean pot and cook in oven on low heat for at least an hour. Stir once or twice. Serves 20 to 30.

Note: I prefer to cook longer, sometimes up to 4 hours at 250°F.

Lee Sweat

Baked Beans

2 large or 3 regular cans pork and beans
1 (14 ounce) can kidney beans
1 cup catsup
1 cup hot barbecue sauce
1 cup corn syrup
1 bell pepper, chopped
2 sections garlic, chopped
1 onion, chopped
Salt, to taste
Bacon

Mix all ingredients except bacon together and pour into 9x13 inch casserole. Top with bacon slices. Bake at 350°F for 1 hour. Serves 8 to 10.

Vicki Bowen
Iuka, Mississippi

Vegetables

Green Beans

½ cup sliced onions
1 tablespoon minced parsley
4 tablespoons butter
2 tablespoons flour
1 teaspoon salt

¼ teaspoon pepper
½ teaspoon grated lemon rind
1 cup sour cream
4 cups green beans, cooked or canned

Cook onion and parsley in butter until tender but not brown. Add flour, salt, pepper and lemon peel. Add sour cream and mix well. Heat slowly (do not boil). Heat beans in their own juice until very hot. Drain beans and toss with sour cream mixture. Serves 8 to 10.

Toxey Smith
Greenwood, Mississippi

Red Beans And Rice

1 can red kidney beans (2 cups)
1 cup water
1 clove garlic, chopped
1 small onion, chopped fine
1 rib celery, chopped
2 tablespoons fresh parsley, chopped
1 large bay leaf, crushed

Ham bone with generous amount of meat, or 1 cup of chopped ham bits
Salt and pepper, to taste
Dash red pepper if hotter seasoning is desired
1 cup rice cooked according to package directions

Add water to beans and heat. Add all other ingredients and simmer over low heat about 1 hour. If beans become too dry, add more water. Stir occasionally. Serve on mounds of rice. Serves 4.

Rosemary T. Williams

Understudy

Broccoli Casserole

2 (10 ounce) packages frozen chopped broccoli
2 tablespoons margarine
2 tablespoons all purpose flour
2 cups milk
¾ cup grated cheese
1 teaspoon salt
1 teaspoon black pepper
¼ cup chopped almonds
4 slices bacon, fried crisp and crumbled
½ cup buttered bread crumbs

Cook broccoli until just tender. Drain and place in a greased 2 quart casserole. Make a sauce of margarine, flour, milk, cheese, salt and pepper. Sprinkle broccoli with almonds. Then pour cheese sauce over broccoli. Spread bread crumbs and bacon on top. Bake uncovered at 350°F about 20 minutes or until bubbling hot and slightly browned on top. Serves 6 to 8.

Mrs. John D. Mercier (Helen)

Broccoli Puff

2 (10 ounce) packages chopped broccoli
3 eggs, separated
1 tablespoon all purpose flour
Ground nutmeg, to taste
1 cup mayonnaise
1 tablespoon butter, softened
¼ teaspoon salt
¼ teaspoon pepper
⅓ cup grated Parmesan cheese

Cook broccoli according to package directions. Beat egg yolks; add flour mixing well. Stir in nutmeg, mayonnaise, butter, salt, pepper and Parmesan. Add broccoli, mixing lightly. Beat egg whites (at room temperature) until stiff but not dry; gently fold into broccoli mixture. Pour into a lightly buttered 9 inch square baking dish. Bake at 350°F for 30 minutes. Cut into squares to serve. Serves 9.

Melinda Hinton Moore

Broccoli Soufflé

2 packages frozen chopped broccoli
1 can cream of mushroom soup
2 tablespoons gr[ated]
1 cup mayonnais[e]
4 eggs

Cook broccoli until tender; drain well. Add all other ingredients and mix with beater. Pour into greased casserole. Bake at 350°F for 45 minutes, or until firm. Can be cut into squares to serve.

Vera Weeks

Broccoli And Rice Casserole

2 packages frozen chopped broccoli
1 large onion, chopped
1 stick butter or margarine
1 (10¾ ounce) can cream of chicken soup
½ cup milk
2 cups cooked rice
1 cup grated sharp cheese
1½ teaspoons salt
¼ teaspoon black pepper

Cook broccoli slightly, drain. Sauté onion in butter. Combine broccoli, soup, milk, rice, onion, cheese, salt, pepper in greased casserole. Sprinkle some cheese on top. Bake at 300°F for 30 minutes. Serves 8.

Brussels Sprouts And Artichokes

1 (10 ounce) package frozen sprouts cooked in ½ cup water
1 (14 ounce) can artichoke hearts, drained
⅔ cup mayonnaise
½ teaspoon celery salt
2 teaspoons lemon juice
¼ cup grated Parmesan cheese
¼ cup margarine, melted

Put artichokes and sprouts in greased casserole. Mix other ingredients, pour over vegetables. Bake at 425°F for 10 minutes.

Miriam R. Propp

Carrot Loaf

12 medium size carrots, peeled
4 eggs
3 tablespoons sugar
1 teaspoon salt

1 rounded tablespoon cornstarch
1 pint half and half cream
3 tablespoons melted butter

Cook carrots in boiling water until tender. Grate them in grater. Beat eggs until light. Add carrots, sugar, salt and melted butter. Mix cornstarch with a little cold water to make a paste. Add to other ingredients. Stir in cream and mix well. Pour into buttered baking dish. Bake in pan of hot water at 350°F for about 45 minutes or until firm. Serves 8.

Helen Moore

Marinated Carrots

5 cups carrots, cooked and drained
1 onion, sliced
1 bell pepper, chopped
1 can tomato soup
½ cup salad oil

½ cup sugar
¾ cup vinegar
1 teaspoon mustard
1 teaspoon Worcestershire
1 teaspoon salt
1 teaspoon pepper

Layer sliced carrots, onion and bell pepper in a a dish, mix the remaining ingredients and heat to boiling point, pour over vegetables, let stand 24 hours. Serve at room temperature.

Mrs. Roderick McCall
Lyons, Georgia

"I never worry about diets. The only carrots that interest me are the number you get in a diamond.", Mae West, stage & screen actress.

Cauliflower Delight

1 head cauliflower
1 tablespoon oil
1 pound yellow squash sliced
½ cup fresh mushrooms sliced
1 bunch fresh green onions, chopped with tops
2 tablespoons soy sauce
1 tablespoon sweet basil

1 tablespoon ground oregano
½ teaspoon thyme
Pepper and salt, to taste
½ cup Parmesan cheese (more if desired)
3 tablespoons butter or margarine

Large skillet is needed. Clean off heavy stems of cauliflower, breaking it into bite size flowerets. Add oil, pan fry for 7 to 8 minutes stirring often on medium to high heat. Add sliced zucchini, continue to fry for about 5 more minutes. Then add mushrooms and onions, continue stirring. This will all soften (but still be firm) very quickly. Add your soy sauce, basil, oregano, thyme, pepper and salt. Toss until mixed. Then add plenty of Parmesan cheese and butter. Toss and serve immediately. Serves 4.

Kathleen A. Masters

Corn Pudding

2 cups canned cream-style yellow corn
1 tablespoon minced green onion
¼ cup minced green pepper
2 ounces minced pimiento

3 eggs
2 tablespoons sugar
1 teaspoon salt
1 tablespoon all purpose flour
1 cup milk
2 tablespoons butter, melted

Butter a casserole. Heat oven to 325°F. Combine corn, onion, green pepper and pimiento. Beat eggs slightly, then stir in sugar and salt. Smooth a little of the milk into the flour, then blend in remaining milk. Combine corn, egg and milk mixtures. Add melted butter. Turn into prepared casserole. Bake at 325°F for 45 to 60 minutes, or until knife inserted near center comes out clean. Serve hot. Serves 6 to 8.

Ruth Malone
Camden, Arkansas

Shoe Peg Corn Casserole

½ cup chopped onion
½ cup chopped celery
¼ cup chopped bell pepper
   (optional)
½ cup grated sharp cheese
1 (12 ounce) can shoe peg
   corn
1 (16 ounce) can French style
   green beans (drained)

1 (10¾ ounce) can cream of
   celery soup
1 cup sour cream
Salt and pepper, to taste
½ cup margarine
1 stack round buttery crackers,
   crushed (24 crackers)

Mix first eight ingredients. Add salt and pepper to taste. Place in 9x13 inch dish. Melt margarine and mix with crackers. Spread on top of vegetable mixture. Bake at 350°F for 45 minutes. Serves 12.

Annie L. Mitchell

Skillet Corn

1 (2½ ounce) jar dried beef
2 tablespoons margarine
2 tablespoons minced onion
2 tablespoons minced green
   pepper
1 tablespoon all purpose flour

¾ cup milk
1 (17 ounce) can cream style
   corn
½ cup shredded Cheddar
   cheese
Toast triangles

Melt margarine in skillet over medium heat. Add onion, green pepper and dried beef which has been shredded. Cook until onion and pepper are soft, stirring often. Stir in flour. Add milk, stir until thickened. Add the corn and cheese, stir until cheese is melted. Serve over toast triangles. Serves 4.

Doris Downs Dixon

Vegetables

Eggplant Or Squash Casserole

2 cups pared, cubed eggplant
 or yellow squash (not pared)
¼ cup chopped onion
1 egg

Corn oil margarine
Bread crumbs
Milk

Cook eggplant or squash and onion in small amount of slightly salted water until tender, about 8 minutes. Soft scramble egg in 1 tablespoon corn oil margarine. Add drained vegetable and about 1 cup of bread crumbs. Pour into an 8x8 inch oiled pan and add enough milk to barely come to top of mixture. Add more bread crumbs. Dot with corn oil margarine. Bake at 350°F for 20 to 25 minutes until bubbly and top is brown.

Loretta D. Greene
Rockdale, Texas

Eggplant Soufflé

1 medium sized eggplant
¼ cup butter or margarine
3 eggs, separated
1 cup cracker crumbs
1 cup grated cheese
1 cup milk

1 tablespoon Worcestershire
 sauce
Salt and cayenne pepper, to
 taste
1 clove garlic

Wash and grease 1 medium sized eggplant. Bake in oven until soft. Let cool and remove outside shell. Mash, and add ½ stick melted butter, yolks of 3 eggs, well beaten, and 1 tablespoon Worcestershire sauce. Add cracker crumbs, cheese and milk. Last, fold in well beaten whites of the 3 eggs. Bake in a greased casserole which has been rubbed with clove of garlic. Bake at 350°F for 30 to 40 minutes, until set and puffed.

Nancy Smith

Understudy

Garlic Grits Casserole

1 cup grits (not instant)
4 cups water
Dash of salt
½ cup of butter or margarine

1 (6 ounce) roll garlic cheese
2 eggs
½ (or more) cup milk

Cook grits in the water according to package directions. Add butter and cheese and stir until completely melted. Break eggs into mixing cup, beat slightly then fill with milk up to 1 cup, stir and add to grits mixture while stirring. Pour into casserole. Heat in 350°F oven until bubbly and thickened, about 30 mintues. Serves 4 to 6.

Lima Beans With Mushrooms

1 (10 ounce) package frozen baby lima beans
4 tablespoons butter
¼ pound fresh mushrooms
1 garlic clove

1 tablespoon lemon juice
Salt and pepper
½ teaspoon basil (dry)
1 tablespoon chopped parsley

Cook the lima beans according to the directions on the package, but do not overcook, they should be fairly firm since they will be cooked again. Drain well and return the beans to the pot. While the beans cook, melt 2 tablespoons of butter in a small skillet. Rinse the mushrooms and thinly slice. Add the mushrooms to the skillet along with a peeled garlic clove stuck on a toothpick. Sprinkle with lemon juice, salt and pepper. Cover and simmer the mushrooms gently for 3 minutes. Remove the garlic from the skillet and scrape the mushrooms into the lima beans. Grind the basil between your fingers until powdery while adding to the pot. Add the 2 remaining tablespoons of butter to the beans and mix gently. Cover and reheat for 1 minute. Add the parsley, mix, recover and simmer for 1 more minute. Serve hot. Serves 4.

Karen Lambert

Vegetables

Herman's Baked Mushrooms

2 cups fresh mushrooms
Stale French bread
½ cup white wine
½ cup melted butter

Clean mushrooms and slice into quarters. Break French bread into bite-sized pieces. There should be 1½ cups. Combine wine and melted butter and then combine all ingredients in an oven-proof casserole dish. Bake at 350°F, uncovered, for 20 minutes. Serves 4.

Herman Brawner

Sweet And Sour Onions

4 large onions
¼ cup cider vinegar
¼ cup butter or margarine
¼ cup boiling water
¼ cup sugar
Salt and pepper, to taste*

Slice onions into rings and arrange in a 1 quart casserole. Mix vinegar, butter and water together and stir until butter melts. Cover and place in preheated 375°F oven. Bake for 45 to 60 minutes. Do not allow it to boil dry. Serves 6 to 8.

*You may omit the salt in this for low sodium diet.

Ms. D. M. Stauffer

Lemon/Parsley Potatoes

2 pounds new potatoes
2 tablespoons lemon juice
2 tablespoons margarine
2 tablespoons parsley, chopped
2 teaspoons grated lemon rind

Wash potatoes and peel a thin strip around the center of each one. Cook in boiling salted water for 15 minutes. Drain water and add mixture of margarine, parsley and lemon rind. Stir potatoes until mixture coats all potatoes. Serves 6.

Brenda Rogers

Understudy

Baked Potatoes Stuffed With Crabmeat

4 Idaho baking potatoes
½ cup butter (use more if desired)
Salt to taste
Pepper to taste
½ (5¾ ounce) can evaporated milk (more if needed to moisten)
1 (6½ ounce) can crabmeat

Bake potatoes in 400°F oven until done (about 1 hour). Scoop out potato pulp, reserving shells. In a medium bowl mash potato pulp, add butter, salt, pepper and evaporated milk. Fold in crabmeat. Bake at 350°F until heated through. May be prepared and frozen if desired. Thaw before heating. Serves 4.

Mrs. J. R. Laughlin, Jr. (Becky)

"What I say is that if a man really likes potatoes, he must be a pretty decent sort of fellow.", A. A. Milne, English dramatist & children's writer.

Creole Peas

2 tablespoons bacon fat
1 large onion, chopped
1 large green pepper, chopped
1 (16 ounce) can tomatoes
Pepper, salt, paprika
1 cup milk
2 tablespoons flour
2 tablespoons butter
2 (16 ounce) cans tiny English peas, drained

Brown onion and green pepper in bacon fat. Add tomatoes to this and simmer slowly until thick. Season with salt, pepper and paprika to taste. Make white sauce with butter, milk and flour. Put layer of peas, white sauce and creole sauce in large 2½ to 3 quart casserole, alternating layers until casserole is filled with creole sauce on top. Dot with butter. Bake slowly 30 to 40 minutes at 350°F. This recipe is over 50 years old and was handed down to me by my mother.

Lee Sweat

Vegetables

Potatoes Au Gratin

6 firm boiled potatoes
½ cup butter
2 cups grated Parmesan cheese
1 cup heavy cream
1 tablespoon butter

Cut potatoes into even cubes. Place layer on flat buttered casserole (1½ quart size). Cover with thin slices of butter. Sprinkle with ½ cup Parmesan cheese. Repeat twice, using 1½ cups cheese in all. Pour over 1 cup cream. Dot with 1 tablespoon butter. Place in 450°F oven until cheese bubbles. Remove and sprinkle with ½ cup cheese. Place under broiler to brown slightly. Serves 6.

Mrs. Ezio Pinza

Spudwisers

6 medium white baking potatoes (or 4 large)
1 pound hamburger meat
1 package brown gravy mix
½ carton sour cream
½ cup grated Cheddar cheese (or more)
½ cup grated Mozzarella cheese (or more)
1 envelope dry onion soup mix

Bake potatoes as usual. Keep warm while browning the hamburger, stirring the hamburger to break up lumps. Add soup mix DRY to the meat. Add gravy mixed according to directions. Add the sour cream. Do not let mixture boil after adding the sour cream. Split the potatoes, fluff, add butter or margarine and spoon beef mixture generously over the potatoes. Cheeses may be served separately. Serves 4 to 6.

Ms. D. M. Stauffer

Understudy

Potato Casserole

½ cup melted butter or margarine
1 teaspoon salt
½ teaspoon pepper
½ cup chopped onion
1 can cream of chicken soup (undiluted)
1 pint dairy sour cream
2 cups grated sharp Cheddar cheese
2 pounds frozen hash brown potatoes
¼ cup melted butter or margarine
2 cups crushed corn flakes

Mix together ½ cup butter, salt, pepper, onion, soup, sour cream and cheese. Add thawed potatoes and blend. Pour into buttered 3 quart casserole. Mix ¼ cup melted butter and corn flakes and put on top. Bake at 350°F for 45 minutes.

Lee Sweat

Creamy Scalloped Potatoes

10 medium potatoes
3 tablespoons butter or margarine
2 tablespoons flour
3 cups milk
1 small onion
1 green pepper
½ pound kielbasa (cut into bite size pieces)
8 slices American cheese
Parmesan cheese
Garlic salt, salt and pepper

Wash and peel potatoes. Slice into medium slices. Melt butter. Blend in flour until creamy. Add milk and stir until sauce is thick. Place a layer of sauce on bottom of pan, then a layer of potatoes, onion, green pepper, cheese, Parmesan cheese, salt and pepper. Continue until half of ingredients are distributed. Continue again but start adding kielbasa. Cover. Bake covered for ½ hour. Then uncover and bake for ½ hour. Serves 6 to 8.

Mrs. Bill Alexander (Lois)

Vegetables

High Society Rice

2 cups raw rice
¼ cup margarine
6 bouillon cubes melted in 2 cups hot water
1 pinch of salt
¾ cup of carrots, chopped fine
¾ cup of parsley, chopped fine
¾ cup of celery, chopped fine
¾ cup of green onions and tops
1 (5 ounce) can water chestnuts sliced thin

Cook rice in bouillon, salt and butter until liquid is absorbed. Then steam in a collander over boiling water until done. When rice is done, mix all raw vegetables in hot rice and serve. Serves 6 to 8.

Martha Ball
New Orleans, Louisiana

Nutty Wild Rice

2 (6 ounce) packages long grain and wild rice mix
¼ cup butter
8 ounces Canadian style bacon, diced (1⅔ cups)
1 (8 ounce) package fresh mushrooms, sliced
½ cup sliced green onion
2 cloves garlic, minced
¼ cup dry white wine
¼ cup snipped fresh parsley
1⅓ cups chopped Brazil nuts or pecans

Prepare rice according to package directions. In large skillet melt ¼ cup butter; add diced bacon, sliced mushrooms, ½ cup onion and minced garlic. Cook and stir about 5 minutes or until bacon is golden and mushrooms and onion are tender. Stir in the ¼ cup white wine, parsley and salt and pepper to taste. Add to cooked rice mixture with the nuts. Toss until well mixed. Bake in a casserole at 325°F for 30 minutes. Can be used in turkey as stuffing. Serves 10 to 12.

Joan Hennessy

Understudy

Mrs. Robbins' Spinach Casserole

4 (10 ounce) packages frozen chopped spinach
1 cup evaporated milk
4 tablespoons margarine
2 tablespoons finely chopped onion
2 tablespoons all purpose flour
½ cup vegetable liquor
4 ounces jalapenô cheese
½ teaspoon black pepper
¾ teaspoon celery salt
¾ teaspoon garlic salt
½ teaspoon salt
1 tablespoon Worcestershire sauce
1½ cups sharp cheese

Cook spinach until done. Drain, saving ½ cup of the vegetable liquor. Melt butter in 3 quart pan. Sauté onion in butter until clear, add flour and stir until bubbly. Add vegetable liquor, stir until smooth. Add milk slowly and stir until smooth and thick, then add seasonings, spinach, jalapeño cheese and ¾ cup sharp cheese. Stir until well mixed. Pour into greased casserole, top with remaining sharp cheese and cook at 350°F for 10 or 15 minutes or until hot. *Strangely enough, even children like this.*

Variation: Scoop out medium or small sized tomatoes, drain well and stuff with the heated spinach. Beautiful and tasty on a plate.

Mrs. Mary Robbins

Spinach And Artichoke Casserole

3 (10 ounce) packages frozen chopped spinach
2 (14 ounce) cans artichoke bottoms or hearts (if hearts, cut in quarters)
1 teaspoon nutmeg
Freshly ground pepper, to taste
2 cups hollandaise sauce

Prepare spinach according to package directions. Squeeze until well drained. Add nutmeg and pepper. Mix well. Arrange artichokes in the bottom of a well buttered casserole dish. Cover with spinach, then top with hollandaise sauce (see below). Can be prepared to this stage several hours in advance. Heat thoroughly in moderate oven or microwave. Serves 12.

Vegetables

Blender Hollandaise Sauce

6 egg yolks
4 tablespoons fresh lemon juice
¼ teaspoonful salt

Pinch cayenne
1 cup butter

Place all ingredients, except butter in the blender. Heat butter in a small saucepan. Cover blender and run at top speed for 2 or 3 seconds. Uncover, still blending at top speed, start pouring in the hot butter in a slow, thin stream. Omit milky residue at bottom of butter pan.

Wanda Witt

Spinach-Artichoke Casserole

3 (10 ounce) boxes chopped spinach
1 (14 ounce) can artichokes (packed in salt water, not in oil)
½ cup melted butter

1 (8 ounce) package cream cheese
1 teaspoon lemon juice
10 crushed round, buttery crackers

Cook spinach and drain. While hot add cream cheese, lemon juice and butter. Stir till smooth. Slice artichokes and line bottom of greased casserole dish. Spoon spinach mixture over artichokes. Crumble crackers over casserole. Bake 25 minutes at 350°F. Serves 6.

Lynn Elliott

Variation: In place of the cracker crumbs, mix ½ cup herb seasoned stuffing and ½ cup Parmesan cheese and sprinkle over the top.

Ann White

Understudy

Company Squash

1 large onion, chopped
½ cup margarine
2½ pounds squash, sliced
1 (10¾ ounce) can cream chicken soup
1 (8 ounce) carton sour cream
1 (6 ounce) can water chestnuts, chopped
1 (12 ounce) stuffing mix
4 tablespoons margarine

Cook onions in margarine until tender but not brown. Cook squash in salted water until tender, drain when done and mash. Add onions, chicken soup, sour cream and water chestnuts to squash. Place ½ mixture in well greased casserole dish. Then cover with ½ of stuffing mix. Add remaining squash mixture and top with rest of stuffing mix. Dot with 4 tablespoons margarine. Bake at 350°F for 30 minutes. Serves 10.

Mrs. Charles Clifton

Summer Squash Casserole

6 medium yellow crooked-neck squash
4 tablespoons butter
Black pepper, to taste
Salt, to taste
½ teaspoon paprika
1 egg, beaten
1 tablespoon grated onion
4 soda crackers, crumbled
¾ cup grated cheese

Cook squash in salted water and mash. Add butter, salt, pepper, paprika, beaten egg, onion and cracker crumbs. Include grated cheese in mixture or add on top, whichever you prefer. Bake at 350°F for 30 to 45 minutes. Serves 4.

Mary Speer
Indianola, Mississippi

Vegetables

Squash Soufflé

1 cup milk
3 tablespoons sifted cornmeal
1 teaspoon salt
¼ teaspoon black pepper
2 cups cooked, mashed yellow squash
3 tablespoons margarine
2 tablespoons minced onion
2 eggs, beaten
½ cup buttered bread crumbs or croutons

Heat milk (low heat), add cornmeal and salt and pepper. Simmer 5 minutes, stirring constantly. Add squash, beat well. Sauté onions in margarine, add to squash mixture. Add eggs. Pour into buttered baking dish. Top with breadcrumbs. Bake at 350°F for 30 minutes.

Margaret Perkins

Squash Dressing

2 cups squash, cooked and mashed
2 cups chopped onion (sauté)
2 cups cooked cornbread
2 eggs
1 (10¾ ounce) can cream of chicken soup
Milk

Cook squash until tender and mash. Sauté onion in small amount of butter or oil. Bake cornbread. Mix eggs, soup, squash, onion and crumbled cornbread. Add enough milk to make right consistency. Bake at 350°F until it tests done. Serves 6 to 8.

Mildred A. Smith

Understudy

Stuffed Yellow Squash

12 medium sized yellow squash
1 large onion, minced
2 tablespoons minced parsley
1 clove garlic, minced or pressed
1 cup butter
2 (10 ounce) packages frozen chopped spinach, cooked and drained well
1½ cups breadcrumbs
1 tablespoon Worcestershire sauce
Salt and freshly ground pepper, to taste
Freshly grated Parmesan cheese

Cut squash in half lengthwise. Scoop out seeds and drop shells in boiling water until just tender, about 2 or 3 minutes. Drain and cool. Sauté onions, parsley and garlic in butter for 5 minutes. Add spinach, bread crumbs and seasonings and mix well. Butter enough flat baking dishes to hold all the squash halves. Stuff each half and top with cheese. Bake at 350°F for 20 minutes or until heated through. Make this dish ahead and cover until ready to heat. Serves 12 to 24.

Wanda Witt

Tomato Pepper Quickie

2 medium green peppers
1 medium onion
3 medium red tomatoes
½ teaspoon basil
1 teaspoon salt
2 tablespoons water

Cut green peppers into ½ inch chunks. Cut onions into ¼ inch slices and separate into rings. In a 1 quart casserole dish, place peppers and layer onion rings on top. Sprinkle seasonings over onions and peppers. Then add the water. Cover and bake in a 350°F oven for 15 minutes until peppers are tender. Cut tomatoes into ¾ inch wedges and arrange over onions. Cover. Bake 10 to 15 minutes longer until tomatoes are hot. Serve immediately. Serves 4.

Judy Martin

Vegetables

Holiday Sweet Potato Bourbon Casserole

4 pounds sweet potatoes
Butter
Milk
Salt

Boil potatoes in skins. Drain. Peel and mash potatoes. Add butter, milk, salt, all to taste. Spread sweet potatoes in a buttered 2 quart casserole. Scoop a 1 inch deep hollow in the center leaving a 1 inch rim around the edge.

Topping

¼ to ½ pound of butter
¾ cup brown sugar, packed
1 beaten egg
3 ounces bourbon
10 to 12 regular or 1 cup miniature marshmallows

Combine butter, sugar, egg and bourbon in top of double boiler, stirring constantly until thickened. Pour into center and over top of sweet potatoes. Place marshmallows around edge and bake at 350°F for 45 minutes. This can be made the day before and warmed up. It actually improves with age. Serves 12.

Dr. Mona Carlyle

Sweet Potato Soufflé

3 cups mashed sweet potatoes
1 teaspoon salt
2 eggs
⅓ stick margarine
½ cup milk
1 teaspoon vanilla
½ cup sugar

In mixing bowl, mix potatoes, salt, eggs, margarine, milk, vanilla and sugar. Pour into baking dish.

Topping

1 cup chopped nuts
1 cup brown sugar
3 tablespoons margarine
½ cup all purpose flour

Mix nuts, brown sugar, margarine and flour in small bowl. Sprinkle on top of potato mixture. Bake at 350°F for 35 minutes. Serves 6 to 8.

Johnnie Callahan

Understudy

Vegetable Casserole

1 (10 ounce) package frozen cauliflower, slightly cooked
2 cups cooked carrots
1 (17 ounce) can green peas with onions, drained
1 (5 ounce) can water chestnuts, drained and sliced
1 small can sliced mushrooms
2 (10¾ ounce) cans cream of mushroom soup, undiluted
8 ounces Cheddar cheese, shredded

Combine vegetables and soup. Toss well. Spoon mixture into 2 quart casserole. Sprinkle with cheese. Bake at 325°F for 30 to 45 minutes or until bubbly. Serves 4 to 6.

Carol Baker
Michie, Tennessee

Zucchini Casserole

1 pound zucchini (¼ inch slices)
2 tablespoons olive oil
2 tablespoons chopped green onion
¼ pound sliced fresh mushrooms
1 tablespoon margarine
1 large tomato, sliced
½ teaspoon oregano
½ teaspoon basil
3 tablespoons seasoned bread crumbs
1 cup shredded Mozzarella cheese

Brown zucchini in oil. Place in 10x8 inch casserole. Sauté onion and mushrooms, add to zucchini. Place tomato slices on top of zucchini. Top with herbs and bread crumbs. Sprinkle cheese on top. Bake at 375°F for 20 minutes. Serves 6.

Dorothy Griffith

Vegetables

Three Vegetable Casserole

4 medium potatoes (1½ pounds), pared and thinly sliced
2 medium onions, peeled and thinly sliced into rings
4 small yellow straightneck squash (1½ pounds) washed, unpared and thinly sliced

Salt and pepper, to taste
½ cup butter
1 cup grated Parmesan cheese
1 cup commercial sour cream

Butter a shallow baking dish, 2½ quart. In it layer ½ the potatoes, sprinkling with salt and pepper; dot with a generous pat of butter. In the same way, layer ½ of the onion and ½ of the squash, sprinkle with salt and pepper and butter. Repeat layers, ending with squash and butter. Cover tightly with foil and bake in preheated 350°F oven until potatoes are very tender when pierced with a fork, about 1 hour and 15 minutes. Stir together the Parmesan cheese and sour cream (the mixture will be thick). Spread over top of vegetables. Broil, watching carefully about 6 to 8 inches from broiler, until topping is browned in spots (3 to 5 minutes). Serve at once. Serves 6 to 8.

Mrs. R. C. Hudson

Apple And Cranberry Crunch

3 cups chopped apples with peeling
2 cups whole cranberries
1¼ cups sugar
1½ cups quick oats

½ cup brown sugar, packed
⅓ cup flour
½ cup pecans, chopped
½ cup melted margarine

In 2 quart casserole mix the first 3 ingredients. Mix next 5 ingredients and put on top. Bake at 325°F for 1 hour until bubbles in the middle. Serves 6 to 8.

Jerry Doran

Understudy

Curried Baked Fruit

1 (27 ounce) can pear halves
1 (20 ounce) can pineapple chunks
1 (27 ounce) can peach halves

½ cup or more sliced maraschino cherries
⅓ cup butter or margarine
¾ cup brown sugar, packed
2 teaspoons curry powder

Drain fruit well and put in a 2 quart casserole. Melt butter, add brown sugar and curry powder. Mix well. Cover fruit with mixture and bake, covered, for 1 hour at 325°F. Great with baked ham. Serves 6 to 8.

Mrs. Robert Jennings (Betty)
Memphis, Tennessee

Hot Fruit Compote

1 heaping cup dried prunes, pitted and chopped
1½ cups undrained pineapple chunks

2 cups dried apricots, cut up
1 cup cherry pie filling
1½ cups water
½ to 1 cup sherry

Mix fruit well. Place in buttered casserole. Combine pie filling, water and sherry. Pour over fruit and bake 1 hour at 350°F. Serves 8 to 10.

Mrs. A. M. Farris

Pineapple Casserole

1 (20 ounce) can of pineapple chunks
1 cup grated Cheddar cheese
½ cup sugar
6 to 8 tablespoons of pineapple juice

3 tablespoons all purpose flour
¼ cup melted butter
1 cup crumbled round buttery crackers

Mix cheese and pineapple well. Mix juice, sugar and flour. Add to pineapple mixture. Pour into a 1 quart casserole dish. Combine butter and crumbs. Spread on top of pineapple mixture. Bake at 350°F for 20 minutes. Serves 6 to 8.

Becky Plaxico

Supporting Roles

SUPPORTING ROLES

Sometimes overlooked on stage, supporting roles should never be slighted when planning a successful menu. While the main entree may be a prima donna and treated as such, careless planning and preparation of the accompanying dishes could spell disaster for the whole meal.

Bread, the staff of life, truly supports and enhances our meals. Bread lends support to many facets of our life. The smell of bread baking lifts our spirits. A loaf of fresh made bread or a basket of muffins has been the beginning of a new friendship between neighbors or brought comfort to the sick.

Attention to the supporting "roll" we serve can turn an ordinary meal into a sensational one.

Breads

Riz Biscuits (Angel)

2½ cups sifted self-rising flour
¼ teaspoon baking soda
3 tablespoons sugar

1 cake or package yeast
1 cup lukewarm buttermilk
⅓ cup shortening

Sift together flour, baking soda and sugar. Dissolve yeast in lukewarm buttermilk. Cut shortening into flour mixture, as for biscuits. Stir buttermilk into dry ingredients quickly. Turn dough out onto floured cloth and knead just until smooth. Roll to ¼ inch thickness and cut with a biscuit cutter. Brush top of each round with melted butter. Place one biscuit on top of another making double discuits. Cover and place in a warm place to rise until light and doubled, about 1 hour. Bake at 375°F for 12 to 15 minutes. Makes about 1½ dozen.

Note: If using plain flour, add 1 teaspoon salt to dry ingredients.

Mrs. Don L. Glisson (Marcia Ann)

Biscuits

2 cups sifted all purpose flour
3 teaspoons baking powder
½ teaspoon salt

⅔ cup skimmed milk
¼ cup vegetable oil

Mix oil and flour until crumbly. You may add salt and baking powder to the flour for easier mixing. Stir in the skimmed milk. Knead two or three times with the heel of the hand. Roll out gently on a floured board. Cut with a round cutter. Prick the tops with a fork. Bake 12 to 15 minutes in a 450°F oven. Yield: 12 biscuits.

These are reduced in calories and cholesterol.

Mrs. Mildred Sawyer

Supporting Roles

Buttermilk Biscuits

2 cups sifted all purpose flour
½ teaspoon baking soda
2 teaspoons baking powder
½ teaspoon salt
½ cup plus 2 tablespoons corn oil margarine
1 cup buttermilk

Sift dry ingredients. Cut corn oil margarine into dry ingredients until mixture is mealy. Add milk, mix quickly. Knead lightly on floured board. Roll ½ inch thick. Cut with floured biscuit cutter. Place on cookie sheet and bake at 450°F for 10 to 12 minutes.

Note: Low cholesterol.

Loretta Greene
Rockdale, Texas

Heavenly Tiny Biscuits

2 cups biscuit mix
½ cup margarine, softened
1 cup sour cream

Mix well. Fill tiny muffin pan. Cook at 350°F about 10 to 15 minutes. These are good cooked ahead and reheated. Makes about 24 tiny biscuits.

Nancy Tenhet

Corn Lightbread With Egg

2 cups cornmeal
½ cup all purpose flour
1 egg
½ cup sugar
1 teaspoon salt
½ teaspoon baking soda
2 tablespoons shortening
2 cups buttermilk

Mix meal, sugar, salt, flour and baking soda. Add 1 cup buttermilk. Add egg slightly beaten, shortening, then other cup of buttermilk. Bake in greased loaf pan at 350°F for 1 hour. Makes 1 loaf.

Estelle Vines
Jackson, Tennessee

Breads

Bread

1 cup sugar
1 cup shortening
1 quart milk
2 packages yeast

9 cups all purpose flour
1 teaspoon salt
1 teaspoon baking soda
2 teaspoons baking powder

Bring to boil the milk, sugar, and shortening. Cool to room temperature and dissolve yeast in milk mixture. Add dry ingredients and stir until well blended. Cover and let rise 1 hour. Shape into 3 loaves and put into 3 greased loaf pans. Cover and let rise 1 hour. Bake at 300°F for approximately 45 minutes. Makes 3 loaves.

Freezes well, makes great toast!

Ann White

Homemade Bread

2 cups scalded milk
¾ cup sugar
⅔ cup oil
4 teaspoons salt

2 eggs
2 packages yeast
1 cup warm water
11 cups all purpose flour

Scald milk in a pan and pour over sugar, salt, and oil. Cool to lukewarm. Add yeast dissolved in warm water to milk mixture. Beat in 2 eggs. Beat in 8 cups of flour until it gets pully. Let stand 10 minutes. Put on a floured board using 3 cups flour and knead at least 5 minutes. Put in a greased bowl, cover and put in the refrigerator for at least 4 hours. Make out the loaves and place in well greased pans, brush tops with melted butter and sprinkle with cornmeal. Let rise in a warm place for 2 hours. Place in a cold oven and bake at 300°F until golden brown. Turn out immediatley. Makes 3 large loaves or 24 individual loaves.

Mary Davis

Supporting Roles

Honey Whole Wheat Bread

4 cups whole wheat flour
½ cup instant non-fat dry milk solids
1 tablespoon salt
2 packages dry yeast

3 cups water
½ cup honey
2 tablespoons vegetable oil
4 to 4½ cups all purpose unbleached flour

Combine 3 cups whole wheat flour, dry milk, salt, and yeast. Heat water, honey, and oil in a saucepan over low heat until warm. Pour over flour mixture. Blend at low speed of electric mixer for 1 minute and then at medium speed for 2 minutes. By hand, stir in the remaining flour. Turn dough onto a floured surface and knead for 5 minutes. Put dough into a greased bowl and let rise until double in size. Punch down and divide into 3 parts. Roll the dough out into a rectangle. Roll up lengthwise jelly roll fashion. Place into a greased 3x7x? inch loaf pan. Cover. Let rise until double. Preheat oven to 375°F. Bake 40 minutes or until sounds hollow when tapped. Cool on a rack. Wrap to store. Can be frozen. Makes 3 loaves.

Barbara Wayne

"Bread, milk and butter are of venerable antiquity. They taste of the morning of the world.", Leigh Hunt, English critic & aphorist.

No Knead French Bread

2 packages dry yeast
½ cup lukewarm water
1 teaspoon sugar
1 cup milk, scalded
3 tablespoons shortening
2 tablespoons sugar

4 teaspoons salt
2 cups warm water
7 cups flour
1 cup flour, if needed
1 egg white mixed
2 tablespoons water

Breads

Mix the yeast in ½ cup lukewarm water, add 1 teaspoon sugar and let stand 5 minutes to proof. Add all other ingredients in the order they are listed. Stir well with a large wooden spoon. Add 1 cup flour if needed - but this is a soft dough and is not kneaded. Place in a large bowl (greased lightly) and let rise 2 hours, or until doubled in bulk. Cover with a cloth, if you wish. Tumble the dough onto a floured surface and divide into four oblongs. Roll each until it tapers on each end. Place on a cookie sheet leaving space to rise between loaves.* Gash the tops. Scissors will snip out the gashes easily. Cover and let rise again until double in bulk. Bake in a preheated 300°F oven about 25 minutes. About 5 minutes before loaves lightly brown, brush with the lightly beaten egg white which has been mixed with the 2 tablespoons water for a crisp crust. Cool on a wire rack. Freezes well. Makes 4 loaves.

The loaves will rise on the cookie sheet but also have a tendency to "spread" side ways. To remedy, make foil pans with double thickness sides, butter well and place loaves in these for their second rise and cooking. This insures the loaves will rise up instead of out.

Ms. Blanche Reiselt
Camden, Arkansas

French Bread

5 cups warm water
2 packs of dry yeast
6 tablespoons sugar
2 tablespoons salt
14 cups of all purpose flour
2 egg whites (slightly beaten)

Mix yeast, sugar and salt in the water and stir until dissolved. Add flour. Knead 10 minutes. Let rise until doubled in bulk. Punch down and knead 3 or 4 times to remove air. Divide into 8 equal pieces. Shape into loaves, place in well greased pans and slash. Brush with egg whites. Let rise. Bake 15 minutes in preheated oven 450°F, then 30 minutes at 350°F. Remove from pans and cool. Wrap in aluminum foil and freeze. To serve, warm in foil for 20 minutes at 350°F, open and cool. Makes 8 loaves.

Dr. T. L. Sweat

Supporting Roles

Chunk O'Cheese Bread

1¾ cups water
½ cup cornmeal
2 teaspoons salt
½ cup molasses
2 tablespoons butter
1 packet dry yeast

½ cup warm water
4 to 4½ cups all purpose flour
1 pound American or Colby cheese cut into ¼ to ½ inch cubes
Heavy duty aluminum foil

In a 2 quart saucepan combine water, cornmeal and salt. Bring to a boil, stirring constantly. Cook until slightly thickened. Remove from heat, stir in molasses and butter. Cool to lukewarm. Soften yeast in water in a large mixing bowl. Blend in cornmeal mixture. Gradually add flour to form a stiff dough. Knead on well-floured surface until smooth and satiny, about 5 minutes. Place in greased bowl and cover. Let rise in a warm place until light and doubled in size, 1 to 1½ hours. Line two 8 or 9 inch round pans with 12 inch squares of foil, edges extending over pan, grease well. Place dough on surface sprinkled with cornmeal. Work cheese into dough, ¼ at a time, until cubes are evenly distributed. Divide into two parts. Shape into round loaves, covering cheese cubes. Place in pans. Let rise in warm place until light and doubled in size, about 1 hour. Bake in moderate oven (350°F) for 45 to 55 minutes until deep golden brown. Makes 2 loaves.

Heather Hamilton

Dutch Babies

3 tablespoons butter
3 eggs
Pinch salt

½ cup all purpose flour
½ cup milk

Preheat oven to 400°F. Place butter in 10½ inch black skillet and heat butter in oven. Mix eggs, salt, flour and milk. Pour melted hot butter into egg mixture, then pour mixture into skillet. Bake at 400°F for 15 to 20 minutes. Cut into wedges; sprinkle with powdered sugar and serve with bacon or ham; (syrup optional). Excellent for breakfast. Children love this. Serves 4 to 6.

Mrs. Phil Nelson
Jackson, Mississippi

Breads

Mexican Cornbread

2 cups self-rising cornmeal
1 egg
Sweet milk
1 (20 ounce) can cream style corn
1 (4 ounce) can green chilies, chopped
2 cups shredded sharp Cheddar cheese
Salt
Garlic salt
1 tablespoon grease (Vegetable oil or bacon grease)

Mix cornmeal, egg, corn, garlic salt and milk to make regular cornbread batter; have skillet with grease hot. Pour in ½ of mixture, cover liberally with cheese and all of green chilies. Add rest of mixture. Cover top with cheese. Bake at 425°F until done. Serves 6 to 8.

Aline Luster

Corn Bread Delicious

1 cup self-rising cornmeal
2 eggs
1 (8 ounce) carton sour cream
½ cup oil
½ cup grated onion

Mix all ingredients and pour into hot, greased skillet. Cook at 400°F until brown. Serves 6 to 8.

Doris Baker

Debbie's Bread

1 large loaf French bread, sliced lengthwise
¾ cup butter
½ cup sliced green onions
2 teaspoons lemon juice
2 tablespoons poppy seed
2 teaspoons Dijon mustard
2 teaspoons seasoned salt
Grated Swiss cheese

Mix all ingredients except cheese and spread on bread. Spread lots of cheese on top. Bake at 350°F until slightly brown, about 15 minutes.

Mrs. Phil Nelson
Jackson, Mississippi

Supporting Roles

Banana Bread - Royale

½ cup shortening
1 cup sugar
2 eggs
1 teaspoon vanilla
1 teaspoon lemon
2 large or 3 medium bananas

2 cups all purpose flour
1 teaspoon baking soda, level
½ teaspoon salt
¼ cup nuts, chopped
Cinnamon and nutmeg may be added

Cream shortening and sugar. Add the mashed bananas. Sift dry ingredients. Add alternately the dry ingredients and unbeaten eggs, 1 at a time. Add flavoring and spices, then nuts. Bake in a greased loaf pan 45 to 60 minutes with oven at 350°F. Yield: 1 loaf.

Mrs. Don L. Glisson (Marcia Ann)

Cranberry Bread

2 cups all purpose flour
1½ teaspoons baking powder
½ teaspoon baking soda
¼ cup orange juice
½ cup chopped pecans
1 banana, mashed

1 cup sugar
1 teaspoon salt
¼ cup shortening
1 egg
1 cup cranberries (coarsely chopped)

Sift together flour, sugar, baking soda, baking powder, and salt. Cut in shortening. Combine egg, orange juice and banana. Add to flour mixture all at once. Mix just enough to moisten. Fold in nuts and cranberries. Spoon into greased loaf pan. Bake 1 hour at 350°F. Makes 1 loaf.

Mrs. Mike Byrnes, III

Breads

Date Nut Bread

1 pound dates, chopped
1 teaspoon baking soda
1½ cups boiling water
2 tablespoons softened butter
1½ cups sugar
2 eggs beaten
¼ teaspoon salt
1 teaspoon vanilla
3½ cups all purpose flour
1 cup chopped walnuts and pecans

Sprinkle baking soda over chopped dates and pour boiling water over all. Stir well and set aside to cool. Cream butter and sugar until light. Add eggs, salt and vanilla and beat well. Add mixture to dates and beat vigorously. Stir in flour, a small amount at a time. Stir in nuts, then spoon batter into 2 greased 8 inch loaf pans. Bake at 300°F for 1 hour. Makes 2 loaves.

Rachel Goddard

Pumpkin Bread

3½ cups sugar
1 cup oil
2 cups of pumpkin (fresh or canned)
4 eggs
3½ cups all purpose flour
2 teaspoons baking soda
1½ teaspoons salt
1 teaspoon each of nutmeg, allspice, cinnamon, and vanilla
1 cup pecans
½ cup raisins (optional)

Blend sugar and oil in a mixing bowl, add the pumpkin and the eggs one at a time. Mix flour, baking soda, salt, nutmeg, cinnamon, allspice and vanilla. Slowly add to other ingredients and continue beating until well mixed. Turn the mixer to slow and add the pecans and raisins. Fill 4 greased 1 pound coffee cans half full or 3 greased loaf pans and bake at 350°F for 1½ hours.

Deborah King

Supporting Roles

Strawberry Bread

3 cups all purpose flour, sifted
1 teaspoon baking soda
1 teaspoon salt
3 teaspoons cinnamon
2 cups sugar

3 eggs, well beaten
2 (10 ounce) packages frozen strawberries, thawed
1¼ cup cooking oil
1¼ cup chopped pecans

Sift dry ingredients together in a large bowl, making a well in center of the mixture. Mix remaining ingredients and pour into well. Stir enough to dampen all ingredients. Pour into 2 greased loaf pans or 1 large tube pan. Bake at 350°F for 1 hour.

Variation: Use 3 cups self-rising flour instead of plain flour, baking soda and salt. Use 4 eggs instead of 3. Proceed as above.

Mrs. Ronnie Jackson (Kay)

Blueberry Bran Muffins

1 cup whole wheat flour
3 teaspoons baking powder
½ teaspoon salt
1 cup bran flakes
⅓ cup sugar

1 egg
3 tablespoons molasses
3 tablespoons oil
1 cup milk
1 cup blueberries

Preheat oven to 425°F. Sift flour, baking powder, salt, and sugar together. Add bran flakes to flour mixture. Beat egg in mixer. Add molasses, oil, and milk to egg and beat until well blended. Add dry ingredients and mix only enough to moisten flour. Fold blueberries in last. Fill greased muffin pans ⅔ full. Bake 16 minutes. Makes 18 muffins. The batter will store in the refrigerator 2 to 3 weeks.

Note: The salt may be omitted entirely which makes this an excellent recipe for a person on a low sodium diet.

Mrs. Rudolph Janzen, Jr. (Donna)

Breads

Buttermilk Orange Muffins

2 cups all purpose flour
¼ teaspoon salt
½ teaspoon baking soda
2 teaspoons baking powder
4 tablespoons unsalted butter

⅓ cup sugar
½ orange peel grated
1 teaspoon vanilla
2 eggs

Sift flour, salt, baking soda and baking powder. Set aside. Cream unsalted butter and sugar until light. Add grated orange peel and vanilla. Beat eggs lightly and combine with buttermilk. Alternately add liquid and dry ingredients to butter mixture and blend well. Put in paper cup or greased muffin tins. Bake in a preheated oven at 375°F for 20 to 25 minutes or until lightly brown on top. Brush immediately with egg white and sprinkle with sugar crystals. Serve warm. Makes 24 small or 12 large muffins.

Mrs. Carl Welch

Wonderful Bran Muffins

2 cups all bran cereal

2 cups boiling water

Combine and set aside.

1 cup shortening
3 cups sugar
4 eggs
1 quart buttermilk

5 cups all purpose flour
5 teaspoons baking soda
1 teaspoon salt
4 cups raisin bran cereal

Cream shortening and sugar, beat in eggs. Add alternately buttermilk, flour, baking soda and salt. Add raisin bran to above and also the mixture that was set aside. Add additional raisins or nuts, if desired. Bake in muffin tins for 15 minutes at 400°F. Store for as long as 4 weeks.

Mrs. Phil Nelson
Jackson, Mississippi

Supporting Roles

Orange Pecan Muffins

1 (3 ounce) package cream cheese
3 cups biscuit mix
½ cup sugar

1 egg, beaten
1¼ cups orange juice
¾ cup chopped pecans

Beat cream cheese until fluffy. Add biscuit mix and sugar. Mix well. Add egg, orange juice and pecans, and stir until all ingredients are moist. Spoon into greased muffin tin. Bake at 350°F for 20 to 25 minutes. Makes 1½ dozen.

Brenda Rogers

Peabody Vanilla Muffins

½ cup margarine or butter, softened
2 cups sugar
4 eggs

4 cups all purpose flour
1 tablespoon baking powder
2 cups milk
2 tablespoons vanilla

Cream margarine and sugar together. Add eggs, one at a time, and beat until well mixed. Add flour, sifted with the baking powder. Mix vanilla into the milk and stir into the flour mixture. Preheat oven to 350°F. Fill tins ¾ full and bake for approximately 30 minutes or until the tops are golden. Makes 36 large muffins.

Variation: To make vanilla nut bread, add 1 cup chopped nuts to muffin mixture. Pour into greased loaf pans and bake about 35 minutes or until "a straw inserted in the center comes out clean". Excellent toasted!

Breads

Martha Hederman's Pumpkin Muffins

3 cups sugar
1 cup salad oil
3 eggs
2 cups canned pumpkin
3 cups all purpose flour
½ teaspoon salt
½ teaspoon baking powder
1 teaspoon vanilla
1 teaspoon cinnamon
1 teaspoon nutmeg
1 teaspoon lemon juice
1 teaspoon baking soda

Mix sugar, oil, and eggs. Add remaining ingredients. Grease and flour regular muffin tins or miniature muffin tins. Fill ½ full. Bake at 350°F for 15 minutes. Mix will keep in refrigerator for 5 days.

Mrs. Barry Cannada (Angelyn)
Jackson, Mississippi

Oatmeal Whole Wheat Muffins

2 cups whole wheat flour
1 cup uncooked oatmeal
4 teaspoons baking powder
½ cup margarine, melted
2 eggs

Mix dry ingredients. Add milk. Break the eggs into the mixture and stir well. (It is not necessary to use mixer or to beat vigorously.) Mix in the melted margarine. Preheat oven to 400°F. Grease the muffin tin and heat it in the oven. Fill muffin tins ¾ full and bake for 15 to 20 minutes. Makes 12 to 15 muffins.

Nancy Smith

Beer Rolls

1 tablespoon sugar
1 (12 ounce) can of beer (not flat)
3 cups biscuit mix

Mix ingredients together. Spoon into oiled muffin tins. Be careful not to fill over half full! Bake 12 to 15 minutes in a preheated 400°F oven. Makes 12 to 15 rolls.

Supporting Roles

Super Muffins

1 cup quick cooking oats, uncooked
¾ cup water
1 cup all purpose flour
¼ cup instant dry milk powder
2 teaspoons baking powder
½ teaspoon salt
½ teaspoon cinnamon
2 egg whites
3 tablespoons brown sugar
2 tablespoons oil
½ cup raisins

Preheat oven to 400°F. Spray twelve 2½ inch muffin pan cups with vegetable cooking spray. Combine oats and water. Combine flour, dry milk, baking powder, salt and cinnamon. In a small bowl beat egg whites, brown sugar and oil. Stir in oats and water. Add to dry ingredients all at once. Fold in raisins. Spoon into prepared pan, filling each cup ¼ full. Bake 12 to 15 minutes. Remove from pan. Cool on wire rack. Can be made ahead and frozen for up to 1 month. Makes 12 muffins.

Etta Mae Vuncannon

Cream Cheese Braids

Dough

1 cup sour cream
½ cup of sugar
1 teaspoon salt
½ cup margarine, melted
2 packages of yeast
½ cup of warm water
2 eggs, beaten
4 cups of all purpose flour

Heat sour cream over low heat until warm. Stir in sugar, salt and melted margarine. Cook stirring, for 3 minutes or so. Cool until mixture is lukewarm. Dissolve yeast in water and add to sour cream mixture. Add beaten egg then slowly add flour. Refrigerate overnight. In the morning, divide dough into 4 equal parts. Roll each into a 12x8 inch rectangle. Spread ¼ filling (recipe follows) on each rectangle and roll up jelly roll fashion. Pinch edges together and fold ends under. Place each roll seam side down on a greased cookie sheet. Slit each roll at 2 inch intervals, about ⅔ way through dough. Cover and let rise 1 hour. Bake at 350°F for 12 to 15 minutes. When done add glaze.

Breads

Filling

2 (8 ounce) packages cream cheese, softened
¾ cup sugar
1 egg, beaten
⅛ teaspoon salt
2 teaspoons vanilla

Mix cream cheese and sugar together. Add beaten egg, salt and vanilla.

Glaze

2 cups powdered sugar
4 tablespoons milk
2 teaspoons vanilla

Mix together. Yield 4 loaves.

Mary Hedges

One Hour Buttermilk Twists

2 packages dry yeast
¼ cup warm water
1½ cups lukewarm buttermilk
¼ cup sugar
½ cup melted shortening
1 teaspoon salt
4½ cups sifted all purpose flour
½ teaspoon baking soda
Coarse salt or poppy seeds to sprinkle on top

Dissolve yeast in the warm water. Add buttermilk, sugar, shortening and salt. Sift the flour and baking soda together (do not remeasure) and mix well. Let stand 10 minutes. Roll out with a rolling pin and cut into 1 inch wide and 5 inch long strips. The dough should be rolled as for biscuits—about ¼ inch thick. Gently take one strip and twist it in one direction. Place on an ungreased cookie sheet. Repeat until all the twists are made and placed on the cookie sheet. Place close together, remembering that these rolls will double in bulk. Let rise in a warm place approximately 30 minutes or until double. Gently brush with melted shortening (butter is best). Now sprinkle generously with coarse salt (or poppy seeds) and place on the middle rack of a preheated 400°F oven for about 10 to 12 minutes. Check to be sure that they do not brown too much. Good for buffet serving because they made delicious ham and turkey sandwiches!

For lower sodium—do not use the coarse salt on top. For lower cholesterol use margarine or vegetable oil.

Ms. Stella Carter

Supporting Roles

All Bran Rolls

1 cup all bran cereal
½ cup shortening
¼ cup sugar
1 teaspoon salt
½ cup boiling water
1 egg

1 package yeast
½ cup warm water
2½ cups all purpose flour
1 teaspoon baking powder
¼ teaspoon baking soda

Pour ½ cup boiling water over first four ingredients. Add 1 egg slightly beaten and mix. Add yeast that has been dissolved in ½ cup warm water and mix. Sift 2½ cups flour; add 1 teaspoon baking powder and ¼ teaspoon baking soda and mix well. Let rise until double in bulk, about 1 hour. Punch down and roll into rolls or cover and put in refrigerator. If refrigerated, use within 3 days. Bake at 450°F in preheated oven for 15 to 18 minutes. Makes 2½ dozen. These rolls freeze well.

Estelle Vines
Jackson, Tennessee

Ella Mae's Rolls

2 cups milk
½ cup shortening
½ cup sugar
1 package yeast
¼ cup water

4 cups all purpose flour
1 teaspoon baking powder
½ teaspoon baking soda
1 teaspoon salt

Heat milk and shortening until shortening melts. Add sugar while mixture is warm. Cool to room temperature. Dissolve yeast in water. Add to milk mixture. Add 1½ cups flour to mixture. Beat until like pancake mix. Add more flour if necessary. Cover and let rise in a warm place until doubled, approximately 1 hour. Add 2 cups flour, baking powder, baking soda and salt. Roll out on a floured board, cut and place on greased pan. Bake at 450°F until light golden in color. Dough can be refrigerated, just allow extra time for rolls to rise before baking.

Rita Strachan

Breads

"Pullit" Coffee Cake

3 (10 count) cans biscuits
½ cup brown sugar
½ cup white sugar
2 tablespoons cinnamon

1 stick margarine, melted
1 cup chopped pecans and/or raisins, optional

Quarter each biscuit. Mix brown sugar, white sugar and cinnamon together. Roll each piece of biscuit in the sugar mixture. Drop in a greased bundt pan. Pour the melted margarine over the top. Bake at 350°F for 40 minutes. (You may add chopped pecans, and/or raisins between the layers.)

Tootsie Dalton

Basic Sweet Dough

1 cup milk
1 envelope dry yeast
2 eggs
1 teaspoon salt

¼ cup sugar
¼ cup shortening
4 cups all purpose flour

Scald milk and cool to lukewarm. Dissolve yeast in lukewarm milk. Slightly beat eggs. Combine milk-yeast mixture, beaten eggs, salt, sugar, shortening, and flour. Turn out on floured board and knead until dough is smooth and satiny. Place dough in greased bowl and let rise until double in size. Punch down, cover and let rest 5 to 10 minutes. Shape into rolls or rings and let rise until light. Bake in 425°F oven 15 to 20 minutes. Serves 12.

Note: This dough is used in the Coconut-Date-Nut Ring recipe which follows.

Mrs. Rudolph Janzen, Jr. (Donna)

Supporting Roles

Coconut-Date-Nut Ring

1 cup chopped dates
Dash of salt
⅓ cup boiling water
¼ cup sugar
1 tablespoon lemon juice
¾ cup coconut

½ cup chopped walnuts or pecans
1 recipe Sweet Dough
½ cup powdered sugar
3 to 4 tablespoons milk
Coconut

Combine dates, salt, water, and sugar. Cook over low heat 8 minutes, stirring constantly. Add lemon juice, coconut and nuts. Have Sweet Dough rolled into a rectangle 12x18 inches. Spread with filling and roll as for a jelly roll, wetting edges to seal. Place on a greased baking sheet, bringing ends together to form a ring. With scissors cut 1 inch slices almost through the ring. Turn each piece on its side. Cover with a dry towel and let rise in a warm place until light. Bake at 375°F for 25 minutes or until done. While still warm, brush top with glaze made from the powdered sugar and milk. Sprinkle additional coconut over top.

Mrs. Rudolph Janzen, Jr. (Donna)

Basic Waffles

2 cups all purpose flour
3 teaspoons baking powder
1 teaspoon salt

2 eggs
1½ to 1¾ cups milk
6 tablespoons vegetable oil

Sift dry ingredients and set aside. Separate whites from yolks of the eggs, beating yolks in mixing bowl. After yolks are well beaten continue to beat and add the milk, then add the dry ingredients and beat until smooth. Add vegetable oil and beat. Beat whites of eggs stiff in a separate bowl and fold into the milk mixture. Follow your waffle maker instructions. Serves 4.

Janice Wilcox Grady

Finale

FINALE

You've planned your show: A dinner party for eight. The cast has been chosen: A four-course menu, within a minimum of serving. The stage is set: All of the preliminary preparations have been made.

But what's for dessert? You still can't decide. Finales can be as versatile as Overtures. They can bring the whole cast back on stage for one last glorious number, or they can whisper away to nothing on a breath of song.

It all depends on the mood of the show. If your piece de resistance was the main entree, you may choose to finish off with fruit and cheese, or even coffee and mints in the livingroom. But if desserts are your strong point, then finish the evening with a bang. After all, who would ever turn down Baked Alaska or Cherries Jubilee?

NUTCRACKER SWEETS
(A CHRISTMAS COOKIE PARTY FOR CHILDREN)

Almond Fingers

Butter Tarts

Iced Caramel Brownies

Chewy Chocolate Cookies

Chocolate Drop Cookies

Cinnamon Sticks

Orange Slice Cookies

Sugar Cookies

Punch - p.89-90

Note: The perfect centerpiece for this party would be a homemade gingerbread house. Invite children to dress up in their Christmas finery to add a grown-up feeling to this special party. Use silver trays to serve cookies and fill crystal or silver bowls with small candies.

Finale

Almond Fingers

1 cup butter, softened (no substitute)
½ cup powdered sugar
1½ cups sifted all purpose flour
Pinch of salt
1 teaspoon almond extract
2 cups chopped toasted almonds
1 cup powdered sugar

In a large bowl with the electric mixer cream together the butter and sugar. Add flour with salt and blend well, then mix in the almond extract. Stir in the almonds. Chill about an hour for easier handling. To bake take a teaspoon of mixture and roll between palms of hands into a cylinder about ½ inch thick. Place on ungreased cookie sheet. Bake at 325°F for 20 minutes. Remove onto a flat pan which has been covered with sifted powdered sugar. Sift more powdered sugar over the cookies. Store in an air-tight container with layers of wax paper between. Makes 6 dozen.

Note: These freeze well.

Mrs. Barbara Wayne

Butter Tarts

Pastry for 2 crusts or 24 small tarts
½ cup butter, softened
1 cup sugar
2 eggs
1 cup currants

Heat oven to 400°F. Line 2 small tart pans (12 holes each) with pastry. Make sure pastry for one shell does not touch pastry lining other shells so the tarts can be easily removed after baking. Cream butter in mixing bowl. Gradually add sugar, beating until light and fluffy. Add eggs one at a time, beating after each addition. Fold in currants last. Fill tart shells ¾ full. Bake at 400°F for 25 minutes or until top of filling browns slightly. Makes 24 tarts.

Ruth Malone
Camden, Arkansas

Menus

Caramel Brownies And Icing

Brownies

½ cup butter
2 cups brown sugar, packed
2 eggs
1¾ cups flour

2 teaspoons baking powder
½ teaspoon salt
2 tablespoons vanilla
1 cup chopped pecans

Cream butter, brown sugar and eggs. Sift dry ingredients together and add to creamed mixture. Add vanilla and pecans. Pour in greased 8x8 inch baking pan. Bake 25 to 30 minutes at 350°F. Makes 16 to 24 servings.

Icing

2 cups sugar
1 stick butter

1 egg
½ cup milk

Heat 1½ cups sugar with egg, butter and milk and set aside. Caramelize ½ cup sugar and add to milk mixture. Cook to soft ball stage. Add 1 teaspoon vanilla and beat. Pour over cooked brownies.

Mrs. Mike Manning
Drew, Mississippi

Cinnamon Sticks

1 cup butter or margarine
1 cup sugar
2 cups flour
1 egg yolk
½ teaspoon cinnamon

½ teaspoon vanilla
Pinch of salt
1 egg white
1 teaspoon water
¾ cup nuts, finely chopped

In a large mixing bowl cream the butter and 1 cup sugar until light and creamy. Add slightly beaten egg yolk. Add the dry ingredients and mix well. Dough will be stiff. Flatten dough out on cookie sheet. In a small bowl beat egg white with 1 teaspoon water. Brush this over the flattened dough. Cover with chopped nuts. Bake in preheated 300°F oven for 30 minutes. Mark and cut in squares or sticks and remove from pan while warm.

Finale

Chewy Chocolate Cookies

1¼ cups butter or margarine, softened
2 cups sugar
2 eggs
2 teaspoons vanilla
2 cups unsifted flour

¾ cup cocoa
1 teaspoon baking soda
½ teaspoon salt
1 cup chopped walnuts or pecans

Cream butter or margarine and sugar in large mixing bowl. Add eggs and vanilla; blend well. Combine flour, cocoa, baking soda, and salt; blend into creamed mixture. Stir in nuts. Drop by teaspoonfuls onto ungreased baking sheet. Bake at 350°F for 8 to 9 minutes. Cool on cookie sheet until set, about 1 minute. Remove to wire rack to cool completely. Makes 4 to 5 dozen.

Mrs. Charles McDonald (Donna)

Orange Slice Cookies

1 cup chopped nuts
1 pound orange slice candy (chopped)
2 cups brown sugar, packed
½ cup butter

3 eggs
2 cups flour
2 teaspoons baking powder
1 (16 ounce) box powdered sugar

Chop candy and nuts and roll in flour to coat. Set aside. Cream sugar and butter. Add eggs. Sift flour and baking powder together and add to mixture. Then add nuts and orange slices that have been rolled in flour. Bake in 9x13x2 inch pan lined with waxed paper for 45 minutes in a 325°F oven. Cool slightly and cut into strips 3 inches long and 1½ inches wide. Remove from pan and roll in powdered sugar. Makes 2 dozen.

Mrs. Leo R. Norman

Menus

Chocolate Drop Cookies

⅔ cup brown sugar, packed
½ cup vegetable shortening
1 egg
1¾ cups all purpose flour
½ teaspoon baking soda
1 teaspoon vanilla
¼ teaspoon salt
½ cup pecans, chopped
2 squares unsweetened dark chocolate
½ cup milk

Cream shortening and sugar. Add egg and beat well. Melt chocolate squares and add to batter. Sift flour, baking soda, and salt. Stir flour and milk alternately into batter. Add chopped pecans. Drop cookie dough 1 teaspoon at a time, about 1 inch apart, on greased cookie sheet. Bake at 350°F for 10 minutes. Set aside to cool. When cool, frost with icing, recipe follows.

Butter "the size of a walnut" (about 2 tablespoons)
1 square unsweetened chocolate
1 cup powdered sugar
2 tablespoons heated milk

Melt butter and chocolate in top of double boiler, over hot water. Add powdered sugar and blend. Gradually add the milk until of spreading consistency. Spread on cookies.

Mrs. Mike Byrnes, III

Sugar Cookies

1 cup vegetable shortening
1 cup sugar
2 eggs
1 teaspoon vanilla
2¾ cups plain flour
¾ teaspoon salt
½ teaspoon baking soda
½ teaspoon baking powder

Cream shortening and sugar. Beat in eggs and vanilla. Gradually blend in dry ingredients which have been sifted together. Chill dough at least 3 hours. Roll ⅛ to ¼ inch thickness on a lightly floured pastry canvas. Cut cookies with floured cookie cutters. Bake on ungreased aluminum cookie sheet at 375°F for 8 to 10 minutes. Makes 2½ dozen.

Ms. Loraine Wammack

Finale

SEASON FINALE DESSERT BUFFET

Dessert Crepes
or
Dessert Waffles

Four Layer Mocha Dessert

Date Nut Roll with Whipped Cream

Lemon Tarts

Cookie Plate:
Mexican Wedding Cakes   *Lace Cookies*
Pecan Pie Squares

Champagne Punch - p.83
or
Henry's Celebration Punch - p.85

Menus

Dessert Crepes

3 eggs, separated
¼ teaspoon vanilla
3 tablespoons melted butter or margarine

½ cup all purpose flour
¼ cup sugar
½ cup milk

In a small mixer bowl, beat the 3 egg yolks with the vanilla and butter. Stir together the flour and sugar. Add dry mixture to liquid mixture alternately with the milk, beating well after each addition. In a large mixer bowl, beat 3 egg whites until they form stiff peaks. Gently fold the batter mixture into the beaten egg whites. Brush a 6 inch skillet or crepe pan lightly with vegetable oil. When hot, spoon a rounded tablespoon of batter into pan. Using back of spoon spread into a 4 inch circle. Brown lightly and flip to other side for just a few seconds. Cool on paper towels or waxed paper. Makes 24 crepes.

Suggested Filling

1 cup whipping cream
¼ cup sugar

1 cup sour cream

Whip cream and sugar until soft peaks form. Fold in sour cream. Spoon about 2 tablespoons of mixture on unbrowned side of crepe and roll into a cone shape.

Topping

1 cup sugar, scant
1 tablespoon flour, rounded
5 teaspoons cocoa, rounded
1 egg yolk

1 cup of milk
Dash of salt
2 tablespoons margarine
1 teaspoon vanilla

Mix all ingredients, except margarine and vanilla, in a saucepan. Cook over medium heat until thickened, stirring constantly. Remove from heat and as the sauce cools stir in the margarine and vanilla.

Note: This is also a good filling for tart shells and served with a whipped topping.

Janice Wilcox Grady

Finale

Dessert Waffles - Made With Timbale Iron

1½ cups sifted flour
2 teaspoons sugar
1 cup milk
2 eggs
¼ teaspoon salt
Salad oil for frying (sufficient to easily cover top of the waffle iron)

Sift flour, sugar, and salt together. Beat eggs slightly and add milk. Pour liquid mixture into the dry ingredients and mix well. Beat or put in blender and blend until smooth. Heat oil to 365°F (or until a cube of bread will brown in 60 seconds). An electric skillet is recommended for oil at an even temperature. Dip the iron into the hot oil and allow it to remain about 30 seconds. Remove, drain by tapping lightly on a folded paper towel. Dip quickly in the batter absolutely to the top and place in the hot oil. When "set" loosen from the iron with a cooking fork. Re-dip iron in batter and quickly put in the hot oil. By loosening the waffles from the iron before they are done and lightly brown, you can process about 4 at a time. You may turn them over to further insure crispness. Drain the waffles in a single layer on paper towels. Can be made ahead and stored in an air-tight container and sprinkled with powdered sugar, cinnamon sugar, or decorated with whipped cream, ice cream or any dessert delicacy. Makes about 55.

Variation: Omit the sugar and use as the base for creamed shellfish, ham, chicken or hot fruit.

Ms. Mallie Norwood

"Exercise is the most awful illusion. The secret is a lot of aspirin and marrons glaces.", Noel Coward, English playwright and actor.

Menus

Four Layer Mocha Dessert

½ cup sugar
2 tablespoons cornstarch
1 envelope unflavored gelatin
2 cups milk
3 eggs, separated
¼ cup sugar
½ cup whipping cream

1 tablespoon instant coffee granules
2 squares unsweetened chocolate
1½ cups crushed chocolate cookies
3 tablespoons melted butter

In saucepan, combine ½ cup sugar, cornstarch, and gelatin. Add milk. Cook and stir until bubbly. Stir 1 cup of mixture into 3 beaten egg yolks and return to pan. Cook and stir until mixture bubbles. Remove from heat. Cover surface with plastic wrap. Cool to room temperature. Beat 3 egg whites to soft peaks. Gradually add ¼ cup sugar, beating to stiff peaks. Whip ½ cup whipping cream. Fold whites and cream into milk mixture. Combine 1½ cups cream mixture with 1 tablespoon coffee granules. Let stand 5 minutes; stir. Add 2 squares chocolate, melted and cooled, into remaining mixture. Combine crushed cookies and melted butter. Reserve ¼ cup crumbs; press remainder into 10x6x2 inch dish. Top with half of chocolate mixture, then coffee mixture, and remaining chocolate mixture. Top with reserved crumbs. Chill several hours.

Mrs. Charles McDonald (Donna)

Date Nut Roll

16 graham crackers
1 cup dates (seeded and cut fine)
1 cup miniature marshmallows

1 cup nut meats, broken
3 tablespoons cream
1 teaspoon vanilla

Roll crackers into fine crumbs, reserve 2 tablespoons for coating the roll. Combine crumbs, dates, marshmallows and nuts. Blend with cream, add vanilla and shape into roll. (This has to be done with your hands.) Coat with cracker crumbs and place in refrigerator for 3 or 4 hours. Serve in slices topped with whipped cream. Serves 8 for dessert.

Note: Rolled into 2 smaller rolls, this will make 20 or more bitesize desserts for a dessert buffet.

Finale

Lemon Tarts

Pastry

1 cup sifted flour
½ cup butter or margarine

2 tablespoons sugar
2 tablespoons milk

Cut or work butter into flour and sugar, stir in milk. Pat small amounts in your smallest muffin tins. Cool in refrigerator while you make the filling.

Lemon Filling

½ cup plus 2 tablespoons sugar
1 tablespoon butter or margarine, melted
1 egg beaten

1 cold cooked medium potato grated
1 tablespoon lemon juice and a little grated rind

Mix all ingredients together thoroughly and fill tarts. Bake in 300°F oven for 8 minutes, raise heat to 375°F and bake a few minutes longer until slightly brown. Don't worry if the potato is slightly lumpy, they turn out fine.

Mrs. T. Y. Williford, Jr.
Greenville, Mississippi

Lace Cookies

¼ cup light corn syrup
¼ cup brown sugar, packed
¼ cup margarine

½ cup flour
½ cup chopped pecans
½ teaspoon vanilla

Line cookie sheets with aluminum foil. Cook syrup, sugar, and margarine until boiling. Remove from heat. Stir in flour, vanilla, and nuts. Drop by teaspoon about 1 inch apart (mixture will be thin and spread). Bake 10 to 15 minutes at 325°F. Cool thoroughly. Peel off foil. Makes 2 dozen.

Mrs. Dorothy Griffith

Menus

Mexican Wedding Cakes

1 cup margarine
2 cups all purpose flour
½ cup powdered sugar

1 cup chopped pecans
1 teaspoon vanilla
Pinch of salt

Preheat oven 350°F. Mix all ingredients except powdered sugar. Roll into small balls. Place on lightly greased cookie sheet ½ inch apart. Bake 12 minutes or until golden brown. Cool slightly and roll in powdered sugar. Makes 4 dozen.

Ms. Permelia Franklin Wallace
Jackson, Tennessee

Pecan Pie Squares

1 package yellow cake mix
   (18.5 ounces)
4 eggs
½ cup melted margarine

1 cup pecans
½ cup brown sugar, packed
1½ cups dark corn syrup
1 teaspoon vanilla

Reserve ⅔ cup cake mix. Mix 1 egg, margarine, and rest of cake mix together well and spread in greased, floured 13x9x2 inch pan. Bake at 350°F for 15 minutes. Mix other ingredients together and pour onto first layer. Bake 30 minutes at 350°F. Cool completely before cutting into squares or bars. Makes 24 large or 48 small squares.

Rosemary Fisher

Finale

TEA FOR (MORE THAN) TWO

Cucumber Sandwiches - p.136

Cheese Angels - p.134

Shortbread

Oatmeal Biscuits

Lady Baltimore Cake

Five Flavor Pound Cake

Chocolate Covered Strawberries

Tea

Menus

Shortbread

2 cups all purpose flour
1 cup unsalted butter, softened
½ cup confectioners' sugar

Dash salt
¼ teaspoon baking powder

Combine all ingredients in a large mixing bowl. Beat with mixer until well blended. Remove dough from bowl and put dough into 9 inch baking pan. Bake in 350°F oven for 30 minutes. Makes 2 dozen.

Lady Baltimore Cake

1 cup margarine
2 cups sugar
8 eggs, separated
3 cups flour

3 teaspoons baking powder
1¼ cups milk
½ teaspoon salt
1 teaspoon vanilla extract

Filling For Cake

1 cup margarine
2 cups sugar
8 egg yolks
Juice of one lemon

2 cups grated coconut
2 cups nuts, chopped
1 pound raisins

Beat egg whites until stiff, then add ½ cup sugar gradually beating after each addition. Cream the margarine, then add remaining sugar and beat until fluffy. Sift flour 3 times with baking powder and salt. Add to butter mixture alternately with milk. Beat until smooth. Fold in beaten egg whites. Bake in two 9x9 inch pans that have been greased; bake in 325°F oven for 35 minutes.

Filling

Cream margarine, add sugar, then egg yolks one at a time. Add lemon juice. Cook in double boiler until thick. Pour this mixture over coconut, nuts, and raisins. Mix well and spread over the cake. Layers may be stacked or iced as two cakes. Makes 32 slices or squares.

Helen M. Moore

Finale

Five Flavor Pound Cake

1 cup margarine
½ cup vegetable shortening
3 cups sugar
5 eggs, beaten
3 cups all purpose flour

1 teaspoon baking powder
1 cup milk
1 teaspoon each of vanilla, lemon, rum, coconut, and butter flavorings

Cream margarine, shortening, and sugar. Add eggs one at a time. Sift baking powder with flour and add flour and milk alternately to creamed mixture; add flavorings. Bake in a greased and floured tube pan for 1½ hours at 300°F.

Glaze

1 cup sugar
½ cup water

1 teaspoon of each of the 5 flavorings

Combine in heavy saucepan. Bring to a boil and stir until sugar is melted. Pour over hot cake in pan. Let sit until cake is cool.

Mrs. Charles Ellington (Sara)

Chinese Almond Cakes (Hang-Yen-Bang)

¾ cup butter, softed
¾ cup granulated sugar
1 egg
2 tablespoons water
1 teaspoon almond extract

2½ cups sifted flour
¼ teaspoon salt
1 teaspoon baking powder
1 egg yolk mixed with 1 tablespoon water

Blend well in mixing bowl the butter, sugar, egg, water, and almond extract. Gradually add flour, salt, and baking powder and blend. Knead into a ball and chill 1 hour or until firm. Roll into 1 inch balls and flatten them on a greased cookie sheet. Place almond on each. With fingers brush each cookie with the egg-water mixture that has been beaten together. Bake at 350°F for 25 minutes. Makes about 3 dozen.

Mrs. Travis M. Nelson (Fae)

Menus

Oatmeal Biscuits

1 cup of margarine
1 cup brown sugar, packed
1 cup white sugar
2 eggs
1½ cups flour, sifted
1 teaspoon salt

1 teaspoon baking soda and dash of cinnamon
1 teaspoon vanilla
3 cups oatmeal
1 cup chopped pecans
½ cup raisins

Cream margarine and sugars together. Add eggs and beat until fluffy. Sift flour, salt, baking soda, and cinnamon together and add to mixture slowly. Add vanilla, nuts and oatmeal and mix well. Drop by the teaspoonful on greased cookie sheet. Bake at 350°F for 10 to 15 minutes. Makes about 4 dozen.

Note: These oatmeal biscuits are, in American terms, chewy oatmeal cookies.

Mrs. Mary W. Bushey

Butter Cookies

4 hard-cooked egg yolks
3 uncooked egg yolks
2 cups sweet butter
4 cups sifted flour
¾ cup sugar

½ teaspoon salt
1 grated lemon rind
2 teaspoons lemon juice
½ teaspoon vanilla

Cream the butter and sugar. Beat well. Add the raw egg yolks and the sieved cooked egg yolks, blending well. Add the dry ingredients sifted together and add the flavoring. Chill. Make small balls and press down. Place pecan half on top or ½ of a red or green cherry. Bake at 350°F for 10 to 15 minutes. Makes 3 dozen.

Mrs. Mary Davis

Finale

Chocolate Covered Strawberries

12 ounces semi-sweet chocolate chips

1 tablespoon corn oil
1 quart large, firm strawberries

Melt the chocolate in the top of a double boiler. Add the oil. Dip the cleaned strawberries in the chocolate. Place them on a cookie sheet lined with waxed paper. Chill. Serves 16.

Tea

A properly brewed pot of tea starts with cold tap water. While the water is coming to a full boil, preheat the teapot by filling it with hot water and letting it stand a few minutes. Now empty the teapot, add your tea bags or loose tea and pour in the boiling water. Cover the teapot and let it brew for five minutes. Remove the teabags or leaves and you are ready to serve.

"Spoil the child, spare the rod, open up the caviar and say, Thank God!", Noel Coward, English playwright and actor.

Cookies

Oatmeal, Orange Slice Cookies

1 cup sugar
1 cup brown sugar, packed
1 cup shortening
2 eggs
1 teaspoon vanilla extract
2 cups all purpose flour
1 teaspoon baking powder
1 teaspoon baking soda
½ teaspoon salt
2 cups oats, uncooked
2 cups orange slice candy, chopped
1 cup coconut, shredded
1 cup nuts, chopped

Cream sugar, brown sugar, shortening, eggs, and vanilla. Add flour, baking powder, baking soda, salt, oats, orange slice candy, coconut, and nuts. Mix well. Roll in small balls and bake at 350°F for 10 minutes. Makes 6 dozen.

Mrs. Louise Clifton

Chocolate Chip Cookies

⅔ cup soft shortening
⅔ cup soft butter
1 cup granulated sugar
1 cup brown sugar, packed
2 eggs
2 teaspoons vanilla
3 cups plain flour
1 teaspoon baking soda
½ teaspoon salt
12 ounce semi-sweet chocolate chips

Cream together shortening, butter, and sugars. Add eggs and vanilla. Sift dry ingredients together and add to creamed ingredients. Stir in chocolate chip pieces. Drop rounded teaspoonful about 2 inches apart on ungreased baking sheet. Bake until delicately browned...cookies should still be soft. Cool slightly before removing from baking sheet. Bake at 350°F for 8 to 10 minutes. Makes 4 to 5 dozen.

Ms. Missy King
Glen, Mississippi

Finale

Chocolate Nut Fingers

2 cups flour
2 tablespoons cocoa
½ cup butter or margarine
3 tablespoons sugar

1 egg, separated
½ teaspoon vanilla
½ cup chopped nuts
¾ cup powdered sugar

Mix together flour, cocoa, and butter. Add sugar, egg yolk and vanilla. Knead dough until it forms one piece. Press into a rectangular cake pan. Mix half the nuts with slightly beaten egg whites and powdered sugar. Spread this over the dough and sprinkle with remaining nuts. Bake in a 375°F oven about 40 minutes. Cool and cut into small strips. Makes approximately 24.

Ms. Judy Martin

Glazed Softies
(Cookies - optional sugarless)

1⅔ cups mashed ripe bananas (about 3 large bananas)
¾ cup margarine, softened
½ cup orange juice
2 eggs
2 teaspoons vanilla
1 teaspoon grated orange peel

2 cups oats (quick or old-fashioned, uncooked)
2 cups all purpose flour
¾ teaspoon baking soda
½ teaspoon salt
½ teaspoon nutmeg
¾ cup raisins (optional)

Glaze

¾ cup powdered sugar or ¾ cup powdered fructose

4 to 5 teaspoons orange juice
1 teaspoon grated orange peel

Cookies

Heat oven to 350°F. Combine mashed bananas, margarine, and orange juice, mix and mash together. In cup mix eggs, vanilla, and orange peel and add to banana mixture, stirring well. In separate bowl combine oats, flour, baking soda, salt, nutmeg, and raisins. Add dry ingredients to banana mixture, mixing thoroughly. Drop by rounded tablespoon onto ungreased cookie sheet. Bake 20 to 22 minutes or until golden brown on bottom of cookie. Cool 1 minute on cookie sheet. Remove to wire cooling rack. Combine powdered sugar, orange juice and peel; drizzle over cookies. Store in tightly covered container. Makes 2½ dozen. (Two or three are almost a breakfast for that finicky youngster who won't eat.)

Ms. Kathleen A. Masters

Lemon Melting Moments (cookies)

1 cup margarine
⅓ cup powdered sugar
1¼ cups flour

½ cup cornstarch
1 teaspoon vanilla

Cream sugar and margarine. Add all other ingredients and mix well. Drop by teaspoon onto an ungreased cookie sheet. Bake for 10 to 12 minutes at 350°F. These cookies should not brown on top.

Icing

¼ cup margarine, melted
1½ cups powdered sugar

2 tablespoons fresh lemon juice
½ teaspoon grated lemon rind

Mix ingredients and pour icing over each cookie. Let set for 30 minutes. Makes about 3 dozen.

Mrs. W. P. Hodges
Washington County (Greenville), Mississippi

Finale

Hello Dolly's
(Seven Layer Cookies)

½ cup margarine
1 cup graham cracker crumbs
1 cup shredded coconut
1 cup chocolate chips
1 cup chopped pecans

1 cup butterscotch chips (optional)
1 (14 ounce) can sweetened condensed milk

Place in layers in a 9x9 inch pan. Don't stir. Over this pour the condensed milk. Bake at 350°F for 30 minutes.

Mrs. Bill Avery (Vicki)

Chokolade Goodies

2½ cups sugar
½ cup cocoa
½ cup milk
¼ cup butter
¼ teaspoon salt

1 teaspoon vanilla
2½ cups quick cooking oats, uncooked
½ cup peanut butter

Combine sugar, cocoa, milk, butter and salt in saucepan and boil 2 to 3 minutes and add the vanilla, oats and peanut butter. Mix well, spread it about ½ inch thick on a baking sheet, until cold and hard. Cut into small bars.

Brigitte
Copenhagen, Denmark
via Kolwezi, Zaire

Easy Brownies

1 cup margarine
3 packed cups dark brown sugar
3 eggs (whole)
3 cups self-rising flour

1 package semi-sweet chocolate chips (6 ounce package)
Vanilla
Butter-nut flavoring, to taste

Cookies

Grease pans (9x13 and 8 inch square). Melt 1 cup margarine, remove from heat and cool. Mix and add all ingredients in order given. Bake at 350°F for 20 to 25 minutes. Makes 25 to 30 servings.

Mrs. Don L. Glisson (Marcia Ann)

Bo Diddly Cookies

4 cups butter
4 cups brown, sugar, packed
4 cups white sugar
6 eggs
1 teaspoon vanilla
10 cups flour

4 teaspoons baking soda
1 teaspoon baking powder
1 teaspoon salt
8 cups oats, uncooked
4 cups raisins

Cream butter, sugars, eggs, and vanilla. Mix raisins with dry ingredients and add to creamed mixture. Drop onto greased cookie sheet. Bake at 350°F for 10 minutes. (You may spread cookie mixture on cookie sheet, bake at 350°F for 10 minutes. Remove from oven and cut while hot.) They are better dropped. Makes 225 cookies (this recipe will yield 112, if divided in half).

Mrs. Carl Welch

Dishpan Cookies

1 cup brown sugar, packed
1 cup white sugar
1 cup liquid shortening
2 eggs
1 teaspoon vanilla flavoring

2 cups of plain flour
¾ cup quick oats, uncooked
1 teaspoon baking soda
2 cups of a rice cereal
½ teaspoon salt

Cream together all the above ingredients. Roll into balls the size of a large marble. Bake at 350°F for 8 to 10 minutes. Makes 8 to 10 dozen.

Connie G. Rast

Finale

Skillet Cookies

2 eggs, beaten
¾ cup granulated sugar
½ cup margarine
1 (8 ounce) package dates chopped
1 teaspoon vanilla

⅛ teaspoon salt
2½ cups rice cereal
½ to 1 cup chopped nuts
Coconut, powdered sugar, or chopped nuts for decoration

Beat eggs, add sugar and beat well. Melt margarine and pour over egg mixture and chopped dates. Cook and stir until mixture thickens and turns dark. Boil 3 to 5 minutes. Remove from heat, add vanilla, rice cereal and nuts. Cool. Pour on wet cloth. Make into long roll. Roll in coconut, powdered sugar or nuts. Refrigerate 2 or 3 hours. Slice and serve.

Ruth Cook

Walnut Lace Cups

¼ cup firmly packed brown sugar
2 tablespoons light corn syrup
3 tablespoons unsalted butter

¼ teaspoon salt
¼ cup all purpose flour
¼ cup chopped walnuts

Combine brown sugar, corn syrup, butter and salt and bring to a boil, whisking. Remove from heat, whisk in flour and walnuts and whisk until well combined. Drop on buttered baking sheets, 1 tablespoon to a mound. Place 6 inches apart. Bake in the middle of a preheated 350°F oven 8 to 10 minutes. Let cool on baking sheet 3 minutes or until set. Lift from cookie sheet with spatula and drape over inverted custard cups. Let cool on cups. Store in air-tight container. To serve fill cups with ice cream. Serves 8.

Helen Moore

Desserts

Dessert Tip

Make a special topping for fresh fruit by combining 1 cup of sour cream with ¼ cup confectioners sugar and 1 teaspoon vanilla. Cover and chill for 2 hours. Try this on strawberries, green grapes, cantelopes and sliced bananas.

Hot Fudge Sundae Dessert

1 (12 ounce) package vanilla wafers, crushed
½ cup finely chopped pecans
¾ cup butter or margarine, melted
½ gallon vanilla ice cream, softened
Chocolate sauce (recipe follows)

Combine vanilla wafer crumbs, pecans, and butter, mixing well. Press half of crumb mixture into a 13x9x2 inch dish. Spread ice cream evenly over crust. Press remaining crumb mixture over ice cream. Cover and freeze until firm. To serve, cut into squares and top each serving with chocolate sauce.

Chocolate Sauce

1 cup sugar
3 tablespoons all purpose flour
¼ cup plus 1 tablespoon cocoa
1 cup milk
2 tablespoons butter or margarine
1 teaspoon vanilla extract

Combine first 4 ingredients in a medium saucepan. Cook over medium heat until slightly thickened, stirring constantly. Remove from heat, and stir in butter and vanilla. Makes about 2 cups. Serves 15.

Alyce W. Richardson
Cleveland, Mississippi

Finale

Easy Chocolate Ice Cream

½ gallon chocolate milk
1 (12 ounce) large carton
  non-dairy topping

1 (14 ounce) can sweetened
  condensed milk

Blend ingredients together and pour into ice cream freezer. Will soft freeze.

Cindi Irwin
Blue Mountain, Mississippi

Frozen Lemon Delight

2 cups vanilla wafers, crushed
1¼ cups sugar
½ stick butter, melted
3 eggs, separated

2 large lemons
1 (14½ ounce) can evaporated
  milk, chilled
1 tablespoon water

Combine vanilla wafers, ¼ cup sugar and butter. Press into freezing pans. Beat egg yolks and add to remaining sugar and water and dissolve on low heat, stirring constantly, about 5 minutes. Set aside to cool. Beat egg whites until stiff. Whip milk and combine with egg whites. When sugar and yolks are cool, fold gently into milk mixture. Add juice of 2 lemons; pour over crust and freeze.

Mrs. John Howard Beall
Lexington, Mississippi

Grape Ice Cream

1 can crushed pineapple (13 ounce)
16 ounces grape juice

3 cups sugar
Juice of 4 lemons
½ pint cream (whipped)

Desserts

Mix all ingredients except cream. Let mixture stand in refrigerator overnight. The next day, put mixture in ice cream freezer and fold in whipped cream. Fill rest of freezer container with milk and freeze.

Nancy N. McLemore

Mocha Ice Cream Dessert

¾ cup crushed vanilla wafers
2 squares unsweetened chocolate
⅔ cup butter
2 cup powdered sugar, sifted
1 cup chopped pecans
1 teaspoon vanilla
2 tablespoons water
2 egg whites, stiffly beaten
½ gallon premium coffee ice cream

Spread crumbs on bottom of a buttered 9x13 inch pyrex dish. Melt chocolate and butter together; cool and stir in sugar, pecans, vanilla, and water. Fold in egg whites. Spread mixture over crumbs. Freeze 2 hours. Soften ice cream and spread on top. Refreeze. To serve, top with hot fudge sauce and crushed heath bars.

Hot Fudge Sauce

1¼ cups sugar
½ cup unsalted butter
½ cup unsweetened cocoa powder
3 ounces unsweetened chocolate
Pinch of salt
1 cup whipping cream
2 teaspoons vanilla

Combine sugar, butter, cocoa, chocolate and salt in heavy small pan over low heat until melted. Slowly add cream, beating until smooth. Blend in vanilla. Can be made ahead. Serves 15.

Note: Can substitute butter pecan, peppermint or chocolate mint ice cream.

Mrs. Barry Cannada (Angelyn)
Jackson, Mississippi

Finale

Lemon Cream Sherbet

1 cup sugar
2 cups milk
Juice of 2 lemons
Grated rind of 1 lemon

2 egg whites
2 tablespoons sugar
½ pint heavy cream

Add sugar to milk and allow to dissolve. When thoroughly dissolved, add lemon juice and rind, stirring while adding lemon juice. Turn into freezing tray and freeze 45 minutes to 1 hour or until mushy. Beat egg whites, adding the 2 tablespoons sugar. Whip the cream to a thick custard consistency. Combine cream and egg whites. Fold lightly into frozen mixture. Return to freezer tray and freeze until hard. Serve garnished with sprigs of mint. Serves 6.

Nancy Smith

Apricot Sherbet

3 oranges
3 lemons
Small can of apricots

1 to 2 cups sugar
1 envelope unflavored gelatin
1 pint whipping cream

Combine juice of oranges and lemons. Drain and mash apricots and add to juice. Add sugar and stir until dissolved. Amount of sugar depends on sweetness of fruit and taste. Add it gradually, tasting to obtain the desired sweetness. Dissolve gelatin in ½ cup boiling water and add to juice mixture. Whip cream and fold into mixture. Pour into freezer container. After it freezes a little, beat well and return to container until frozen.

Blanche W. Beall
Lexington, Mississippi

Desserts

Caramel Bavarian Cream

2 tablespoons unflavored gelatin
½ cup cold water
1½ cups sugar
1 cup boiling water
2 eggs
1 cup milk
2 teaspoons vanilla
1½ cups whipping cream

Soften gelatin in cold water 5 minutes. Heat 1 cup sugar slowly in heavy skillet or pan until browned, stirring constantly. Add boiling water and heat until browned sugar dissolves, stirring constantly. Add gelatin and stir until dissolved. Beat eggs and combine with remaining sugar, milk and vanilla and add browned sugar mixture. Cook over boiling water, stirring constantly, until mixture coats spoon. Chill and when mixture begins to thicken, fold in whipped cream. Turn into a single or individual molds. Serve plain or with caramel sauce. Dessert is very good with whipped cream and a bit of fruit added to a caramel topping. Serves 12.

Mrs. R. M. Brunet

Macaroon Pudding

6 eggs, separated
1 cup sugar
2 cups milk
2 envelopes unflavored gelatin
1 cup chopped nuts
1 (6 ounce) bottle maraschino cherries, drained and chopped
1 pound macaroons
2 jiggers whiskey

Combine yolks of eggs and sugar. Add milk and cook in a double boiler until thickened like custard. Dissolve gelatin in cold water and add to hot custard. Cook about 5 minutes, stirring constantly. Add nuts, whiskey, cherries and crushed macaroons. Beat egg whites until stiff and gently stir into mixture. Serve well chilled and topped with whipped cream and a cherry. Serves 14.

Mrs. George S. Beall
Lexington, Mississippi

Finale

Pineapple Ozark Pudding

1 cup margarine
2 cups powdered sugar
6 eggs, separated
1 (16 ounce) can crushed pineapple, drained
1 cup pecans
1 (12 ounce) box vanilla wafers, crushed
1 (8 ounce) carton frozen whipped non-dairy topping

Melt margarine and add powdered sugar. Beat egg yolks and add to margarine and sugar while margarine is hot. Stir well. Add pineapple and nuts. Beat egg whites until stiff and fold into pineapple mixture. Layer vanilla wafers in 9x13 inch pyrex dish. Top with pineapple mixture. Repeat layers ending with vanilla wafers on top. Spread cool whip on top. Keep in refrigerator.

Louise Clifton

Bread Pudding

3 cups milk
3 eggs
¼ teaspoon salt
½ cup sugar
10 slices day-old bread
½ cup chopped dates
2 tablespoons sugar
1 teaspoon cinnamon

Scald milk. Cool to room temperature. Combine milk, beaten eggs, salt, and sugar. Tear bread into chunks. Add dates to bread. Pour milk mixture over combined bread chunks and dates. Press bread down into liquid. Let stand 10 minutes. Combine sugar and cinnamon. Sprinkle over top of bread mixture. Bake in 350°F oven till knife inserted in center comes out clean. Serves 6.

Mrs. Rudolph Janzen, Jr. (Donna)

Desserts

Cup Custard

6 egg yolks
1 cup sugar
¼ teaspoon nutmeg

¼ teaspoon salt
2 cups milk
1 teaspoon vanilla

Beat egg yolks until lemon-colored; add ½ cup of the sugar, nutmeg and salt. Scald milk and pour slowly into egg mixture, beating well. Stir in vanilla. In small iron skillet, rapidly heat remaining ½ cup sugar, stirring until lightly caramelized. Divide caramelized sugar into 6 individual custard cups. When sugar is cool, pour custard into custard cups; place cups in baking pan containing 1 inch of hot water. Bake in 350°F oven for 40 to 45 minutes. Chill before serving. Unmold upside down on dessert plate. Serves 6.

Mrs. O. B. Wooley, Jr. (Easie Mercier)
Jackson, Mississippi

Sherry-Mint Melon Balls

3 or 4 sprigs fresh mint
⅔ cup sugar
½ cup orange juice
⅓ cup sweet sherry
3 tablespoons lemon juice

Dash of salt
6 servings of melon balls
  (watermelon, honeydew, cantaloupe)

Crush mint and put in saucepan with sugar and orange juice. Bring to a boil, stirring in sugar. Simmer 5 minutes. Add sherry, lemon juice and salt. Chill. At serving time, put chilled melon balls in individual serving dishes (I use small brandy snifters). Pour chilled syrup over melon. Pretty and good. Serves 6.

Mrs. John D. Mercier (Helen)

Finale

Meringue With Fruit

Meringue

10 egg whites, beaten stiffly
3 cups sugar
1 teaspoon cream of tartar

2 teaspoons vanilla
½ teaspoon salt

Other Ingredients

2 cups heavy cream, whipped

8 cups fresh cut-up peaches, strawberries or blueberries

Preheat oven to 450°F. To make meringue, beat egg whites until stiff. Beat sugar gradually into egg whites. Add cream of tartar, vanilla and salt. Spread into greased 9x13 inch pan. Put in oven, turn oven off, and leave for 4 hours. Do not open oven. When meringue has completely baked and cooled, spread whipped cream on top. Refrigerate all day. When ready to serve, top with fresh fruit and cut into squares. Serves 16.

Note: Meringue should be made on a clear day. It can be made well ahead. Normally, I make this in the strawberry season, but those marvelous southern peaches would be delicious, too! Meringues can be the base for many wonderful desserts. Another option is to use ice cream, kiwi, and whipped cream.

Alice Mary Pierce
Portland, Maine

Lemon Cheese

½ cup margarine
1½ cups sugar
Grated rind of 2 lemons

½ cup lemon juice
6 eggs, slightly beaten

Put in top of double boiler over simmering water, stirring constantly until fairly thick. Cool and store in refrigerator. Serve on toast, ice cream, cake or almost anything.

June Cassibry
Cleveland, Mississippi

Desserts

Apple Crisp

½ cup finely chopped walnuts
7/8 cup flour
⅓ cup brown sugar, packed
4 teaspoons granulated sugar
⅛ teaspoon cinnamon
⅓ cup salted butter

3 medium Granny Smith or Winesap apples (peel, core and slice)
⅛ cup granulated sugar
⅛ teaspoon cinnamon

Place chopped walnuts in a small shallow baking dish. Roast walnuts in a 250°F oven for 30 to 45 minutes. After roasting, remove from oven and cool thoroughly. Preheat oven to 375°F. In a small bowl combine flour, brown sugar, granulated sugar, cinnamon, and butter. Mix well. Add cooled walnuts and mix again. Arrange apple slices in an unbuttered shallow baking dish. Sprinkle with remaining sugar and cinnamon. Evenly cover apples with the topping mixture. Bake for 35 to 45 minutes or until apples are tender and topping is crisp.

Karen Lambert

Banana Split Dessert

3 cups vanilla wafer cookies, crushed
½ cup butter, melted
¼ cup sugar
16 ounces cream cheese
1 (16 ounce) box powdered sugar
1 teaspoon vanilla

4 or 5 bananas, sliced in round
Lemon juice to coat bananas
1 (20 ounce) large can crushed pineapple
1 (12 ounce) large carton whipped topping
1 cup crushed pecans
Sliced red cherries

Mix first three ingredients and put in bottom of pan for crust. Combine cream cheese, powdered sugar and vanilla and spread on crust. Distribute bananas on top of cream cheese mixture and cover with pineapple. Spread whipped topping on top. Sprinkle with pecans and garnish with cherries. Refrigerate overnight.

Lisa Golotte
Biloxi, Mississippi

Finale

Rum Babas

1 envelope active dry yeast
½ cup lukewarm water
  (between 105 to 115°F)
1¾ cups sifted flour
3 eggs, beaten (room temperature)
⅓ cup lukewarm milk
½ cup butter, room temperature
½ teaspoon salt
1 tablespoon sugar
2 tablespoons raisins (optional)
Rum syrup
Apricot pureé

Dissolve yeast in warm water. Allow to proof for 10 minutes or until it appears spongy. Put flour into a warm mixing bowl and add dissolved yeast, eggs, and milk. Mix together well. Dough will be soft and more like a batter than a dough. Beat it vigorously until it becomes less sticky and feels springy. Cover bowl and put it in warm place to rise until it doubles in bulk, about 45 minutes. While babas are rising, make apricot pureé. Cream butter until it is very soft. When dough has risen, punch it down and fold in butter, salt, and sugar. Add raisins. When thoroughly combined, divide among 12 well-buttered baba molds, or use popover pans, half filling them. Let rise again in a warm place until dough almost reaches the tops of the molds, about 45 minutes. While babas rise, finish the apricot pureé and start rum glaze. Set the molds on a baking sheet and bake in a preheated 425°F oven for 18 to 20 minutes or until they are nicely brown and have shrunk slightly from the sides of the molds. Before cooled completely, turn them out of molds and place in a deep dish. Prick tops and sides with a skewer. Pour warm rum syrup over cakes and let soak for 1 hour, basting occasionally. Drain babas and brush the apricot glaze over the tops. Move the babas to a serving dish by sliding with two wide spatulas under them. Babas are best eaten the day they are prepared, but will keep in the refrigerator for several days. Optional garnishes: a dollop of whipped cream topped with a strawberry, a wedge of kiwi, toasted almonds, or glacéed cherries.

Rum Syrup

2 cups sugar
2 cups water
½ cup rum or kirsch

Bring sugar and water to a boil and cook briskly for 8 minutes. Add rum. Any syrup which is not used can be stored in a covered jar in the refrigerator.

Cakes

Apricot Pureé

½ pound dried apricots
½ cup sugar

2 tablespoons kirsch or brandy

Cover apricots with cold water and leave them to soak for several hours. Put them, with the water, into a heavy saucepan and simmer until soft, stirring occasionally. (They stick to the pan very easily.) Cool and pureé in the food processor. Rub through a fine sieve, return to the saucepan, and add sugar. Cook, stirring, until mixture is thick enough to hold up when spread on a cake. Add kirsch or brandy. Serves 12.

Mrs. James Y. Palmer (Sheila)
Jackson, Mississippi

Kentucky Cherry Pecan Loaf Cake

2 cups butter or margarine
3 cups sugar
½ teaspoon mace
8 eggs, separated, at room temperature
3 cups sifted all-purpose flour

⅓ cup bourbon (use more if desired)
1 pound red glaced cherries, finely chopped
4 cups pecans, finely chopped

Grease well and flour 2 loaf pans (10x5x3 inch). In a mixing bowl (very large bowl) thoroughly beat the butter with a little more than half of the sugar and the mace until light and fluffy. Gradually and thoroughly beat in the egg yolks. Stir in the flour, (reserving ¼ cup) alternately with the bourbon. Sprinkle remaining ¼ cup flour over the chopped cherries and toss. Stir into the cake batter with the pecans. Beat egg whites until soft peaks form. Gradually beat in remaining sugar and continue beating until very stiff. Fold into cake batter. Turn into prepared pans. Bake at 350°F for 1¼ to 1½ hours (test for doneness with toothpick). Place cakes in pans on wire racks to cool for 1 hour. Turn out. Store in refrigerator. (They slice much easier when cold.) Loafs may be frozen - just wrap in foil and plastic wrap.

Helpful Hint: Cherries are easily chopped with a hand-held pastry (or dough) blender.

Mrs. Robert (Betty A.) Jennings

Finale

Japanese Fruit Cake

Cake Ingredients

2 cups sugar
1 cup vegetable shortening
3 cups flour
3 teaspoons baking powder
Pinch of salt

1½ cups milk
1 teaspoon vanilla
8 egg whites
1 teaspoon cloves
1 teaspoon cinnamon

For cake: Sift flour with baking powder and salt. Cream sugar and shortening. Add flour mixture alternately with milk until both are used. End with flour. Add vanilla and mix well. Beat egg whites until stiff and gently fold into batter. Pour ⅓ of batter in 1 greased and floured 8 inch round pan and ⅓ into another. Mix cinnamon and cloves with remaining ⅓ batter and pour into third prepared pan. Bake at 300°F for 25 to 30 minutes until done.

Filling

Meat of 2 fresh coconuts, ground and divided
2 cups dates
3 cups pecans, chopped
1 (8¼ ounce) can crushed pineapple

3 cups dark brown sugar, packed
1½ cups milk
Juice of 1 lemon

For filling: Reserve meat of 1 coconut to cover cake. Grind dates with pecans and mix with remaining coconut and the pineapple (use juice). Add lemon juice. Set aside. Mix sugar and milk in large saucepan. Bring to boil and cook, stirring until soft ball will form in ice water. Then add ground mixture and cook over medium heat stirring constantly until thick enough to spread (will leave sides of the pan). Cool until warm and spread between layers, top and sides of cake. Use 1 white layer on bottom, the spice layer in the center, the other white on top. Press on coconut over cake.

Doris D. Dixon

Cakes

Apple-Pecan Cake With Cinnamon Frosting

2 eggs
2 cups sugar
½ teaspoon salt
2 teaspoons vanilla extract
1½ cups vegetable oil
2 tablespoons strained lemon juice and 1 tablespoon grated lemon rind

3 cups flour
1 teaspoon baking soda and cinnamon - each
¼ teaspoon nutmeg
3 cups peeled Granny Smith or Pippin apples, grated
2 cups chopped pecans or walnuts

Frosting

4½ ounces cream cheese, softened
¾ cup unsalted butter, softened

1½ cups powdered sugar
¾ teaspoon cinnamon and vanilla extract - each

Preheat oven to 325°F. In large mixing bowl, beat eggs with rotary beater; beat in sugar, salt, vanilla, oil, lemon juice and rind until well blended; set aside. Sift flour, baking soda, cinnamon and nutmeg in separate bowl. Gradually add dry ingredients to egg mixture. Combine well; stir in apples and nuts until well combined. Butter and lightly flour bottom and sides of angel food cake pan - tube pan. Shake out excess flour; fill with batter. Bake about 1½ hours or until toothpick comes out clean. Remove from oven; invert on cooling rack. Cool several minutes before removing from pan. In a large bowl, combine all frosting ingredients except nuts. Using electric mixer, beat until light and fluffy. Spread with spatula on completely cooled cake. Decorate with 8 to 10 whole nuts. Serves 15.

Martha T. Kabbes

Finale

Fresh Apple Cake

2 eggs
2¼ cups sugar
1 tablespoon vanilla
1¼ cups cooking oil
2½ cups flour (plain)

1 teaspoon salt
1 teaspoon baking soda
2 teaspoons baking powder
1 cup chopped pecans
3 cups peeled, chopped apples

Icing

½ cup margarine
2 tablespoons milk

1 cup brown sugar, packed
Powdered sugar

Beat eggs at high speed on mixer. Add sugar and vanilla and beat again. Add oil. Sift flour, salt, baking soda, and baking powder together. Dredge pecans in flour mixture. Add ½ of flour mixture, mix well; then add other half and mix well. Mix apples in with spoon. Bake in 8x8 inch pyrex dish at 350°F for 1 hour.

Icing: Melt margarine, add milk, brown sugar and enough powdered sugar until thick enough to spread smoothly.

Mrs. Pete Pannell (Sara)

German Bundt Cake

Cake

1 (18.5 ounce) box yellow cake mix
1 (3 ounce) box vanilla instant pudding mix
¾ cup corn oil
¾ cup water

1 teaspoon butter flavor extract
1 teaspoon vanilla extract
4 eggs
½ to ¾ cup chopped pecans
2 teaspoons ground cinnamon
¼ cup sugar

Combine cake mix, pudding, oil, water and flavorings in a large mixing bowl. Add eggs, one at a time, beating after each addition. Beat 3 minutes. Grease Bundt pan with shortening. Sprinkle ¼ cup of pecans in the bottom of pan. Combine remaining pecans, cinnamon and sugar for filling. Pour ⅓ of batter into prepared pan; sprinkle ⅓ filling. Repeat procedure two more times. Bake at 350°F for 40 to 45 minutes or until done. Let cook in pan for 25 minutes.

Cakes

Glaze

1 cup powdered sugar
½ teaspoon butter flavor extract

½ teaspoon vanilla extract
2 tablespoons milk

Sift the powdered sugar. Add the flavorings and milk. Stir until mixed and pour over cake.

Mrs. Bob (Carol) Lee

Banana-Black Walnut Cake

2 cups all purpose flour
1 teaspoon baking powder
1 teaspoon baking soda
¼ teaspoon salt
½ cup coarsely chopped black walnuts
¼ cup granulated sugar
½ teaspoon ground cinnamon
½ cup butter or margarine, at room temperature

1 cup granulated sugar
2 large eggs
1 cup mashed very ripe bananas
½ cup plain (no salt-no sugar) yogurt
½ teaspoon vanilla

Heat oven to 350°F. Generously grease a 9x8x12 inch pan. Mix flour, baking powder, baking soda, and salt on waxed paper. On another piece of waxed paper mix nuts, ¼ cup sugar, and the cinnamon. In medium size bowl beat butter and sugar with electric mixer on medium until well-blended. Add eggs, beat 2 minutes until pale and fluffy. Add bananas, yogurt, and vanilla (mixture will look curdled). Beat about 2 minutes until batter is smooth. With wooden spoon stir in flour mixture, one third at a time, until blended. Sprinkle half the nut mixture over bottom of prepared pan, top with half the batter; spread smooth. Repeat layers. Bake 40 to 50 minutes or until pick inserted in center comes out clean. Cool in pan 10 minutes and turn out or leave in pan and slice and serve from pan. Freezes great.

Bess Fisher
Covington, Tennessee

Finale

Holiday Nut Cake

6 eggs
1 teaspoon cream of tartar
1½ cups butter
1½ cups light brown sugar
¾ cup milk
1 teaspoon vanilla
7 tablespoons brandy or sherry
3⅓ cups self-rising flour, sifted
¼ teaspoon nutmeg
1 pound pecans, coarsely chopped
½ pound almonds, coarsely chopped
½ pound walnuts, coarsely chopped

Grease a 10 inch tube pan (or 2 large loaf pans) and line bottom with brown paper. Grease bottom and grease and flour sides. Separate eggs, beat whites stiff and add cream of tartar. Beat yolks lightly. In a large bowl cream butter and sugar till light and fluffy. Add yolks and beat until light and fluffy. Mix milk, vanilla, and brandy; set aside. Sift flour and nutmeg together. Alternate adding flour mixture and milk mixture to butter and sugar mixture, beating well after each addition and scraping sides often. Pour batter over nuts and mix by hand. Fold egg whites into batter and turn batter into pan. Bake on center rack of 275°F oven for 2½ hours. Let cake cool in pan for 30 minutes. Sprinkle with 3 tablespoons brandy or sherry. Take out of pan and allow to cool overnight. Cover with towel soaked in brandy or sherry and wrap tightly with plastic wrap. Makes 1 large cake (20 to 25 servings) or 2 loaves.

Mrs. Rosemary Fisher

Buttermilk Pound Cake

3 cups flour
1 cup butter or margarine
2¾ cups of sugar
4 eggs
1 tablespoon lemon juice
1 cup buttermilk

Measure flour and place in a bowl and set aside. Cream butter and sugar until well blended. Add eggs, one at a time, beating well on high speed after each addition until light and fluffy. Mix lemon juice and buttermilk. Add flour alternately with milk to creamed mixture, adding flour in 3 portions and milk in 2. Mix only until all flour is moistened. Pour into greased 10 inch pan. Bake at 300°F for 1 hour and 10 minutes.

Carolyn Whitehurst

Cakes

Chocolate Chip Pound Cake

1 cup margarine
2 cups sugar
5 eggs
2 cups flour

½ cup cocoa
1 (12 ounce) bag chocolate chips

In electric mixer, cream together margarine and sugar until the consistency of whipped cream. Add eggs, one at a time, beating well after each addition. Add flour and cocoa, which have been combined. Beat for about 15 minutes. Then add chocolate chips. Bake in a greased 10 inch tube or Bundt pan at 325°F for 1 hour. Let cool in pan.

Alternate Instructions: Combine all ingredients except chocolate chips in mixer bowl and beat at medium speed for 15 minutes. Add chocolate chips and mix. Bake in a greased 10 inch tube or Bundt pan at 325°F for 1 hour. Let cool in pan.

Nancy Smith

Cream Cheese Pound Cake

1 (8 ounce) package cream cheese
1½ cups margarine
3 cups sugar

6 eggs
3 cups plain flour
2 teaspoons vanilla

Have all ingredients at room temperature. In a large mixing bowl cream margarine and cream cheese thoroughly. Add sugar to mixture and beat well again. Add eggs, one at a time, beating well after each addition. In small amounts, beat in flour. Add vanilla. Mixture will be thick. Be sure to beat well. Bake in a greased and floured 10 inch tube or bundt pan at 300°F for 1 hour and 25 minutes. Do not overcook.

Mrs. Johnny R. Purvis (Katie)

Finale

Coconut Pound Cake

3 cups all purpose flour
1 teaspoon baking powder
1 cup margarine, softened
¼ cup shortening
2½ cups sugar

5 eggs
1 cup milk
1 teaspon vanilla
1 cup shredded coconut

Sift together flour and baking powder. Set aside. Cream margarine, shortening, and sugar. Add eggs one at a time, beating after each addition. Add flour mixture and milk alternately. Add vanilla and fold in coconut. Pour into a tube pan which has been greased and floured. Bake in 325°F oven for 1½ hours.

Mrs. Dolan Bugg (Rita)

Chocolate Mousse Cake

7 ounces semi-sweet chocolate
½ cup unsalted butter
7 eggs, separated

1 cup sugar
1 teaspoon vanilla extract
⅛ teaspoon cream of tartar

Whipped Cream Frosting

½ pint whipping cream (1 cup)
⅓ cup powdered sugar

Preheat oven to 350°F. In small saucepan, melt chocolate and butter over low heat. In a large bowl, beat egg yolks and ¾ cup sugar until very light and fluffy, about 5 minutes. Gradually beat in warm chocolate mixture and vanilla. In another large bowl, beat egg whites with cream of tartar until soft peaks form. Add remaining ¼ cup sugar, 1 tablespoon at a time. Continue beating until stiff. Fold egg whites carefully into chocolate mixture. Pour ¾ of the batter into an ungreased 9x13 inch springform pan. Cover remaining batter and refrigerate. Bake cake 35 minutes. Prepare frosting and set aside. Remove cake from oven and cool. Cake will drop as it cools. Remove outside ring of pan. Stir refrigerated batter and spread on top of cake. Frost.

Mrs. Charles McDonald (Donna)

Cakes

Tunnel Of Fudge Cake

Cake

1¾ cups margarine or butter, softened
1¾ cups granulated sugar
6 eggs
2 cups powdered sugar

2¼ cups all-purpose flour
¾ cup cocoa
2 cups chopped walnuts or pecans*

Glaze

¾ cup powdered sugar
¼ cup cocoa

1½ to 2 tablespoons milk

Heat oven to 350°F. Grease and flour 12 cup bundt or tube pan. In large bowl, beat margarine and granulated sugar until light and fluffy. Add eggs, one at a time, beating well after each addition. Gradually add powdered sugar; blend well. By hand, stir in remaining ingredients until well blended. Spoon batter into prepared pan; spread evenly. Bake at 350°F for 58 to 62 minutes.** Cool upright in pan on cooling rack 1 hour; invert onto serving plate. Cool completely. In small bowl, combine glaze ingredients until well blended. Spoon over top of cake, allowing some to run down sides. Store tightly covered. 16 servings.

Tips: *Nuts are essential for the success of the recipe.

**Since this cake has a soft tunnel of fudge, ordinary doneness test cannot be used. Accurate oven temperature and bake time are critical.

Frances N. Morgan

Finale

Easy Chocolate Cake And Icing

2 cups sugar
2 cups sifted flour
1 teaspoon baking soda
½ cup buttermilk
1 cup water

½ cup butter or margarine
4 tablespoons cocoa
¼ cup shortening
2 eggs, slightly beaten
1 tablespoon vanilla

Combine sugar and flour; dissolve baking soda in buttermilk and set aside. Combine water, margarine, cocoa, and shortening and bring to a boil. Add to sugar and flour mixture. Blend well. Add eggs, buttermilk and vanilla. Bake in a 375°F oven 20 to 25 minutes.

German Chocolate Icing

1 cup sugar
1 (14½ ounce) can evaporated milk
½ cup margarine

3 egg yolks, beaten
1 (7 ounce) can flaked coconut
1 cup pecans
1 teaspoon vanilla

Mix sugar, milk, margarine, and egg yolks and cook slowly in skillet until thick, stirring constantly. Set off heat, add pecans, coconut and vanilla. Cool and spread on cake.

Ms. Avetta King
Glenn, Mississippi

Italian Cream Cake

½ cup butter or margarine
½ cup vegetable oil
2 cups sugar
5 eggs, separated
1 cup buttermilk

1 teaspoon baking soda
2 cups plain flour
1 teaspoon vanilla
1 cup shredded coconut
½ cup nuts, chopped

Cream butter, oil, and sugar. Add egg yolks one at a time, beating after each addition. Stir baking soda into buttermilk. Add flour into batter, alternating with buttermilk mixture. Add vanilla, coconut, and chopped nuts. Beat egg whites and fold into mixture. Pour into three greased and floured 8 or 9 inch layer pans. Bake at 325°F for approximately 25 minutes. (This cake can also be baked in a 9x13 inch cake pan. Bake at 325°F for approximately 45 minutes.)

Cakes

Icing

1 (8 ounce) package cream cheese
½ cup butter or margarine, softened
1 teaspoon vanilla
1 (16 ounce) box powdered sugar
½ cup nuts, chopped

Beat cream cheese and butter. Add vanilla, powdered sugar, and nuts. Continue to beat until of spreading consistency. (Sometimes I double the icing.)

Mrs. Mary Hedges

$30.00 Cake

5 eggs, separated
2½ cups sugar
1 cup margarine or butter
1 teaspoon vanilla
2 tablespoons boiling coffee
2 tablespoons cocoa
3 cups flour
1½ teaspoons baking soda
1 cup buttermilk

Beat egg whites stiff with ½ cup sugar. Set aside. Cream butter and sugar well. Add egg yolks one at a time. Add vanilla and coffee. Mix well. Sift cocoa and flour. Add baking soda to buttermilk. Then add milk and flour alternately. Fold in egg whites. Grease and flour two 10x10 inch cake pans. Preheat oven to 300°F and bake 40 to 50 minutes (makes a large cake).

Icing

1 (16 ounce) box powdered sugar
2 tablespoons cocoa (not level)
½ cup margarine
1 teaspoon vanilla
Use enough coffee to make spread

Sift sugar and cocoa. Melt margarine and add to sugar mixture. Use the cold coffee left from cup fixed to get the amount needed for cake. Use enough coffee to make the spreading easy. Add vanilla.

Mrs. Mike Byrnes, III

Finale

Mini-Sheath Cake

2 cups self-rising flour
2 cups sugar
¼ teaspoon salt
½ cup margarine
½ cup shortening
4 tablespoons cocoa

1 cup water
½ cup buttermilk
2 eggs, lightly beaten
1 teaspoon baking soda
1 teaspoon cinnamon
1 teaspoon vanilla

Sift together in large bowl flour, sugar and salt. In saucepan place margarine, shortening, cocoa, and water. Bring to boil (rapid boil) and pour over flour mixture. Stir well. Add, mixing by hand, the remaining ingredients; mix well. Batter will be quite thin. Pour into greased and floured 16x11 inch pan or 2 smaller pans. Bake 20 minutes at 400°F. Icing for cake: stir 2 cups sugar, ½ cup margarine, 1 teaspoon vanilla, 3 tablespoons cocoa, and ½ cup milk in saucepan, bring to full boil and cook for 2 minutes. Beat with electric mixer until stiff. Pour over warm cake.

Mrs. Billy R. Briggs, Jr. (Carol)

The "Original" Coca Cola Cake

2 cups unsifted flour
2 cups sugar
1 cup butter or margarine
2 tablespoons cocoa
1 cup coke
½ cup buttermilk

2 eggs
1 teaspoon baking soda
1 teaspoon vanilla
2 cups miniature mashmallows
1¼ teaspoon salt

Bring butter, coke and cocoa to a boil. Pour over sifted flour and sugar. Add marshmallows, these will float and batter will be thin. Bake in a 9x13 inch greased and floured pan 30 to 35 minutes. Check for doneness. Bake at 350°F.

Cakes

Icing

½ cup butter
2 tablespoons cocoa
6 tablespoons coke

1 (16 ounce) box powdered sugar
1 cup nuts
1 teaspoon vanilla

Heat coke, cocoa, and butter to boiling point. Pour over powdered sugar. Add nuts and vanilla. Put on cake while hot.

Giny Hulbert

Oatmeal Cake

1 cup oats, uncooked
½ cup margarine
1¼ cup boiling water
1 cup brown sugar
1 cup white sugar
2 eggs, beaten

1 teaspoon baking soda
1½ cups all purpose flour
1 teaspoon baking powder
1 teaspoon salt
1 teaspoon nutmeg
1 teaspoon cinnamon

In saucepan, bring water to a boil. Add oatmeal and margarine and cook as directed on oatmeal package. Let oatmeal mixture stand 30 minutes. Sift together, white sugar, baking soda, flour, baking powder, salt, nutmeg, and cinnamon. Add sifted ingredients, brown sugar, and eggs to oatmeal mixture. Blend all together. Bake in broiler pan for 1 hour at 350°F.

Icing

1 cup brown sugar
½ cup margarine
3 teaspoons milk

½ teaspoon vanilla
½ cup chopped nuts
½ cup coconut

For the icing, boil brown sugar, margarine, and milk for 1 minute. Add vanilla, chopped nuts, and coconut and stir. Let cake cool for 15 minutes before icing.

Mary Pierce Jones
Memphis, Tennessee

Finale

Classic Haresch (hair reese ah) Cake

1 tablespoon butter
2 eggs
⅔ cup sugar
4 tablespoons milk

⅔ cup self-rising flour
1½ teaspoons baking powder
1 cup coconut

In bowl cream together butter, eggs and sugar. Add milk; mix well. In a separate bowl mix flour, baking powder and coconut. Add ½ dry mixture to batter at a time. Pour into buttered and floured pan. (Makes 1 small layer cake—double recipe for 13x9 inch cake pan.) Heat oven to 350°F. Let cake sit out in pan for 20 minutes before placing in 350°F oven. Bake for 30 to 35 minutes or until done. If you want to double the recipe, double all ingredients except coconut. Use 1¾ cups coconut only and only 3 eggs.

Topping

⅔ cup sugar

⅔ cup water

Bring sugar and water to a boil, simmer for a few minutes. Pour over cake while cake is still hot from the oven. Start pouring around the edges of the cake first and then cover the top. This is a rich dessert, so cut into small pieces. (Middle Eastern cake recipe.)

Short Cut Version

1 box Butter Cake mix
1 egg

1 cup coconut or for variety add pecan pieces

Use box of butter cake mix, following directions on the box, except use only 1 egg. Optional: Add coconut or pecan pieces. Bake according to box directions and pour topping over cake as previously instructed.

Ms. Faye Shaalan

Pies

Basic Pastry

1 cup all purpose flour, plain
¼ teaspoon salt
⅓ cup shortening
3½ tablespoons water

Sift flour and salt into mixing bowl. Cut shortening into flour mixture with pastry blender until texture is like coarse meal. Add water; mix with spoon then with hand, taking up all the flour. Roll out on floured board. Double or triple this recipe as needed.

Margaret Perkins

Food Processor Pie Crust

1 stick butter or margarine, frozen
2 cups of plain flour
¾ cup of ice water

Cut frozen butter into 6 pieces. Put into bowl or processor with knife blade. Add 2 cups of plain flour. Process until the consistency of cornmeal. Add ice water through tube with processor going. Turn off when a ball begins to form.

Note: This will make enough for a two crust pie. The dough can be frozen as is and rolled out later.

French Coconut Pie

4 eggs, beaten
1½ cups sugar
½ cup butter
Pinch of salt
2 teaspoons vanilla
½ cup milk
1 cup of coconut, shredded
Unbaked pie shell

Mix all ingredients together and pour into unbaked pie shell. Bake at 300°F for 1 hour.

Dr. Robert E. Crowe

Finale

Ole Miss Hot Fudge Pie

4 eggs
1½ cups sugar
½ cup butter
3 squares unsweetened chocolate

3 tablespoons corn syrup
1 teaspoon vanilla
1 9" unbaked pie shell

Beat eggs well. Add sugar and beat. Melt chocolate and butter in double boiler. Cool slightly and add to egg mixture. Add corn and vanilla; mix well. Pour into pie shell. Bake at 350°F for 30 to 40 minutes. Serve hot with vanilla ice cream.

Mrs. Barry Cannada
Jackson, Mississippi

Chocolate Pie With Oatmeal Crust

½ cup butter
¾ cup all purpose flour
¼ cup oats

½ cup chopped pecans
2 tablespoons sugar

Melt butter and stir in remaining ingredients. Bake in 9 inch pie pan at 400°F for 12 to 15 minutes or until lightly brown. Cool.

1 (8 ounce) plain chocolate bar
1 (8 ounce) container non-dairy whipped topping

Melt chocolate bar in microwave (on high) or in the top of a double boiler, over hot water. Cool. Stir into slightly thawed whipped topping. Spoon into pie shell and refrigerate until serving time.

Note: Double the pie crust ingredients, bake and freeze 2. You can then make this pie in less than 10 minutes. A great time saver!

Permelia Franklin Wallace
Jackson, Tennessee

Pies

Macaroon Pie

3 egg whites, room temperature
1 cup sugar
¼ teaspoon baking powder
1 teaspoon almond extract

12 single soda crackers
12 dates, cut fine
½ cup chopped nuts

Roll soda crackers until fine. Mix with dates and nuts. Set aside. Beat egg whites until stiff. Add sugar, baking powder, and extract gradually. Beat very stiff. Mix cracker mixture with egg white mixture. Put white butcher paper or foil on cookie sheet. Drop mixture in about 6 parts on paper. Spread out as with meringues. Cook in 300°F oven about 30 minutes. Serve with whipped cream.

Mrs. R. C. Liddon

Walnut Pie

1 cup white corn syrup
1 cup dark brown sugar
½ teaspoon salt
⅓ cup melted butter

1 teaspoon vanilla
3 whole eggs
1 heaping cup shelled walnuts

Beat the eggs with the brown sugar, corn syrup, salt, melted butter and vanilla and stir in the walnuts. Pour into an unbaked pastry shell and bake at 350°F for 45 minutes.

Billie Wadlington

To Reduce Calories

Reduce sugar by ¼ to ⅓ without harming baked product. Cinnamon and vanilla also give the impression of sweetness. (H.N.S.)

Finale

Butterscotch Pie

¾ cup brown sugar, packed
5 tablespoons all purpose flour
½ teaspoon salt
2 cups milk

2 egg yolks, slightly beaten
2 tablespoons butter
1 teaspoon vanilla

Combine sugar, flour, and salt. Stir in milk slowly. Cook over boiling water until thickened, stirring constantly. Cover and cook 10 minutes longer, stirring occasionally. Add mixture to egg yolks, stirring vigorously; cook 1 minute longer. Add butter and vanilla and cool. Place filling in cooked pastry shell and cover with whipped cream.

Mrs. Mike Byrnes, III

Crustless Buttermilk Pie

1½ cups sugar
3 eggs
½ cup biscuit mix

1 cup buttermilk
1 teaspoon vanilla
½ cup melted margarine

Mix together ingredients with electric mixer. Pour into well greased 9 inch pie pan. Bake at 350°F for 30 minutes. Yield: 8 servings.

Julie Chambers

Peanut Butter Pie

1 (8 ounce) package cream cheese, softened
1 cup crunchy peanut butter
1 (16 ounce) container whipped topping

1½ cups sifted powdered sugar
2 (9 inch) graham cracker crusts

Combine cream cheese and peanut butter in a large mixing bowl; beat at medium speed until light and fluffy. Gradually add whipped topping and powdered sugar, and beat until smooth. Spoon filling into prepared crusts. Freeze. Makes two 9 inch pies.

Ann French Coker

Pies

Lemon Meringue Pie

1½ cups sugar
⅓ cup cornstarch
1½ cups water
3 egg yolks, slightly beaten

3 tablespoons butter
¼ cup lemon juice
1 tablespoon grated lemon rind
1 (9 inch) pie shell, baked

Mix sugar and cornstarch in saucepan. Gradually stir in the water and cook over medium heat, stirring constantly, until the mixture boils. Boil for 1 minute. Remove from the heat and slowly stir at least half the hot mixture into the egg yolks. Blend the rest of the mixture into the egg yolks, return to the heat and boil (stirring constantly) for about 1 minute longer. Remove from the heat and continue stirring until smooth. Blend in butter, lemon juice and lemon rind. Pour into a baked pie shell, cover with meringue and place under broiler until golden brown.

Jerrie Doran

Lime Pie

3 cups sweetened condensed milk
4 egg yolks

⅔ cup lime juice
½ cup whipping cream
1 (9 inch) pie shell (baked)

Beaten egg yolks and milk are gradually added to the lime juice while stirring. Pour into (9 inch) pie shell, baked. After 2 hours in the refrigerator the filling is solid enough to be served. Add small rosettes of whipped cream over each serving.

Ms. Rachel Goddard

Finale

Strawberry Fluff Pie

Crust

½ cup margarine, melted
¼ cup sugar

4 cups rice cereal squares crushed to 1 cup

Preheat oven to 350°F. Grease a 9 inch pie plate. Combine margarine, sugar; add crumbs and mix well. Press evenly into the bottom and sides of pan. Bake 8 minutes and cool.

Filling

1 envelope unflavored gelatin
½ cup milk
20 large or 2 cups small marshmallows

1 package frozen strawberries, chopped (do not drain)
¼ cup sugar
2 cups whipped topping, thawed

Soften gelatin in milk in a 3 quart saucepan. Heat over low heat to dissolve gelatin; add marshmallows. Cook over low heat and stir until marshmallows are melted. Remove from heat. Stir together strawberries and sugar until sugar is dissolved. Add, a small amount at a time, to marshmallow mixture. Chill 5 to 10 minutes then stir often. Beat on high speed of mixer for 1 minute. Beat in topping over low speed. Spoon into crust and chill about 2 hours.

Etta Mae Vuncannon

Betty Ruth's Speedy Peach Pie

2 cups fresh peaches
½ cup sugar
¾ cup butter
½ cup flour

½ cup milk
½ cup sugar
1 teaspoon baking powder

Mix fresh peaches with ½ cup sugar; let set while preparing crust. Dot bottom of 3 quart baking dish with butter. Mix next four ingredients. Pour in baking dish and add peaches on top. DO NOT MIX. Bake 40 minutes at 350°F or until set.

Claire Stanley

Pies

Strawberry Pie

1 quart fresh strawberries, hulled and washed
3 tablespoons cornstarch
1 cup sugar
2 tablespoons lemon juice
1 baked 9 inch pie crust
½ cup heavy cream, whipped

Crush half of berries (use a fork or pastry blender). Stir in cornstarch, sugar, and lemon juice. Stir over medium heat until thick and clear. Cool. Halve rest of berries. Fold into cooled mixture. Pour into crust. Chill thoroughly. Before serving spread with whipped cream. This is a beautiful pie. Stored in refrigerator will keep at least 2 days. Serves 6.

Doris D. Dixon

Peach Cobbler

½ cup corn oil margarine
1 cup all purpose flour
2 teaspoons baking powder
1 cup sugar
¾ cup milk
2 cups sliced peaches, fresh or frozen (If peaches are juicy, substitute juice for part of milk.)
⅛ teaspoon almond extract
½ teaspoon butter flavoring
½ cup sugar

Melt margarine in a 8x12x2 inch baking pan. Sift flour, baking powder and 1 cup sugar together. Add flavorings to milk. Mix with dry ingredients and pour into melted margarine without stirring. Add peeled, sliced (or thawed) peaches over this. Sprinkle remaining ½ cup sugar over peaches. Bake at 300°F for 1 hour, then bake at 350°F about 20 minutes.

Note: For apple cobbler, substitute 2 cups sliced apples. Add ½ teaspoon cinnamon to dry ingredients. Omit almond flavoring.

Loretta D. Greene
Rockdale, Texas

Finale

Ambrosia Pie

2 prepared graham cracker crusts
1 can sweetened condensed milk
½ cup lemon juice
1 (12 ounce) carton non-dairy topping
2 cans mandarin orange sections, drained
2 cans crushed pineapple
1 (14 ounce) package frozen coconut
Nuts, optional

Mix milk, lemon juice, and topping; fold in other ingredients, reserving orange sections for garnish. Pile into crusts and refrigerate for 2 hours. Garnish with whipped topping and orange sections.

Rosemary Fisher

Pineapple Glazed Apple Pie

1½ cups of unsweetened pineapple juice
¾ cup sugar
7 tart medium apples, cored, peeled and cut in wedges
3 tablespoons of cornstarch
1 tablespoon margarine
½ teaspoon vanilla
¼ teaspoon salt
1 (9 inch) pie crust, baked and cooled

Combine 1¼ cups pineapple juice and sugar in a saucepan. Bring to a boil, add the apple wedges. Simmer, covered 3 or 4 minutes or until the apples are tender, but not soft. With slotted spoon lift the apples from pineapple juice; set aside to drain. Blend the remaining pineapple juice slowly into cornstarch; add to liquid in saucepan. Cook and stir until mixture thickens and bubbles; cook 1 minute more. Remove from heat. Stir in margarine, vanilla and salt. Cover. Cool for 30 minutes. Do not stir. Pour half of the pineapple mixture into pie shell. Spread to cover the bottom. Arrange cooked apples on top. Spoon remaining mixture over apples. Cover and refrigerate until chilled. Garnish with whipped cream before serving.

Deborah King

Pies

Creme De Menthe Cheesecake

1½ cups chocolate wafer crumbs
¼ cup melted margarine
3 (8 ounce) packages cream cheese
1½ cups sugar
4 eggs, plus 1 egg yolk

3 tablespoons cream de cacao (clear)
¼ cup plus 2 tablespoons creme de menthe (green)
4 (1 ounce) squares semi-sweet chocolate
1 cup sour cream

Mix chocolate crumbs and margarine. Press in 9 inch springform pan. Set aside. Beat cream cheese at medium speed until light and fluffy. Gradually add sugar; heat. Add eggs one at a time and the yolk. Add creme de menthe and cream de cacao. Mix well. Spoon into crust. Bake at 350°F for 55 to 60 minutes. Cool thoroughly. Melt chocolate in double boiler and allow to cool. Stir in sour cream and spread on top of cake. Chill covered.

Mrs. Barry Cannada

Italian Cheese Cake

Crust

1 cup all purpose flour
½ cup butter

2 tablespoons sugar

Blend above ingredients with pastry cutter and pat into 9 inch pie pan.

Filling

20 ounces of well drained Ricotta cheese
1½ teaspoons almond extract
3 eggs

1 cup sugar
¼ cup chocolate chips (optional)

Mix together above ingredients and pour into pie pan. Bake at 350°F for 1 hour.

Linda Gunther
Glen, Mississippi

Finale

Refrigerated Cheese Cake

Crust

2 cups graham cracker crumbs
2 heaping tablespoons sugar
½ cup melted butter
½ teaspoon cinnamon

Filling

1 (3 ounce) package lemon gelatin
1 cup boiling water
1 (14½ ounce) can evaporated milk
1 (8 ounce) package cream cheese
½ cup sugar
2 teaspoons vanilla

Combine ingredients for crust and press in the bottom of 8x11 inch pan or dish. Dissolve gelatin in boiling water and set aside to cool. Place milk in a bowl and place in freezer until icy. Remove and whip. Next mix cream cheese and sugar and add to cooled gelatin. Fold in whipped milk and vanilla and pour into prepared crust. Top with leftover crumbs.

Mrs. James (Kathleen) Brickey
Jackson, Tennessee

Coffee Chiffon Pie

1 envelope unflavored gelatin
½ cup sugar, divided
⅛ teaspoon salt
1½ tablespoons instant coffee
4 eggs, separated
1 cup water
1 teaspoon vanilla
1 (9 inch) crumb crust

Mix gelatin, ¼ cup sugar, salt, coffee in double boiler. Beat egg yolks and water together, add to gelatin mixture, cook over boiling water, stirring constantly until thickens, about 5 minutes. Remove from heat, add vanilla, chill. Beat egg whites stiff, add ¼ cup sugar and fold into mixture. Put in crust, chill, cover with whipped cream, shaved chocolate.

Miriam Propp
Corinth, Mississippi

Epilogue

EPILOGUE

At some point in their culinary experience most cooks decide to venture away from the ordinary, mundane world of meat and potatoes. For some, the art of making pickles and relishes is their next challenge, while for others, candy making has more appeal.

There is a continuing challenge in cooking to use the knowledge and expertise gained through past experience and to apply it to learning new techniques in areas not yet explored.

Candies

Buttery Peanut Brittle

2 cups sugar
1 cup light corn syrup
½ cup water

1 cup butter
2 cups raw peanuts
1 teaspoon baking soda

Combine sugar, corn syrup and water in a 4 quart saucepan. Cook and stir until sugar dissolves. When syrup boils, blend in butter. Stir frequently after mixture reaches the syrup stage, 230°F. Add nuts when temperature reaches the soft crack stage, 280°F. Stir constantly until temperature reaches hard crack stage, 305°F. Remove from heat. Quickly stir in baking soda, mix well. Pour onto 2 buttered cookie sheets. As the candy cools, stretch it out thin by lifting and pulling from the edges. Loosen as soon as possible. Turn candy over and break in pieces. Store in airtight containers. Makes 2½ pounds.

Louise Clifton

Date Roll

3 cups sugar
1 cup milk
1 teaspoon vanilla
Pinch of salt

1 cup dates, chopped
1 cup nuts
3 tablespoons butter

Cook sugar and milk slowly about 20 minutes. Add chopped dates. Cook until soft ball forms in cold water. Stir constantly or dates will burn. Take off heat. Add vanilla, nuts and butter. Beat vigorously until hard enough to form a loaf. Pour on wet cloth, roll up and cool. Refrigerate. The candy is better to slice as needed.

DeEtta Wigginton

Epilogue

English Toffee I

Pecans, finely chopped
6 chocolate bars, plain
1 cup butter

1 cup sugar
3 tablespoons water
1 teaspoon vanilla

Cook in very heavy skillet, stirring constantly until mixture turns a coffee color. (Temperature should be set at hot.) Turn into a lightly buttered large flat 13x11 inch pan. Lay 6 plain Chocolate bars on top. Use spatula to spread chocolate over brittle. Cover top with finely chopped pecan nuts.

Roberta Wiggins
Cleveland, Mississippi

English Toffee II

2 cups butter
2 cups sugar
Pinch cinnamon
1 teaspoon cold water
½ teaspoon vanilla

1 cup sliced almonds
1 (6 ounce) package chocolate chips
Ground almonds

Combine butter and sugar in heavy saucepan. Cook over medium heat. When mixture reaches rolling boil, add cinnamon and cold water. Bring mixture to hard crack stage (300°F on candy thermometer). Remove from heat. Add vanilla and sliced almonds. Pour into a greased cookie pan and cool completely. Melt chocolate chips in double boiler or microwave. Spread top of toffee with ½ of chocolate. Sprinkle with ground almonds. When chocolate dries, turn toffee over and frost other side. Let chocolate dry completely (3 to 4 hours). Break into bite-sized pieces. Makes 2 to 3 dozen pieces.

Audrey McWhirter

Candies

Creamy Pecan Fudge

3 (12 ounce) packages
 semi-sweet chocolate morsels
1 (7 ounce) jar marshmallow
 cream
1 cup margarine

4½ cups sugar
1 (13 ounce) can evaporated
 milk
3 to 4 cups pecans, chopped

Combine chocolate morsels, marshmallow cream, and butter in a large bowl. Combine sugar and evaporated milk in a heavy saucepan. Bring to a boil. Reduce heat and cook over low heat for 9 minutes, stirring constantly. Pour hot mixture over chocolate morsel mixture. Stir until the chocolate melts and mixture is smooth. Add pecans and stir until well blended. Spread mixture in a lightly buttered 15x10x1 inch pan. Chill until firm. Cut into squares when cool and firm. Makes 10 dozen pieces.

William McMullin

Deluxe Three Chocolate Fudge

4½ cups sugar
1 (15 ounce) can evaporated
 milk
½ cup butter
1 (12 ounce) bar of chocolate
 candy, without almonds
1 (12 ounce) package of
 chocolate chips

2 squares baking chocolate
1 (16 ounce) jar marshmallow
 cream
2 cups pecans, chopped
1 teaspoon vanilla

In a two quart saucepan combine sugar, milk and butter. Cook until it reaches soft ball stage on candy thermometer. Stir constantly. Remove from heat and add candy bar, chocolate chips, baking chocolate and marshmallow cream. Stir until well blended. Add nuts and vanilla. Pour into a well greased 11x13x2 inch glass dish. Cool for an hour and cut into small pieces. Makes 4 pounds. *This is very rich!*

Lynn Wroten

Epilogue

Minute Fudge

2 cups sugar
3 tablespoons cocoa
⅓ cup white corn syrup
½ cup sweet milk
1 tablespoon margarine

1 heaping teaspoon cornstarch
1 teaspoon vanilla extract
1 pinch of salt
1 cup broken nuts

Blend sugar and cocoa; add corn syrup, milk, and margarine. Bring to a full boil. Boil 1 minute. Remove from heat; add cornstarch, salt, and vanilla. Beat until thick; add nuts. Drop by teaspoonfuls onto waxed paper.

Margaret Perkins

Mystery Fudge

1 pound pasteurized processed cheese
2 cups margarine
4 (1 pound) boxes powdered sugar

1 cup cocoa
2 teaspoons vanilla
2 cups pecans, chopped

Melt margarine and cheese in a double boiler. Pour over powdered sugar and cocoa. Stir in nuts and vanilla. Pour into 2, lightly greased, 9x13 inch pans. Chill and cut into small squares. Makes close to 150 pieces. Recipe may be halved.

Mary Louise Burns
Brookhaven, Mississippi

Candies

White Fudge

2 cups sugar
⅓ cup light corn syrup
½ cup milk

Pinch salt
2 tablespoons butter

Cook ingredients until a soft ball forms in ice water. Remove from heat. Add 1 teaspoon cornstarch. Beat until ready to pour on a greased plate. To make chocolate add 1½ squares of chocolate or 3 tablespoons cocoa. This is candy and also used for icing.

This recipe is 55 years old and was handed down to me by my sister-in-law.

Mrs. Frank Hinton

Pralines

3 cups sugar
1 cup buttermilk
1 teaspoon baking soda
¼ cup butter or margarine

1 teaspoon vanilla
3 cups pecans (preferably halves)

Put all ingredients except pecans and vanilla into a big boiler and boil until mixture turns brown and forms a soft ball in cold water. Add vanilla and beat a little. Stir in pecans and drop on buttered waxed paper. Candy sets up very fast when it reaches right temperature. When hard, remove from paper and wrap each individually in waxed paper. Do not attempt in humid weather.

Rosemary Williams

"Appetite, a universal wolf!", William Shakespeare, English dramatist and poet.

Epilogue

Melt A Ways

1st Layer

½ cup butter
1 square baking chocolate
¼ cup sugar
1 teaspoon vanilla

1 egg, beaten
2 cups crushed graham crackers
½ cup chopped pecans

2nd Layer

¼ cup butter
1 tablespoon milk

2 cups powdered sugar
1 teaspoon vanilla

3rd Layer

2 squares baking chocolate

2 tablespoons butter

To assemble: 1st Layer: Melt butter and chocolate, add sugar, vanilla, egg, mix well and pour over graham cracker crumbs and pecans. Mix well and press into greased 11x13 inch baking dish. 2nd Layer: Melt butter and mix well with milk, powdered sugar and vanilla. Press onto 1st layer evenly. 3rd Layer: Melt butter and chocolate and dribble over the 2nd layer. Cool. Cut into small squares. Delicious!

Vicki Wroten
Orlando, Florida

Christmas Nuts

1 egg white
2 tablespoons cold water
½ teaspoon salt
½ teaspoon cinnamon
¼ teaspoon cloves

¼ teaspoon allspice
½ cup sugar
2 cups whole nuts, pecans or walnuts

Beat together egg, water, salt and spices until soft and peaks. Gradually add sugar, beating until very stiff peaks form. Fold in a few nuts at a time, stir gently to coat. Place nuts one at a time on a greased baking sheet. Cook at 275°F for 40 minutes. Store in a very tight container.

Mrs. Boyd Armstrong

Candies

Orange Pecans

2 cups sugar
⅓ cup white corn syrup
½ cup water
Juice and grated rind of 1 orange
2 cups pecans

Cook all ingredients except pecans until soft ball forms in cold water or 230°F. Add pecans. Beat until creamy. Pour on waxed paper. Break apart with fork.

De Etta Wigginton

Baked Caramel Corn

2 cups butter or margarine
2 cups firmly packed brown sugar
½ cup corn syrup (light or dark)
1 teaspoon salt
½ teaspoon baking soda
1 teaspoon vanilla
6 quarts popped corn

Melt butter, stir in brown sugar, syrup and salt. Bring to a boil stirring constantly. Boil 5 minutes without stirring. Remove from heat. Stir in baking soda and vanilla. Gradually pour over popped corn, mixing well. Turn into 2 large shallow pans or cookie sheet with sides. Bake at 250°F for 1 hour, stirring every 15 to 30 minutes. Remove from oven. Cool completely. Break apart and store in tightly covered container.

Linda Gunther
Glen, Mississippi

Epilogue

Granola

6 cups rolled oats
1 cup unsweetened coconut
2 cups nuts (any combination)
1 cup wheatgerm
1 cup honey
½ cup vegetable oil

Combine all dry ingredients. Mix in honey and oil. Spread out on cookie sheets. Roast in 300°F oven until golden brown. Sprinkle with raisins. Stir occasionally while cooling to prevent lumping. This is a really loose recipe and can be altered to fit your taste.

Sandy Hanson
Clearwater, Florida

Whiz Energy Balls

½ cup butter, melted
1 cup honey
1 cup powdered dry milk
1 cup wheatgerm
1 cup flaked coconut
1 cup chopped walnuts

Mix honey and butter well in a large mixing bowl. Add remaining ingredients. Roll into small balls. Refrigerate. Yield 2 to 3 dozen.

Dale Bishop

All-Purpose Creole Seasoning

1 (26 ounce) box salt
1½ ounce black pepper
1 ounce red pepper
1 ounce pure garlic powder
1 ounce chili powder
1 ounce monosodium glutamate

Mix well and use like salt.

Billie Wadlington

Pickles & Seasonings

Better Than Zest

¾ cup water

1 cup coarsely chopped lemon rinds

Save lemon rinds after you extract the juice! Place 1 cup coarsely chopped rinds in the blender with ¾ cup water. Grind and then pureé. Place 1 tablespoon of mixture in individual ice cube tray sections and freeze. Put into a plastic bag and save. One cube added to white sauce or one or more added to chicken soup is "better than zest". Makes 1 cup.

Mr. Jonnie Norwood
Oxford, Mississippi

Candied Garlic Dills

1 gallon dill pickles, whole or sliced
5 pounds of sugar

1 can pickling spices (1½ ounces)
5 cloves of garlic

In a crock or one gallon jar place sliced, drained pickles, spices, garlic and sugar. Let set for 5 days. Remove from jar and remove garlic. Put into 8 pint or 16½ pint jars. This is a festive, relish type pickle, best served with a full meal.

Rosemary Fisher

Epilogue

Green Tomato Pickle

1 peck green tomatoes, cut into thin slices
12 large onions, peeled and cut into thin slices
1 cup salt
3 quarts cider vinegar
12 green peppers, sliced thin
6 sweet red peppers, diced
12 cloves garlic, minced

4 pounds brown sugar
2 tablespoons dry mustard
2 tablespoons whole cloves
2 tablespoons stick cinnamon, broken
2 tablespoons powered ginger
1 tablespoon salt
1 tablespoon celery seed

Sprinkle the cup of salt over the tomatoes and onions. Let them stand for 12 hours. Wash them in clear water, drain. Heat to boiling point, vinegar, peppers, garlic, and brown sugar. Add rest of the ingredients to tomatoes and onions, cook slowly until the tomatoes are transparent, about 1 hour. Do not overcook, tomatoes will be mushy.

Jotham Pierce
Falmouth Foreside, Maine

Icicle Pickle

7 pounds sliced, green tomatoes (unpeeled)
2 cups household lime
2 gallons water
4½ pounds sugar
3 pints vinegar

2 teaspoons each, celery seed, whole cloves, whole allspice
4 sticks cinnamon
2 cups raisins
Salt, to taste, optional

In a crock, add lime to water and pour over the tomatoes, let soak 24 hours. Drain well, then soak the tomatoes in clear water for 3 hours. Make a syrup of the sugar, vinegar, and the spices. Drain the tomatoes well, put back in crock and pour the syrup over them and let stand 24 hours. Put in heavy pot, add the raisins, and salt and cook until the tomatoes are clear. Seal in jars while hot. Yield 7 to 8 pints.

Mrs. H. W. Hobbs (Sarah)
Brookhaven, Mississippi

Revivals

CORINTH AND THE ARTS

To satisfy the demand for culture and entertainment, the performing arts have been a part of Corinthians' daily lifestyle since the 1860's. The last half of the nineteenth century and the first quarter of the twentieth century saw the rise of several opera houses where both dramatic and musical performances, concerts and lectures were held.

Today, Corinth boasts an active and successful community theatre, the Northeast Mississippi Community Concert Association, the Corinth Area Arts Council and a magnificent twenty-voice community choral group who work together with others to keep the arts very much alive in our town.

HOLIDAY MENU

Oyster Soup or Fresh Fruit Cup

Turkey   Ham In A Blanket

Bread Dressing   Cornbread Dressing

Giblet Gravy

Water Chestnut Gravy

Scalloped oysters (p.193)

Cranberry Fluff Salad

Sweet Potato Soufflé   Au Gratin Vegetables

Sweet and Sour Green Beans

Spiced Oranges

Assorted Pickles and Olives

Ice Box Rolls

Ambrosia   Pumpkin Pie

Big Mama's 3-Flavor Pound Cake

Boiled Custard   Dried Apple Cake

Revivals

Oyster Soup

1 medium onion, chopped
½ bell pepper, chopped
2 ribs celery, chopped
3 tablespoons butter

1 (12 ounce) jar oysters, drained
2 cups milk
1 cup half and half
Salt, to taste

Sauté the onion, bell pepper and celery in butter on low heat until transparent. Add the drained oysters. Cook on low heat until oysters curl and are done. Turn heat to simmer and add the milk and half and half. Cover and let heat. Do not add salt until soup is served into the bowl or it will curdle. Serves 4 to 6.

Mrs. W. B. Herring
Pascagoula, Mississippi

Cranberry Fluff

2 cups raw cranberries, ground in blender
3 cups miniature marshmallows
¾ cup sugar
2 cups diced unpared tart apples

½ cup seedless grapes
½ cup broken walnuts
¼ teaspoon salt
1 cup heavy cream, whipped (unsweetened)

Combine cranberries, marshmallows and sugar. Cover and chill overnight. Add apples, grapes, walnuts and salt. Fold in whipped cream. Chill. Turn into serving bowl. This recipe was handed down to me by my mother, Mrs. Wilford (Jean) Johnson. Serves 8 to 10. *We always serve this at Thanksgiving or Christmas.*

Mrs. Charles McDonald (Donna)

Cooking A Turkey In An Electric Roaster

1 turkey, about 20 pounds, completely thawed (if frozen)
Salt and pepper, to taste
1 to 2 teaspoons celery salt
¼ teaspoon garlic salt, sprinkled on any time
1 cup butter or margarine, at least
4 cups water, at room temperature
2 stuffings

Remove giblets from the cavity of the turkey and reserve for making Giblet Gravy or Water Chestnut Gravy. Gently lift the skin on the breast and ease the skin away from the breast as far as you can. Salt, pepper and celery salt the breast under the loosened skin. Salt and pepper the inside of the main body cavity. Lightly stuff the breast cavity with bread stuffing, filling under the loosened skin. Pull the skin over the cavity and pin to close securely. Tuck the wings under the bird. Stuff the main cavity of the bird loosely with cornbread stuffing (or any other stuffing of your choice). Close the cavity and tie the legs together. Place on the rack of the roaster and butter generously. Put the lid on the roaster and turn control to 450°F for 15 to 20 minutes or until the bird begins to cook. Add more butter all over the top of the bird, replace lid, add 1 cup water and turn heat down to 350°F. Cook for 30 minutes more. Open roaster and place thermometer in the bird being careful not to let the tip touch the bone. Continue cooking adding more water 1 cup at a time if needed. Baste with pan juices every 20 minutes. Be generous with the amount of butter or margarine brushed on the breast. The turkey should be perfectly browned when the thermometer reaches 185°F. Remove from roaster on the rack and cool to room temperature. Remove the stuffings and refrigerate if you are not serving immediately. The pan juices may be added to the already prepared gravys. (You may need to thicken them before adding to the gravys.)

Note: You can tell when you need to add more water to the pan during the cooking period because you will hear a slight "sizzling" sound when the water evaporates. Do not be afraid to add more water to the pan, especially if you are cooking a wild turkey.

Revivals

Country Ham In A Blanket: A Real Show Stopper

1 large, deep boiler (a lard can is perfect)
1 (16 to 20 pound) country cured ham only
Water to cover by 2 inches
3 (33 8/10 ounce) bottles of gingerale

Water to add to the gingerale to cover the ham
Cloves for decoration
2 tablespoons mustard
1 cup brown sugar
1 cup cider vinegar

Put ham in container and completely cover with water. Bring to a rolling boil and cook for 1 hour. Cool enough to handle. Discard the cooking water. Place the ham back into the boiler. Pour in the 3 bottles of gingerale and enough water to cover the ham. Bring to a boil, turn heat to simmer and cook once more, this time 1½ hours. Remove from heat. Put a heavy lid on the boiler. Cover the boiler and ham and cooking liquids completely in a blanket or two. Leave the covered ham for 72 hours without "peeking". After 72 hours, uncover the ham, drain off the liquid and discard. Remove the skin and excess fat. Score the ham fat you leave on in diamond shapes. Decorate each diamond with a whole clove. Mix the mustard, sugar and vinegar to a paste and brush over the fat side of the ham. Now bake the ham, uncovered in a 350°F oven for 1 hour to glaze. Remove from oven and allow to cool to room temperature before slicing.

Mrs. Preston Biggers

"There is nothing wrong with sobriety in moderation",
John Ciardi, critic.

Menu

Chicken Or Turkey Bread Dressing Supreme

2 regular size loaves of fresh, white bread
½ cup butter plus ¼ cup for topping
4 cups boiling water
8 eggs
Sage leaves (fresh or dried)

2 cups finely chopped celery
2 cups finely chopped onion
1½ cups milk
Salt and pepper, to taste
1 cup chopped parsley adds a little glamour

Break up the pieces of bread in a large mixing bowl, placing the ½ cup of butter on top. Pour the 4 cups of boiling water over and stir until the butter melts. Beat the eggs and stir into the mixture. Add salt and pepper and enough crumbled sage "until you can smell it". Add celery and onion and the milk. Taste! Mix the parsley into the dressing. Place in a large casserole, dot with ¼ cup butter, cover and cook in a preheated 325°F oven for about 1 hour. The dressing will rise during the cooking. Uncover for the last 15 minutes to brown. The dressing can also be lightly stuffed in your fowl, spooned around the bird and cooked together. Serves 8 to 10.

Ms. Joyce Turner
Laredo, Texas

An Old Fashioned Guide To Oven Temperatures

Very slow oven	250 to 275 degrees
Slow oven	300 to 325 degrees
Moderate oven	350 to 375 degrees
Hot oven	400 to 425 degrees
Very hot oven	450 to 470 degrees
Extremely hot oven	500 to 525 degrees

Revivals

Cornbread Dressing For Turkey Or Chicken

Cornbread

2 cups cornmeal, self-rising
1 cup buttermilk

2 eggs
2 tablespoons oil

Dressing

1 recipe cornbread
1½ cups seasoned breadcrumbs (½ package if using bought)
½ cup butter or margarine
¾ cup chopped onion
¾ cup chopped celery

1 tablespoon dried sage, or to taste (optional)
1 tablespoon poultry seasoning, or to taste (optional)
Salt, pepper
1 quart turkey or chicken stock, more or less

Make cornbread by mixing first three ingredients in bowl. Heat the oil in an iron skillet until very hot, coat bottom and sides of skillet and pour rest into batter, stir and pour batter into the very hot skillet, place in 375°F oven and bake until firm and lightly brown on top, about 25 to 30 minutes. Mix cornbread (crumbled) and breadcrumbs in large bowl. Cook onion, celery in butter until tender. Pour into crumb mixture, add seasonings to taste. Next pour in stock and mix. The amount of stock depends on how moist you want the dressing. This fills a 9x13 inch casserole; if you are stuffing the bird, do not make dressing as moist as it will become more moist during cooking. Serves 12.

Turkey - Water Chestnut Gravy Without Giblets

1 (8 ounce) can water chestnuts
Broth from Giblet Gravy recipe

Yellow food coloring
Salt, pepper and garlic salt, to taste

Drain and thinly slice the water chestnuts. Stir into the broth. Taste for seasoning. Add one or two drops yellow food coloring.

Menu

Giblet Gravy

Liver, neck and gizzard from the turkey (also heart if there is one)
3 quarts water
Salt and pepper

1 medium onion, chopped
1 stalk celery (with leaves) chopped
¼ cup butter or margarine
2 hardboiled eggs

Cook the liver, neck and gizzard of the turkey in the 3 quarts of water. The gizzard can be tough so simmer the poultry for about 2 hours. Season the broth with the onion, celery and salt and pepper. The butter or margarine is just to insure a richer broth. When the meats are done, remove from the broth and cool. Taste the broth and let it cook down to one half. Divide the gravy in half. For giblet gravy, chop the giblets very finely. Some do not include the gizzard. Chop the eggs and add to the gravy. Taste for seasonings.

Thickening

8 teaspoons flour (more if a thick gravy is wanted)
½ cup cold water

Shake together in a jar with a lid. Pour into boiling liquid gradually. Let simmer at least 5 minutes to cook away the "uncooked" taste.

Note: Canned, drained, mushroom caps and pieces may be added as well as snipped parsley.

Sweet And Sour Beans

2 (10 ounce) packages frozen green beans (or 2 - 16 ounce cans)
6 strips of bacon

2 tablespoons finely chopped onion
5 tablespoons brown sugar
4 tablespoons vinegar
3 tablespoons bacon drippings

Cook the beans according to directions. Cook bacon until crisp, drain reserving 3 tablespoons drippings. Drain beans, then add brown sugar, vinegar and drippings, cook until the sugar is dissolved and beans are hot through. Serve with the crisp bacon crumbled and mixed with the onion on top. Serves 6.

Revivals

Stella's Sweet Potato Soufflé

4 cups coarsley ground raw sweet potatoes (about 2 large potatoes)
1 cup milk
1 (20 ounce) can crushed pineapple, with juice
¾ cup butter or margarine, melted
1 teaspoon vanilla
1 cup chopped pecans (which have been toasted in butter)
1 cup sugar
1 cup frozen grated coconut
¼ cup frozen grated coconut, for garnish
2 ounces bourbon

Grind the potatoes on the coarse blade of hand grinder (your food processor can be used). Place in the milk to prevent discoloration. Stir in the crushed pineapple, butter or margarine, vanilla, pecans, sugar and the cup of coconut. Mix well and fill a 3 quart casserole and bake in a preheated 350°F oven, uncovered, for 40 to 55 minutes. Remove from oven and sprinkle with the ¼ cup coconut. Return to oven, and broil briefly to lightly brown. Remove from oven and cool for 30 minutes. Pour the bourbon evenly over the top. This is a slightly crunchy casserole and can be served hot or at room temperature. Serves 10 to 12.

Stella Carter

Au Gratin Vegetables

2 cups carrots, cooked and diced
1 cup cooked peas
3 tablespoons melted butter
⅓ cup grated cheese
1 cup sweet milk
1 egg, beaten
½ teaspoon salt
1 cup buttered crumbs

Mix all the above, except crumbs, together, place in greased baking dish and top with the buttered crumbs. Bake in moderate oven 30 minutes. Serves 4 to 6.

This is a recipe of my great grandmother, Mrs. T. E. Beck of Union City, Tennessee. So good and so easy.

Mrs. Stephen M. Bell
Jackson, Mississippi

Menu

Spiced Oranges

8 whole medium oranges (juicy, thin skinned ones are best)
5 cups sugar
3 cups water

1 ¼ cups cider vinegar
24 whole cloves
2 sticks cinnamon

Simmer whole oranges, uncovered, in enough water to cover. This will take about 30 minutes. Cool and drain. Combine the sugar, water, vinegar and spices in a large pan. You may cut the oranges in halves, quarters or slices and place in the syrup. Simmer for 20 minutes. Remove the cinnamon sticks. Spoon into 6 hot pint jars. Cover with the liquid. Seal and refrigerate. The halves are beautiful on the tray with your turkey and the quarters look beautiful with duck or chicken. They have an unusual sweet and tart flavor and the rind is a real treat. Tip: You may want to double the syrup recipe to be certain you have enough. Keeps refrigerated several weeks. Heat slightly at serving time. Serves 8 or more.

Mallie Vesta Knight

Ambrosia

8 to 10 oranges (or enough to make 4 or 5 cups of sections)

½ to 1 cup sugar (or to taste)
1 cup grated fresh or frozen coconut

Peel oranges, remove seeds and membrane, and section. Add sugar to taste (this varies with the sweetness of the oranges). Toss with the coconut and refrigerate until sugar dissolves. This will keep as long as a week and improves with sitting. Serves 4 to 6.

Revivals

Ice Box Rolls

1 quart sweet milk
1 cup shortening
1 cup sugar
1 yeast cake (or 2 packages of granulated yeast)

1 teaspoon baking soda
1 tablespoon baking powder
1 teaspoon salt
All purpose flour
Butter or margarine

Put milk, sugar and shortening in the top of a double boiler. Heat on slow heat until shortening melts. Cool. When lukewarm add the yeast and enough flour to make a stiff batter (like a heavy cake batter). Beat until very light, cover, and let rise in a warm place 2 or 3 hours. You need a large crock or mixing bowl for this. Punch down, add baking powder, baking soda, salt and enough flour to make a stiff dough. Work until smooth. Place in refrigerator until needed. This will still rise a little. Keep it covered. When you are ready to use, roll out as you do for biscuits using flour to keep from sticking to rolling pin or board. Brush on melted butter, or dip in butter, and fold over for pocketbook rolls. Make 3 little balls and place in greased muffin pans for clover leaf rolls. Let rise in a warm place for 1 hour. Bake at 450°F until lightly browned. I find that 3 cups of flour is about right for the batter and about 3 more for the dough. If you add enough flour to be able to handle it, the dough will be very floury and will be dry when you bake the rolls. When you roll out the rolls, use just enough flour to be able to handle well. If you want 12 rolls, make them and put back the scraps of dough. Keep the rest of the dough in the refrigerator. Makes 6 or more dozen.

This recipe is over 50 years old and handed down to me by my sister-in-law, Freddie Virginia Warriner Thompson, who got it from her mother.

Mrs. Richard B. Warriner

Menu

Clara Dove Brasher Ward's Boiled Custard

2 quarts whole milk, plus ½ cup
5 large eggs
1 teaspoon salt

1 cup sugar
2 tablespoons cornstarch
2 teaspoons vanilla extract

Heat the 2 quarts of milk with ½ of the sugar in it. Heat until near boiling but never let it boil. Set the milk aside. Separate the eggs and beat the whites and yolks separately. Beat the remaining sugar into the yolks. Then fold the sweetened and beaten yolks into the beaten egg whites, gently. Do not beat. Dissolve 2 tablespoons cornstarch in ½ cup whole milk. Beat this into the hot sweet milk. Lightly fold the egg mixture into the warm milk and heat in double boiler for about 5 minutes with very little and very gentle stirring and folding. Add the vanilla. Do not stir much. Do not at any stage let the milk boil. Chill overnight in a jug or covered container. Stir well before serving in a cup and flavor with bourbon to taste. Serves about 16.

Dr. Dennis Ward

Pumpkin Pie

2 large eggs or 3 small eggs
¾ cup sugar
2 cups pumpkin
1 cup milk
½ teaspoon ginger

1 teaspoon cinnamon
½ teaspoon nutmeg
½ teaspoon salt
1 tablespoon cornstarch

Beat eggs and sugar until fluffy. Add other ingredients and beat slowly till blended. Pour in shell. Bake at 450°F for 10 minutes then reduce heat to 325°F for 50 minutes for two 9 inch pies. Add 10 minutes for deep dish at the end of the baking time.

This recipe is 50 years old and was handed down to me by my grandmother.

Lynn Elliott

Revivals

Dried Apple Cake

Home dried apples, sufficient to make 2½ cups sauce
1 cup bourbon
1 cup black seedless raisins
1 cup finely chopped English walnuts
2 cups sugar
1 cup butter
½ teaspoon salt
1 teaspoon vanilla extract

2 teaspoons cinnamon
2 teaspoons nutmeg
1 teaspoon cloves (ground)
1 teaspoon allspice
4 cups all purpose flour
4 teaspoons baking soda
2 cups sugar
1 cup whole milk
1 teaspoon vanilla
1 cup bourbon

On day prior to making cake cook home dried apples into a sauce and chill overnight. (Commercially dried apples do not do as well.) Also on day before, cover a cup of black seedless raisins with the 1 cup of bourbon to soak. When ready to make the cake, preheat oven to 350°F and grease 3 (9 inch) cake pans with shortening and dust with flour. Drain and reserve the bourbon off the raisins and dust them with flour. In large bowl, cream 2 cups sugar into cup of real butter. Blend into this the bourbon off the raisins, ½ teaspoon salt, the vanilla and all the spices and lastly the 2½ cups of applesauce and 1 cup of flour. Knead in the nuts and raisins. Sift together 3 cups flour and 4 teaspoons soda. Knead this into the mixture rapidly by hand. It is thick and sticky. Divide into three equal portions and "smash" into pans (no need to spread evenly). Quickly get this into the oven and bake for 5 minutes at 350°F. Reduce heat to 225°F and bake until done, about 45 minutes. Glaze while hot.

Glaze: Mix 2 cups sugar, cup of whole milk in large saucepan and boil gently with constant stirring until it forms a soft ball when dropped into a glass of cold water. Stir in teaspoon of vanilla. Rapidly spread this over the still warm cake, between layers and over top and sides while it is still very hot. Let cake stand in open air overnight until glaze is dry. Tightly wrap in plastic wrap and aluminum foil. Some 5 days after making the cake, unwrap it and drench the top and sides with the remaining cup of bourbon. Reseal cake. Do not refrigerate. Cut cake when two weeks old and serve with boiled custard.

This recipe is over 200 years old. Handed down from my grandmother, Bertie Bingham Ward, and has been traditionally served at Christmas.

Dr. Dennis Ward

Menu

Big Mama's 3-Flavor Pound Cake

3 cups sugar
½ cup oil
1 cup margarine
6 eggs
3 cups all purpose flour

1 teaspoon baking powder
1 teaspoon vanilla flavoring
1 teaspoon butter flavoring
1 teaspoon coconut flavoring

Cream sugar and shortening (oil). Add eggs, one at a time. Beat after each addition. Add flavoring. Continue beating. Alternate flour and milk (ending with flour). Pour into greased and floured 10 inch tube pan. Start in cold oven and bake 1¼ hours at 325°F.

This recipe is many years old and was handed down to me by my mother from her mother.

Mrs. Carl Welch

Cheese Icebox Wafers

½ pound sharp Cheddar cheese, shredded
¼ pound butter

½ teaspoon salt
Small pinch cayenne pepper
1½ cups sifted all purpose flour

Cream together cheese, butter, salt and cayenne and flour. Make into roll, wrap in wax paper and place in refrigerator. When needed, slice into thin rounds, bake in a moderate oven. Top each with a pecan, salt and paprika. Makes about 4 dozen.

When I make these I always make two recipes as the rolls will freeze well. This was my grandmother's recipe and is over 75 years old.

Mrs. Edward S. T. Hale

Revivals

Old Southern Chicken Cracklings

Cut the fat from a chicken into small pieces. Render over low heat until "cracklings" are golden crisp. Do not try to rush or cracklings will be tough. Lift cracklings from liquid fat and drain on paper towels. Add to your favorite cornbread recipe.

From: Kathleen Forrest Bradley
Memphis, Tennessee
(Great-Granddaughter of Gen N. B. Forrest)

Old Roosevelt Hotel Remoulade Sauce

2 egg yolks
1 cup creole mustard
¼ cup vinegar
Juice of 1 lemon
Salt and pepper

2 cups salad oil
1 bunch green onions, minced
½ stalk celery, minced
4 pounds peeled, cleaned, boiled shrimp

Blend egg yolks, mustard, vinegar, lemon juice, salt and pepper. Add oil slowly, beating constantly as when making mayonnaise. When sauce has thickened, add green onions and celery; soak shrimp in this sauce for 4 hours; serve on lettuce. Serves 12 to 16.

Mrs. C. J. Richardson
Cleveland, Mississippi

Heirloom Recipes

Chicken Sauce Piquant

5 cooking spoons (long handled stirring spoon) cooking oil
3 cooking spoons all purpose flour
4 (large) chopped onions
1 (17 ounce) can peas
1 (6 ounce) can mushrooms, or fresh
1 (3 to 4 pound) chicken
1 (28 ounce) can tomatoes
½ pod minced garlic
Red pepper and salt, to taste

Brown flour in oil, then add onions, minced garlic and cook to golden brown. Add tomatoes. Let this fry until well cooked, then add the chicken, cut into pieces, and enough water to make gravy. Cover and cook slowly until the chicken is ready to leave the bone. Remove bones and skin. Just before serving, add mushrooms and sweet peas. Serve over rice. Serves 6.

This is an old Cajun recipe.

Alyce Richardson
Cleveland, Mississippi

Baked Sauerkraut And Chicken

1 chicken cut into pieces
¼ cup oil
1 large chopped onion
4 slices bacon
1½ pounds sauerkraut (drained and rinsed)
2 bay leaves
1 teaspoon pepper corns
1½ cup chicken broth (can be made with bouillon cube)
Butter, to taste
Salt, to taste

Fry onions and bacon in oil for 15 minutes on low flame. Add sauerkraut, bay leaves, pepper corns and broth. Simmer ½ hour. Arrange chicken pieces over top. Rub a little butter and salt on chicken. Bake 2 hours at 350°F. Goes great with mashed potatoes and a hardy full grained bread. Serves 4.

This recipe was given to me by my grandmother.

Kathleen A. Masters

Revivals

Spaghetti Deluxe

2½ pounds beef
2½ pounds pork
3 pounds onions, peeled and chopped
1 (46 ounce) can tomato juice
1 (6 ounce) can tomato paste
1 (2 ounce) bottle olive oil
1 (1½ ounce) package chili mix
2 (¾ ounce) packages dried mushrooms

½ teaspoon cumin powder
½ cup parsley flakes
2 tablespoons paprika
1 tablespoon spaghetti spices
1 raw carrot, grated
1 stalk celery, chopped very fine
3 cloves garlic, minced
Salt and pepper, to taste
4 pounds spaghetti

Cook meats in just enough water to cover, until it falls apart, several hours. (Or pressure cook according to cooker directions.) Add all other ingredients, except spaghetti, and simmer for 30 to 40 minutes, adding more water if necessary for thick sauce consistency. Serve over spaghetti, cooked according to package directions. Serves 25.

This recipe was handed down to me by my in-laws.

Mrs. Travis Nelson

Tourtiere Canadian Meat Pie

2 pounds ground pork
1 medium onion, chopped
½ teaspoon cinnamon
½ teaspoon ground cloves

Salt and pepper, to taste
1 pound potatoes, peeled, quartered, boiled and mashed
Pastry for 2 (9 inch) crust pies

Heirloom Recipes

Sauté pork and onion until browned. Pour off fat and add water almost to the top of the meat. Add salt, pepper, cinnamon and cloves and simmer 1 hour. Meanwhile, peel and cut up potatoes and boil until done. Drain and mash coarsely with hand potato masher. Add to meat mixture. Place uncooked pie dough (a 10 inch circle) in 9 inch pie pan. Spoon half the meat-potato mixture into it and cover with top crust. Crimp edges to seal and cut decorative vents in the top. Repeat with second pie using other half of the filling. Brush tops with beaten egg. Cook at 350°F in the oven approximately 1 hour or until the crust is done. These freeze well. If frozen, to reheat, place in slow oven for about 1 hour. Makes 2 pies. Each Serves: 6.

This recipe is over 100 years old and was handed down to me by my husband's Canadian born mother, who later moved to Vermont.

Mary Bushey

Yorkshire Pudding

1 cup all purpose flour
1 cup milk
2 eggs
½ teaspoon salt

Roast beef drippings, supplemented with butter or margarine

Mix flour and milk to a smooth paste in medium mixing bowl. In separate bowl beat eggs and salt until thick and lemon colored. Gradually pour beaten eggs into milk mixture, blending well. Beat for 2 minutes. Preheat oven to 425°F. Heat an 8 cup muffin tin with 1½ teaspoons of drippings in each cup until the drippings are hot. Drop batter into cups until half full. Bake for 20 minutes or until lightly browned. May be made as one pudding by heating 1 inch of drippings in an 8 inch cake pan. Serves 6.

This recipe is a century old and was handed down to me by my Great-Aunt, Mrs. Angus Findlay (Mary), originally from Struan Park, Scotland.

Janice Wilcox Grady

Revivals

Creole Gumbo

2 tablespoons bacon drippings (rendered bacon fat)
3 tablespoons all purpose flour

2 quarts chicken broth (canned may be used)

Make a Roux

Make a roux by cooking flour in bacon fat on low heat. This takes time and must not burn! (If it burns start over.) The flour should be nicely browned. Add broth, stirring to prevent lumping. After it thickens slightly, set aside, to be used later.

The Gumbo

3 strips bacon
2 large onions, finely chopped
2 cloves garlic, peeled and minced
1 small green pepper, minced
3 cups chopped okra, fresh or frozen
1 (16 ounce) can tomatoes, chopped, drained, reserve juice
4 bay leaves

2 pounds shrimp, uncooked, cleaned
1 pound crabmeat, or 6 cleaned fresh crabs
1 pint (2 cups) oysters
1 teaspoon salt
1 teaspoon pepper
1 dash Louisiana hot sauce
1 dash cayenne (red) pepper
1 dash Worcestershire sauce

Fry bacon, which has been cubed. Add chopped vegetables including chopped, drained tomatoes. Sauté until onion is golden, stirring occasionally. Add the roux, juice from the tomatoes and all of the seasonings. Cook very slowly (and watchfully) for 2 hours. About 30 minutes before gumbo is to be served, add seafood and additional salt, if necessary, and barely simmer. Gumbo will become darker with the addition of the seafood.

Serve piping hot over a mound of cooked rice. (This recipe is over 50 years old and was handed down to me by my grandmother, Mrs. W. B. Herring of Pascagoula, MS.)

Lenoir Stanley

Heirloom Recipes

Corn Lightbread

2 cups boiling water
2 cups cornmeal
2 cups cold water
½ teaspoon baking soda
1 teaspoon salt
1 cup buttermilk

½ teaspoon baking soda
1 teaspoon salt
½ cup sugar
1 egg
½ cup lard
Handful of cornmeal

2 cups boiling water and 2 cups plain cornmeal made into mush. Add 2 cups cold water, ½ teaspoon baking soda, 1 teaspoon salt; stir into mush until thick. Set in a warm place until morning. Add 1 cup buttermilk, ½ teaspoon baking soda, 1 teaspoon salt, ½ cup sugar, 1 egg, ½ cup lard and a handful of meal. Stir well and pour it on a hot greased 6x5x3 inch loaf pan and bake immediately. Bake at 325°F for 30 minutes. Makes 1 loaf.

This recipe is 125 years old and was handed down to me by my grandmother, Mrs. Pearl Ferguson, of Chapel Hill, Tennessee.

Mrs. David DeVaughn

Hot Water Cornbread

1½ cups cornmeal
Pinch of salt
1 tablespoon sugar

2 tablespoons bacon drippings, melted
1 to 1½ cups boiling water

Mix all ingredients together and drop onto baking sheet or pat out and place on baking sheet. Bake at 400°F for 20 minutes. Makes 1 dozen pieces. This old-timey cornbread is delicious with fresh country vegetables or at a fish fry, in place of hush-puppies. Makes 1 dozen pieces.

This recipe is 100 years old, handed down to me by my mother, Mrs. Ellis Latimer, Jr., formerly Dorothy Dowlen of Corinth and Okolona, Mississippi.

Rosemary Fisher

Revivals

Mama Ream's Rolls

4 cups milk
1 cup shortening
1 cup sugar
1 package yeast
¼ cup lukewarm water

8 cups all purpose flour, divided
1 heaping teaspoon baking powder
1 teaspoon baking soda
1 tablespoon salt

In a large saucepan slowly boil milk, shortening and sugar for 2 to 3 minutes. Let this cool. Dissolve yeast in warm water. Add to cooled mixture along with 4 cups of flour. Cover this and set aside in a warm place to rise for 2 hours. Then add baking powder, baking soda, salt, and remaining 4 cups of flour. Work this all together with hands, cover and refrigerate. Roll into clover leaves or cut into rolls. Let rise again 2 to 3 hours. Be sure to grease your pan. Bake at 375°F for 10 minutes. Then bake loaves of bread at 325°F for 1 hour. I put a little grease and flour on my hands when working with dough. This dough stays good in refrigerator for a week. Makes 100 rolls or 3 loaves of bread.

Mary Hedges

Sweet Potato Biscuits

1 cup all purpose flour
3 teaspoons baking powder
½ teaspoon salt

⅓ cup shortening
1½ cups mashed sweet potatoes
3 tablespoons sweet milk

Combine dry ingredients and cut in shortening. Add potatoes and the milk to make a soft dough. Turn out on floured board and knead lightly and roll to ½ inch thickness. Cut in your favorite style. Cook at 450°F for 15 to 20 minutes. Makes 15 medium size biscuits.

My mother's recipe, at least 100 years old.

Mrs. C. B. Sawyer, Mildred

Heirloom Recipes

Grandmother's Spoon Bread

3 cups milk
¾ cup cornmeal
1 teaspoon salt

3 tablespoons butter
3 well beaten eggs
1 teaspoon baking powder

Heat milk in saucepan until hot. Gradually add cornmeal to hot milk, stirring constantly to prevent lumps. Cook until mixture has thickened. Cool. Add salt, butter, eggs, and baking powder. Mix well, and turn into greased 1 quart casserole. Bake in 375°F oven for 30 minutes. Serves 6. A real southern specialty.

This recipe is 75 years old and was handed down to me by my grandmother, Zena Burns.

Lynn Wroten

Buttermilk Pancakes

2 eggs
2 cups all purpose flour
2 teaspoons baking powder
½ teaspoon baking soda

3 tablespoons sugar
2 cups sour milk (buttermilk)
4 tablespoons melted butter

Separate 2 eggs. Whip the whites until standing in peaks - set aside. In another bowl sift together flour, baking powder, baking soda and sugar. Add the egg yolks, sour milk and melted butter, stirring until well mixed (Bill uses an electric mixer up to this point, Grandma didn't!) Gently fold in the egg whites, spoon batter onto a hot griddle to form 5 inch round pancakes. Cook cakes till golden and turn. Serve hot off the grill with warm maple syrup. Serves 4 to 6.

This recipe is more than 75 years old handed down to me by Joan's grandmother, Martha Gerszewski.

Bill Hennessy

Revivals

Fruit Salad With Cooked Sauce

¾ cup sugar
2 tablespoons flour
2 egg yolks, beaten
Juice of 1 medium lemon
1 (8 ounce) can pineapple chunks, reserve juice

4 tart apples, peeled, cored and cut into bite size pieces
1 banana, sliced
2 cups red grapes, seeded and cut into halves
1 cup pecans, broken

Make sauce before preparing fruit. Mix sugar and flour, add pineapple juice, egg yolks and lemon juice. Cook over medium heat until very thick, stirring constantly. Must be very thick because juice in the fruit will dilute it. Cool in refrigerator. Mix with fruit. Great with Christmas meals, brunch or dinner. Serves 6.

This recipe is 100 years old and was handed down to me by my mother, Mrs. Paul Wiles, Memphis, Tennessee, given to her by her aunt, Mrs. C. M. Mount, Franklin, Tennessee.

Wanda Witt

Stewed Georgia Peaches

8 firm ripe peaches
1½ cups sugar

6 whole cloves
Water, enough to cover peaches

Peel peaches (leave whole) and put in a pot. Add enough water to cover peaches. Add sugar and cloves. Simmer uncovered until peaches are easily pierced with a fork and begin to appear translucent. Remove cloves and serve warm or chilled. Serves 8.

This recipe is 65 years old and was handed down to me by my mother, Mrs. George Archer, Jr., of Greenville, MS. It was her mother's favorite recipe for Georgia peaches.

Mrs. Hull Davis (Bitsy)

Heirloom Recipes

Marble Cake

White Part

½ cup butter
1½ cups sugar
½ cup milk
2½ cups all purpose flour

4 egg whites, beaten until stiff
1 teaspoon baking powder
1 teaspoon lemon extract

Mix butter and sugar until light colored; sift flour and baking powder together; add lemon extract to milk then mix alternately with flour to butter mixture until thoroughly mixed.

Dark Part

½ cup butter
½ cup molasses
2 cups brown sugar
½ cup "sour milk"
½ teaspoon baking soda

2 cups all purpose flour
4 egg yolks
1 whole egg
1 teaspoon ground cloves
1 teaspoon ground cinnamon

Mix butter, molasses and brown sugar thoroughly; sift baking soda, flour, cloves and cinnamon together; beat egg yolks, plus whole egg well; add to sour milk and then mix alternately with flour to butter-sugar mixture. Using large well buttered pan, alternate large spoonfuls of white mixture with dark mixture until all is used. Bake in moderate oven (350°F) until done. About 35 to 40 minutes. Serves 12.

This recipe is over 80 years old and was handed down to me by my grandmother, Persis Garland Warner, Lake Village, Arkansas. She took it from a newspaper in the summer of 1902.

Helen R. Foster
Jackson, Tennessee

Revivals

Old Fashioned Jelly Roll

1 cup sifted all purpose flour
¼ teaspoon salt
¾ teaspoon baking powder
5 eggs, separated
1 teaspoon grated lemon rind

2 tablespoons lemon juice
1 cup sugar
1 cup currant jelly (or any other tart jelly)

Sift together the salt and baking powder. Beat egg yolks until thick as mayonnaise. Stir in lemon rind and juice. Beat well. Gradually add sugar, beating until thickened. Whip egg whites until stiff but not dry. Add the flour to the yolk mixture alternately with egg whites, folding in gently and thoroughly. Pour into a 15½x10½x1 inch jelly-roll pan that has been lightly greased, lined with waxed paper and greased again. Spread batter evenly and bake in hot oven, 400°F for 12 to 14 minutes or until it springs back from the touch. Turn cake out onto a cloth that has been dusted with powdered sugar. Quickly remove paper and trim edges of the cake. Roll up in towel and cool. Break up jelly in a bowl with a fork. Unroll cake onto waxed paper and spread jelly evenly. Roll up again and place on serving plate, seam side down. Glaze and decorate as desired. Serves 6 to 8.

This recipe is old and handed down to me by a friend in military travels.

Mrs. Travis M. Nelson (Fae)

Old Fashioned Light Fruit Cake

1 pound shelled pecans
1 pound blanched almonds
1 pound candied pineapple
1 pound candied cherries
1 pound seedless white raisins
½ pound ready-mix candied orange and lemon peel
½ pound soft butter
2¼ cups sugar

1½ teaspoons cinnamon
1 teaspoon salt
1 teaspoon baking soda
4 cups flour
6 whole eggs
1 teaspoon nutmeg
1 tablespoon vanilla
1 teaspoon baking powder

Heirloom Recipes

Mix all fruit and nuts with 2 cups flour. Set aside. Mix butter, sugar, eggs, and flavoring until creamy. Sift together all remaining ingredients; add to butter-egg mixture. Work into batter with hands the fruit and nuts. Fill foil-lined tube pan ⅔ full. Cook at 250°F for 3 hours. Cook remainder in loaf pan at 250°F for 2 hours. (Line loaf pan with foil.) Keep in cool place after cakes are done. Season with grape juice and wrap carefully. (Option: season with preferred spirits.) Makes 1 tube cake and 1 small loaf cake.

Note: Make cake 3 weeks before Holidays!

Mrs. Margaret F. Smith

Lemon Cake-Pudding

3 tablespoons of butter or margarine
1 cup sugar
4 tablespoons all purpose flour
⅛ teaspoon salt

5 tablespoons lemon juice
1 or 2 rinds of lemon, grated
3 eggs, separated
1½ cups milk
Oil

Cream butter, sugar and flour. Add salt, lemon juice and lemon rind. Mix in egg yolks and milk. Beat egg whites until stiff and fold them into mixture. Oil 7 custard cups with vegetable oil. Pour mixture into cups and place the custard cups into a 9x13 inch pan. Add about 1 inch of water to pan around cups. Cook uncovered 45 minutes at 350°F. Top of cakes will be lightly browned. Remove custard cups from pan and chill. Serves 7.

This recipe is 75 years old and handed down to me by my husband's grandmother, Mrs. W. C. Hull.

Mrs. Hull Davis

Revivals

Potato Cake

2 cups sugar
1 cup butter or margarine, softened
4 eggs, separated
4 tablespoons cocoa
2 cups plain flour
½ teaspoon salt
2 teaspoons baking powder

½ teaspoon ground cloves
½ teaspoon ground cinnamon
½ teaspoon ground nutmeg
⅔ cup milk
1 cup hot mashed potatoes
1 teaspoon vanilla
1 cup chopped pecans

In a large mixing bowl, cream sugar and butter. Add egg yolks and cream well. Sift together the dry ingredients. Add alternately with the milk to the creamed mixture. Add the potatoes. Fold in stiffly beaten egg whites. Add the nuts and vanilla. Pour into 2 greased and floured 8 inch cake pans. Bake at 350°F for 25 to 30 minutes or until a toothpick comes out clean when inserted in the center. Cool completely before frosting.

This recipe is 60 years old and was handed down to me by my grandmother, Mrs. Pearl Ferguson.

Mrs. David DeVaughn

Date Cake

4 pounds dates, pitted
2 pounds English walnuts
2 cups sugar
2 cups all purpose flour

2 teaspoons baking powder
Pinch of salt
8 eggs, beaten separately
1 teaspoon vanilla

Mix dry ingredients with dates and nuts. Add beaten egg yolks. Fold in stiffly beaten egg whites last. Bake in angel food type cake pan, greased and lined with greased brown paper. Bake in 250°F oven for 4 hours - more or less - WATCH IT.

This is a favorite Christmas cake as it appeals to those who do not ordinarily care for fruit cake. The recipe is at least 60 years old.

Mrs. Walker Tanner
Union City, Tennessee

Heirloom Recipes

Mystery Cake

2 tablespoons shortening
1 cup sugar
1 egg
1 (10¾ ounce) can condensed tomato soup
1½ cup plain flour
1 teaspoon baking soda
¼ teaspoon salt
1 teaspoon cinnamon
1 teaspoon cloves
1 teaspoon nutmeg
1 cup seedless raisins
½ cup chopped pecans

Mix first 10 ingredients and beat well. Then add 1 cup seedless raisins, ½ cup chopped pecans. Pour batter into slightly greased cake pan, bake at 375°F for 30 minutes, ice with caramel icing.

This recipe is 55 years old.

Mrs. Frank Hinton

Aunt Lala's Pie Crust

2½ cups all purpose flour
½ teaspoon salt
¾ cup to 1 cup shortening
8 to 10 tablespoons heavy cream

Mix flour and salt. Cut shortening into flour mixture with two knives until it is pea size. Add cream, tablespoon by tablespoon, stirring with a fork until you can make a ball that holds together. (If dough falls apart add more cream.) Roll out on floured board. Makes enough for a 2 crust pie.

This recipe is at least 90 years old and was handed down to me by my great-aunt, a marvelous cook who lived in northern Maine.

Deborah Pierce Nicklas
Falmouth, Maine

Revivals

Old Fashioned Chess Pie

2 cups sugar
5 whole eggs
½ cup melted margarine

1½ teaspoons vanilla
1 (9 inch) unbaked pie crust

Mix sugar and eggs. Add melted margarine gradually; add milk; add vanilla. Make certain all ingredients are mixed well. Preheat oven to 325°F. Put mixture in pie shell and bake approximately 45 minutes, or until the center is firm.* Makes 1 large pie.

*This recipe is 100 years old and was handed down to me by my grandmother, Adelaide Wheeler Walker.

Mrs. C. B. Sawyer

Mom's Coconut Pie

1 cup sugar
3 tablespoons all purpose flour
1 (7 ounce) package coconut
3 egg yolks

2½ cups milk
Pinch salt
2 tablespoons butter
1 teaspoon vanilla

Mix sugar and flour. Add other ingredients (reserving a bit of the coconut for garnish on the meringue). Cook, stirring constantly, until thickened. Pour into cooked pie shell. Top with meringue from your own favorite recipe, sprinkle with reserved coconut, and bake until meringue and coconut are golden brown.

This recipe is 65 to 80 years old and was handed down to me by my mother.

Mrs. Travis M. Nelson (Fae)

Heirloom

Mamaw's Pecan Pie

1 cup sugar
1 cup white corn syrup
⅓ cup butter
3 eggs

1 cup pecans
Dash salt
1 teaspoon vanilla

Cream butter and sugar. Add eggs one at a time beating well after each addition. Then add other ingredients and mix well. Bake in unbaked pie crust 1 hour in slow oven (about 350°F).

This recipe is 70 years old and was handed down to me by my grandmother.

Claire Stanley

Gran's Pie

1½ cups sugar
3 eggs
¾ cup raisins
¾ cup pecans
2 tablespoons cold water

1 teaspoon vinegar
½ stick of butter or margarine
½ teaspoon cinnamon or any other spice desired
1 unbaked pie shell

Cream sugar and butter. Add well beaten eggs. Add remaining ingredients. Bake in a 350°F oven for 30 minutes or until done in an unbaked pie shell.

This recipe is many years old and handed down to me by my grandmother.

Mrs. Rivers Ulmer

Old South Pecan Custard Pie

½ cup plus 1 tablespoon sugar
2 tablespoons cornstarch
½ teaspoon salt
1 cup white corn syrup
3 large eggs
1½ tablespoons vanilla
¼ stick margarine
2 cups pecans
1 deep dish pie crust

Combine sugar, corn starch and salt in a large bowl. Add corn syrup and mix. Beat eggs with mixer and add. Stir in vanilla and melted margarine. Run pecans through food chopper (fine grind) and add to mixture. Beat with electric mixer (medium speed for about 30 seconds) until well mixed. Pour into deep pie crust. Bake in a preheated 400°F oven for 15 minutes. Lower to 325°F and bake for 40 to 45 minutes until set.

Kathleen Forrest Bradley
Memphis, Tennessee
Great-granddaughter of
General N. B. Forrest

Emily's Chocolate Pie

3 eggs
1 cup sugar
2 cups milk
2 teaspoons cream
2 tablespoons cocoa
3 teaspoons butter or margarine
2 teaspoons flour
1 teaspoon almond extract
1 (9 inch) baked pie shell

Beat egg yolks well. Add flour and cocoa to sugar. Stir in the dry mixture into the beaten egg yolks and beat well to get all ingredients well blended. Heat mixture in top of a double boiler until the mixture is thick. Add the butter to hot filling. Then add the almond flavoring. Pour filling into a baked pie shell. Cover the top of the pie filling with the beaten egg whites and brown the whites slowly. One may add nuts or coconut in the filling for variety.

Heirloom Recipes

Topping

3 egg whites   3 tablespoons sugar

Beat egg whites to a stiff froth and add sugar and beat until stiff. Spread over pie filling and brown the meringue for 2 to 4 minutes in 450°F oven.

This recipe is 60 years old and was handed down to me by my mother, Mrs. James Walker (Olga). This is an original recipe.

Mrs. Don L. Glisson (Marcia Ann)

Date Pie

Crust

1½ cups flour   ½ teaspoon baking soda
⅓ cup oatmeal   1 cup brown sugar
¾ cup butter   1 teaspoon vanilla

Cream butter and sugar. Add flour and oatmeal. Mix well. Add baking soda and vanilla. Mix well. Pinch off small amounts of dough and flatten with palms of hands. Place pieces in bottom and along sides of 10 inch pie pan letting the pieces overlap.

Filling

1 (1 pound) box chopped dates   ¾ cup cold water
1 cup sugar

Simmer on top of stove until dates are done and the mixture has thickened. Pour into the oatmeal crust. Bake at 300°F for 30 minutes. Serves 8 to 10.

This recipe is over 50 years old and was handed down to me by my mother, Mrs. Henry Arnold of Corinth, Mississippi.

Mrs. Faye A. Hodges
Columbus, Mississippi

Revivals

Zweiback Pie

1 (4 ounce) package Zweiback toast, crust crushed
¾ cup sugar
1 teaspoon cinnamon
½ cup melted butter

Mix all ingredients together and pack in a 9 inch buttered pie plate (reserve ½ cup for the top of pie). In packing the crust down also force it up the sides of the pie plate to the top. Cook in a 300°F oven for 8 minutes. Cool.

Pie Filling

1 (5 5/8 ounce) package vanilla pudding made according to package instructions
2 egg whites
4 tablespoons sugar
½ pint whipping cream
2 tablespoons sugar

Make pie filling according to instructions; cool to room temperature and pour or spoon evenly into cooled crust. Beat the egg whites, gradually adding 4 tablespoons sugar until stiff peaks are formed. Spread over pie and bake in a 400°F (preheated) oven until lightly browned. Cool! Beat the whipping cream, gradually adding the 2 tablespoons sugar until peaks form. Spread and swirl over the top of the pie. Sprinkle with the reserved crust mixture.

Note: The meringue may be omitted if you are counting calories. And whipped topping may be used. (But it won't be nearly as wonderful!) Classic filling - below may be used.

Mrs. T. Y. Williford, Sr.
Cleveland, Mississippi

Pastry Cream

4 eggs
¾ cup sugar
⅓ cup cornstarch
2 cups milk
3 tablespoons Amaretto (can substitute 1 tablespoon vanilla)

Heirloom Recipes

Mix eggs, sugar and cornstarch in a bowl. Bring milk to a boil. Whisking constantly, pour milk slowly into the sugar mixture. Pour mixture back in the saucepan and place over medium high heat, whisking constantly until thickened. Remove from heat and cool to room temperature. Add Amaretto (or vanilla), cover and refrigerate until ready to use. This pastry cream will keep for 3 days. Makes about 3 cups. May use with Zweiback Pie.

Pastry Chef
Plaza Hotel
New York City, New York

Tea Cakes

2 eggs, beaten well
1 teaspoon vanilla
2 tablespoons sweet milk
1 cup shortening

1 cup sugar
4 cups all purpose flour
2 teaspoons cream of tartar
1 teaspoon baking soda

Mix together eggs, vanilla and milk. Cream shortening and sugar and add egg mixture to it. Mix flour, cream of tartar and baking soda together and add to egg mixture. If dough isn't stiff enough to roll out, add more flour. Cut out cookies with cookie cutters. Bake until slightly brown around edges, at 350°F. Makes 4 dozen.

This recipe is 75 years old and was handed down to me by my mother, Priscilla Nelson King.

Imogene King Stanley

"Rightly thought of there is poetry in peaches, even when they are canned.", Harley Granville Barker, English dramatist.

Revivals

Peach Sherbet

2 eggs
2 cups sugar
1 quart milk

1 quart crushed peaches
Juice of 1½ lemons

Beat eggs slightly and add 1½ cups of the sugar. Add to milk. Put in freezer. When it begins to chill, add peaches to which the other ½ cup of sugar and all the lemon juice have been added. Continue to freeze until firm. Serves 6.

This recipe is 50 to 75 years old and was handed down to me by Mrs. J. C. Tucker, Ecru, Mississippi.

Nancy Smith

Great Grandmother's Fruit Sherbet

3 cups sugar
3 cups water
1 (15 ounce) can crushed pineapple

Juice of 6 lemons
Juice of 3 oranges
3 large bananas, mashed
Milk

The day before: In a saucepan heat sugar and water almost to a boil to dissolve sugar. Let cool overnight in refrigerator to shorten freezing time. Add remaining ingredients (except milk), and pour into a 5 quart hand crank or electric freezer. Pack freezer with ice and rock salt according to freezer directions. Run freezer for 10 to 15 minutes, then open and add milk to the fill line or to within 2 inches from top of container. Continue freezing until hard to crank or until electric freezer seems to "labor" and slow. Repack around freezer with ice and rock salt and cover with heavy towel and allow to "season" an hour or two. Leftovers may be put in pint or quart size plastic containers and stored in freezer. However, it gets very hard, so you will need to take them out of freezer about 10 or 15 minutes before serving. Serves 6.

Ms. Betty A. Jennings
Memphis, Tennessee

Heirloom Recipes

Orange Ice

3 cups water
2 cups sugar
4 cups orange juice

4 tablespoons lemon juice
2 egg whites, beaten

Boil sugar and water together 5 minutes. When cooled add orange juice and lemon juice to sugar and water mixture. Fold in beaten egg whites and freeze in electric or hand freezer. Serves 8 to 10.

This recipe was given to me by my mother, Priscilla Nelson King. It was given to her by her sister, Nell Nelson Young.

Mrs. Imogene King Stanley

Five Three's Frozen Sherbet

3 pints water
3 cups sugar
3 lemons

3 oranges
3 bananas

Make a syrup of the sugar and water. Let it cool. Extract the juice from the lemons and oranges. Mash the bananas well. Mix the fruit with the cooled syrup. Freeze at once. Remember all frozen mixtures should stand several hours before serving in order to ripen. Serves 6 to 8.

This recipe is 72 years old and was handed down to me by my mother, Mrs. Dewitt Mercier.

Mrs. Clifford Worsham

Revivals

Custard Ice Cream

2 quarts milk
2 cups sugar

6 eggs
2 tablespoons vanilla

Scald milk slowly (never let it boil!). In mixer, beat eggs well and slowly add sugar. Pour egg and sugar mixture slowly into the hot milk, stirring constantly. Cook on low heat until the custard thickens (only a few minutes) let cool to room temperature. Cooling in the refrigerator will cause the mixture to curdle or to separate. When cool, pour into an ice cream freezer and proceed to freeze. Makes 4 quarts. Serves 12, but don't count on it!

This recipe is 115 years old and was handed down to me by my mother, Mrs. T. Y. Williford.

Mrs. Corinne Pierce

Boston Cream Candy

3 cups sugar
1 cup white corn syrup
1 cup whole cream

2 tablespoons margarine or butter

Combine sugar, syrup and cream in heavy saucepan and cook until forms a firm ball. Add butter and cook until hard ball stage. Remove from stove, place pan in cold water and beat constantly until candy is creamy and looses its gloss. Pour in a buttered 9x9 inch baking dish. Allow to cool. Cut into squares. Don't try this on a rainy day. Makes 64.

This recipe is many years old and was handed down to me by Granny Gertrude Flynn.

Peggy Woodhouse

Heirloom

Caramel Candy

1 (16 ounce) bottle white corn syrup
2 cups sugar
1 cup butter

1 (13 ounce) can evaporated milk or comparable amount of half and half
2 cups nuts (optional)
1 teaspoon vanilla

Boil sugar, corn syrup and butter in a large skillet for 5 minutes. Slowly add milk, stirring constantly. Cook for approximately 45 minutes over low heat until a drop forms a firm ball in water, or to 240 to 244°F on candy thermometer. Remove from heat, add nuts and vanilla and pour in a greased 14x9 inch glass dish. Let stand 4 hours. Cut to desired size, wrap in wax paper, and store in air-tight container.

This recipe is over 50 years old and was handed down to me by a friend of my mother's (Betty Feemster) who gave us these caramels for Christmas every year until she died.

Lee Sweat

Date And Nut Candy

3 cups sugar
1 cup milk
2 tablespoons butter

Package of pitted dates
1 cup pecans, chopped
1 teaspoon vanilla

Cook sugar, milk and butter until it forms a hard ball when put in cold water. Put dates into mixture and cook for a few minutes, remove from heat, add vanilla and nuts, beat until hard, pour on a damp cloth, shape into a roll and cool. Slice. Makes 24 pieces.

This recipe is over 60 years old, given to me by my mother, Mrs. N. C. Rinehart.

Mrs. Frank Hinton

Orange Marmalade

9 oranges
2 grapefruit
3 lemons
Sugar

Wash fruit and quarter. Cut out centers, removing seeds and any membrane easily detached. Grind oranges, grapefruit, and lemon pulp. Do not grind lemon skins. Weigh the pulp. It should weigh about 6 pounds. Add 1 quart of water for each pound of pulp. Let stand for 24 hours. Boil for 2 hours uncovered. Then measure the amount of pulp. There should be 6 or 7 pints. Add 3 cups of sugar for every pint of fruit. Boil for about an hour, stirring frequently, until mixture begins to jell when tested on a cold saucer. Cook to desired consistency and skim. Fill hot, sterilized jars and seal with paraffin. Makes 12 to 14 pints.

This recipe was brought to America by my Scottish grandmother in the early part of this century. It has been a staple in the pantries of our family for at least 5 generations. My mother Americanized it by adding grapefruit and lemon for tartness when "bitter oranges" were no longer available.

Audrey Muir McWhirter

Peach Conserve

5 pounds firm peaches, peeled and cubed
3 oranges, juice and chopped pulp
1 lemon, juice and chopped pulp
1¼ pounds seeded raisins, chopped
9 cups sugar
8 ounces walnuts, broken

Combine all ingredients except walnuts. Cook slowly, stirring frequently, until the conserve is fairly thick. Add walnuts and cook 10 minutes longer. Pour into sterilized jars while hot. Makes about 5 to 6 pints.

Heirloom Recipes

Peach Marmalade

5 cups firm peaches, peeled and sliced
5 cups sugar

1 orange, seeded and minced (do not peel)

Mix all together and let stand for 2 to 3 hours. Boil in heavy pot, stirring frequently, until the syrup is heavy. Pour into sterilized jars. Makes about 3 pints.

Tracy Hale Bell
Jackson, Mississippi

Tomato Preserves

2 pounds tomatoes
2 pounds sugar
2 lemons, thinly sliced
½ teaspoon salt (optional)

¼ teaspoon ground cloves
¼ teaspoon allspice
1 stick cinnamon
½ teaspoon ground pepper

Scald, skin, and weigh 2 pounds of small red tomatoes. Cover with sugar and let stand overnight. Next day, drain off juice and add lemons, salt and spices. Boil for 5 minutes. Add tomatoes and cook until tomatoes are clear and fairly thick (the tomatoes will cook to pieces). Pour the boiling preserves into hot jars and seal at once. Makes about 3 to 4 pints.

Mrs. Edward Hale

Celery Relish

1½ cups chopped celery
4 teaspoons sugar
1 teaspoon salt

½ teaspoon mustard
¼ cup vinegar

Cover and let stand in a cold place 1½ hours. Drain before serving. Serves 6.

Loraine Wammack

Revivals

Sweet Cucumber Pickles

7 pounds cucumbers, washed and sliced crosswise
2 gallons water
3 cups lime
5 pounds sugar
1 teaspoon cloves
3 quarts vinegar
1 teaspoon ginger
1 teaspoon ground allspice
1 teaspoon celery seed
Raisins, if desired

Soak cucumber slices 24 hours in water and lime. Drain. Soak in plain water 3 to 4 hours. Drain. Make a syrup of the rest of the ingredients and let come to a boil. Pour over cucumbers and let stand for 24 hours. Put on stove and boil for 1 hour. (Add a box of raisins during last 15 minutes, if desired.) Pack in 1 dozen sterile pint jars.

This recipe was given to me by my grandmother, the late Alma Dowlen of Corinth. I can remember helping her prepare these pickles when I visited her in the summer.

Rosemary Fisher

Sweet Pepper Relish

12 red peppers
12 green peppers
4 hot peppers
8 medium size onions
1 bunch carrots
3 pints vinegar
6 cups sugar

Grind all ingredients. Add salt and let set 2 hours. Squeeze out juice then add vinegar and sugar. Let set 1 hour. Bring to boil and can in sterilized jars. Makes 4 pints.

This recipe is 60 years old and was handed down to me by my mother, Mary Griffin Ward.

Amy Foster
Jackson, Tennessee

Revivals

Aunt Ruby's Relish

2½ pounds cabbage
1 pound onion
1 large bunch celery
3 large bell peppers
Salt
2 cups sugar

1 quart vinegar
½ cup dry mustard
¾ cup flour
1 tablespoon celery seed
1 tablespoon tumeric
Cayenne, to taste

Chop cabbage, onions, celery and bell pepper coarsely. Sprinkle lightly with salt. Put vinegar and sugar in pan and bring to boil. Mix dry ingredients, add a small amount of liquid mixture to dry ingredients to remove lumps then add this slowly to rest of liquid mixture. Cook until thick. Add all vegetables and cook until vegetables don't seem raw. Pack boiling relish into clear, hot jars to ½ inch of top of jar. Adjust jar lids. Process in boiling water for 5 minutes. Remove jars. Set jars upright, several inches apart on a wire rack to cool, to store at room temperature, or pack jars and store in the refrigerator. Makes 2 pints.

This recipe is 50 years old and was handed down to me by my grandmother, Mrs. B. W. Wadlington of Sledge, Mississippi.

Lenoir Stanley

Tomato Relish

24 large, ripe tomatoes, peeled and cut in quarters
2 (1 pound) boxes brown sugar
5 cups apple cider vinegar

8 large white onions, sliced
3 cinnamon sticks
1 tablespoon salt
1 hot pepper, or more

Mix all the above together. Cook slowly in heavy pan to desired consistency, about 1 hour and 15 minutes. Makes about 6 pints.

Mrs. T. Y. Williford, Sr.
Cleveland, Mississippi

Revivals

Cabbage Pickle

3 or 4 hard white heads
   cabbage
Sugar

White mustard seed
White vinegar
Boiling water

Grind white cabbage in a food chopper (do not use a food processor). In a large crock, layer the cabbage with a handful of salt over each layer. Cover with boiling water (handle very carefully) and leave overnight or 24 hours. Drain. Squeeze water out until quite dry. (I put in a sack and squeeze like a jelly bag.) In a pint jar put a layer of cabbage, about an inch. Add about 2 tablespoons of sugar and a few mustard seeds. Add another layer of cabbage and so on until the jar is ¾ full. Cover with white vinegar and let stand overnight. Taste to see if sweet enough. Add more sugar if necessary and seal jar. This relish is not hard to make but is time consuming. It is worth it if you like a sweet sour relish. It is good with any meat and especially with turkey. Keep in the refrigerator after opening. Makes 5 pints.

This recipe is 125 or more years old and handed down to me by my grandmother, who got it from hers. I have never seen this recipe anywhere else.

Mrs. Richard B. Warriner

Pepper Sherry

Fresh hot peppers

Dry sherry

Wash peppers and place them in a jar. (An empty catsup bottle would be nice.) Cover with dry sherry and put top on jar. Use the sherry to season meats, soups, stews and cheese dishes. Use the peppers to boil beans, blackeyed peas, anywhere a hot pepper is indicated. Sherry and peppers may be replaced in bottle as they are used. Of course, the sherry will become more and more peppery as time goes by.

This recipe is several hundred years old and was handed down to me by Claire Chalaron. Miss Chalaron is now deceased. I knew her in New Orleans in the 1950's.

Nancy Smith

Index

Index

$
$30.00 Cake 359

2
24 Hour Slaw 116

A
After Theatre Punch 83
All-Bran Rolls 312
All-Purpose Creole Seasoning 382
Alley Galley's Beef Burgundy 166
Almond Fingers 318
Amaretto Cheesecake 24
Amaretto Liqueur 86
Ambrosia 395
Ambrosia Pie 370
APPETIZERS
  CANAPES
    Cucumber Sandwiches 136
    Vegetable Sandwich Spread 66
  COLD
    Cheese Bits 57
    Cheese Icebox Wafers 399
    Elegant Vegetable Tray 53
    Marinated Mushrooms 52
    Marinated Shrimp 62
    Melon Balls in Port Wine 44
    Mexican Caviar 75
    Mississippi Caviar 76
    Old Roosevelt Hotel Remoulade
      Sauce 400
    Oyster Cracker Tidbits 72
    Texas Trash 77
    Walnut Sour Cream Diamonds 64
  DIPS
    Artichoke Dip 61, 74
    Coconut Dressing 57
    Cream Cheese Dip 78
    Curry Dip for Crudities 74
    Delicious Dip 73
    Fruit Dip 58
    Hummus Bi Tahini 75
    Redeal Fruit Dip 93
    Ron's Favorite Shrimp Dip 50
    Salmon Dip 70
    Seafood Dip 67
    Shrimp Party Spread 71
    Spinach Dip 73
    Tex-Mex Dip 76
  HOT
    Artichoke Dip 61
    Burgundy Mushrooms 69
    Chafing Dish Mexicali Tamale Balls 68
    Chafing Dish Sweet and Sour Meatballs 51

    Cheese and Ham Puffs 60
    Chinese Ribs Norman 68
    Elegant Beef Bits for Cocktails 214
    Georgetown Brie 52
    Hot Crab Canape Pie 61
    Hot Crabmeat Canape 67
    Hot Crabmeat Dip 55
    Miniature Mushroom Pies 26
    Mushroom and Herb Rolls 70
    Mushroom Roll Ups 69
    Mushrooms Elegant 54
    Mushrooms Stuffed with Snails 41
    Oysters Rossi 62
    Rumaki 56
    Seafood Dip 67
    Spinach Dip 73
    Spinach Rolls 50
    Spinach Squares 55
    Super Sausage Balls 74
  SPREADS AND MOLDS
    Bar Cheese 80
    Blue Cheese Ball 80
    Braunschweiger Mold 71
    Camembert Appetizer, Frozen 78
    Cheese Ball 79
    Cheese Ball with a Difference 78
    Cucumber Mousse 110
    Curried Cream Cheese Spread 77
    Daube Glace 65
    Mock Daube Glace 66
    Mushroom Sausage Spread 63
    Mushroom-Liver Pate 49
    Salmon Mousse 36
    Savory Cheesecake 58
    Shrimp and Crab Salad in Cream Puffs 52
    Shrimp and Salmon Terrine 12
    Shrimp Cheese Ball 79
    Shrimp Mold 56
    Smoked Salmon Tartare 43
    Susan's Cheese Ball 79
    Tuna Mold 72
    Warm Goat Cheese Terrine 17
    Wonderful Cheese and Apples 63
APPLES
  Apple and Walnut Tart, Carmelized 19
  Apple Cranberry Crunch 293
  Apple Crisp 347
  Apple Pecan Cake with Cinnamon
    Frosting 351
  Apple Tart 46
  Dried Apple Cake 398
  Fresh Apple Cake 352
  Pineapple Glazed Apple Pie 370
  Wonderful Cheese and Apples 63

Index

Apricot Cream Dressing 128
Apricot Sherbet 342
ARTICHOKES
  Artichoke Casserole 271
  Artichoke Dip 61, 74
  Artichoke Madrilene 105
  Artichokes A La Redmont 106
  Brussels Sprouts and Artichokes 275
  Shrimp and Artichoke Casserole 197
  Spinach and Artichoke Casserole 286
  Spinach-Artichoke Casserole 287
  Tomato Aspic with Artichoke Hearts 118
ASPARAGUS
  Asparagus Casserole 271
  Asparagus with Mushrooms and
    Toasted Almonds 94
  Cheese-Asparagus Soup 142
Au Gratin Vegetables 394
Aunt Lala's Pie Crust 413
Aunt Ruby's Relish 427

B

Bacon, Ham Quiche 253
Baked Bean Casserole 272
Baked Beans 272
Baked Caramel Corn 381
Baked Crab and Shrimp 196
Baked Fish with Vegetables 187
Baked Fondue 250
Baked Potatoes Stuffed with Crabmeat ... 282
Baked Sauerkraut and Chicken 401
Baked Seafood 203
Baked Stuffed Fish 188
BANANAS
  Banana Black Walnut Cake 353
  Banana Bread Royale 304
  Banana Split Dessert 347
Bar Cheese 80
Barbecued Brisket 215
Barbecue Sauce for Chicken 206
Barbecued Spareribs with Orange Sauce 181
Barkley's Chicken Casserole 222
Barley Soup 144
Basic Pastry 363
Basic Sweet Dough 313
Basic Waffles 314
Bass and Cashews 187
BEANS
  Baked Bean Casserole 272
  Baked Beans 272
  Creole Bean Soup 142
  Hamburger and Bean Casserole 174
  Kidney Bean Salad 110
  Lima Beans with Mushrooms 280

  New Orleans Style Red Beans and Rice 176
  Red Beans and Rice 273
  Sweet and Sour Beans 393
BEEF
  Alley Galley's Beef Burgundy 166
  Barbecued Brisket 215
  Beef Brisket in Beer 165
  Beef Eggplant Curry 168
  Beef Shish-Kabobs 211
  Beef Stew 169
  Beef Stroganoff 170
  Beef Tenderloin 212
  Beef Tenderloin, Buffet 213
  Busy Day Pot Roast 166
  Ed's Roast 216
  Elegant Beef Bits for Cocktails 214
  Garnished Beef Stroganoff 171
GROUND
  Chafing Dish with Sweet and Sour
    Meat Balls 51
  Delicious Lasagna 261
  El Dorado Casserole 172
  Hamburger and Bean Casserole 174
  Hamburger Pie 172
  Italian Mini Meat Loaves 173
  Italian Spaghetti 262
  Jalapeno Chile 148
  Meat 'N Pepper Cornbread Skillet 174
  Peppery Mexican Crescent Pie 173
  Spaghetti Deluxe 402
  Spaghetti Ring 263
  Lazy Creamy Swiss Steak 167
  Oven Swiss Steak 167
  Smoked Roast 215
  Spicy Beef Tenderloin 37
  Steak Au Poivre 28
  Sure Fire Rib Roast 165
  Swedish Beef Stew 168
  Swiss Bliss 170
Beer Batter Fried Fish 191
Beer Rolls 309
Beet Salad 105
Bernaise Sauce 213
Better Than Zest 383
Betty Ruth's Speedy Peach Pie 368
BEVERAGES
  Amaretto Liqueur 86
  COLD
    After Theatre Punch 83
    Bourbon Slush 82
    Champagne Punch 83
    Cranberry Rum Slush 84
    Diet Pina Colada 88
    Henry's Celebration Punch 85

Index

Lemon Tea	88
Mocha Punch	84
Orange Smoothie Punch	90
Pink Punch	89
Quick Lemonade	88
Southern Mint Juleps	85
Spiced Cider Punch	90
Surprise Punch	89
Tea Punch	90
World Famous Bloody Mary Mix	86

HOT

Christmas Mull	81
Hot Buttered Rum	81
Hot Spiced Tea	82
Instant Mocha	82
Tea	332
Kaluah	87
Peach Brandy	87
Big Mama's 3-Flavor Pound Cake	399
Biscuits, Reduced Calorie	297
Black Cherry Salad	99
Blue Cheese Ball	80
Blue Cheese Special Dressing	128
Blueberry Bran Muffins	306
Blueberry Salad	99
Bo-Diddly Cookies	337
Boston Cream Candy	422
Bourbon Slush	82
Braunschweiger Mold	71
Bread	299
Bread Dressing Supreme	391
Bread Pudding	344

BREADS

Banana Bread Royale	304
Basic Sweet Dough	313

BISCUITS

Biscuits, Reduced Calorie	297
Buttermilk Biscuits	298
Heavenly Tiny Biscuits	298
Riz (Angel) Biscuits	297
Sweet Potato Biscuits	406
Bread	299
Chunk O'Cheese Bread	302

COFFEE CAKE

Coconut Date-Nut Ring	314
Cream Cheese Braids	310
Pullit Coffee Cake	313
Corn Light Bread	298
Corn Light Bread	405
Cornbread Delicious	303
Cranberry Bread	304
Date Nut Bread	305
Debbie's Bread	303
Dutch Babies	302

French Bread	301
Grandmother's Spoon Bread	407
Home Made Bread	299
Honey Whole Wheat Bread	300
Hot Water Corn Bread	405
Mexican Cornbread	303

MUFFINS

Blueberry Bran Muffins	306
Buttermilk Orange Muffins	307
Martha Hederman's Pumpkin Muffins	309
Oatmeal Whole Wheat Muffins	309
Orange Pecan Muffins	308
Peabody Vanilla Muffins	308
Super Muffins	310
Wonderful Bran Muffins	307
No Knead French Bread	300

PANCAKES

Buttermilk Pancakes	407
Pumpkin Bread	305

ROLLS

All-Bran Rolls	312
Beer Rolls	309
Ella Mae's Rolls	312
Ice Box Rolls	396
Mama Ream's Rolls	406
Old-Fashioned Yeast Rolls	38
One Hour Buttermilk Twists	311
Strawberry Bread	306
Sweet Potato Rounds	33

WAFFLES

Basic Waffles	314
Yorkshire Pudding	403

BROCCOLI

Broccoli and Cauliflower Salad	105
Broccoli and Rice Casserole	275
Broccoli Bisque	143
Broccoli Casserole	274
Broccoli Puff	274
Broccoli Salad	108
Broccoli Souffle	275
Fresh Broccoli Salad I	107
Fresh Broccoli Salad II	107
Ham and Broccoli Roll-Ups	176
Browned Noodles	171
Brownies (Easy)	336
Brownies (Quick and Easy)	336
Brunch Casserole	246, 247
Brunswick Stew	223
Brussels Sprouts and Artichokes	275
Brussels Sprouts Cream Soup	143
Burgundy Mushrooms	69
Busy Day Pot Roast	166
Butter Cookies	331
Butter Tarts	318

432

Index

Buttermilk Biscuits 298
Buttermilk Orange Muffins 307
Buttermilk Pancakes 407
Buttermilk Pound Cake 354
Butterscotch Pie 366
Buttery Peanut Brittle 375

C
CABBAGE
24 Hour Slaw 116
Cabbage Pickle 428
Cruise Street School Slaw 115
Freezer Slaw 115
Vera's Cabbage Salad 114
CAKES
$30.00 Cake 359
Chocolate Cake and Frosting (Easy) 358
Chocolate Mousse Cake 356
FRUIT
Date Cake 412
Dried Apple Cake 398
Japanese Fruit Cake 350
Kentucky Cherry Pecan Loaf Cake 349
Old Fashioned Light Fruit Cake 410
German Bundt Cake 352
Italian Cream Cake 358
Layer
Lady Baltimore Cake 329
Marble Cake 409
Mystery Cake 413
Oatmeal Cake 361
Old-Fashioned Jelly Roll 410
Potato Cake 412
POUND
Big Mama's 3-Flavor Pound Cake 399
Buttermilk Pound Cake 354
Chocolate Chip Pound Cake 355
Coconut Pound Cake 356
Cream Cheese Pound Cake 355
Five Flavor Pound Cake 330
SHEET
Apple Pecan Cake with Cinnamon
  Frosting 351
Banana Black Walnut Cake 353
Classic Haresch Cake 362
Fresh Apple Cake 352
Hakesch Cake, Shortcut 362
Holiday Nut Cake 354
Mini Sheath Cake 360
The "Original" Coco-Cola Cake 360
Tunnel of Fudge Cake 357
Camembert Appetizer, Frozen 78
Candied Garlic Dills 383
CANDY
Baked Caramel Corn 381
Boston Cream Candy 422
Buttery Peanut Brittle 375
Caramel Candy 423
Christmas Nuts 380
Creamy Pecan Fudge 377
Date Roll 375
Date and Nut Candy 423
Deluxe Three Chocolate Fudge 377
English Toffee I 376
English Toffee II 376
Melt A Ways 380
Minute Fudge 378
Mystery Fudge 378
Orange Pecans 381
Pralines 379
White Fudge 379
Caramel Bavarian Cream 343
Caramel Brownies and Icing 319
Carbonara 260
CARROTS
Carrot Loaf 276
Carrot Souffles, Individual 41
Carrot Soup 144
Carrot-Cauliflower Cream Soup 145
Marinated Carrots 276
CASSEROLES
CHEESE
Baked Fondue 250
Fabulous Cheese Casserole 249
EGGS
Brunch Casserole 246
Brunch Casserole 247
Creole Eggs 249
Ham Strata 252
Scrambled Egg Casserole 251
FRUIT
Apple Cranberry Crunch 293
Curried Baked Fruit 294
Hot Fruit Compote 294
Pineapple Casserole 294
MEAT
Beef Eggplant Curry 168
Cheezy Sausage Casserole 182
Chinese Casserole 183
Curried Sausage and Rice Casserole
  181
El Dorado Casserole 172
Hamburger and Bean Casserole 174
Hamburger Pie 172
Meat 'N Pepper Cornbread Skillet 174
Peppery Mexican Crescent Pie 173
PASTA
Pasta Casserole 257

433

Index

POULTRY
Barkley's Chicken Casserole 222
Chicken and Wild Rice Casserole 235
Chicken Livers and Brown Rice 234
Chicken Noodle Casserole 230
Curried Chicken Divan 223
Hot Chicken Salad 226
Quail in Casserole 241
Vol Au Vent 236

SEAFOOD
Baked Seafood 203
Crabmeat Casserole 186
Eggplant and Shrimp Casserole 198
Holiday Newberg 202
Salmon Casserole 195
Scalloped Eggplant and Oyster
  Casserole 192
Shrimp and Artichoke Casserole 197
Wild Rice and Shrimp Casserole 201

VEGETABLE
Artichoke Casserole 271
Asparagus Casserole 271
Au Gratin Vegetables 394
Baked Bean Casserole 272
Broccoli and Rice Casserole 275
Broccoli Casserole 274
Carrot Loaf 276
Eggplant or Squash Casserole 279
Garlic Grits Casserole 280
Mrs. Robbin's Spinach Casserole 286
Potato Casserole 284
Shoe Peg Corn Casserole 278
Spinach and Artichoke Casserole with
  Blender Hollandiaise Sauce 286
Squash Casserole 289
Stella's Sweet Potato Souffle 394
Summer Squash Casserole 288
Sweet Potato Souffle 291
Three Vegetable Casserole 293
Vegetable Casserole 292
Zucchini Casserole 292

CAULIFLOWER
Broccoli and Cauliflower Salad 105
Carrot-Cauliflower Cream Soup 145
Cauliflower Delight 277
Cauliflower Salad Bowl 108
Cauliflower Salad Bowl Dressing 109
Celery Relish 425
Celery Seed Dressing 129
Chafing Dish Mexicali Tamale Balls 68
Chafing Dish Sweet and Sour Meat Balls . 51
Champagne Punch 83
Champagne Sorbet 27
Charlengne Salad with Hot Brie 109

Cheekwood Port Wine Salad 103
CHEESE
Baked Fondue 250
Bar Cheese 80
Blue Cheese Ball 80
Camembert Appetizer, Frozen 78
Cheese and Ham Puff 60
Cheese and Potato Omelet 247
Cheese Angels 134
Cheese Ball 79
Cheese Ball with a Difference 78
Cheese Bits 57
Cheese Icebox Wafers 399
Cheese Souffle 248
Cheese Soup 145
Cheese-Asparagus Soup 142
Cheesy Onion Pie 252
Cheezy Sausage Casserole 182
Chunk O'Cheese Bread 302
Country Cheese Pie 253
European Cheese Soup 146
Fabulous Cheese Casserole 249
Georgetown Brie 52
Ham Strata 252
Nutty Cheese Sandwich 135
Pimento Cheese Spread 139
Shrimp and Cheese Strata 197
Shrimp Cheese Ball 79
Susan's Cheese Ball 79
Tal's Pimento Cheese Goodies 139
Wonderful Cheese and Apples 63
Chess Pie (Old Fashioned) 414
CHICKEN
Baked Sauerkraut and Chicken 401
Barkley's Chicken Casserole 222
Brunswick Stew 223
Chicken and Dumplings 226
Chicken and Snow Pea Pasta Salad 256
Chicken and Wild Rice Casserole 235
Chicken Breast Supreme 222
Chicken Cerese 224
Chicken Gertrude 227
Chicken Jambalaya 230
Chicken L'Orange 229
Chicken Livers and Brown Rice 234
Chicken Loaf 228
Chicken Mimosa 231
Chicken Noodle Casserole 230
Chicken Salad 122
Chicken Salad for Sandwiches 135
Chicken Salad Mousse 121
Chicken Sauce Piquant 401
Chicken Spaghetti 264
Chicken Tetrazzini 264

434

Index

Chicken Tomatoes 121
Chicken with a Twist 255
Chicken with Pasta and Curry Sauce .. 254
Cold Chicken Pasta 255
Cornish Hens 236
Country Captain 225
Curried Chicken Divan 223
Good Time Chicken Salad 94
Hot Chicken Salad 226
Lemon Chicken 228
Mallie's Chicken Soup with "Better
 Than Zest" 97
Mrs. Donald's Chicken 225
Old Southern Chicken Cracklings 400
Oriental Chicken 232
Pecan Chicken 232
Rolled Chicken Breasts 234
Ruth Malone's Chicken Pie 233
Southern Fried Chicken with a
 Difference 231
Stan's Charcoaled Chicken 205
Vermicelli Salad 257
Vol Au Vent 236
Chilled Spinach and Cucumber Soup ... 152
Chinese Almond Cakes (Hang-Yen-Bang) 330
Chinese Casserole 183
Chinese Ribs Norman 68
Chinese Salad 110
Chive Sauce 13
CHOCOLATE
 Brownies (Easy) 336
 Brownies (Quick and Easy) 336
 Chocolate Cake and Frosting (Easy) .. 358
 Chocolate Chip Cookies 333
 Chocolate Chip Pound Cake 355
 Chocolate Cookies (Chewy) 320
 Chocolate Covered Strawberries 332
 Chocolate Drop Cookies 321
 Chocolate Mousse 39
 Chocolate Mousse Cake 356
 Chocolate Nut Fingers 334
 Chocolate Pie (Emily's) 416
 Chocolate Pie with Oatmeal Crust 364
 Chocolate Terrine 42
 Chokolade Goodies 336
 Creamy Pecan Fudge 377
 Deluxe Three Chocolate Fudge 377
 Easy Chocolate Ice Cream 340
 Four Layer Mocha Dessert 325
 Hello Dollys 336
 Hot Fudge Sunday Dessert 339
 Medallions of Chocolate Mousse with
  Kumquats, Orange and Lavender
  Sherbet 15

Melt A Ways 380
Minute Fudge 378
Mocha Ice Cream Dessert 341
Mystery Fudge 378
Ole Miss Hot Fudge Pie 364
Tunnel of Fudge Cake 357
Christmas Brunch Quail 239
Christmas Mull 81
Christmas Nuts 380
Chunk O'Cheese Bread 302
Cinnamon Sticks 319
Clam Chowder 156
Clara Dove Brasher Ward's Boiled Custard 397
Classic Haresch Cake 362
Classic Rustic Inn Dressing 133
COCONUT
 Coconut Date-Nut Ring 314
 Coconut Dressing 57
 Coconut Pie 363
 Coconut Pie (Mom's) 414
 Coconut Pound Cake 356
Coffee Chiffon Pie 372
Cold Chicken Pasta 255
Cold Glazed Duck 238
Cold Spinach Soup 151
Cold Zucchini Soup 154
Come Back Sauce 129
Company Squash 288
Confetti Fettucini 267
COOKIES
 Almond Fingers 318
 Bo-Diddly Cookies 337
 Brownies (Easy) 336
 Brownies (Quick and Easy) 336
 Butter Cookies 331
 Butter Tarts 318
 Caramel Brownies and Icing 319
 Chinese Almond Cakes
  (Hang-Yen-Bang) 330
 Chocolate Chip Cookies 333
 Chocolate Cookies (Chewy) 320
 Chocolate Drop Cookies 321
 Chocolate Nut Fingers 334
 Chokolade Goodies 336
 Cinnamon Sticks 319
 Dishpan Cookies 337
 Glazed Softies 334
 Hello Dollys 336
 Lace Cookies 326
 Lemon Melting Moments 335
 Mexican Wedding Cakes 327
 Oatmeal Biscuits 331
 Oatmeal-Orange Slice Cookies 333
 Orange Slice Cookies 320

Index

Skillet Cookies 338
Sugar Cookies 321
Tea Cakes 419
CORN
  Corn Light Bread 298
  Corn Lightbread 405
  Corn Pudding 277
  Cornbread Delicious 303
  Cornbread Dressing 392
  Grilled Parmesan Corn 218
  Nana's Corn Salad 111
  Shoe Peg Corn Casserole 278
  Skillet Corn 278
Corned Beef Salad 123
Cornish Hens 236
Cottage Cheese and Pineapple Salad 103
Country Captain 225
Country Cheese Pie 253
Country Ham in a Blanket 390
CRAB
  Baked Crab and Shrimp 196
  Baked Potatoes Stuffed with Crabmeat 282
  Crab and Spinach Timbale 26
  Crab Stew 155
  Crab with Sherry 185
  Crabmeat Casserole 186
  Eastern Shore Crabcakes 185
  Hot Crab Canape Pie 61
  Hot Crabmeat Canape 67
  Hot Crabmeat Dip 55
  Shrimp and Crab Salad in Cream Puffs 52
  Stuffed Crabs 186
  West Indies Salad 125
CRANBERRIES
  Apple Cranberry Crunch 293
  Cranberry Fluff 388
  Cranberry Bread 304
  Cranberry Rum Slush 84
  Cranberry Salad 101
Cream Cheese Braids 310
Cream Cheese Dip 78
Cream Cheese Pound Cake 355
Cream Puffs 53
Creamy Pecan Fudge 377
Creamy Potato Soup 149
Creamy Scalloped Potatoes 284
Creme De Menthe Cheesecake 371
Creole Bean Soup 142
Creole Eggs 249
Creole Gumbo 404
Creole Peas 282
Crescent City Oyster Soup 157
Crispy Coconut Shrimp 198
Cruise Street School Slaw 115

Crustless Buttermilk Pie 366
CUCUMBER
  Cucumber Mousse 110
  Cucumber Sandwiches 136
  Cucumber Sauce 196
  Sweet Cucumber Pickles 426
Cup Custard 345
Curried Baked Fruit 294
Curried Chicken Divan 223
Curried Cream Cheese Spread 77
Curried Sausage and Rice Casserole 181
Curry Dip for Crudities 74
Curry Vegetable Salad 122
CUSTARD
  Clara Dove Brasher Ward's Boiled
    Custard 397
  Cup Custard 345
  Custard Ice Cream 422

D

DATE
  Date and Nut Candy 423
  Date Cake 412
  Date Nut Bread 305
  Date Nut Roll 325
  Date Pie 417
  Date Roll 375
Daube Glace 65
Debbie's Bread 303
Delicious Dip 73
Delicious Lasagna 261
Delmonico Sandwiches 137
Deluxe Ham Sandwich 138
Deluxe Three Chocolate Fudge 377
Dessert Crepes 323
Dessert Waffles 324
DESSERTS
  Ambrosia 395
  Apple Crisp 347
  Banana Split Dessert 347
  Cheesecake
    Amaretto Cheesecake 24
    Creme De Menthe Cheesecake 371
    Italian Cheesecake (Pie) 371
    Peanut Butter Pie 366
    Refrigerated Cheese Cake 372
  Chocolate Covered Strawberries 332
  Chocolate Mousse 39
  Chocolate Terrine 42
  Clara Dove Brasher Ward's Boiled
    Custard 397
  Date Nut Roll 325
  Dessert Crepes 323
  Dessert Waffles 324

Index

Four Layer Mocha Dessert 325
FROZEN
   Frozen Lemon Delight 340
   Hot Fudge Sunday Dessert 339
   Mocha Ice Cream Dessert 341
Grand Marnier Mousse Cake 30
Lagniappe 218
Lemon Cake Pudding 411
Lemon Tarts 326
Medallions of Chocolate Mousse with Kumquats, Orange and Lavender Sherbet 15
Meringue with Fruit 346
Mexican Flan 34
Rum Babas 348
Sherry Mint Melon Balls 345
Walnut Lace Cups 338
Diet Pina Colada 88
Dining Car Special Sandwich 138
Dishpan Cookies 337
Dove Breats 207
Doves Elegant 238
Dried Apple Cake 398
DUCK
   Cold Glazed Duck 238
   Duck Gumbo 147
   Duck Shish-Kabob 207
   Mississippi Delta Duck 239
Dutch Babies 302

E

Easie's Cucumber Salad 111
Eastern Shore Crabcakes 185
Easy Chocolate Ice Cream 340
Ed's Roast 216
Eddie Knight's Barbecue Sauce 208
EGGPLANT
   Beef Eggplant Curry 168
   Eggplant and Shrimp Casserole 198
   Eggplant or Squash Casserole 279
   Eggplant Souffle 279
   Moussaka 178
   Scalloped Eggplant and Oyster Casserole 192
EGGS
   Bacon, Ham Quiche 253
   Brunch Casserole 246, 247
   Cheese and Potato Omelet 247
   Creole Eggs 249
   Fancy Egg Scramble 250
   Ham Omelet Supreme 248
   Sausage Souffle 182
   Scrambled Egg Casserole 251
   Zucchini Flan 34

El Dorado Casserole 172
Elegant Beef Bits for Cocktails 214
Elegant Vegetable Tray 53
Ella Mae's Rolls 312
English Toffee I 376
English Toffee II 376
European Cheese Soup 146
Exotic Luncheon Salad 127

F

Fabulous Cheese Casserole 249
Fancy Egg Scramble 250
FISH (Also See Individual Fish Listings)
   Baked Fish with Vegetables 187
   Baked Stuffed Fish 188
   Bass and Cashews 187
   Beer Batter Fried Fish 191
   Fish and Vegetable Salad 32
   Fish Chowder 160
   Fish Filets or Steaks 216
   Fish Stock 158
   Oven Fried Catfish 191
   Salmon Steaks with Sauce Picante 190
   Snapper Soup 158
   Stuffed Flounder 189
   Stuffed Red Snapper 188
   Trout with Almonds 190
Five Flavor Pound Cake 330
Five Fruit Salad 101
Five Three's Frozen Sherbet 421
Food Processor Pie Crust 363
Four Layer Mocha Dessert 325
Freezer Slaw 115
French Bread 301
French Dressing, Special 37
French Onion Soup 95
Fresh Apple Cake 352
Fresh Broccoli Salad I 107
Fresh Broccoli Salad II 107
Fresh Tomato Soup 153
Fresh Vegetable Marinade 119
Fried Rice with Pork and Shrimp 179
Frozen Banana Salad 99
Frozen Fruit Salad 98
Frozen Fruitcake Salad 102
Frozen Lemon Delight 340
Frozen Tomato Salad 117
FRUITS
   Fruit Dip 58
   Fruit Marinade 130
   Fruit Salad 100
   Fruit Salad with Cooked Sauce 408

437

Index

G

GAME
Brunswick Stew 223
Christmas Brunch Quail 239
Cold Glazed Duck 238
Dove Breasts 207
Doves Elegant 238
Duck Gumbo 147
Duck Shish-Kabob 207
Mississippi Delta Duck 239
Pheasant Breast Marinade 242
Quail and Wild Rice 241
Quail in Casserole 241
Roast Leg of Venison 184
Roasted Quail 240
Trail's End Quail 240
Garlic Grits Casserole 280
Garnished Beef Stroganoff 171
Gazpacho 151
Georgetown Brie 52
German Bundt Cake 352
Giblet Gravy 393
Glazed Softies 334
Good Time Chicken Salad 94
Good Winter Soup 156
Gran's Pie 415
Grand Marnier Mousse Cake 30
Grand Slam Congealed Salad 94
Grandmother's Spoon Bread 407
Granola 382
Grape Ice Cream 340
Grapefruit Salad 100
Gratin Dauphinois 29
Great Grandmother's Fruit Sherbet 420

GREEN BEANS
Green Bean Sandwich 134
Green Beans 273
Haricots Vert 28
Sweet and Sour Beans 393
Green Tomato Pickle 384
Grilled Parmesan Corn 218
Grilled Shrimp Kabobs 211
Gruyere Salad with Dressing 29

H

HAM
Bacon, Ham Quiche 253
Country Ham in a Blanket 390
Deluxe Ham Sandwich 138
Good Winter Soup 156
Ham 'N Potato Salad 124
Ham and Broccoli Roll-Ups 176
Ham Chowder 146
Ham Loaf 175

Ham Loaf with Sweet and Sour Sauce 175
Ham Omelet Supreme 248
Ham Sandwich Loaf 137
Ham Steak 209
Ham Strata 252
Holiday Ham and Sauce 177
Hamburger and Bean Casserole 174
Hamburger Pie 172
Haresch Cake (Shortcut) 362
Haricots Vert 28
Heavenly Tiny Biscuits 298
Hello Dollys 336
Henry's Celebration Punch 85
Herbed Pork Roast with Sour Cream Sauce
.... 44
Herman's Baked Mushrooms 281
High Society Rice 285
Holiday Ham and Sauce 177
Holiday Newberg 202
Holiday Nut Cake 354
Holiday Sweet Potatoes 291
Hollandaise Sauce 287
Home Made Bread 299
Honey Dressing 131
Honey Whole Wheat Bread 300
Hot Bacon Dressing 116
Hot Buttered Rum 81
Hot Chicken Salad 226
Hot Crab Canape Pie 61
Hot Crabmeat Canape 67
Hot Crabmeat Dip 55
Hot Fruit Compote 294
Hot Fudge Sunday Dessert 339
Hot Spiced Tea 82
Hot Water Corn Bread 405
Hummus Bi Tahini 75

I

Ice Box Rolls 396

ICE CREAM
Custard Ice Cream 422
Easy Chocolate Ice Cream 340
Grape Ice Cream 340
Icicle Pickle 384
Instant Mocha 82
Italian Cheesecake (Pie) 371
Italian Cream Cake 358
Italian Mini Meat Loaves 173
Italian Spaghetti 262

J

Jalapeno Chile 148
Japanese Fruit Cake 350
JELLIES AND PRESERVES

438

Index

Lemon Cheese 346
Orange Marmalade 424
Peach Conserve 424
Peach Marmalade 425
Tomato Preserves 425

K

Kaluah 87
Kentucky Cherry Pecan Loaf Cake 349
Kidney Bean Salad 110
Kiwi Dressing 42

L

Lace Cookies 326
Lady Baltimore Cake 329
Lagniappe 218
LAMB
    Lamb Tenderloin 18
    Moussaka 178
    Roasted Leg of Lamb 184
Layered Salad 112
Lazy Creamy Swiss Steak 167
Leek Soup 96
Leeks, Sauteed 45
LEMONS
    Lemon Cake Pudding 411
    Lemon Cheese 346
    Lemon Chicken 228
    Lemon Cream Sherbet 342
    Lemon Melting Moment 335
    Lemon Meringue Pie 367
    Lemon Parsley Potatoes 281
    Lemon Tart 326
    Lemon Tea 88
Lima Beans with Mushrooms 280
Lime Pie 367
Louie's Special Barbecue Sauce 204
Louis Dressing 130

M

Macaroon Pie 365
Macaroon Pudding 343
Macedonian Salad 112
Mallie's Chicken Soup with "Better
    Than Zest" 97
Mama Ream's Rolls 406
Mamaw's Pecan Pie 415
Mandarin Orange Salad with Tarragon
    Dressing 113
Marble Cake 409
Marinated Carrots 276
Marinated Italian Salad 22
Marinated Mushrooms 52
Marinated Shrimp 62

Martha Hederman's Pumpkin Muffins 309
Mary Ann's Hodge Podge Soup 148
Mayonnaise 131
Meat 'N Pepper Cornbread Skillet 174
Meat Sauce for a Crowd 265
Medallions of Chocolate Mousse with
    Kumquats, Orange and Lavender
    Sherbet 15
Melon Balls in Port Wine 44
Melon Balls, Sherry Mint 345
Melt A Ways 380
Meringue with Fruit 346
Mexican Caviar 75
Mexican Cornbread 303
Mexican Flan 34
Mexican Wedding Cakes 327
Mike's Peel 'Em and Eat 'Em Shrimp 200
Mini Sheath Cake 360
Miniature Mushroom Pies 26
Minute Fudge 378
Mississippi Caviar 76
Mississippi Delta Duck 239
Mixed Salad Greens with Vinaigrette 45
Mocha Ice Cream Dessert 341
Mocha Punch 84
Mock Daube Glace 66
Mollie's Remoulade Sauce 132
Moussaka 178
Mrs. Donald's Chicken 225
Mrs. Robbin's Spinach Casserole 286
MUSHROOMS
    Burgundy Mushrooms 69
    Herman's Baked Mushrooms 281
    Lima Beans with Mushrooms 280
    Marinated Mushrooms 52
    Mushroom and Herb Rolls 70
    Mushroom Liver Pate 49
    Mushroom Roll Ups 69
    Mushroom Salad 113
    Mushroom Sausage Spread 63
    Mushrooms Elegant 54
    Mushrooms Stuffed with Snails 41
Mystery Cake 413
Mystery Fudge 378

N

Nana's Corn Salad 111
Nancie's Salad 126
New Orleans Style Red Beans and Rice .. 176
Nick's Shrimp Givesti 267
No Knead French Bread 300
Nutrition Concepts 9
Nutty Cheese Sandwich 135
Nutty Wild Rice 285

Index

O

OATMEAL
- Oatmeal Biscuits 331
- Oatmeal Cake 361
- Oatmeal-Orange Slice Cookies 333
- Oatmeal Whole Wheat Muffins 309
- Old Fashioned Light Fruit Cake 410
- Old Roosevelt Hotel Remoulade Sauce ... 400
- Old South Pecan Custard Pie 416
- Old Southern Chicken Cracklings 400
- Old-Fashioned Jelly Roll 410
- Old-Fashioned Yeast Rolls 38
- Ole Miss Hot Fudge Pie 364
- One Hour Buttermilk Twists 311

ONIONS
- Cheesy Onion Pie 252
- French Onion Soup 95
- Sweet and Sour Onions 281
- Opening Night "Showoff" 268

ORANGES
- Ambrosia 395
- Buttermilk Orange Muffins 307
- Orange Ice 421
- Orange Marmalade 424
- Orange Pecan Muffins 308
- Orange Pecans 381
- Orange Pineapple Salad 101
- Orange Salad with Kiwi Dressing 42
- Orange Slice Cookies 320
- Orange Smoothie Punch 90
- Spiced Oranges 395
- Oriental Chicken 232
- Oriental Salad 125
- Oven Fried Catfish 191
- Oven Swiss Steak 167

OYSTERS
- Crescent City Oyster Soup 157
- Oyster Chop Suey 192
- Oyster Cracker Tidbits 72
- Oyster Soup 388
- Oyster Stew 157
- Oysters Rockefeller 194
- Oysters Rockefellow 194
- Oysters Rossi 62
- Scalloped Eggplant and Oyster Casserole 192
- Scalloped Oysters 193

P

PASTA
  COLD
  - Chicken and Snow Pea Pasta Salad .. 256
  - Chicken with a Twist 255
  - Chicken with Pasta and Curry Sauce 254
  - Cold Chicken Pasta 255
  - Shrimp Pasta Salad for a Crowd 256
  - Vermicelli Salad 257

  HOT
  - Browned Noodles 171
  - Carbonara 260
  - Chicken Spaghetti 264
  - Chicken Tetrazzini 264
  - Confetti Fettucini 267
  - Delicious Lasagna 261
  - Italian Spaghetti 262
  - Meat Sauce for a Crowd 265
  - Nick's Shrimp Givesti 267
  - Opening Night "Showoff" 268
  - Pasta Casserole 257
  - Pasta Mustardo 259
  - Scampi Sauce 23
  - Seafood Lasagna 266
  - Shrimp Fettuccini 268
  - Shrimp Stroganoff 201
  - Spaghetti Deluxe 402
  - Spaghetti Ring 263
  - Spaghetti with Veal and Peppers 266
  - Spinach Lasagna 258
  - Stuffed Shells Florentine 258

PASTRY
- Basic Pastry 363
- Cream Puffs 53
- Date Pie 417

PIE CRUST
- Aunt Lala's Pie Crust 413
- Chocolate Pie with Oatmeal Crust 364
- Food Processor Pie Crust 363
- Shrimp and Crab Salad in Cream Puffs 53
- Zwieback Pie with Pastry Cream 418
- Peabody Vanilla Muffins 308

PEACHES
- Betty Ruth's Speedy Peach Pie 368
- Peach Brandy 87
- Peach Cobbler 369
- Peach Conserve 424
- Peach Marmalade 425
- Peach Sherbet 420
- Stewed Georgia Peaches 408
- Peanut Butter Pie 366
- Pear Salad 102
- Peas, Creole 282
- Pecan Chicken 232
- Pecan Pie Squares 327
- Pepper Sherry 428
- Peppery Mexican Crescent Pie 173
- Pesto 260
- Pheasant Breast Marinade 242

PICKLES AND RELISHES

Index

Aunt Ruby's Relish 427
Cabbage Pickle 428
Candied Garlic Dills 383
Celery Relish 425
Green Tomato Pickle 384
Icicle Pickle 384
Pepper Sherry 428
Sweet Cucumber Pickles 426
Sweet Pepper Relish 426
Tomato Relish 427
PIES
Butterscotch Pie 366
Chess Pie (Old Fashioned) 414
Chocolate Pie (Emily's) 416
Chocolate Pie with Oatmeal Crust 364
Coconut Pie 363
Coconut Pie (Mom's) 414
Coffee Chiffon Pie 372
Crustless Buttermilk Pie 366
FRUIT
Ambrosia Pie 370
Apple and Walnut Tart, Carmelized 19
Apple Tart 46
Betty Ruth's Speedy Peach Pie 368
Date Pie 417
Lemon Meringue Pie 367
Lime Pie 367
Peach Cobbler 369
Strawberry Fluff Pie 368
Strawberry Pie 369
Gran's Pie 415
Italian Cheesecake (Pie) 371
Macaroon Pie 365
Mamaw's Pecan Pie 415
Old South Pecan Custard Pie 416
Ole Miss Hot Fudge Pie 364
Peanut Butter Pie 366
Pineapple Glazed Apple Pie 370
Pumpkin Pie 397
Walnut Pie 365
Zwieback Pie with Pastry Cream 418
Pimento Cheese Spread 139
PINEAPPLE
Pineapple Casserole 294
Pineapple Glazed Apple Pie 370
Pineapple Ozark Pudding 344
Pink Punch 89
Polish Sausage Subs 140
PORK
Barbecued Spareribs with Orange Sauce 181
Chinese Ribs Norman 68
Fried Rice with Pork and Shrimp 179
Herbed Pork Roast with Sour Cream 44

Pork Chops 210
Pork Ribs 210
Pork Tenderloin Picante 180
Pork-Apple Salad 123
Skillet Pork Chops and Rice 180
Sweet and Sour Pork 179
Tourtiere (Canadian Meat Pie) 402
POTATOES
Baked Potatoes Stuffed with Crabmeat 282
Cheese and Potato Omelet 247
Creamy Potato Soup 149
Creamy Scalloped Potatoes 284
Gratin Dauphinois 29
Ham 'N Potato Salad 124
Lemon Parsley Potatoes 281
Potato Cake 412
Potato Casserole 284
Potato Salad 114
Potato Soup 149
Potato Soup, Low Cholesterol 150
Potatoes Au Gratin 283
Spudwisers 283
Vichyssoise 150
Pralines 379
Pretzel Salad 104
PUDDINGS
Bread Pudding 344
Caramel Bavarian Cream 343
Lemon Cake Pudding 411
Macaroon Pudding 343
Pineapple Ozark Pudding 344
Pullit Coffee Cake 313
Pumpkin Bread 305
Pumpkin Pie 397

Q

QUAIL
Christmas Brunch Quail 239
Quail and Wild Rice 241
Quail in Casserole 241
Roasted Quail 240
Trail's End Quail 240
Quick Gazpacho 151
Quick Lemonade 88

R

Red Beans and Rice 273
Red Wine Tomato Sauce 259
Redeal Fruit Dip 93
Reducing Soup 147
Refrigerated Cheese Cake 372
RELISHES (See Pickles and Relishes)
RICE
Broccoli and Rice Casserole 275

441

Index

Chicken and Wild Rice Casserole 235
Curry Vegetable Salad 122
Fried Rice with Pork and Shrimp 179
High Society Rice 285
Nutty Wild Rice 285
Quail and Wild Rice 241
Red Beans and Rice 273
Skillet Pork Chops and Rice 180
Wild Rice and Shrimp Casserole 201
Wild Rice Salad 120
Rich's Barbecue Sauce 205
Riz (Angel) Biscuits 297
Roast Leg of Venison 184
Roast Turkey (In Electric Roaster) 389
Roasted Leg of Lamb 184
Roasted Quail 240
Rolled Chicken Breasts 234
Ron's Favorite Shrimp Dip 50
Roquefort Cheese Dressing 132
Royal Sandwich Loaf 140
Rum Babas 348
Rumaki 56
Russian Dressing 132
Ruth Malone's Chicken Pie 233

S

SALAD DRESSINGS
Apricot Cream Dressing 128
Blue Cheese Special Dressing 128
Cauliflower Salad Bowl Dressing 109
Celery Seed Dressing 129
Classic Rustic Inn Dressing 133
Coconut Dressing 57
Come Back Sauce 129
French Dressing, Special 37
Fruit Marinade 130
Fruit Salad with Cooked Sauce 408
Gruyere Salad with Dressing 29
Honey Dressing 131
Hot Bacon Dressing 116
Kiwi Dressing 42
Louis Dressing 130
Mayonnaise 131
Mollie's Remoulade Sauce....................... 132
Roquefort Cheese Dressing 132
Russian Dressing 132
Salad Dressing A La Steak House 128
Sweet Salad Dressing 133
Tangy Lemon Mustard Dressing 32
Tarragon Dressing 113
Thousand Island Salad Dressing 133
Vinaigrette 45
Zesty French Dressing 130
SALADS

CONGEALED
Artichoke Madrilene 105
Beet Salad 105
Black Cherry Salad 99
Blueberry Salad 99
Broccoli Salad 108
Cheekwood Port Wine Salad 103
Chicken Salad Mousse 121
Cottage Cheese and Pineapple Salad   103
Cranberry Salad 101
Cucumber Mousse 110
Grand Slam Congealed Salad 94
Grapefruit Salad 100
Orange Pineapple Salad 101
Pretzel Salad 104
Strawberry Nut Salad 104
Tomato Aspic with Artichoke Hearts .. 118
Tomato Soup Aspic 117
Vegetable Mold 120

FROZEN
Frozen Banana Salad 99
Frozen Fruit Salad 98
Frozen Fruitcake Salad 102
Frozen Tomato Salad 117
Tomato Ice 118

FRUIT
Cranberry Fluff 388
Five Fruit Salad 101
Fruit Salad 100
Fruit Salad with Cooked Sauce 408
Mandarin Orange Salad with Tarragon
  Dressing 113
Orange Salad with Kiwi Dressing 42
Pear Salad 102

GREEN
Charlengne Salad with Hot Brie 109
Gruyerè Salad with Dressing 29
Mixed Salad Greens with Vinaigrette ... 45
Spinach Salad with Hot Bacon
  Dressing 116

MEAT
Corned Beef Salad 123
Ham 'N Potato Salad 124
Pork-Apple Salad 123
Taco Salad 124

POULTRY
Chicken Salad 122
Chicken Tomatoes 121
Exotic Luncheon Salad 127
Good Time Chicken Salad 94
Hot Chicken Salad 226
Turkey-Wild Rice Salad 127

Index

SEAFOOD
Fish and Vegetable Salad 32
Nancie's Salad 126
Oriental Salad 125
Shrimp Topped Salad 126
West Indies Salad 125

VEGETABLE
24 Hour Slaw 116
Artichokes A La Redmont 106
Asparagus with Mushrooms and Toasted Almonds 94
Broccoli and Cauliflower Salad 105
Cauliflower Salad Bowl 108
Chinese Salad 110
Cruise Street School Slaw 115
Curry Vegetable Salad 122
Easie's Cucumber Salad 111
Freezer Slaw 115
Fresh Broccoli Salad I 107
Fresh Broccoli Salad II 107
Fresh Vegetable Marinade 119
Kidney Bean Salad 110
Layered Salad 112
Macedonian Salad 112
Marinated Italian Salad 22
Mushroom Salad 113
Nana's Corn Salad 111
Potato Salad 114
Sweet and Sour Salad 119
Vera's Cabbage Salad 114
Wild Rice Salad 120

SALMON
Salmon Casserole 195
Salmon Dip 70
Salmon Loaf 195
Salmon Loaf with Cucumber Sauce 196
Salmon Mousse 36
Salmon Steaks with Sauce Picante 190
Shrimp and Salmon Terrine 12

SANDWICHES
Cheese Angels 134
Chicken Salad for Sandwiches 135
Cucumber Sandwiches 136
Delmonico Sandwiches 137
Deluxe Ham Sandwich 138
Dining Car Special Sandwich 138
Green Bean Sandwich 134
Ham Sandwich Loaf 137
Nutty Cheese Sandwich 135
Pimento Cheese Spread 139
Polish Sausage Subs 140
Royal Sandwich Loaf 140
Tal's Pimento Cheese Goodies 139
Tuna Fish Salad for Sandwiches......... 141

Vegetable Sandwich Spread 66

SAUCES AND SEASONINGS
All-Purpose Creole Seasoning 382
Barbecue Sauce for Chicken 206
Bernaise Sauce 213
Better Than Zest 383
Chive Sauce 13
Cucumber Sauce 196
Eddie Knight's Barbecue Sauce 208
Giblet Gravy 393
Hollandaise Sauce 287
Louie's Special Barbecue Sauce 204
Meat Sauce for a Crowd 265
Old Roosevelt Hotel Remoulade Sauce 400
Pepper Sherry 428
Pesto 260
Red Wine Tomato Sauce 259
Rich's Barbecue Sauce 205
Sauce for Ham Steak 209
Swine Lake Ballet Barbecue Sauce 208
Turkey Water Chestnut Gravy 392
White Wine Tomato Sauce 262

SAUSAGE
Cheezy Sausage Casserole 182
Chinese Casserole 183
Curried Sausage and Rice Casserole ... 181
New Orleans Style Red Beans and Rice 176
Polish Sausage Subs 140
Sausage Souffle 182

Sauteed Leeks 45
Savory Cheesecake 58
Scalloped Eggplant and Oyster Casserole 192
Scalloped Oysters 193
Scampi Sauce 23
Scrambled Egg Casserole 251

SEAFOOD
Baked Seafood 203
Creole Gumbo 404
Holiday Newberg 202
Seafood Dip 67
Seafood Gumbo 158
Seafood Lasagna 266

SHERBET
Apricot Sherbet 342
Champagne Sorbet 27
Five Three's Frozen Sherbet 421
Great Grandmother's Fruit Sherbet 420
Lemon Cream Sherbet 342
Orange Ice 421
Peach Sherbet 420

Sherry Mint Melon Balls 345
Shoe Peg Corn Casserole 278
Shortbread 329

Index

SHRIMP
- Baked Crab and Shrimp 196
- Crispy Coconut Shrimp 198
- Eggplant and Shrimp Casserole 198
- Fried Rice with Pork and Shrimp 179
- Grilled Shrimp Kabobs 211
- Marinated Shrimp 62
- Mike's Peel 'Em and Eat 'Em Shrimp . 200
- Nancie's Salad 126
- Nick's Shrimp Givesti 267
- Old Roosevelt Hotel Remoulade Sauce 400
- Opening Night "Showoff" 268
- Oriental Salad 125
- Ron's Favorite Shrimp Dip 50
- Scampi Sauce 23
- Seafood Lasagna 266
- Shrimp and Artichoke Casserole 197
- Shrimp and Cheese Strata 197
- Shrimp and Crab Salad in Cream Puffs 53
- Shrimp and Salmon Terrine 12
- Shrimp Cheese Ball 79
- Shrimp Creole 199
- Shrimp De Jonghe 200
- Shrimp Fettuccini 268
- Shrimp in Beer 202
- Shrimp Mitchell 199
- Shrimp Mold 56
- Shrimp Party Spread 71
- Shrimp Pasta Salad for a Crowd 256
- Shrimp Stroganoff 201
- Shrimp Topped Salad 126
- Wild Rice and Shrimp Casserole 201
- Skillet Cookies 338
- Skillet Corn 278
- Skillet Pork Chops and Rice 180
- Smoked Roast 215
- Smoked Salmon Tartare 43
- Snapper Soup 158

SOUPS
   COLD
   - Broccoli Bisque 143
   - Chilled Spinach and Cucumber Soup 152
   - Cold Spinach Soup 151
   - Cold Zucchini Soup 154
   - Gazpacho 151
   - Quick Gazpacho 151
   - Tomato Dill Soup 153
   - Vischyssoise 150
   - Zucchini Soup, Cold 22
   - Fish Stock 158

   HOT
   - Barley Soup 144
   - Brussels Sprouts Cream Soup 143

- Carrot Soup 144
- Carrot-Cauliflower Cream Soup 145
- Cheese Soup 145
- Cheese-Asparagus Soup 142
- Clam Chowder 156
- Crab Stew 155
- Creamy Potato Soup 149
- Creole Bean Soup 142
- Creole Gumbo 404
- Crescent City Oyster Soup 157
- Duck Gumbo 147
- European Cheese Soup 146
- Fish Chowder 160
- French Onion Soup 95
- Fresh Tomato Soup 153
- Good Winter Soup 156
- Ham Chowder 146
- Jalapeno Chile 148
- Leek Soup 96
- Mallie's Chicken Soup with "Better Than Zest" 97
- Mary Ann's Hodge Podge Soup 148
- Oyster Soup 388
- Oyster Stew 157
- Potato Soup 149
- Potato Soup, Low Cholesterol 150
- Reducing Soup 147
- Seafood Gumbo 158
- Snapper Soup 158
- Taco Soup 152
- Teedee's Vegetable Beef Soup 154
- Veloute of Garlic Soup Gratine 16
- Vichyssoise 150
- Wonton Soup 155
- Southern Fried Chicken with a Difference 231
- Southern Mint Juleps 85
- Spaghetti Deluxe 402
- Spaghetti Ring 263
- Spaghetti with Veal and Peppers 266
- Spiced Cider Punch 90
- Spiced Oranges 395
- Spicy Beef Tenderloin 37

SPINACH
- Chilled Spinach and Cucumber Soup . 152
- Cold Spinach Soup 151
- Crab and Spinach Timbale 26
- Mrs. Robbin's Spinach Casserole 286
- Spinach and Artichoke Casserole with Blender Hollandaise Sauce 286
- Spinach Dip 73
- Spinach Lasagna 258
- Spinach Rolls 50
- Spinach Salad with Hot Bacon Dressing 116
- Spinach Squares 55

444

Index

Spinach-Artichoke Casserole 287
Stuffed Shells Florentine 258
Spudwisers 283
SQUASH
  Company Squash 288
  Eggplant or Squash Casserole 279
  Squash Casserole 289
  Squash Dressing 289
  Squash Souffle 289
  Stuffed Yellow Squash 290
  Summer Squash Casserole 288
Stan's Charcoaled Chicken 205
Steak Au Poivre 28
Stella's Sweet Potato Souffle 394
Stewed Georgia Peaches 408
STRAWBERRIES
  Strawberry Bread 306
  Strawberry Fluff Pie 368
  Strawberry Nut Salad 104
  Strawberry Pie 369
Stuffed Crabs 186
Stuffed Flounder 189
Stuffed Red Snapper 188
Stuffed Shells Florentine 258
Stuffed Yellow Squash 290
STUFFINGS
  Bread Dressing Supreme 391
  Cornbread Dressing 392
Sugar Cookies 321
Summer Squash Casserole 288
Super Sausage Balls 74
Super Muffins 310
Sure Fire Rib Roast 165
Surprise Punch 89
Susan's Cheese Ball 79
Swedish Beef Stew 168
Sweet and Sour Beans 393
Sweet and Sour Onions 281
Sweet and Sour Pork 179
Sweet and Sour Salad 119
Sweet Cucumber Pickles 426
Sweet Pepper Relish 426
SWEET POTATOES
  Holiday Sweet Potatoes 291
  Stella's Sweet Potato Souffle .. 394
  Sweet Potato Biscuits 406
  Sweet Potato Rounds 33
  Sweet Potato Souffle 291
Sweet Salad Dressing 133
Swine Lake Ballet Barbecue Sauce .. 208
Swiss Bliss 170

T
Taco Salad 124

Taco Soup 152
Tal's Pimento Cheese Goodies 139
Tangy Lemon Mustard Dressing 32
Tarragon Dressing 113
Tea 332
Tea Cakes 419
Tea Punch 90
Teedee's Vegetable Beef Soup 154
Texas Trash 77
Tex - Mex Dip 76
The "Original" Coco-Cola Cake 360
Thousand Island Salad Dressing 133
Three Vegetable Casserole 293
TOMATOES
  Fresh Tomato Soup 153
  Frozen Tomato Salad 117
  Tomato Aspic with Artichoke Hearts 118
  Tomato Dill Soup 153
  Tomato Ice 118
  Tomato Pepper Quickie 290
  Tomato Preserves 425
  Tomato Relish 427
  Tomato Soup Aspic 117
  Tomatoes Provencale 45
Tourtiere (Canadian Meat Pie) 402
Trail's End Quail 240
Trout with Almonds 190
Tuna Fish Salad for Sandwiches 141
Tuna Mold 72
Tunnel of Fudge Cake 357
TURKEY
  Exotic Luncheon Salad 127
  Roast Turkey (In Electric Roaster) 389
  Turkey Breast Mole 237
  Turkey Water Chestnut Gravy 392
  Turkey-Wild Rice Salad 127

V
VEAL
  Spaghetti with Veal and Peppers 266
  Veal Bouchet 183
  Veal Chops in Apple Mustard Sauce 41
  Veal Medallions "Pot Pourri" ... 13
VEGETABLES
  Au Gratin Vegetables 394
  Elegant Vegetable Tray 53
  Fresh Vegetable Marinade 119
  Gazpacho 151
  Mary Ann's Hodge Podge Soup 148
  Quick Gazpacho 151
  Reducing Soup 147
  Teedee's Vegetable Beef Soup ... 154
  Three Vegetable Casserole 293

Index

Vegetable Accompaniments for
  the Grill 217
Vegetable Casserole 292
Vegetable Mold 120
Vegetable Sandwich Spread 66
Veloute of Garlic Soup Gratine 16
Vera's Cabbage Salad 114
Vermicelli Salad 257
Vichyssoise 150
Vinaigrette 45
Vol Au Vent 236

Whiz Energy Balls 382
Wild Rice and Shrimp Casserole 201
Wild Rice Salad 120
Wonderful Bran Muffins 307
Wonderful Cheese and Apples 63
Wonton Soup 155
World Famous Bloody Mary Mix 86

Y

Yorkshire Pudding 403

W

Walnut Lace Cups 338
Walnut Pie 365
Walnut Sour Cream Diamonds 64
Warm Goat Cheese Terrine 17
West Indies Salad 125
White Fudge 379
White Wine Tomato Sauce 262

Z

Zesty French Dressing 130
ZUCCHINI
  Cold Zucchini Soup 154
  Zucchini Casserole 292
  Zucchini Flan 34
  Zucchini Soup, Cold 22
Zwieback Pie with Pastry Cream 418

Reorder Additional Copies

CRITICS' CHOICE
P.O. Box 435
Corinth, Mississippi 38834

Please send me ___ copies of **CRITICS' CHOICE** at $15.95 per copy plus $2.00 per copy of postage and handling to:

Name _____

Address _____

City _____ State _____

Zip _____

(Mississippi residents add sales tax.) Custom Gift Wrapping $.50 per copy. All proceeds from the sale of this book go to support of Corinth Theatre Arts.

CRITICS' CHOICE
P.O. Box 435
Corinth, Mississippi 38834

Please send me ___ copies of **CRITICS' CHOICE** at $15.95 per copy plus $2.00 per copy of postage and handling to:

Name _____

Address _____

City _____ State _____

Zip _____

(Mississippi residents add sales tax.) Custom Gift Wrapping $.50 per copy. All proceeds from the sale of this book go to support of Corinth Theatre Arts.

CRITICS' CHOICE
P.O. Box 435
Corinth, Mississippi 38834

Please send me ___ copies of **CRITICS' CHOICE** at $15.95 per copy plus $2.00 per copy of postage and handling to:

Name _____

Address _____

City _____ State _____

Zip _____

(Mississippi residents add sales tax.) Custom Gift Wrapping $.50 per copy. All proceeds from the sale of this book go to support of Corinth Theatre Arts.